John McCaldin Loewenthal: Letters Home from a Victorian Commercial Traveller, 1889 - 1895

John McCaldin Loewenthal: Letters Home from a Victorian Commercial Traveller, 1889 - 1895

Editors

MICHELLE FINK AND ROBERT BOYD

MOORE & WEINBERG
ANN ARBOR, MICHIGAN, USA

It is available in the following editions:

ISBN 979-8-9854286-1-2 (Ebook)

ISBN 979-8-9854286-0-5 (Paper)

Online at https://loewenthal.pressbooks.com/

Downloadable PDF on Humanities Commons: http://dx.doi.org/10.17613/2y1n-xr59

Library of Congress Control Number: 2022930300

Published by Moore & Weinberg, Ann Arbor, Michigan, USA

To contact the publisher, visit https://mooreweinberg.com/

Note: The formatting of the transcripts mirrors the formatting of the original letters to the degree possible. An image of each letter is linked above the transcript. The complete set of images can be found at https://hcommons.org/groups/loewenthal-letters-project/ The originals of the images shown in the book are assumed to be in the Public Domain on account of their age, but the publisher invites any potential rightsholders to be in contact via the details found on its website.

For Miss Jane McCully

Art thou not charmed by the dead-working deep

Not woo'd, by the land-lymning shore.

That thou longest to leave, thy sea-gladdened Hall,

That resounds with the Ocean's roar!

Stay, stay, is roll'd on the hoarse breakers' voice –

The deep-mutt'ring caves bid thee stay.

And the shell-skirted rocks thy stay invite,

As they drink the fish-feeding spray!

For who would exchange the wild shout of waves,

For the city's incessant din, —

The sparkle of spray, and the foam wrapt rocks,

For the **house** where the Plague has been?

Thine eye can descry the peaked martial land

Where the wild-voiced Ossian raves

Whence the song yet streams from his awful Harp

Charioted on its kindred waves!

'Tis sweet to behold the dark, spangled sea,

How, lit up the Polar Blaze,

And to hear the song that they sang of old,

Mid' the **Chants** of ancient days.

Thy lullaby is sung by a white-capt Band

*By ten thousand blue-**skinned** waves*

That embalming the ear, soft Call to sleep

As they turn in their brethren's graves!

Jane, this spot might be a much-cherished home —

Here, thy wing-fluttering soul might soar,

Mid sea foaming rocks, and echoing Caves,

Mid the surge and the torrents' roar

Stay, stay, is rolled on the hoarse breakers' voice —

The deep-muttering caves bid thee stay,

And the shell-skirted rocks thy stay invite

As they drink the fish-feeding spray!

This poem was sent to Jane McCully, it is thought by Julius Loewenthal, and is marked with the date 10th November 1854, which is seven years prior to their marriage on 10th July 1861. It was transcribed by JMcC's granddaughter, Sarah Watkinson. The words marked in bold represent best guesses where the writing is unclear. An image of the letter can be seen here: https://doi.org/g9fp

Contents

Part V. The Letters: Voyage to South America, 1893-1894

Part VI. The Letters: Brazil and Argentina 1894-1895

Preface

This is a collection of travel letters written by my maternal grandfather John (Jack) McCaldin Loewenthal, known as JMcC, to his mother Jane at their home in Lennoxvale, Belfast, between 1889 and 1895, when he was in his mid to late 20s.

They were written during his journeys to South America and the West Indies, where he had been sent as a "traveller" by Isaac Weinberg, co-founder of the firm "Moore and Weinberg", Linen and Jute traders, based in Dundee and Belfast. His role was to represent the firm and secure commercial contracts for both Dundee (run by Weinberg) and Belfast (run by his father, Julius Loewenthal, Isaac Weinberg's business partner).

The reason these letters survived for posterity is that he had specifically asked his mother to keep them as a record of his travels, for him to look back on after his return home to Belfast.

The letters are a diary-like account of his travels and travel impressions, also containing little anecdotes, as well as more personal interactions with his mother to do with family and friends in Belfast and Dundee, as well as social chit chat. They were part of a regular correspondence between him and Jane.

They were separate to those he wrote to his father which were reserved for matters of "business".

Sadly, neither the letters from Jane to JMcC, nor the letters to Julius were kept.

These travel letters reflect how this descendent of Irish and Scottish Presbyterians and German Jewish merchants perceives himself and the world in the Victorian colonial trade environment.

We see a refined, self-confident, well-read, multilingual young bachelor who thinks of himself through and through as an "English gentleman", except on St Patrick's day, when he is definitely an Irishman. His views mirror those of the epoch, and at times can be jarring to present-day sensibilities.

We sense the perception of superiority of imperial English society with respect to other colonists ("natives"), let alone indigenous people or descendants of recently enslaved African people ("blackies" and "niggers"). Guests at a party in Brazil referred to as "*Many of the guests were coloured – not black – but with a touch of tar*".

We hear of "English Clubs", and "English guest houses" where "good English food" can be found, and good company can be kept. Women are either "young", "young and pretty", or good conversationalists. But serious company is kept with male peers ("good young fellows"). There are dinner parties, dances, picnics and theatre outings.

The letters provide a fascinating window into the world of "upmarket" international sea travel in the 19th century, the extent of the network of British and German influence in South American and West Indian economic and early industrial life, local political events and skirmishes, and social mores.

Being able to transcribe these letters and immerse myself into JMcC's world at the time has been the most sustaining and pleasurable occupation of the prolonged Melbourne pandemic lockdown of 2020-2021.

Michelle Fink
Melbourne, November 2021

Genealogy

JMcC and His Siblings

John McCaldin Loewenthal (known as "JMcC" by the family) was born on the 29th February 1864 (a leap year baby) in Belfast. He was the second child and first son of Jane Rea née McCully (or McCulla) and Julius Löwenthal (or Loewenthal). He was named John McCaldin after Jane's maternal grandfather (b 1777, d 1858) and/or uncle (both John McCaldin). JMcC's siblings were:

- Minna (b 1863, d 1880) – named after Julius' mother – died age 17 of heart valve disease
- Ferdinand Adolphus (b 1865, d 1942) – named after Julius' brother – known as "Addie", and changed his surname to "Lowell" – the black sheep of the family – died in London
- Anne Isabella (b 1867, d 1922) – named after Jane's mother – known as "Annie"- never married and said to have committed suicide – died in London
- Emma Flora (b 1869, d 1948) – named after Julius' sister – never married – died in Edinburgh
- Olga (b 1870, d 1955) – married Claude Hardy in 1900 – died in Cheshire
- Julius (b 1872, d 1896) – known as "Julie" – died of yellow fever in Brazil at age 23
- James Moore (b 1874, d 1919) – known as "Jim" – named after the senior partner in "Moore and Weinberg" (James Moore from Holywood, County Down, b 1811, d 1884) – Jim was JMcC's trusted business partner (the only reliable surviving male sibling) – he died of the "Spanish Flu" and was unmarried.

His Parents

JMcC's father, Julius Löwenthal, was born on the 7th December 1834 in Ludwigslust, in the Duchy of Mecklenburg-Schwerin (now Mecklenburg-Vorpommern, Germany). His father Israel (b 1804, d 1835) died at the age of 30 one year after Julius' birth. Both his father (Israel) and grandfather (Meyer Israel, b 1771) were Jewish merchants, residing in Ludwigslust, where they were among a very small cohort of so-called "protected (court) Jews". His mother Minna née Samson (b 1803, d 1887) was born in the then "territory" of Hanover. There was a longstanding connection of marriages between the Hanover Samson and Mecklenburg-Schwerin Löwenthal families (including Elsa Iklé's maternal grandmother Louise Derenberg née Samson having been Minna's sister).

Julius had a brother, Ferdinand Adolph (b 1833, d 1902), and a sister Emma (b 1831, d 1913). Ferdinand Adolph, later known as "Adolph", was also a merchant ("commission merchant colonial produce") and lived in London (at 205 Adelaide Road, Hampstead) with his wife Caroline née Goldschmidt, and their three children, Nanny (b 1871, d 1943), Edgar (b 1872, d 1957), and Clara (b 1873, d 1943). Emma was born and died in Ludwigslust, she never married.

Julius arrived in Belfast in 1856 to work as an assistant to Isaac Julius Weinberg in his business, Moore and Weinberg, founded only one year earlier. He had been recommended by Mr Weinberg's uncle, Philip Simon, in whose company he had worked in Hamburg[1]. More recently Julius had been working with his maternal uncle, Leopold Samson (his mother Minna Samson's brother), a merchant in Manchester. On arrival in Belfast Julius stayed at the same "boarding house for gentlemen" as Mr Weinberg, which was run at 10 College Square East, by a Mrs McCulla. This is where he likely first

---

1. Simon May & Company: In 1842 in Hamburg, Simon May and Phillip Simon organized a small mercantile house specializing in textiles, concentrating on lace. Jacob Weinberg (I. J. Weinberg's brother) opened a branch in Nottingham, the principal source of lace, in 1849.

came to know her younger daughter, Jane. Jane Rea McCulla was born 17th March 1836 in Belfast into a Presbyterian family. Her siblings were Isabella (m Hall) and James McCulla. Her father was William McCulla about whom we know little, except that he was no longer alive at the time of her wedding to Julius Löwenthal on 10 July 1861. Her mother, Ann Isabella McCulla, née McCaldin, (b 1803, d 1892), lived out her life with Julius and Jane. Ann Isabella's siblings were Andrew, Martha, James, Hugh, and John McCaldin. Jane and Julius were married in Malone Presbyterian Church in 1861.

His Marriage and Children

JMcC married his second cousin Elsa (Louise Helene) Iklé in Hamburg, on the 21st April 1903. Elsa had been born on the 15th August 1874. She was the granddaughter of Louise Derenberg (née Samson), the sister of JMcC's grandmother Minna Löwenthal (née Samson). Elsa's mother, Clara Iklé (née Derenberg) had always had a very warm relationship with JMcC, her cousin Julius Löwenthal's son. Her father was Julius Iklé, the fourth of the 15 children of Sara née Jonas, and Moses. Both families came from Hamburg. Elsa's siblings were:

- Robert Max Julius (b 1873, d 1893 suicide)
- Olga (Sara Olga) [m Jacoby], her twin sister (b 1874, d 1913)
- Charles (Carl) Felix (b 1879, d 1963)
- Amélie Marie [m Lewandowsky] (b 1882, d 1963)

JMcC and Elsa lived in Belfast where they had and raised four daughters:

- Helen Olga Lowenthal (b 1904, d 1993)
- Amélie Clara Boyd (b 1906, d 1998). Mother of:
  - John Dixon Iklé Boyd
  - Robert David Hugh Boyd
  - Stephen Andrew Colin Boyd
  - Richard (Charles Adam Richard) Boyd
- Joan Elsa Day (b 1911, d 2004). Mother of:
  - Sarah Caroline Watkinson
  - Thomas Kevin Day
- Peggy (Margaret Grace) Fink (b 1913, d 2013). Mother of:
  - (Anne) Michelle Fink

End of life

JMcC lived in the family home in Lennoxvale until his death on 20th January 1951. Elsa had a recurring mental illness since her young adult days, and despite the most attentive and loving care given by JMcC at home in Lennoxvale, Belfast, needed to move to residential care in Edinburgh in 1932. She was cared for at Vogrie House nursing home, where she died on the 7th November 1959.

The Letters: An Intergenerational Voyage

7 Lennoxvale, off the Malone Road, in Belfast, always "Lennoxvale" to the family, was the home of Julius Loewenthal, his Belfast-born wife Jane, the recipient of these letters, and their 8 children. 'Lennoxvale' was also a sufficient address for mail from another continent; the boat chosen for its voyage being indicated above the address on the envelope. The back of each envelope is usually dated in a different hand, presumably Jane's.

Front and back of the envelope containing a letter sent by JMcC to his mother from Pernambuco, dated 1st February 1894, postmarked 3rd February 1894. Online version: https://doi.org/hbtx

The writer, John McCaldin Loewenthal, Jack to his friends and JMcC to family to distinguish him from another John, his cousin, John Jacoby (JJ), was their eldest son.

After the period of the voyages, vividly described in these letters, JMcC settled down in Belfast in University Square. His beloved younger brother "Julie" died in Brazil of yellow fever during a similar voyage in 1896. Whether his death played a role in JMcC's decision to settle we do not know. Settle he did, followed by marriage at the age of 39. The wedding was in Hamburg, to Elsa, a cousin on Julius' side of the family. The couple moved to Marlborough Park, Belfast, where they had four daughters – in sequence: Helen, Amélie, Joan, and Margaret (always known as Peggy).

When Julius died in 1916 the young family moved into Lennoxvale. Something of life there is brought alive in the youngest daughter's memoir, *From Belfast to Belsen and Beyond*. Lennoxvale, a much-loved house, remained the family home until, in turn, JMcC's death in 1951 (the picture shows Lennoxvale with two of JMcC's daughters; Peggy seated, and Joan standing).

Amélie, their second daughter must have acquired the letters when that home of two generations of Loewenthals was broken up. The Vice-chancellor of Queen's University had his residence in Lennoxvale too. The Loewenthal home went to the University and became its School of Psychology, and in 2015, by now an administration building, the house still bore a plaque memorialising JMcC who had, long after the voyages, been honoured in 1939 with a Queen's University M.A. in recognition of his contributions to Belfast life.

Elsa Loewenthal's battered suitcase, in which the letters were stored

Amélie was always a hoarder of letters. Forty years later she, widow of an academic, in turn left her house, in Cambridge. The move meant another clear-out and distribution of items to her four sons. One of these items was a battered old suitcase of Elsa's which ended up in, second son, Robert's Macclesfield garage.

The suitcase was stuffed with letters and other memorabilia; Robert's school reports, childhood postcards, some photographs and many negatives. The bulk of the letters were between Amélie and Dixon Boyd and their friends and relatives. Their courting missives, wartime correspondence and later holiday reports predominated. There was, however, some earlier material. When leaving the suitcase, Amélie drew specific attention to a group of her father's letters from South America – those which now form this volume.

But, Robert was a busy man or thought himself a busy man. Amélie died. The garage became cluttered with mid-life bicycles, garden tools, and the detritus of university-leaving children; yet another generation. The contents of the suitcase migrated to a cupboard in the ex-bedroom of one of these, JMcC's great-grandson. Robert had read a few of the letters at the time of that migration and even transcribed a summary of one voyage but did no more until the cycle of life brought Amélie's four children – four sons – into their phase of retirement and more imminent death. More time and less time!

Robert began to share the contents of the suitcase with his brothers, especially letters between their parents in coping with war-time separation as young parents and, with John, the eldest, who was then dying in his turn, evidences of his early life. Some of the letters were from friends and relatives and in German

A selection of the letters, laid out on the kitchen floor

The letters brought out of storage, ready to be photographed and sent to Michelle

Enter Michelle, Peggy's daughter and JMcC's youngest grandchild born the year before he died. She was home in Cambridge from Australia. She came to Macclesfield and, brought up in Vienna, kindly translated, including difficult early missives in "Kurrent" (German cursive) script from Julius' family. The same visit, she and Robert began to seriously engage with the letters of JMcC's voyages. It was clear she had the skills and interest to take engagement with them to an entirely new level: the boats, the friends, the peripatetic life. But, her stay was short.

Came the pandemic. Robert was locked down on the island of Tiree, one of the smaller Hebrides. He had the letters with him. Michelle was stuck in Melbourne unable to come to Cambridge. What better Covid project? Robert could image and send, using WhatsApp, letters laid out on the kitchen table, with the help of low denomination weights from ancient kitchen scales. This had to be done at mid-day when the light was sufficiently bright to avoid blurring. Michelle could decipher occasionally faded handwriting using her expertise as a radiologist in handling imaging tools. She could then, with the help of the internet, integrate the letters into their local and wider context. After a morning swim, WhatsApping for Michelle became a daily pleasure. A century and more since their writing did not seem very long. It was also poignant to remember that another of JMcC's brothers, Jim, had died in 1919, twenty years after the voyages, in another pandemic, the Spanish Influenza of 1918

Covid, and John's death which brought cousins together, also provided an unexpected stimulus for all JMcC's surviving grandchildren to get together on Zoom and contemplate our shared grandparent. And, as we discussed the possibility of sharing more widely aspects of 19th-century commerce brought alive in JMcC's vivid prose (and occasional verse), we realised that a great-grandchild (Charles Watkinson) might enable us to reach that goal. This volume is the result.

Memories of JMcC

Sarah Watkinson

My clearest memory of my Loewenthal grandfather is of his bending down to my level from his armchair, to feel if there was enough room for my toes in my new slippers. I was three, in my place on the hearthrug beside the black dog Hamlet. In my toddler memory from 76 years ago, this was the centre of the house, a completely happy place next to Bampa's feet in shiny black shoes and legs in dark trousers. Peat smouldered in the hearth under its massive fossiliferous black marble surround, the scent mingling with his cigar smoke. Perhaps a clock ticked. The drawing room stretched darkly behind us, divided in two by a vast velvet curtain. The ceiling was out of sight and I sometimes found it agreeable to sit under the grand piano; whenever I hear *Kinderszenen* now, a strong memory of Lennoxvale comes back; my mother Joan told me that her friend Elizabeth Kinnaird's boyfriend might have played it as I sat beneath.

Next to the drawing-room, and also opening off the square hall, was the sunny dining room where I had FruGrains for breakfast, alone with Joany at a long shiny table; a memory of this room is strongly triggered by the smaller dining room at the Reform Club in London, which at lunchtime has the same smell of last night's good dinner, cigar smoke and red Turkey carpet. The red carpet with its blue and green lozenge pattern also covered the stairs and the landing where Big Sarah, the maid, gave me rides on the carpet sweeper. You could look down from the bannisters around the landing into the hall below and watch people from on top. In the higher regions of the house I had my cot where I spent ages looking at the ceiling with its crack in the plaster, although once, intolerably bored, I danced in the cot with my doll and crashed through its base onto the floor. Another little room up here was the sewing room, with a ragbag of old petticoats you could dress up in – I never saw anybody sewing in there.

It was as if I could go anywhere and come across people who might, like Big Sarah, find me delightful, or be less responsive – like Margaret the other maid, who inhabited the kitchen. Then it was better to go out into the garden, where Colin the gardener would be busy but friendly among the vegetables and fruit trees, and where a peach tree grew against the house wall. Once there was a single peach in the net hung to catch the fruit, and I was told it was Bampa's – the only thing I remembered ever having been denied to me in that Arcadian household. A veranda stretched along another side of the house. There were lawns, under big trees alongside the drive, and a copper beech towards the back of the house with a rope swing suspended from a high branch. Round the left side of the house from the drive, a grassy slope made a good place to roll down (perhaps the one on which JMcC and his youngest daughters were photographed; see below). Somebody once made me a snowman there, which Hamlet came and peed on, making a terrible yellow stain.

On my third birthday – February 1945 – Joany stuck red and yellow whirligigs into the grass to spin in the wind and brought in crocuses – purple and gold – arranged in a bowl of sand so that they opened in the warmth of the dining room. All for me! But with hindsight, I wonder if her relief at the prospect of the war ending, and my father Tom's expected return, contributed to the atmosphere of pure happiness that day, which is one of my strongest memories of Lennoxvale. It was a house full of delight in life; its comfortable security felt proof against what I understood was a dangerous and uncertain world outside.

Oxford, November 2021

Robert Boyd

Yes indeed. Hamlet – though loved, he had halitosis, my first unpleasant breath experience; I think of him whenever I add garlic. Despite this, I, too, liked being on Hamlet's level. Cigars yes; I think of Bampa (allegedly named because toddler eldest-grandchild John couldn't say Grandpa) on the now rare occasions the smoke of one comes my way. The dining room too, on whose shiny, and enormous, table napkin rings rolled so enticingly to the irritation of my father, and the grassy slope to roll down round the corner from the veranda. Between rolls, Bampa showed me how he dug out dandelions from the slope with a special knife.

Four years older than cousin Sarah, there were additional excitements. The curving bannisters were a joy to slide down – until I fell the wrong side and landed on my head on the tiles of the Palladian hall round which they ran. I had learnt from someone, probably older brother John, that damaged horses were shot. "Shoot me it's worse than a bomb" was, once I had stopped crying, my war-time response to the fall.

Later, after peace had come, John and I stayed at Lennoxvale with Amélie who was recuperating from Jaundice. Learning bridge with Bampa was a high spot. So was Margaret's delicious food – no meat rationing in Northern Ireland. So was a side trip I had to stay with a Kinnaird brother in Carrowdore Castle. Earlier-generation Kinnairds are a feature of the letters (this was George Young Kinnaird's son, George Young Kinnaird Jr, who owned Carrowdore Castle, see the Index to People).

Later still, John and I went without Amélie. Bampa was, by then, restricted to his upstairs sitting room but the household had its comforting sense of permanency. We played endless monopoly with the Ashby boys in the Vice-chancellor's residence across the way and, to (Big) Sarah's outrage, squirted our water pistols there. We didn't dare in Sarah's domain. Margaret served our meals in the dining room. Lennoxvale friends entertained us – Elizabeth Kinnaird, Dorothea McDowell, or Nascio Llubera. Supportive loyalty to our grandfather and his daughters I suppose.

Not long before his death, I went on my own, a memorable visit. From Sarah's "Good morning Master Robert" when she raised the blind and placed tea by my bed (I was 12) until bedtime it was a delightful grown-up experience. A purse had been bought for me. In it, a half-crown was "to spend as you like". I beat Dorothea at Canasta – to her annoyance. I sat on the floor beside Bampa's armchair (which I still have) and gained praise by solving a crossword clue for him with the help of his encyclopaedia. I walked round to Elizabeth's house. I also explored Lennoxvale's downstairs at my leisure. In my possession as I write is a particularly lovely pack of cards I found in a drawer and surreptitiously purloined; sorry Bampa!

Many decades later three grandchildren returned to Lennoxvale. We were to Rathlin Island to scatter Peggy's ashes, his centenarian daughter and Hamlet's owner. No 7 was now University offices. Trees on the slope had overgrown the dandelions of memory. Half as old as these letters, they were already as high as the house. But, for me too, memories of John McCaldin Loewenthal, and of the house to which he directed his letters, trump, indeed, the flow of time.

Tiree, November 2021

JMcC with his four daughters in a car at Rock Cottage, Newcastle, County Down.

Informal photograph of JMcC sitting on a flowery bank with his two youngest daughters, Joan (left, b 1911) and Peggy (right, b 1913).

A photograph of Lennoxvale, JMcC's house. Taken around 1922 by Robert John Welch. Peggy and Joan are standing on the windowsill and Amélie on the ground to the side of Peggy.

A photograph of the side of Lennoxvale, JMcC's house in Belfast, with his four daughters. Helen, sophisticated (not in pinafore), and Amélie next to her – the two "little" ones in front, Joan sitting and Peggy standing. The picture was taken around 1922 by Robert John Welch.

Robert John Welch (b 22nd July 1859, d 28th September 1936) was the leading photographer in the north of Ireland at the time. He specialised in outdoors photography and took thousands of photographs of the towns and scenery of Ireland, as well as industrial scenes such as the construction of RMS "Olympic" and "Titanic" at the Harland and Wolff shipyards: https://en.wikipedia.org/wiki/Robert_Welch_(photographer).

PART I
THE LETTERS: WEST INDIES VOYAGE, 1889-1890

Map of the 1889-1890 voyage by John McCaldin Loewenthal, showing the places mentioned in the letter and an approximate route for his travels from Plymouth to South America and then to New York. A high-res version is available online: https://doi.org/10.17613/2mfc-hz92. (Original map by Thomas Bachrach)

1. Letter from SS Medway sailing to Barbados, 1st-10th December 1889

18891201 See an image of the original letter, http://dx.doi.org/10.17613/8nr8-6w78

S.S. Medway

Sunday 1st Dec.

My dear Mother,

I wrote you a few hurried lines & sent you a wire from Plymouth, as directed, both of which I trust were duly delivered.

We are now three days out, so I shall begin to note down a few incidents of the voyage so as to have a fairly long account to post to you by first opportunity.[1]

As cabin companion I found I had a little Frenchman from Martinique, – tolerably clean – as French West Indians go – which isn't saying much;

Providence helps those who help themselves & it is very useful to bear this principle in mind when travelling. And so I went to the Purser & told him I didn't relish the little Frenchman very much, & as there were not many passengers perhaps he could give me a cabin to myself. Now he has given me one of the best cabins on the ship – a three-berth one, large & well ventilated – in fact one that costs half as much again as the one my ticket entitles me to, with the further advantage that I have it all to myself – which makes a wonderful difference to one's comfort.

The first two days of the voyage were calm, y'day & today have been very rough & just now the ship is rolling so that I can scarcely sit on my campstool, & I have to clutch my inkbottle to prevent a spill. The crockery on board is having a high old time of it & the trunks are performing a war dance in the neighbouring cabins. All this is not conducive to polite letter writing, so you must excuse if both style & characters are rather jerky.

Many of the passengers are still lying wedged in their berths, with groanings that cannot be uttered. One man has just told me that he wd cut his own throat for sixpence, from which I take it that he doesn't find existence under these circumstances an unmixed joy. – Another charitably hopes my time will come too.

Monday 2nd Dec.

Much calmer today; my porthole is open & a pleasant breeze comes in. Temperature just pleasant, neither too hot nor too cold. Several fresh faces have shown themselves on deck today, – I mean fresh in the sense of new – for they still look very green.

The Most Reverend The Archbishop of Trinidad is playing quoits with an old French priest, – reminds me of Mrs Black & Mrs Byers at the potato game. There is bad whist going on in the smoking room. I was looking on for a bit, but when the best player of the four held king, queen, & four small trumps & didn't lead them, I got disgusted & came away. Well for him he hasn't somebody we know for a partner!

I had intended reading some German poetry, but this exhibition brought on a paroxysm of nervous excitement, so I

---

1. 3 days out from Plymouth on 1st December – therefore left around 27-28th November 1889. Azores in sight on 2nd December – 1/3 of the way to Barbados. Arrive in Barbados on 10th December. Thus approximately two weeks' voyage.

came down to my cabin to work it off by writing and munching chocolates out of the boys' hamper. I have just given a couple of sweets to a dirty-faced little urchin outside – I hope he won't choke over them – On second thoughts, I don't mind if he does, if it's the same one that howls at nights. I wanted to persuade him to say "thank you" & I tackled him in Spanish, German & French, but without eliciting a sound, so I have come to the conclusion that, whatever he speaks, he does not speak it with Castilian, Parisian, or Hannoverian accent.

The Azores are in sight, so we have about one third of our voyage over. Till noon today we had run some 1250 miles since leaving Southampton. Today's run was 340 miles, just over 14 knots per hour – a very fair pace.

I have finished "Hypatia" since I came on board – & I shouldn't care to have to read it again. It doesn't increase the small admiration I ever had for Kingsley.[2] I suppose the picture it gives – not very flattering one – of Alexandrian life & the Christian Church in the fifth century is tolerably correct, & in so far it is interesting, but the book as a whole is undeniably tedious. Kingsley's inflated style is very different from George Eliot's compressed thought.

Tuesday 3rd Dec.

It is a lazy life on board ship, sleeping & feeding take up most of the time.

The latter goes on pretty well all day long. At 6 in the morning there is a tea or coffee for those that want it; breakfast at 9, luncheon at 1, dinner at 6 & tea & coffee again at 8.

I have my salt-water bath at abt. 8 o'clock, & most refreshing it is. I always begin breakfast with stirabout,[3] as at home, then chop, steak, or bacon & eggs, & wind up with marmalade. We have fresh milk every morning – not from the cow, but from the refrigerator, where it is stored in frozen blocks. Fish & meat are kept in the same way. For luncheon there is soup, sardines, cold beef, ham, mutton etc, sweets, fruit, cheese.

As for dinner, I send you the bill of fare for last Sunday, from which you will see that we are not in any immediate danger of starving. The oyster patties were very fair & the pheasant was excellent. See what hardships a poor traveller has to put up with! Then I have your jolly plum-cake to fall back on. Half of it has already gone the way of all plumcakes, & the rest of it will ere long dissolve & leave not a wrack behind. I gave some of it last night to three fellows with whom I played whist, & they appreciated it muchly. One of them thought it rather rich to eat at night, or, to continue the quotation, that it was "such stuff as dreams are made on", but he took another piece all the same.

The Royal Mail's steamship Medway was launched in 1877.

Thursday 6th Dec.

We are just a week out today. Only last Thursday we were shivering in our top coats & winter clothes. Today those who are lucky enough to have brought tennis flannels have put them on & we place our chairs in the coolest corners under the awning on deck. There is scarcely a ripple on the water & not a cloud in the sky.

There are about a hundred saloon passengers – a very comfortable number. There are not many ladies on board & only two or three young & pretty ones – of these one is said to have a nice little dot of £150,000! A dragon-like "Mamma" keeps the strictest watch over her & never lets her out of sight. The "heiress" as she is called, does not seem so grateful for this motherly care in keeping the men at a distance as a right-thinking young woman ought to.

2. "Hypatia", or "New Foes with an Old Face" is an 1853 novel by the English writer Charles Kingsley. Intended as Christian apologia, it reflects typical 19th-century religious sentiments of the day. For many years the book was considered one of Kingsley's best novels and was widely read.
3. porridge

There is another fair one with a "cocky" straw hat & a suspicion of paint about the eyes, who flirts in the most outrageous fashion, in the opinion of all sober matrons, with the officers of the ship from the Captain down.

There is, of course, the ubiquitous "yachting man", got up – regardless of expense from the yellow leather boots up to the blue knitted cap of that inverted–jelly–strainer form, which is popularly supposed to be the exclusive property of yachtists & Italian bandits.

His wife is rigged out "to match". She is a tall fine-looking woman & the couple <u>pose</u> for the benefit of the rest of the passengers. Mr H. tells me that his wife enjoys an evening cigarette in the cabin of one of the officers. She doesn't smoke it elsewhere for fear of "treading on the toes" of the other passengers.

Sat. 7th Dec.

Father's birthday: – many happy returns to him.[4] I shall drink his health at luncheon in XX or Pilsener.[5] When at Adelaide Road I heard that the usual box was coming over from Germany – with marzapan, goose-breast & I suppose other good things.[6] They will last longer through my absence. The savoury Limburg cheese will be supplanted for a time.[7] You will quite miss its all-pervading fragrance & you will have to partly fill the void by going in heavily for Fynan haddock; – not your poor fresh stuff with no more smell that singed hair, but good venerable haddock of mellow aged odour, compared with which "Ceylon's spicey breezes"

or "The sweet South

That breathes upon a bank of violets" are but as gilded tinsel to "refined gold" or as a "taper" to "the burnished eye of heaven."[8]

Sunday 8th Dec.

These reflections on haddock & cheese were cut short by the steward who came to settle my cabin, & turned me out of it.

At the end of our first week out everyone was agreed that we were having a very dull voyage, so on Thursday it was voted by common consent that the do-nothing-ness had lasted long enough & that an effort should be made towards mutual entertainment during the rest of the trip.

We now have a daily sweep-stake on the run of the ship during the 24 hours. The entrance is 4/- & there is a first prize of £1 for the holder of the winning number posted up by the Captain at the entrance to the saloon at noon each day, & two second prizes of 10/- each for the numbers immediately above & below the winning one. The surplus goes into the box for the fund on behalf of the widows & orphans of the Royal Mail Co's sailors.

On Thursday evg. we had a concert in the Music Saloon, which is a kind of round gallery above the Dining Saloon. There was no extraordinary talent, but the proceedings were made lively by several good comic songs & one or two amusing incidents. One young man forgot an accompaniment he had volunteered to play for another fellow, & after half a dozen false starts they both retired amidst considerable laughter.

At the request of the Archbishop, who is himself an Irishman, an Irish priest sang Killaloo in the most rollicking fashion, while a broad appreciative grin spread itself over the big round red face of the Archbishop.[9]

After the concert there was dancing on the quarter-deck to the music of a concertina, a banjo, & a guitar, played by three of the sailors. The ship was rolling pretty well, & it was very funny to see erratic revolutions of the dancers, & their helpless rushes first to one side, then to the other. I danced a Schottische (that word doesn't look right somehow) with

4. Julius Sr's 55th birthday (b 7/12/1834)
5. Dos Equis XX Special Lager: A crisp, refreshing, light-bodied malt-flavored beer.
6. The residence of Ferdinand Adolf Loewenthal Sr ("Uncle Addie") was at 205 Adelaide Road, Hampstead, London. See Index to people. "Marzapan" is JMcC's spelling.
7. Limburger is a strong-smelling Belgian cheese.
8. A wry reference to Orsino's speech in Shakespeare's "Twelfth Night".
9. "Killaloe" was written in 1887 by Irish composer Robert "Ballyhooly Bob" Martin for "Miss Esmeralda", a burlesque production based on "The Hunchback of Notre Dame".

an indefatigable Scotch girl, & she nearly killed me. I wouldn't give in, & we danced the music out, earning the applause of the onlookers.[10]

A young chap who occupies the next cabin to me told me his partner valsed him till he was ready to drop. He did not like to ask her to stop, but he squeezed her gloved hand very hard, hoping that would have the desired effect, but in vain. It was only afterwards he found out that she had a mechanical arm & that he had been squeezing an india rubber hand!

On Friday evg. the concert was repeated, & as it was too rough for dancing, one of our amateur musicians afterwards gave us a selection of comic songs with banjo accompaniment. Among others he sang that one about the young lady "whose age it was red & whose hair was nineteen."[11]

Y'day afternoon we had athletic sports. They began with a "grasshopper race" in which the candidates for distinction had to run on "all fours". Then followed a potato race – similar to our potato game, but with about a dozen potatoes & no spoons. The next item was an egg-race, the egg being placed on a tea-spoon which the racer held in his mouth. After that came a tug of war between the passengers & the officers, the latter winning after a very hard pull. There was to have been a race for the ladies to see who could drink a lemon squash most quickly through a straw, but as there were no entries, that did not come off. One very amusing competition was ducking for eggs in a large tub – two men ducking at the same time burying themselves – up to the shoulders – in the tub, & butting each other's head under water. As two fellows had succeeded in securing an equal number of eggs it was arranged that they should decide the match by fishing for one more, and that there might be no advantage to either they were to put down their heads over the tub & the egg was to be dropped in between them. But in their excitement & without knowing it they smashed the egg between their heads, & when the first man came up to breathe he had it all plastered over his ear, but all unconscious of the fact he dived into the tub again to search for the missing egg, while the spectators fairly shrieked with laughter.

The meeting concluded with an obstacle race, the impediments consisting of a sail full of water, to be waded through, stools to be gone under, lifebelts & a long wind-sail, or canvas tube used for ventilating the hatches, to be crept through. Two fellows were wriggling in the middle of this tube when the chief officer turned the hose into the far end of it. I thought the fellows would have been smothered &, as it was, they came out looking like drowned rats. Fortunately they had rigged themselves out for a wetting, so no harm was done.

It becomes hotter & hotter. This afternoon the breeze died away & I felt that I sh$\underline{^d}$ like to take off my skin & sit in my bones. Still I prefer it what you are probably having at home.

This Sunday, as well as last, the Captain conducted the Church of England Service in the Saloon. First the crew is mustered on the quarter deck in their Sunday best, & the roll is called; then the bos'n pipes for prayers & they all troop below.[12] The Doctor presides at the harmonium, having previously got a choir together. As there is no Church of England clergyman on board we have no sermon.

Roman Catholic service was held at the same time in the fore-saloon, the Archbishop officiating.

Once a week there is a "fire drill"; the fire bell is rung, the crew all rush to their places, some to lower the boats, some to pass buckets or carry blankets, some to the pumps, & some to the hose, with which they try to put out the sea.

When the Captain considers that everyman has done his duty & the sea is duly extinguished, the bell is rung again & all danger is over.

---

10. The schottische is a partnered country dance that apparently originated in Bohemia. It was popular in Victorian era ballrooms as a part of the Bohemian folk-dance craze.

11. The song was called "The Maid of York Beach". It is featured in William H. Hills' *Students' Songs*, first published in 1880: https://hdl.handle.net/2027/hvd.32044043901040.

12. A boatswain, bo's'n, bos'n, or bosun, also known as a Petty Officer, deck boss, or a qualified member of the deck department, is the seniormost rate of the deck department and is responsible for the components of a ship's hull. Other names: Bosun; Petty Officer; Chief rate. Department: Deck department.

<u>Tuesday morng</u> <u>10th Dec</u>. 6 a.m.

We shall be at anchor in Barbados in half an hour or so. I shall now bring this letter to a close & post it as soon as we land, on the chance of it catching a mail via New York.

With best love all round

Your affectionate son

Jack.

P.S. I add Xmas & New Year good wishes in case my letter sh^d arrive in time for them to be seasonable. Many happy returns also of birthdays to Julie, Grannie & Emma.[13]

13. Birthdays: Julie = Julius Loewenthal Jr, b 17th December 1872. Grannie = Ann Isabella McCully (Jane's mother) b 25th December 1803. Emma Loewenthal, b 2nd January 1869.

2. Letter from Barbados, 14th-22nd December 1889

18891214 See an image of the original letter, http://dx.doi.org/10.17613/0cma-yf06

By Royal Mail
Barbados

Sat. Dec. 14th 1889

My dear Mother,

The night before arriving at Barbados I brought to a close the long letter I had written during the voyage. Next day I posted it via New York, but you will not have it much before this one though I shan't post this for another week. Unfortunately the outward steamer of the Royal Mail just misses the homeward-bound ship, reaching Barbados the day after the departure of the other, so that our letters lose a fortnight. The contract-day for the arrival of the outgoing Mail is Wednesday, but almost all the steamers arrive on Tuesday, & might easily do so on Monday. But as there is not competition on the route the Company instruct their captains to use as little coal as possible. Besides if the Post office sees that the voyage can be done in 10 days instead of 12, it will shorten the time when giving out the next contract.

When we anchored on Tuesday at day break it was raining heavily. The island looked very fresh & green, & everyone was pleased to see land once more. A Yankee who had suffered from sea sickness during the whole voyage came on deck with beaming face & "guessed he'd go ashore" & have a "square meal".

The "Medway" lies in the middle of a small fleet of the Royal Mail Intercolonial steamers that meet the Packet & convey passengers & cargo to the various islands & to Demerara. She is about half a mile from the shore, & all around her are dusky boatmen clamouring for fares, & imps of darkness in cockle shells of their own construction, who dive for the pennies thrown into the water by those of the passengers to whom the scene is fresh. As the coin touches the water over go the "little nigger boys" & for a few moments you can see only the white soles of their black feet down through the blue water. Then they turn upwards & you catch the gleam of the whites of their eyes. The one who gets the penny – for they never miss it – holds it up triumphantly; then they clamber into their cockleshells again & recommence the chorus "Master! Throw in a penny, Master!"

After breakfast I came ashore got comfortable quarters at the Ice House. The place that enjoys this refreshing name is the depot where the ice is stored & retailed, & is also the principal hotel in the town.

As it was Packet Day I was not able to do very much; still I made a few business calls & met with a most friendly reception from old acquaintances.

In the evening, while sitting in the verandah of the hotel I was told that someone wanted to speak to me at the telephone. This was Mrs Da Costa who had heard of my arrival, at which she was good enough to say she was very pleased.[1] She very kindly invited me to dinner the following evening, saying she has something to tell me. I accepted the invitation & spent a very pleasant evg. The "something" was that they were going to have a dance on the 31st & hoped I w‌ᵈ be present. Unfortunately there is no chance of that & I am very sorry indeed. I am told they give awfully jolly dances in "a" style & that the girls here know how to dance!

---

1. The Da Costa family is believed to be of Portuguese origin. The earliest Da Costas in the Caribbean are believed to have been Sephardic Jews from Europe. The family home was Dalkeith House, a large mansion in the centre of Bridgetown. "Mr and Mrs Da Costa" were probably Darnley Da Costa (b 1844) and his wife Ellen Mary Jeany née Clements. See Index to People.

Mrs Da Costa promised to fix a day for tennis. I imagined playing tennis at Christmas & finding it almost too hot work. Dalkeith is the name of their place & they have improved it greatly since my last visit.

The drawing room is square & about as large as our two rooms with a wide open verandah round three sides of it. The verandah will be lighted by Chinese lanterns, & Mrs Da Costa has arranged to have bright moonlight on the occasion.

Mr Da C. has put my name down as hon. member of the Club during my stay. I had first rate whist there the other evg. & several games of billiards.

Next day I met one of the youngest Professors of the Harrison College.[2] He asked me out to dine there this evg. It was very likely this College that young Craig thought of coming to. There is another, the Codrington College, at the other side of the Island.[3] I don't know much abt it, but in any case Craig did not know what he was refusing.

I also met old Mr Braithwaite, my cabin companion on the way home; – a friend of Dr Brown & of Taylors of Drum.[4] He is out of town but will be back in Bridgetown in a few days, when he says he will show me some attention.

I have made a beginning in business & hope I shall do fairly well. Among other things I have an order for G.Y.K. for collars & cuffs.[5]

Tuesday Dec. 17th Many happy returns to Julie[6]

Although it is only 12 o'clock I have had 3 invitations already this morning! How is that for Barbadian hospitality? A note from Mrs Da Costa asking me for tennis this afternoon. An invite for tea from a Mrs Cumings, whom I don't know. She is the aunt of one of the heads of departments at Harrison's store.[7] Thirdly a dinner-party at Mr Braithwaite's on Friday evg.

Have got along very well so far in business. I have made up my mind to go to Demerara before visiting Trinidad. The steamer goes tomorrow week. I shd like to get an earlier one & be back here for Da Costa's dance – for I must come back to get the steamer for Trinidad – but there is none before the 25th Xmas day, & business is the first consideration.

I must be off now to finish taking Harrison's order.[8]

2. Founded in 1733, Harrison College takes its name from Thomas Harrison, a Bridgetown merchant, who intended it to serve as "A Public and Free School for the poor and indigent boys of the parish". Even in the nineteenth century it was recognised as perhaps the most prestigious secondary school in the British West Indies, attracting boys from neighbouring islands, including Pelham Warner who later went on to become the "Grand Old Man" of English cricket. Described as "The Eton College of Barbados", since Barbados' independence in 1966, five out of Barbados's eight Prime Ministers have been alumni of Harrison College, among whom are also numbered the national poet Kamau Brathwaite and Alan Emtage the co-inventor of Archie, the world's first Internet search engine.

3. Codrington College is an Anglican theological college in St. John, Barbados now affiliated with the University of the West Indies at Cave Hill. It is the oldest Anglican theological college in the Americas. It was affiliated to the University of Durham from 1875.

4. How old is old? There is a John Braithwaite in Barbados – b 1849 – so just around 50 then.

5. George Young Kinnaird – father of Elizabeth Kinnaird - (George Kinnaird & Co, linen merchants, Belfast ; Kinnaird, George Y & Co., collar & cuff manufacturers). See Index to People.

6. Julius Loewenthal Jr (JMcC's younger brother) 17th birthday – b 17th December 1872. See Index to People.

7. A store on Broad Street, Bridgetown, Barbados called the HARRISONS. It was owned/founded by a C. F. Harrison in 1875.

8. Our lack of the parallel set of business letters to his father means that we can only surmise JMcC's business in Barbados. However, possibly he is setting up business deals with both Da Costa & Co and Harrison, C. F., & Co for jute ropes. Both companies are listed as Ship Chandlers in the "Commercial Directory of the American Republics" of 1898.

"Street Scene, Barbados: Throwing Money." An illustration from Owen T. Bulkeley's The Lesser Antilles, published in 1889.

STREET SCENE, BARBADOS; THROWING MONEY.

Sat'day 21st Dec.

Owing to heavy rain the tennis did not come off on Tuesday. I went to Mrs Cummins's for tea & found that my hostess was a tall middle aged coloured lady with a cafe au lait complexion. She was very kind but rather melancholy, for she had lost her only son not long ago. There were three young coloured ladies & one ditto gentleman. We had some music of very fair quality, & I had to taste all the fruits & preserves of the country. So many different sweets nearly made me sick, but it w^{d} not have been polite to refuse to try them as Mrs Cummins took considerable trouble in bringing them out.

The dinner-party last night at Mr Braithwaite's was most delightful. He has a nice villa about 2 miles out of town. The hour was 7.30 & we sat down 10 to table. There were Mr Braithwaite & a lady related to him, who did the honours, a Capt. & Mrs Saddler, a Dr Anthony, from the garrison, & his wife, Mr, Mrs, & Miss Austin & myself. Mr Austin is agent here for the Royal Mail.

I took Miss Austin in to dinner – to borrow a description from Fred Boas [9] "one of the most charming girls I ever met", not exactly very pretty, & yet distinctly not plain looking. She talked & listened well – she did not "ejaculate" but she "conversed", so she was different from the most of young ladies one meets – the interjectional fair ones whom Andy Bell objects to so strongly. But Miss Austin's "greatest charm" was a perfect ease of manner & an absence of all affectation.

And now I will tell you who these Austins are. Mrs A. is a sister of Mrs John Taylor of Drum, & I don't know what relation to Dr Jack Brown – the Fergusson's Dr Brown. Mr Braithwaite is also related to the Austins & Taylors by marriage I think. I am not very clear about the whole connection, but possibly you may know more about it. Mrs Austin & also her son & daughter have been in Belfast at different times staying with the Taylors at Windsor. [10]

I am going to the Austins' to-night for dinner. As I have finished my business & am now waiting for my steamer, I am lucky in getting so many – almost too many – invites, as the time goes very pleasantly.

9. See Index to People
10. The social networks of the Victorian colonies are on full display here. Mr Braithwaite was related to the Austins and Taylors by marriage. Capt. & Mrs Saddler, Dr Anthony (from the garrison), Mr Austin (agent for the Royal Mail), and Mrs Austin a sister of Mrs John Taylor of Drum.

<u>Sunday evg. 22nd Dec.</u>

Y'day afternoon I went to an Agricultural Exhibition held in the grounds of the Harrison College. The show itself was not very remarkable, consisting chiefly of poultry & vegetables, but it was well worth going to see the collection of gorgeously arranged negro beauty & fashion. It is quite impossible to convey any idea of the display of multi-coloured dresses, along side of which Joseph's coat would have looked dowdy. The proudest "ladies" were those who had most hues in their skirt & most flowers in their bonnets. The latter were botanic gardens in miniature & as for the former, the effects produced by the combination of the most flaming blues, greens, yellows, reds & pinks, baffle all attempt at description. Over all the tiny parasol festooned with embroidered muslin, carried, no doubt, to shade those exquisitely chiselled (out of one block!) full round lips, which suggested to the intelligent observer the probability of there being a face behind them.

After the exhibition I came to the Hotel & dressed for Austins'. It was a very pleasant little dinner, menu clear soup, flying-fish, eggs, boiled mutton, roast chicken, & English pheasant. There were two other fellows there & the conversation was lively, though it began rather uncannily with deaths & funerals at sea, & the delightfulness of being drowned.

Unfortunately I had to leave early, about 9 o'clock, to carry out a second engagement (!) – being such a popular man, as Mr Austin put it! The other was for tea, & I did not enjoy it for I was too horribly sleepy. – You see I am up at half past six every morning here, & have my bath over when my cup of tea is brought up at seven.

One more dinner brings the list up to date. It was this afternoon & my host was a Mr Challenor, a well-to-do sugar planter & merchant, who has a nice place on the outskirts of the town.[11] He has 7 children – one daughter married, & a son in England; the rest are youngsters. The dinner was like a family English meal; – giblet soup, roast beef, & roast turkey, with plum-pudding to finish up.

Tomorrow the mail goes & I must now bring this letter to a close. On Tuesday the steamer arrives from England, & brings, I hope, letters with good news from you all.

On Christmas-day I leave for Demerara, so I shall eat my Xmas dinner on board. After Barbados I am afraid I shall have a dull time at Demerara, as it is my first visit & I have not introductions. Still we shall see.

> "When other lips & other eyes
> Than mine shall feast on your mince-pies
> Then you'll remember me."[12]

With which touching couplet I stop.
Best love all round.
Your affectionate son.
Jack

---

11. The Challenors were one of the established English families on the island and were frequently listed among Barbados's leading citizens.

12. JMcC is parodying "Then You'll Remember Me", a song from M. W. Baife's opera *The Bohemian Girl*, 1863: https://digitalcommons.conncoll.edu/sheetmusic/1081/

3. Letter from Georgetown, Demerara, 27th December 1889–3rd January 1890

18891227 See an image of the original letter, http://dx.doi.org/10.17613/xnt6-wa33

Georgetown, Demerara.

Friday 27th Dec. 1889

My dear Mother,

Before leaving Barbados on Xmas-day, I recvd. your welcome letters of 2nd & 9th Dec. Together with the family budget of good wishes for the season. Many thanks to all for their letters, which I hope to answer by degrees.

Much interested to hear about Fuhrs' dance.[1] It is reported out here that the "heirloom" swallow-tail made such an impression on one of the heiresses that she proposed to Julie right away, but he replied that he must first see if his brother James w^{d} take over a young lady whose affections they had jointly engaged at a fashionable seaside resort.[2]

It is well that Mr Willie Brown's life was so fully assured. I suppose his widow will be comfortably provided for. Have you heard anything more about Miss Brown's reported engagement? Are Jack Sinclair's friends subscribing to make him a wedding present? If so I sh^{d} like to join. I shall write to Father about it.

By this time I trust you have all quite recovered from the consequences of the Christmas festivities.

I was invited to take pot luck on Xmas-day at Mr Rickford's where I spent a most pleasant evg. during my previous visit to Barbados. As I sailed that day I c^{d} not accept.

The letter which I posted by last mail, brought me as far as Monday 23rd. On Tuesday afternoon I played tennis at Da Costas'. I met there a Miss Haines, a very nice lively girl. She drove me into town in her carriage & asked me to call at their house on my return. Of all the places I know Barbados takes the palm for hospitality.

Earlier the same afternoon I had called at the Austins to pay a digestion visit, & had mentioned that I might be passing through Barbados again abt Janry. 6th on my way from Demerara, whereupon Mrs Austin asked me to dine with them that evg. (Janry. 6th) & go with them to an amateur pantomime – Blue-beard – in which one of the children was taking part.

To anyone who reads my list of invitations at Barbados I must seem a very "uncommercial traveller". But it all helps business to take a low view of it, & need not at all interfere with one's work.

The "Eden" sailed for Demerara about noon on Xmas-day. There were only some four passengers on board & we had rather a dull time of it. There was a heavy sea on, & none of us seemed to enjoy very much the turkey & plum pudding served up in honour of the occasion.

After dinner I paced the decks & wondered how you were getting on at home. It was too warm to go below so I stretched myself in someone's deck-chair & slept there till abt. 4 in the morning, when I turned into my cabin.

---

1. The Fuhrs (see Index to People) are Ernest Augustus and Dorothea (née Hanney) Fuhr. They had a very large number of children, both older and younger than those of Jane and Julius (among them "Harry Fuhr" the civil engineer who JMcC meets on his voyages). They live in Belfast and in 1880 are to be found at 1 Mount Pleasant, Strandmillis Road (9 minutes walk from Lennoxvale). In 1901 one of their unmarried daughters is at 52 Malone Avenue (4 minutes walk away).
2. These are neighbours of the Loewenthals (the Blacks) – and appear in various letters – but not further identified.

We were in Demerara early this morning – 27th – a two days' run. I know no one here & have only a couple of rather valueless introductions, so I am rather doubtful as to how I shall fare – but Nil Desperandum!

I must tell you rather a good thing about a fellow passenger by the Medway – a young man with a shrill squeaky voice. It seems that when leaving Waterloo Station for Southampton, he took, by mistake, someone else's portmanteau instead of his own, but did not find out the error till the steamer had started for the West Indies! His own contained a complete new rig-out, new suits, new boots, new shirts, new handkerchiefs with his name (as he pathetically told me) nicely embroidered in the corners. He hoped he might find an equivalent in the other portmanteau but what were his feelings when he discovered that the wardrobe was that of a lady, & that it comprised a ball-dress of some white material, a black silk dress, & a variety of nondescript garments, belonging to some Miss Mary Burgess!

Miss Burgess's feelings may also be imagined when she finds- instead of her ball dress & her black silk – the new shirts & boots, two pairs of – "divided skirts" of grey tweed with their complementary vests & jackets, not to mention the handkerchiefs nicely marked "J.Smiths".

1st Janry. 1890   A happy New Year to you all – & many birthday wishes to Emma for tomorrow.[3] It is already tomorrow with you, for it is abt 10pm here, which would make it something like 2 a.m. in Belfast.

For the past week we have had almost continuous downpours of tropical rain making everything, even in one's bedroom, feel horribly damp. One's boots become mildewed if not worn for a day, & one's trunk has a blue-mouldy smell.

To-day a pleasant change has come with the New Year, & after a single day's sunshine the roads look as if it had not rained for weeks.

British Guiana is a prosperous colony. Its principal export is sugar, but gold has latterly been found in fair quantities on the Demerara River & the search for it seems to be a growing industry, though hitherto the yield has barely paid expenses. The present Governor is an Irish peer from County Galway.[4]

Georgetown, the capital, is a place of considerable importance. It is on the Demerara River, which is navigable for some distance. It is a swift-flowing muddy current, about half a mile wide at its mouth, & rolling over its shallow bar it discolours the water for many miles. In fact the first indication that you are approaching Demerara, coming from Barbados, is the change in the sea from deep blue to turbid yellow. The country all around is quite flat, mud is abundant, & mosquitoes have here their home. The houses are all build of wood, as the ground is not solid enough to support stone walls. Some of the best houses look very fine from the outside, with their open verandahs, elaborate venetians or "jealousies" (Fr jalousies) & square turrets; – wood lends itself better than stone to light ornamental architecture for it is so much more easily worked with. The gardens surrounding these houses are very beautiful – thanks more to Nature than to art. The climbing plants, the many coloured crotons, & the infinite variety of palms & other tropical trees, make such a garden seem one vast hothouse & all the air so heavy with the perfumes that we know only in a cactus or orchid house at home.

Along the middle of the wider streets run canals or trenches which serve to carry the rains of the wet season into the river. Several of these trenches are covered with the magnificent Victoria Regis lily, which is now in bloom.[5] I remember seeing sketches of it in the Illustrated London News last year, by Melton Prior.[6] The leaves are quite three feet across, round, with an upturned brim like a large tea-tray. The upper surface is green, but the under, as seen on the reverse of

---

3. Emma is Jack's sister – later known as "aunty Em". The birthday he refers to has Emma turning 21 (b 2 Jan 1869).

4. Jenico William Joseph Preston, 14th Viscount Gormanston, GCMG (1st June 1837 – 29th October 1907), was an aristocratic Anglo-Irish colonial administrator. In 1885 Gormanston was appointed Governor of the Leeward Islands, a post he held until 1887, and then served as Governor of British Guiana from 1887 to 1893 and as Governor of Tasmania from 1893 to 1900.

5. Victoria is a genus of water-lilies, in the plant family Nymphaeaceae, with very large green leaves that lie flat on the water's surface. Victoria amazonica has a leaf that is up to 3 metres (9.8 ft) in diameter, on a stalk up to 8 metres (26 ft) in length. The genus name was given in honour of Queen Victoria.

6. Melton Prior (12 September 1845 – 2 November 1910), was an English artist and war correspondent for The Illustrated London News from the early 1870s until 1904.

the rim, is a deep red colour beautifully veined. The large blossoms open at night, the outer petals of pure white falling back on the water, the inner, graduating from light pink to dark crimson, rising in a cluster in the centre.

There is a preponderating Scotch element in the business population here. The merchants seem to have retained their old-country characteristics. They are canny & suspicious with a you're-trying-to-get-the-better-of-me-but-I'm-too-wide-awake- kind of air. I don't like them nearly so well as the Barbadians.

New Year's day was a holiday here, & rather a dull one I found it. The niggers seemed to enjoy themselves though, as they paraded the streets in bands of about a dozen, with masks & all kinds off fancy costume, dancing, shouting, & playing drums, fifes, & tambourines.

<u>Friday 3rd Janry. /89</u> By this time you will likely have rcvd. my first letter & on Monday you ought to have my second. You will have this one abt. Monday 20th I expect.

I mean to leave this place on Sunday for Trinidad, & then go on to Curaçao.

I am taking a direct steamer to Trinidad – a quicker way than by Barbados so I shall miss the Austins' dinner& pantomime, which I regret. But I want to push on as quickly as I can.

I noticed a nice house here called Norwood Tower, & struck by the name I asked whose it was; I was told that it belongs to a Mr McGowan, of Belfast origin.[7] He has a store here, but is said to be in difficulties & to have gone home to arrange with his creditors.

The mail closes to-night & I have still to write some business letters, so I shall now close my "Fortnightly Review". I shall not have your letters (written abt Xmas-eve) till this day week in Trinidad. I hope they will bring good news.

Best love to all

Your affectionate son

Jack

A letter to Olga goes under separate cover.[8]

7. David Hugh McGowan (b Belfast ca 1849). He was listed as a "West India Merchant" in the Walthamstow Census of 1891.
8. Olga is Jack's sister.

4. Letter from Trinidad, 7th–14th January 1890

18900107 See an image of the original letter, http://dx.doi.org/10.17613/yg3c-xh29

Trinidad, Tuesday 7th Jany. 1890

My dear Mother,

It is 5 o'clock on a wet afternoon; business is over for the day, & there is still an hour till dinner, so I shall begin my letter for next mail, which leaves some 10 days hence.

This morning I sent you a postcard telling you I had just arrived from Demerara. I wrote you already about the sugar estates there. Some of the largest are owned by a Mr Quintin Hogg, brother of Sir J. McGarrel Hogg.[1] He is also the proprietor of extensive estates in Ceylon, & of the Polytechnic in London & has founded a "New Religion". These facts I have from the (R.C.) Bishop of Demerara who was my fellow passenger on the French boat. You will notice that I have latterly become quite "chummy" with the West Indian Dignitaries of the Roman Catholic Church. To meet his lordship there came on board the steamer my old acquaintance the Archbishop of Trinidad, who smilingly & politely lifted his hat to me. The Bishop asked me to go & see him on my return to Demerara. On the steamer we had a discussion about the old bones of contention – free trade – which I firmly upheld while the Bishop advocated protection. He then started "evolution", – physical, intellectual, & spiritual, but I held my tongue – venturing only to make an occasional remark – partly out of respect for the old gentleman & partly from a wholesome fear of getting out of my depth.

There were several very interesting men on board the French Steamer. They were returning from Cayenne & Salut (Dutch or French Guiana I think) where they had gone to observe the eclipse. Salut is a penal settlement & very unhealthy place.[2] It was there that Father Perry from Liverpool, who was sent out by the English Government to watch the eclipse, took dysentery, of which he died on the man of war "Comus".[3] Among them were Professor Schaeberle & another, from Lick Observatory, San Francisco, commissioned by the Govt. of the United States, Count de la Baume, by the French Govt., & a gentleman named Rockville from New York, who had gone down to see the eclipse for himself.[4]

They were able to make their observations with complete success, & I heard several most interesting conversations about eclipses, the velocity of light, the spectroscopic photography as applied to astronomy, & so on.

---

1. Quintin Hogg (b 14th February 1845, d 17th January 1903) was a tea merchant and philanthropist. Having made his fortune, he became concerned with educational reform. In 1864 he founded York Place Ragged School for boys in rented rooms off The Strand. In 1882, he founded the Young Men's Christian Institute, later renamed the Regent Street Polytechnic. It is now the University of Westminster, the largest provider of adult education in London with headquarters still at the same location on Regent Street.
2. The Salvation Islands (French: Îles du Salut). Between 1852 and 1953, the islands were part of a notorious penal colony for the worst criminals of France.
3. Stephen Perry (1833-1889) was a Jesuit priest, astronomer, and educator. His life is described in an article by George Bishop in the *Journal of British Astronomical Association* 1979, 89 (5) 473-84.
4. John Martin Schaeberle (b 1853, d 1924) was a graduate of the University of Michigan who served as Astronomer at Lick Observatory from 1888-1898. His obituary by J. M. Hussey appeared in the *Publications of the Astronomical Society of the Pacific*, December 1924, Vol. XXXVI, No. 214. The eclipse described is the total eclipse of December 1889, which Schaeberle and his colleague Burnham were sent to Cayenne to observe. It was this eclipse that led Schaeberle to formulate a mechanical theory of the solar corona. The Lick Observatory is now owned and operated by the University of California. It is on the summit of Mount Hamilton, in the Diablo Range just east of San Jose. Count Aymar Eugène de la Baume Pluvinel (b 6 November 1860, d 18 July 1938) was a French astronomer and professor in the École supérieure d'optique.

This Mr Rockville has travelled all he world over, & has met a lot of well-known people. He was telling me about a day he had spent in Edison's laboratory in New York. It was at the time when Edison was perfecting the phonograph. Mr Rockville was impressed with a feeling akin to awe at the wonderful invention & its far-reaching possibilities. It seemed to bring home to him that every word that a man uttered would be brought into judgement against him, & he realized how careful of his words a man should be. Just then Mr Edison shouted in a squeaky voice &, as he turned the handle, the phonograph repeated, in a still shriller way

> "There was a little girl
> And she had a little curl
> Right in the middle of her forehead"
> & then told how she "lost this little curl"
> "And it made her look perfectly horrid".

What a come-down from lofty moral reflection to absurd reality, was it not? I think the anecdote is worth preserving as one more illustration of the short step from the sublime to the ridiculous.[5]

I've just read a book called Macaria by an American authoress – one Augusta Evans.[6] She wrote another book – Infelice – & I think I remember seeing the name in the library or at home. All the characters, without exception, quote poetry by the yard, without the slightest provocation. This kind of idiocy is only laughable at first, but as you go further into the book, it becomes horribly irritating, & you are kept in a state of nervous dread the whole time, just as in a game of "snap", wondering who will succeed first in flinging a quotation at somebody else. Out of curiosity I noted a <u>few</u> of the outbreaks of the most violent cases.

Young woman "A" refuses a proposal & quotes, to the rejected suitor, <u>9 lines</u> of blank verse; young man takes refusal philosophically, & in next chapter discusses fame with young woman "A" & quotes <u>11 lines</u>; young woman "B", star-gazing at 1 a.m. is told by her uncle she ought to be in bed, – she says she won't go & quotes <u>6 lines</u>; Uncle takes tea with a young man, tells him not to work too hard & quotes <u>9 lines</u>; Family Doctor condemns charitable societies & quotes <u>18 lines</u> (!); young woman "B" defends them & quotes <u>6 lines</u>, gives a book to a small boy & quotes <u>6 lines</u>, talks of woman's sphere & quotes <u>15 lines</u>; Family Doctor goes to the wars, & quotes <u>8 lines</u> as he says good-bye to young woman "B", who quotes <u>3 lines</u>; young women "A" & "B" both in love with same young man – he is killed – B faints – A brings her round by quoting <u>9 lines</u>; A paints a picture & quotes <u>9 lines</u>, B looks on & quotes <u>4 lines</u>, & the chapter closes with <u>11 lines</u>.

I don't think I shall read "Infelice".

Friday 10th Jany.

The mail is in & I have just recv[d] two welcome letters from you, one from Father, & one from Julie; – no papers, please ask Father to send me the Weekly Whig.[7]

Your letters bear date 16th & 22nd Dec. & you are impatient at not having heard from me. I told you before I left that you would not have any news from me before Jany. 6th, but you seem to have forgotten this.

What Finlay was it that you had for whist along with Richard Wallace, Mrs Dods, & Mrs Rogers? I had a fair game the other evg. with some young fellows here & won renown & 4/-

---

5. Edison later developed a talking doll that repeated the words. It is preserved by the US National Parks Service, which has also put the recording online: https://www.nps.gov/edis/learn/photosmultimedia/there-was-a-little-girl-edison-talking-doll-cylinder-brown-wax-rolfs-colleciton.htm

6. Augusta Evans Wilson, (b 8th May 1835, d 9th May 1909) was an American Southern author and one of the pillars of Southern literature. She wrote nine novels: *Inez* (1850), *Beulah* (1859), *Macaria* (1863), *St. Elmo* (1866), *Vashti* (1869), *Infelice* (1875), *At the Mercy of Tiberius* (1887), *A Speckled Bird* (1902), and *Devota* (1907). These are all available free online at https://www.gutenberg.org/ebooks/author/1399.

7. The Northern Whig was a regional newspaper first published in Belfast in 1824. In its early years the paper as its editor and owner Finlay was in favour of Catholic Emancipation and supported the disestablishment of the Church of Ireland. Its editorial line was liberal and unionist and it was seen as reflecting a Presbyterian slant on the news.

The Blacks at your tea night were, I suppose, the heiresses from over the way. What do you think of them on closer acquaintance?[8]

The winter gaieties are in full swing & now that I have been away for two seasons & Julie is taking my place, I shall be quite forgotten. Besides you get to know new people & I should be quite a stranger now. When I come back I shall say, like the travelled young man from Cookstown in Grannies' evergreen 'd story, "Are these the chucks that were the chicks when I left?". I don't know half the people that were at your hen-party.

Did the young people go to Newetts'? I should not have done so. It was kind of Mrs Newett to ask them, but she was aware that the proper thing to do was to call, & when people know that, their invitation is more an affront than a compliment. It is not necessary to give the many reasons why.[9]

I am particularly stiff – if you like to call it so – about such matters.

Julie & the family swallow-tail are in great demand. If he has as much fun while he wears it as I had when it was my property he may be quite satisfied. He seems to have enjoyed Mrs Parfitt's two dances very much.

So Miss Brown's reported engagement is not a fact. By the way, I met a young fellow in Demerara, Higinbotham by name, whose home is a place called Guelph, some 12 miles from Toronto. A very decent chap, – connected with a Canadian Insurance Co. I asked him if he know Miss Molesworth (Toronto is where she lives, is it not?) but he said not. However he has not been much in Canada for some time, but was going back to Toronto in a month or two.

How is Miss M'Hinch after her long stay in London? Please give her my kind regards. I await your account of Xmas eve. You must have been a jolly party.

Sunday 12th Jany.

Heavy rain still continues to fall here, though the dry season should have begun before Christmas. The people cannot dry their cocoa & some of it has already gone bad. If the rain does not cease very soon the loss will be severe.

What an extraordinary thing is that epidemic of influenza which is spreading over all Europe.[10] I hope none of you have been troubled by it. Y'days telegram says the little King of Spain is dangerously ill with it; poor little chap, I hope he will get over it.[11] If not, I am afraid there will be another struggle in Spain among the many factions. Castelan & the moderate Republicans would probably throw in their lot with Zorilla, & the extreme section & succeed in bringing about a Republic. The movement w^d be aided by recent events in Brazil.

The Carlist regime is a thing of the past, & I don't think the Spain of today would tolerate a restored Inquisition.

We had a sharp little shock of earthquake the night before last at a little after seven o'clock. We were at dinner at the time. It was a sudden bump with a short vibration afterwards lasting only a few seconds. I thought something very heavy had fallen in the room overhead. The astronomer immediately noted the time & particulars. He said they had, in Lick Observatory, an earthquake about once a month, & that this one was probably caused by a displacement in the earth's surface of one sixteenth of an inch.

By the way, I am told that this Mr Schaeberle, the astronomer, has discovered some comets, one of which bears his name.

Today I have turned to good account an accomplishment that I never expected to come in useful, – the deaf & dumb alphabet. There are three new arrivals in the hotel, a gentleman, his wife & her brother. The two latter are deaf-mutes.

8. We know little about the heiresses – except their worth as it has come up several times. Also Addie and JMcC go to the wedding of James Black (possibly related, as it is a very posh affair) in NY on 28th January 1891. See Index to People.
9. Probably Jane Newett (b 1845) of Dunluce Avenue off the Lisburn Road.
10. The 1889–1890 flu pandemic, also known as the "Asiatic flu" or "Russian flu", was a pandemic that killed about 1 million people worldwide, out of a population of about 1.5 billion. It was the last great pandemic of the 19th century and is among the deadliest pandemics in history. A 2005 genomic virological study says that "it is tempting to speculate" that the virus might not have been an influenza virus, but human coronavirus OC43. In 2020, Danish researchers reached a similar conclusion in a study that had not been published in a peer-reviewed academic journal as of November 2020. They described the symptoms as very like those of COVID-19.
11. At the beginning of January 1890, King Alfonso XIII of Spain fell ill, who was at the time five years old. His health deteriorated but, eventually, the king recovered: https://www.ncbi.nlm.nih.gov/pmc/articles/PMC3867475/.

I made the acquaintance of the deaf & dumb brother & went out for a walk with him. We carried on a most animated conversation by means of the finger alphabet. He is a most intelligent fellow, sketches, botanizes & so on. He laughs & cracks jokes, seemingly quite indifferent to his affliction. He is a man of about 30, & he comes from Co Wicklow.

We were talking about deaf-mute education, & to illustrate the rapidity that comes with practice in the finger-language the gentleman who is not deaf told me that when he was married to this deaf & dumb lady the service was conducted simultaneously by two clergymen, one viva-voce reading the usual Church of England service, & the other, himself a deaf-mute, using the finger alphabet & going through the same service. Neither clergyman knew where the other was in the ritual, but the deaf & dumb one got ahead & came in first at the finish!

Tuesday Jany. 14th

I shall close & post this letter now, for I shall probably sail for Curaçao by a steamer due tomorrow, & I have a lot of things to square up still.

I can't say when you will get my next letter – probably it will go by New York, so don't expect any by the next Royal Mail Packet.

Best love to all.

Your affectionate son.

Jack

5. Letter from Curaçao, 24th-28th January 1890

18900124 See an image of the original letter, http://dx.doi.org/10.17613/nm7g-5274

Curaçao 24th Jany. 1890

My dear Mother,

I left Trinidad on Wed. week, 9 days ago. I was only a week in that island & I left it rather hurriedly, for had I missed my steamer, there was no other for a week or 10 days, so I was obliged to finish up my business with some speed. Travelling out in this part of the world one must look ahead & see what means there are of getting on to the next stage. The steamers come only once a week or once a fortnight, – in Spain I could always get at least one train a day from one place to another, so I could finish my business & go, but here I must go sometimes with my business only three quarters finished.

The steamer was the "Australian" of the "West Indian & Pacific Line", a small boat but comfortable, & I spent a very pleasant week on board.[1] There was a young engineer named Copperthwaite, going to Colombia, & I found him a very pleasant companion.[2] He comes from Yorkshire & has lived for some time in Mexico where he was in charge of some railway works. He is now going out to make arrangements for the construction of a railway near the Magdalena River. I wrote to Harry Fuhr to apply to him for a post in case he – Harry – has not decided on anything else meanwhile.[3]

Old Captain Peters, the skipper, did his best to make us comfortable. We used to play whist & dominoes with the aid of a little fat Scotchman, agent for Clark's Cotton.

The first night Copperthwaite & the Scotchman played together. Having lead from a single card, returned his opponent's lead, & generally shown his utter ignorance, at the conclusion of the hand the latter said in broad Scotch, to his partner who plays really well "I think we did pretty well there. I see we play exactly the same game."

Copperthwaite exchanged a look with me & then proceeded to point out several cases in which they did not "play the same game", but the only satisfaction he could get from the Scotchman was "Well, that's the way we play in Glasgow"!

We touched at the ports of La Guayara, & P^{to} Cabello, but I am leaving those places for the way back.[4] I wanted to come on quickly to this place & Colombia.

The people in Curaçao who were so attentive to me last time seem pleased to see me back. I like the island very well, if it were not such a hungry place, but I mean to forage on board the steamers, & get tinned biscuits & German sausages.

Sat. 28th Jan.

The mail v N.York is just in & brings letters from London of the 28th Dec. but none from you. I hope to have a big lot by next mail.

---

1. The Australian was built in 1867 and scrapped at Amsterdam in 1893. It operated the following routes: 1881 - 1899 Liverpool - West Indies - Colon - Mexico - New Orleans. Previously, 1864 - Inter-island service St. Thomas - La Guaira - Puerto Cabello - Curacao.
2. William Charles Copperthwaite. b ~ 1856, from York. See Index to People.
3. Henry Augustus Robert Fuhr b 17 May 1868 Belfast. Civil engineer. See Index to People.
4. La Guaira is the capital city of the Venezuelan state of Vargas and the country's main port. It was founded in 1577 as an outlet for Caracas, 30 kilometres to the southeast. Puerto Cabello is a city on the north coast of Venezuela. It is located in Carabobo State, about 210 km west of Caracas.

I must end this very short, as the outgoing mail closes in about 2 hours & my correspondence is not yet finished. My next letters will be longer.[5]

Best love to all

Jack

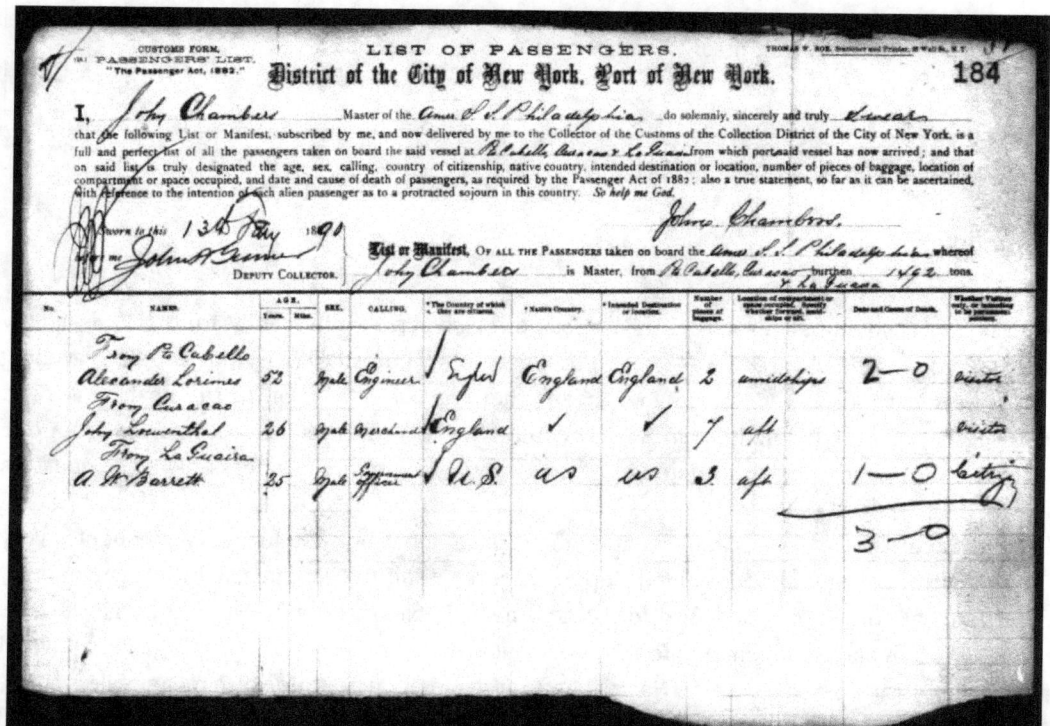

List of passengers on SS Philadelphia arriving New York 13th February 1890

5. This is the last letter we have from this trip. The next evidence in the trail of this particular voyage is that he is on the transit passenger list of the "Philadelphia" which arrives in New York on 13th February 1890 from Curaçao and La Guairá and Puerto Cabello, Venezuela. He is presumably on his way home – especially as we know that his next journey to S America starts only 2 months later on 16th March 1890!

PART II
THE LETTERS: SOUTH AMERICAN VOYAGE, 1890

Map of the 1890 voyage by John McCaldin Loewenthal. Note that JMcC refers to Brazilian cities by the names of the states that they are part of. These are shown in parentheses on the map. A high-res version is available: https://doi.org/10.17613/h5nb-6a20 (Original map by Thomas Bachrach)

6. Letter from Dundee, 14th March 1890

18900314 See an image of the original letter, http://dx.doi.org/10.17613/rmzg-1w45

Headed notepaper: Fernbrae, Dundee[1]

Crest: **W A I**   *(intertwined)*[2]

Friday 14th March 90

My dear Mother,

Father sent me Addie's letter, & I now return it with the one I had from him for my birthday.[3]

I can't get away till tomorrow morng. Renny comes to dinner, also a Spanish buyer from Santander whom I know very well.[4]

My train leaves at 8 tomorrow morng. reachg. London at 7. I think I shall drive right across to Waterloo & leave my luggage. I shall go & see the Boases on Sunday morning, if I can possibly manage it.[5]

I shall write you a line from either London or the steamer, & shall wire you when I get safely on board with my goods & chattels.

The Coleridge will touch at Madeira abt. the 21st & sh[d] be wired from Montevideo or Buenos Ayres abt. Monday 7th April.

Hope to have a line from you to Adelaide Rd.[6]

Best love to all

Jack

---

1. Fernbrae House, 329 Perth Road, Fernbrae, Dundee. Style of William Scott, circa 1860. 2-storey classically detailed ashlar villa. South Elevation: 5-bay, central entrance porch corniced on square piers and Roman Ionic columns in antis. Windows in architraves, with consoled cills and cornices at ground floor. 1st floor cill band, mutule cornice and blocking course. Quoined angles. Built for Julius Weinberg, merchant. http://portal.historicenvironment.scot/designation/LB25567

2. W A I intertwined = Weinberg Agnes Isaac (Isaac Julius Weinberg & wife Agnes)

3. Addie is his brother Ferdinand Adolphus. See Index to People and Family Tree

4. Likely to have been William John Renny – b 11th Feb 1841 in Russia, naturalized British – Flax Merchant and Artist in Dundee. Son of William Warden Renny of Broughty Ferry (b 26th March 1809 in Arbroath, Scotland, d 1882 Broughty Ferry). He was "one of the oldest and most honourable of Dundee's merchants. He lived a life steeped in the knowledge, workings and trading of flax, both here in Scotland and also in Russia." "William Warden Renny enjoyed a long and successful career as a flax merchant. Known as a peace-maker, he was frequently sought as an arbiter in disputes where his opinions and decisions carried weight. His name was as familiar in the flax trade throughout Russia as it was at home on the streets of Dundee." https://mcmanus168.org.uk/mcmanus168entry/w-w-renny-esq/#source2

5. Fred Boas and his wife Henrietta. See Index to People.

6. 205 Adelaide Road is the residence of Julius' brother Ferdinand Aldolf Loewenthal ("uncle Addie") and his wife Caroline (nee Goldschmidt) – JMcC only once mentions his uncle by name – they frequently appear in his letters as he uses their home as a place to stay overnight before setting off from London.

7. Letter from Southampton, 16th March 1890

18900316 See an image of the original letter, http://dx.doi.org/10.17613/rntd-2231

Headed notepaper:[1]

London and South Western Railway. (167*)

Parcels Department,

Waterloo Station (S.E.)

_____ 188

Written at right angles to heading in pencil

12.25 train Sunday

My dear Mother

Havg. begged a sheet of paper from the Railway Co I now proceed, under difficulties to scribble you a few lines, as I may not have time on board. I am on the way to Southampton & the carriage is shaking about tremendously.

Fred & Bertie came to see me off by the 8 o'c train y'day morng [2]. In the same carriage the whole way, were three ladies. I thought of appealing as an unprotected male, to the guard for protection, but contented myself with taking a seat on the side of the alarm communicator.

They did not molest me, though they cast hungry looks at the luncheon basket I bought at Preston, & I did not conquer my nervousness till I had demolished the half chicken, ham, salad, rolls, butter, cheese, & pint of Bass.

The day was pleasantly warm, no rain, & the train reached Euston punctually at 7 p.m. Havg. driven to Waterloo & left my luggage I proceeded to Adelaide Rd & found the inhabitants of 205 in usual good health & spirits. They gave me a nice tea-dinner & I had a good night's rest.[3]

I was glad to get your note. Don't get laid up with your back – let someone else nail down the carpets. After what you wrote abt. Fred's play, I gave up the idea of callg on Boases. Enclosed a critique cut from the Sunday Times.[4] Burn it please. Very sorry.

Called for a moment at Goldschmidts, who asked abt. the health of the family.[5] Reassured them, & took a cab for the station. A lot of people there, but I have no idea yet how many go with us.

Opposite me in the carriage I have a "Johnny" who has already informed me that he is from York, goes to B. Aires to

1. Sent from Southampton after boarding the "Coleridge" (heading for Buenos Aires) but written on the train from Waterloo to Southampton – on notepaper from London and South Western Railway, Parcels Dept, Waterloo Station
2. Fred & Bertie were sons of Isaac Julius Weinberg, co-founder of Moore & Weinberg : Frederick Simon b 1865 Belfast. Herbert James b 1868 Belfast d Perth, Scotland 1896. See Index to People
3. These were his uncle (Julius' brother) Ferdinand Adolf, his wife Caroline and their children Nanny, Edgar and Clara.
4. The play referred to was The Favourite of the King, by F. S. Boas and Jocelyn Brandon, a comedy about George Villiers, Duke of Buckingham, that ran between March 11 and March 15 1890 to poor reviews. Frederick Samuel Boas, OBE FRSL (1862–1957) was an English scholar of early modern drama. He was born on 24th July 1862, the eldest son of Hermann Boas of Belfast. His family was Jewish. Hermann Boas is found living in Windsor Park in the 1901 Census (and listed as Jewish). He died in Belfast in 1917. b ca 1828 in Germany and listed as "retired manufacturer." His wife was called Caroline. So, Frederick Samuel was a contemporary of JMcC's and Father Hermann, 6 years older than Julius. Likely family friends, thus the great embarrassment re the play. Interestingly Frederick Samuel was baptised in London in 1890.
5. Ferdinand Adolf Loewenthal of 205 Adelaide Road was married to a Caroline née Goldschmidt in Brunswick (Braunschweig). So these must be family of hers. Ferdinand Adolf (Julius' brother) was in business with them.

"look round". If he makes money well & good, if not he comes back, his coat cost him £1, the first owner of it committed suicide, the second was drowned. Wants to share my cabin, but I think not.

Too communicative. Rattles away like a "hundred of bricks".

Calm & warm, some rain (our special meteorological reporter).

Close this on the tender. Goods & Chattels all on board.[6]

Best love to all

Jack

(Enclosed review of play by Messrs Boas & Brandon)

Plays and Players

Messrs. Bores-no, Boas and Brandon have held possession of the Comedy every afternoon this week since Tuesday with their historical play, "The Favorite of the King." This is in four acts, with eight changes of scene, each of which is preceded by the fall of a curtain – a very tedious arrangement; and when it is added that the dialogue is written in blank verse, "inebriated with the exuberance of its verbosity," and that a tiresome and invertebrate plot if dragged along with dramatic inconsequence, it will be seen that our repertory of historic dramas is not enriched by this ambitious effort. The hero (?) of the play is George Villiers, Duke of Buckingham, and his career as set forth by Messr. Boas and Brandon, presents him in anything but a heroic light, for he is faithless in love and loyalty, and mean-spirited into the bargain. But his rural sweetheart, whom he forsakes for a court lady, is a very extraordinary young woman, for there is no suggestion that Villiers has done more than break off a virtuous, but seemingly incompatible engagement, yet she poses as a Nemesis, denounces him in ambiguous terms to his fiancee, and betrays him to his enemies, and then falls a-weeping upon his dead body, and on every possible occasion recites a dream. Mr. Royce Carleston was brave in bearing and forcible in manner as Villiers; but Miss Dorothy Dene was, except in one or two moments of the play, as uninteresting as her part. Her voice lacked tone, and her delivery of the verse was monotonous. Miss Louise Moodie as Villier's mother, a part that at one time promised to run on the lines of Lady Macbeth, gave all possible significance to her lines, both by expression and suggestion. Miss Annie Rose as the Duke's fiancee, and, later, his wife, showed that she has studied to improve her acting, with gratifying results. She was pleasantly sympathetic. Mr. Bassett Roe, as a mysterious and murderous alchemyst of the burning cauldron brand, revealed considerable capacity for pantomime; Mr. J. R. Crauford was good as a soldier with a grievance. Mr. Allen Beaumonth did not the heavy father too much of a bore, and Mr. Laurence D'Orsay was ridiculous in a ridiculous part. Mrs. Carson was industriously engaged in trying to solve the puzzle, where to find the comedy? But it was not her fault that the answer remained unrevealed. Mr. Thomas Lewen was a pretty page. There is some fair verse of the college exercise order in the play, but the authors have yet to learn the whole art of dramatic writing.

---

6. The Coleridge was the ship JMcC embarked on – and he is listed on the passenger list as travelling to Buenos Aires, sailing 16th March 1890. It is interesting that JMcC listed as a "foreigner" on the passenger list, not English, Scotch, nor Irish.

Telegram

Sent from Southampton on 16th March

POST OFFICE TELEGRAPHS
Handed in at the Southampton *Office at* 9.5 pm *received here at* 9.15 pm
Rubber stamp: BELFAST C   MR 16 90
TO   Loewenthal
Lennoxvale   Belfast

Safely on board au revoir Jack

8. Letter from aboard the S.S. Coleridge sailing to Montevideo, 21st March 1890

S.S. Coleridge[1]

21st March 1890

My dear Mother,

As soon as I was safely on bord at Southampton, with all my luggage, I sent you a wire to let you know that I had started.

As the rain was falling steadily, the work of getting the things onto the tender, & thence to the steamer, was very disagreeable. We sailed abt. 4 o'c. & had a smooth run down Channel, but next day the Bay of Biscay justified its reputation by giving us a stiff gale.

The waves washed the deck, & the water came through ventilators & between planks, in copious streams, into the cabins, wetting everything & putting everybody in a bad temper. For two nights I had to sleep in the saloon. The third day we sailed into calm water again & the sun came out bright & strong. All the beds & bedding, cushions, curtains, coats, rugs, were taken up & spread out on deck, or hung on lines, till the place looked like the side garden at Ashley Avenue on drying-day or during the Spring house-cleaning.[2].

Fortunately my things escaped without serious damage, though my dress-clothes, new coat, & tall hat ran no slight risk for some time, as there was not a dry place on the ship. Now all is pleasant again & we may expect fine weather & calm seas for the rest of the voyage.

My cabin is a large one & well ventilated & my companion is a decent fellow who keeps his chattels in order & does not get sick. There are some 60 passengers (saloon), a somewhat mixed lot at first sight, but I can't say much abt. them yet.

I shall tell you more abt. the other passengers in my first letter from Buenos Ayres.

The Dr is a jolly fat little Irishman from Dublin. He gave me a sprig of shamrock which I wore on the 17th in your honour & St. Patrick's.

Here I may take this opportunity to send my best wishes for Annie's birthday.[3]. Some time ahead, but you won't get another letter from me till beginning of May. You may hear from D^ee that they have had telegrams from me.

The steamer ought to reach Montevideo any day from the 7th till the 10th or 11th & the Company have undertaken to wire you on her arrival.

---

1. SS Coleridge: built 1875 ex-Mira, Lamport and Holt Line, 1889 purchased from Rathbone Bros, Liverpool renamed Coleridge, 1890 transferred from Belgian subsidiary, 1892 reverted to British flag, 1893 scrapped. 2 610 tonnes http://www.theshipslist.com/ships/lines/lamport.shtml

2. Ashley Avenue, Belfast: A street of terrace houses off the Lisburn Road. It seems to have developed over a number of years starting before 1880. As opposed to the large villas of Lennoxvale.

3. His sister Anne Isabella, born 24th April 1867.

We are just abt. to anchor now at Madeira, so I must cut this very short. While the vessel was rolling & pitching it was absolutely impossible to write.

I am very well indeed, & have not been sea-sick. On Tuesday evg. I was one of four passengers, out of sixty, who turned up for dinner.

To my great joy & satisfaction the plumcake, safe in my waterproof hold-all, passed uninjured through the ordeal, & I now have two big pieces a day. It is excellent, & my cabin-companion, who gets a slice at night, praises it enthusiastically.

I have had some of the sweets & they are tip top. With this big tinful (one l or two?) I hope to make friends with some nice children on board, particularly with one baby of two years, really a nice baby, very different from ordinary babies.

I intend getting some stamps on shore & shall decorate the envelope.

This is written in a hurry, so don't be critical.

Hope you are all A[1]

Best love all round.

Your affectionate son Jack

9. Letter from aboard S.S. Coleridge sailing to Montevideo, 23rd March 1890-7th April 1890

18900323 See an image of the original letter, http://dx.doi.org/10.17613/kfvw-n765

Sketch enclosed with letter

S.S. Coleridge
Posted Montevideo
Montevideo Apl 7th, 1890

Sunday 23rd March 1890

My dear Mother,

Just one week out to-day, & about one third of the voyage over.

I posted a letter to you two days ago in Madeira. We had about five hours on shore at Funchal & in that time we managed to see about everything that was to be seen.

The first visit was to the post office where I was disappointed, on account of the collectors, to find Madeira no longer has stamps of her own, but has to be satisfied with the ordinary Portuguese ones.[1]

We formed a party of three to do the place, my cabin companion (of whom more hereafter), a young fellow called Hayes (son of one Major Hayes, Inspector of Irish Fisheries), & myself.

After posting our letters we set out to look for Reid's Hotel & in making enquiries as to its whereabouts I had an opportunity of airing my best Portuguese. We were beset by beggars & guides, who seemed to form no inconsiderable part of the whole population.

We had the greatest difficulty in getting rid of one disgusting fellow & had finally to appeal to a dirty little policeman to prevent him from pestering us.

The guide was argumentative but the policeman was peremptory. The scene was very amusing, but we did not wait for the issue, but left them at the corner of the square & walked diagonally across the pretty garden in the centre.

When we came to the far corner we saw that the persevering guide had gone round one side of the garden & was making for us again, but the suspicious little policeman had dodged round the other side & Greek met Greek at the corner!

This time the Bobby would admit of no palaver, but sent the guide right about, & we got rid of him at last.

We found Reid's hotel a bright comfortable place, with tennis-court & pretty garden, & over part of the house a flat roof, forming a kind of verandah, covered, & decorated with shrubs & climbing plants. From this spot we had a splendid view of the town of Funchal, & of the steep hills that rise behind it, covered with vines & terraced by stone walls to prevent the scanty soil from being washed down by the heavy rains.

At the hotel we were told that the correct thing to do was to take a ride in a sledge to the convent up on the hill & then slide down again.

---

1. "the collectors" are his stamp-collecting siblings.

Se we precured a light basket-sledge with the seat facing back, drawn by two bullocks (as per sketch!) & having taken our places we Started. The bullocks were strong & used to their work & they drew us up the very steep hill at a pace that our guides & drivers (of whom there were five!) found some difficulty in keeping up.

Sketch of sled and bullocks used to ascend the hill above Funchal, and then descend it (without bullocks).

The narrow streets are paved with small hard stones, in about twelve-inch waves so as to give men & animals foot-hold (Refer again to sketch). There are no wheel-carts or carriages in the place. All the traffic is done in sledges with runners of hard wood that slide over the smooth pavement, polished by the constant friction, as easily as they would over snow.

As we gradually rose we had a bird's eye view of the town below us, & the amphitheatre of hills sloping down to the calm blue bay, on which the vessels looked like toy boats. It was a magnificent panorama.

We spent ten minutes in the dingy old convent & church at the top. I think our guide was disappointed that we did not evince more admiration at the sight of the dusty tinsel on the alters & the daubs hung on the walls.

We then took our seats again in the sledge from which the bullocks were un-yoked, & off we went down-hill at a merry pace, three men running with us & guiding the sledge by means of ropes fastened two to the sides & one at the back. When we came to a long straight slope they w$^{\underline{d}}$ jump on behind, & give an occasional shove with one leg.

In less than ten minutes we were at the foot of the hill that took us an hour & a quarter to go up.

After our excursion, our appetites, already sharpened by a week's sea air, were phenomenal, & I think we ate the biggest lunch on record at Madeira. Hayes said he felt as if he had swallowed a cave, & to judge by the havoc he wrought among the cutlets, cold chicken, salad, cheese & fruit, it must have been the Mammoth one.

At four o'clock we were on board again & we found the quarter deck of the "Coleridge" covered with chairs & sofas of all imaginable shapes, made of the wicker work for which Madeira is famous. They are sightly, comfortable, & very cheap, & both passengers & officers had purchased freely.

The sun-awning was now spread for the first time, & soon tweeds & serges were changed for tennis flannels.

The next land we sighted was the Cape de Verde Islands. We sailed between St Vincent & San Fernando, I think, signalling our name to the station as we passed. What we saw of the Islands was all brown-black lava, twisted up into the most fantastic shapes, entirely without vegetation. On San Fernando there are numberless little craters of extinct volcanoes.[2] On St Vincent the mountains rise to a considerable height & on their jagged ridges we could make out several resemblances of a man's face.

I never saw a more barren uninviting place than these Islands.

The signal station is on a conical rock, & behind it is the little harbour of St Vincent, in which two or three steamers were coaling.

2. There doesn't seem to be a "San Fernando" – I think the other island was actually "Santo Antão" with St Vincent they are the 2 north-west most islands.

Four days later we crossed the line, & the heat became very oppressive, particularly in the cabins. To cool our heads a little Hayes & I agreed to cut each other's hair. I was the first operator. H. sat on a camp-stool on the lower deck, with an old shirt over his coat. The performance caused much amusement & we had an admiring crowd round us. We were sketched by two amateur artists & photographed by another. The enclosed is a copy of one sketch made by a very nice fellow, Pearce Edgecumbe L.L.D. He has been in the River Plate bore, & has written a book about his trip, under the title of Zephyrus, a very readable volume containing interesting information about ranching, politics, & railways, in the Argentine & Uruguay. In the railways he seems to take a particular interest; he is a banker by profession & I suppose he has something to do with some of the lines.

He tells me he has also written two law books & a little book on Political Economy. The latter was published by the Cobden Club & is used as a text-book at Harrow.

I should think he can't be more than 35, but he is already a widower, with two youngsters.

He also tells me he is the proud possessor of two Reynolds & some other good pictures.[3]

But to come back to the hair-cutting, it is not by any measures easy. I thought before I tried it. I snipped a little piece out of my own finger & brought blood to both of Hayes' ears & after all there was a touch want of uniformity about his head when I had done, one side was almost bald & the other was in white & black patches. The thinness of his hair, & the rolling of the ship, together with my inexperience, produced such a sorry result that I wanted to back out of my part of the bargain, but Hayes would not let me off, & when he had done I was told by another passenger that my head suggested the penitentiary.

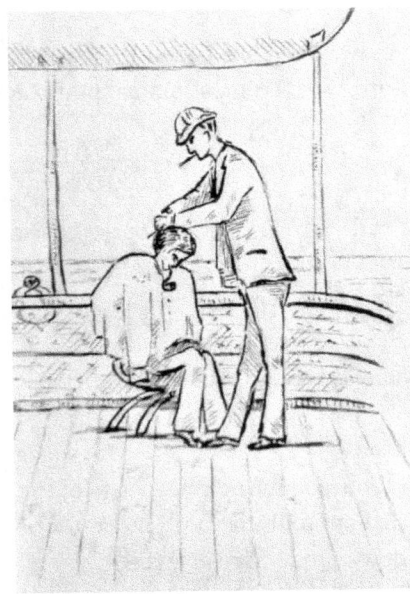

A sketch of haircutting on board the SS Coleridge, drawn by Edgecumbe

The only entertainments that have been arranged on board were two concerts.

The first was a very mediocre performance; more trouble was taken with second, the programme being settled beforehand so that singers & accompanists had some days to practice.

3. Sir Edward Robert Pearce Edgcumbe (b March 13, 1851 , d September 29, 1929) was a British politician, author and lawyer. Edgcumbe was considered an art lover who collected African and South American art while travelling through South America and Africa. He indeed published several books including: *The Law of Bills of Sale. The Bills of Sale Acts, 1878 and 1882*, H. Sweet, London, 1882; *Zephyrus. A holiday in Brazil and on the River Plate*, Chatto & Windus, London 1887; *Popular Fallacies Regarding Trade and Foreign Duties* (together with Frédéric Bastiat), Cassell, London 1888; *The parentage and kinsfolk of Sir Joshua Reynolds*, Chiswick, London, 1901. He was actually 39 when JMcC wrote.

The Manager was a man called Deeming, – a chap who has been everywhere & done everything at some period of his life. He started as an engineer on a steamer, was wrecked in Australia, worked at gold & diamond mines in South Africa, floated companies, & so on. He wears huge diamonds on his fingers & his shirtfront, & has a large nugget on his watch-chain.

He drops his h's in the most reckless fashion, a little habit that has afforded much amusement on the ship. His singing of "The place where the hold orse died" was immense, & made many of the audience almost choke with laugher though the song is really most pathetic.[4]

One line

"Hi was <u>hup</u> in alf a minute"

has been seized upon & is now quoted at every propos.

Another amusing item in the concert was the topical song, a parody on Killaloo (?), written by Edgecumbe, really a clever composition.[5] It related the various incidents of the trip – the storm in the Bay of Biscay – the sickness – the leaky cabins – the hair-cutting – etc. etc. – & contained most of the passengers. I shall not copy it as you w^d not understand the allusions, but I may mention that I was referred to in the flowing couplet.

> "Oh come now. Blow it all!
> Said graceful Lowentall."

Needless to say that "graceful Lowentall" has stuck to me during the rest of the voyage.

A minstrel troupe was made up by some of the passengers, with aide from the crew. They blackened their faces, collected banjo, tambourine & hornes, & made a very good show. The second steward was the most amusing of the crowd. He sang an utterly absurd ditty, the chorus of which was

> "Oh I weep-ye-were & I wander-were
> Overhills-es-es & mountains
> Where the bees-es-es & the wops-es-es (wasps!)
> And the nanny goats do baa!"

He also gave us a capital stump speech on that "insect the world", appealing every now & then to that his "Brethren & Sistren"

Altogether the concert was very successful.

I have read quite a lot of books in the last 3 weeks. Uncle Adolph gave me "Darwin's Journal during the voyage of the Beagle." It is about South America, & is a most delightful book. Though written in 1835, I am told that nothing better or more complete has been published since. I w^d be glad if Father w^d mention to Uncle how much I have enjoyed it.[6]

My cabin companion is the most orderly chap. He had tacks & strings arranged about the cabin to hang things on & all kinds of ingenious contrivances. He keeps everything very clean & altogether is about as pleasant a room-mate as I could have got.

There is a Dr Siddal with his wife, from Nottingham, on board.[7] I had a long conversation with him last night & heard some curious facts. He is a horsey man & is just now going to Buenos Ayres to settle up some difficulties into which he has got through young Buckly. This must be Miss Buckly's brother, the one who ran through their money. Dr Siddal formerly practised in Nottingham & says he was a friend of Dr Buckly, the father. The son was, he thought, a decent fellow, but he went to the bad. Dr Siddal got him employment in Buenos Ayres on the Harbour works, & I think got him

---

4. How Mr Deeming (Beaming Deeming) portrayed himself to the admiring crowd is described in a later letter.
5. "Killaloo" Actually Killaloe – you can find the words to the song here: https://en.wikipedia.org/wiki/Killaloe_March
6. "Uncle Adolph" was Ferdinand Adolphus of 205 Adelaide Road, Julius' brother.
7. Dr Sidall is listed on the passenger list as "Doctor G.O. Siddall" – he was a surgeon (b 3rd March 1837), with his wife Eiza.

to bet for him (Dr S.) on horse-races, backing horses sent out by friends of Siddal's. Buckly seems to have exceeded his powers, lost some money & given Siddal's name for it. The amount is not great, but Dr S. is going to settle it personally & also to attend to some business he has in rubber tires for wheels.

I expect it was Dr Siddal & his set that had a good deal to do with Bucklys' going wrong.

You had better not say anything about this to Dora Sinton. It might give pain to Miss Buckly if she knew about it.[8]

Monday April 7th

We are now in the River Plate, nearing Monte Video where I shall post this.

Easter Monday, I suppose the youngsters are in the Gardens. I hope to have letters from you in a week or so. I shall write again very soon, & by the way, I sh^{d} like you not to destroy my letters, but to keep them for me. There are some things that I might like to refer to again, & my home letters are the only diary I keep.

Best love all round

Jack

---

8. The Sintons are Quaker Linen merchants, and friends of the family: https://en.wikipedia.org/wiki/John_Sinton. I can find no trace of Dr Buckly, his son who "went wrong", or Miss Buckly, nor how they are connected to Dora Sinton (See Index to People).

10. Letter from Buenos Aires, 13th April 1890

18900413 See an image of the original letter, http://dx.doi.org/10.17613/0gg9-ma79

Buenos Ayres
13th April 1890

My dear Mother,

As we dropped anchor in Montevideo I brought to a close the letter written during the voyage, & posted it the same afternoon.

The health officers came on board abt 9 o'clock, & with them an official who turned out to be one of the chiefs of police. A protracted consultation was held in the Captain's cabin, & then the male passengers were ordered on the quarter deck & the names were called. I thought this proceeding was merely a kind of "passing the Doctor", but immediately after the order was given to put Mr Deeming's luggage on the tender. This Deeming was the man who arranged the second concert & sang "The place where the hold orse died." In the topical song he was referred to as "Mr Deeming, Whose face is always beaming".

At that moment his face was anything but beaming, & with good cause, for he had just been arrested, on the strength of a telegram from the Foreign Office, for the robbery of some 74 diamonds worth about £5000.[1]

When the news ran round the other 49 passengers, which it did like lightening, you might have knocked them down with 49 feathers. For a long time we could scarcely believe it, as the man did not look at all like a common swindler. On the night of the concert he made an eloquent speech, saying that a collection wd be taken up for the Steamers' Orphan Society, on whose behalf he made a touching appeal, afterwards heading the list with £2.

It seems his real name was Parsons or Lawson. The diamonds were found in his luggage, & he has confessed, & will be sent back to England for trial. Very likely you will have read something about the affair in the papers. On the voyage he had shown his diamonds all round & spoken freely of them. That very morning another passenger had jokingly advised him to take off a large diamond ring, else he might be arrested for having stolen it! The incident caused great excitement.

We landed at Montevideo about noon. As I shall be visiting it again later on, I shall defer my description till then.

After attending to some business I joined a few of the passengers at a nice hotel on the outskirts of the town, & we had dinner in the garden, under the plane-trees, while the fountains close by sparkled in the light of the lamps & splashed with a pleasant music. It was a glorious night, with a bright full moon & the delightful surrounding, & the relief of getting ashore, not to mention the excellent dinner, made us feel at peace with the world.

We spent all the next day in Montevideo, & in the evening sailed for Buenos Ayres.

La Plata is something like a River. I don't know its exact width here, but it is between 60 & 90 miles. It is very shallow, so much so, the Captain said, that we were half sliding over the soft mud most of the night. It was not, when we crossed it, of that clear silver colour that its name implies, but a pale brick hue that looked like honest clay.

Landing at Buenos Ayres was quite a complicated operation. The steamer anchored fully ten miles out in the river, &

1. Frederick Bailey Deeming (b 30th July 1853 - d 23 May 1892, hanged) was a serial criminal. Before leaving England he had swindled a jeweler in Hull. After being arrested in Montevideo, he was extradited to England. On release from prison, he eventually moved to Australia where he was convicted of other crimes including murder and executed in 1892: https://en.wikipedia.org/wiki/Frederick_Bailey_Deeming

we were transferred to a steam launchcraft that brought us in an hour's time to within half a mile of the shore. Then the launch could come no nearer & we were transhipped into a sailing boat, in which we managed to shorten the distance to about a hundred yards. The water was now only a couple of feet deep & the last stage had to be done in small rowing boats or in carts! So owing to the shallowness of the water we had to change in all three times to come ashore!

Fortunately we had not to look after our luggage through all these changes. There is a Transport Company whose employees come on board the steamer & take charge of your trunks, passing them through the customhouse & putting them in your room, for a small charge.

They are now busy with extensive harbourworks at Buenos Ayres. It is to be hoped that these will facilitate the, at present, rather disagreeable undertaking of disembarking.

Buenos Ayres is a very large town. The streets are straight & intersect one-another at right angles, cutting up the town into blocks. The pavements are simply shocking, I never saw anything to equal them & I wonder how any wheels can stand them.

There is little or no stone here, & almost all the houses are built of sun dried brick, covered with plaster which is much more durable in this climate than in England, for there is no frost to crack it. Many of the buildings are highly ornamental.

There are tramways along most of the principal streets; the drivers use high pitched horns to give warning of their approach, & the din is hideous.

I have put up at the "Provence", a fairly comfortable French Hotel. Later on I may take a furnished room if I find that the natives are disposed to lunch & dine me very often, as in the Hotel they don't make any allowance for that.

I have been awfully busy since my arrival & there are so many important matters to attend to that I scarcely know what to do first.

I have no time for more just now. This goes by Royal Mail "Elbe". Weather is delightful & I feel very well.

I hope you are all first rate.

Best love

Jack

11. Letter from Buenos Aires, 16th-22nd April 1890

1890416 See an image of the original letter, http://dx.doi.org/10.17613/trd1-fv05

No 3 Buenos Ayres.

16th April 1890

My dear Mother,

I sent you a letter y'day. by the Royal Mail, & another last week from Montevideo. In order that you may know whether you get all my letters, perhaps the best way will be for me to number them, which will save my referring – like a systematic man of business – to the dates of the various letters already on the way; so I will call this one No3.

I had an invitation to join a party y'day. to visit the Port of La Plata, a harbour, about 30 miles from Buenos Ayres, where important works have recently been completed. The invitation was given me by Mr Ogilvie, who came out by the "Coleridge".[1] He is acting on behalf of some Company in London owning one of the Railways here; his father was a large railway contractor & had, I rather think, something to do with the Forth Bridge.

Very unfortunately some Dundee business, that could not be postponed, prevented my accepting the invitation. There were about twenty people, – among them the managers of the Great Southern & Ensenada Railways & other Railway bosses, some local capitalists, a few of the nicest of the Coleridge passengers &, not least, Mr Uriburro, the new finance minister (Chancellor of the Exchequer), – altogether people whom it would have been very pleasant & useful from me to meet.[2] They went by special train abt 10 o'clock to the Puerto, had a champagne breakfast, were conducted round the harbour works in a steam launch, & were brought back again by special train in the afternoon, having spent, I understand, a most enjoyable day.

---

1. Probably Campbell Patrick Ogilvie son of Alexander Ogilvie: "Contractors Peto and Betts got their first railway concession in 1862 and Brassey, with partners Wythes, Wheelwright and Alexander Ogilvie, followed in 1864, just after the completion of the Grand Trunk Railway in Canada. Patrick Ogilvie was one GTR agent who moved to Argentina. With its nineteenth-century history one sees how the British engineers in Argentina were to be more numerous there than in most of dominions in 1890. This was in part a reflection of the dominance of British trade in the area" https://www.arct.cam.ac.uk/Downloads/ichs/vol-1-675-694-chrimes.pdf. Alexander 1812-1886: Civil engineer and contractor. https://www.gracesguide.co.uk/Alexander_Ogilvie. Son: Campbell Patrick b ~ 1856 Civil Engineer.

2. Actually Francisco Uriburu, Finance Minister 18th April 1890, resigned 7th June 1890.

At the breakfast Mr Uriburro announced, for the first time, his appointment to the Treasury, & several gentlemen present, knowing what a favourable impression the news would produce on the money market, at once tried buying local stocks, some of which advanced 35% since yesterday.

22nd April 1890

Very glad to have news from you. Your letter of 24th came y'day. with enclosure from Mrs Gotto for which I am much obliged. When I can find time I shall send a few words of thanks to Mrs Gotto.[3]

I am very sorry indeed to hear you were so unwell on your birthday. I hope you will feel much stronger & better now that Spring is almost over. (Here it is Autumn).

When you have Harry Fuhr's address I hope you will send it to me.[4] I might perhaps see him here or at Rosario.

I have been awfully busy since my arrival, but I have not time to tell you of my doings – that must wait till next mail.

By this one I send a ten page letter to Dundee, & a few lines to M & W Belfast.

Mr Hirschberg is here, but leaves next week for England.[5] He has been collecting money from his customers & says he has been fairly successful. Still he must have had some losses.

An oil portrait of Francisco Uriburu, the Brazilian politician, by the Spanish artist Joaquin Sorolla y Bastida (1863-1923).

I hope you will keep me well supplied with home news.

Best love all round

Jack.

3. Margaret Gotto b 1853, wife of Arthur Charles Gotto, lived on the Malone Road, Belfast. Arthur Charles Gotto was the brother of Percy Murly Gotto (See Index to People), who was a Civil engineer in Rio de Janeiro. JMcC frequently visited the Murly Gottos in Rio de Janeiro. I imagine he must have had an introduction to them from Margaret Gotto. Their father Edward Gotto had founded the Rio de Janeiro City Improvements Company in 1862. From the obituary: https://www.icevirtuallibrary.com/doi/pdf/10.1680/imotp.1897.19422.

4. See Index to People: Harry Agustus Robert Fuhr (b 17 May 1868 Belfast, d 1942 King William's Town, Cape Colony, South Africa). Father: Ernest Agustus Fuhr, Mother: Dorothea Hannay (1836-1894). In "List of Associate Members of The Institution of Civil Engineers" in 1900: https://www.forgottenbooks.com/en/download/CharterSupplementalChartersbyLawsandListofMembersoftheInstitutionofCivilEngineer_10672245.pdf

5. Edward Hirschberg (See Index to People): a German merchant naturalized in Dundee in 1887. Eduard Hirschberg (Itzig Eduard Hirschberg – born Lauenburg, Pomerania – was Germany now Poland –(Lebork) 30th December 1851 - died Lancashire 1914. Married Selma Hedwig Zander (1861-1946) born in Belgard, Pomerania (now Poland) 15 km north of Lauenburg. Children: Alfred Ewald died age 3 months, Erika Josephine 1887-1940, Frederick Rudolf 1890 -1963.

12. Letter from Buenos Aires, 25th-28th April 1890

18900425 See an image of the original letter, http://dx.doi.org/10.17613/19zf-b458

Nº 4 Buenos Ayres April 1890
29th
Royal Mail "Atrato"

<u>25th</u>

My dear Mother,

Since posting my last, 22nd, I received your welcome letter of 31st. No doubt my lines from Madeira reached you a few days later; – very likely they had to wait some time there for a homeward mail.

I hope you went to Portrush for a day or two at Easter & enjoyed the change.

Bertie Weinberg will be glad to go to you for a week, & I am sure he will be popular at Lennoxvale. I like Bertie, he is a good-natured fellow.[1]

To show you how international my private correspondence has become, the last post brought me a letter from Spain, one from Italy, one from the Canaries, one from Central America, a card from Paris & another from Curaçao, not to mention a letter from Mrs Weinberg[2] & the home budget, – a fairly cosmopolitan list.

My Italian acquaintance is Monsieur Saverio (otherwise the Duke of) Veltri – It is not everyone who receives autograph letters from a "gilded Duke", even though it be an Italian one, & very slightly gilded! He hopes I'll go to Naples!

My old friend Don Nicolas Polo hopes I'll go to Spain & pay him a visit in his country house. As an inducement he offers to regale me with brook trout rolled up in paper & roasted with butter in the oven; – very good they are!

My young friend Juanito Carlo hopes I'll go to the Canaries! He is a youngster about 14 & his letter is very entertaining, it begins (in Spanish of course): "My esteemed & distinguished friend" (Impertinently familiar correspondents please copy!) "My joy at receiving your welcome letter was extremely great, not only because it brought me ever-welcome news from you but also because it proved to me that your have not forgotten your young friend, who is so proud of the friendship you extend to him." To be told that one's friendship inspires feelings of pride is to have the assurance that one has not lived in vain!

Mr Iklé hopes I'll go to Paris, & finally a very decent fellow called Nixon hopes I'll go to San Salvador![3]

So you see I have a nice little circular tour already planned for me after leaving Buenos Ayres.

The Salvador letter is dated 22nd Nov. It was sent to Belfast, thence to Curaçao, back to Belfast, & out here, so it has travelled a distance equivalent to once round the World, & has taken five months to find me.

---

1. Herbert Weinberg. See Index to People
2. Agnes Weinberg, wife of Isaac Julius Weinberg. See Index to People.
3. Mr Iklé in Paris may have been Julius Iklé (b 1842, d 1896), the husband of JMcC's first cousin once removed Clara, and the father of his future wife Elsa (he was the 4th of the 15 children of Sara and Moses Iklé). It may also have been Ernst Iklé, Julius Iklé's brother (the 9th child). Ernst was born in 1848 and settled in Paris in 1871, where he married Emma Stern on 21st March 1875. On the marriage bans his address was given as Rue Montmartre 161. Their daughter Marthe Karolina was born in Paris 1st June 1876 and was Anne Queyras' grandmother (she married Max Jacoby, brother of John Jacoby; both sons of Bertha Iklé, the 3rd child, born in 1840, m Siegfried Jacoby).

Yesterday I met a man on the street who first looked hard at me & then spoke to me by name, reminding me that we had been together in Lisbon some three years ago.

Mr Hirschberg has been here for about two months; he goes home by the same steamer that takes this.[4] You know he is giving up his Manchester business; he has had an advantageous offer to open an import-house here, & will possibly accept it, he says all depends on the health of his wife who is at present in Italy.[5]

<u>26th</u> My linen has just returned from the wash, accompanied by a little bill for $7.50. With gold at par this would be 30/- but at the exchange of to-day it is only 12/6.

The currency in the Argentine Republic is all paper & there are bank-notes of all values down to 5 cents – worth just now about 1^{d}.

For about a year & a half these notes have gradually depreciated in value. Their par value is 4/2, but they fell steadily till at the end of last year they were worth about 2/6 & as the crisis became more acute they dropped heavily, until about a fortnight ago when they were equivalent to only 1/3. That is, that a merchant who wanted to send money to Europe to pay for goods imported had to give 15 dollars paper for every 5 dollars (or £1) gold. As he had probably already sold these goods calculating that he would not have to pay more than 7 or 8 paper dollars for the £1 you can easily imagine what heavy losses a large majority of the merchants have suffered; – many of them could not meet their engagements.

The Stock exchange is open from 12 till 1, & from 3 till 4, & as gold or shares are bought & sold the rate & amount of each transaction are chalked by clerks on a large black-board. I happened to be in the Exchange the day the banknotes reached their lowest point, – when it took 315 paper dollars to buy 100 dollars gold.

Speculation had been indulged in recklessly all round. Taking advantage of the large credits given so easily in Europe, men of all trades & professions, who ought to have confined themselves to their legitimate occupations, speculated feverishly in worthless stocks & in land that had not been & probably never could be cultivated, until both stocks & land had attained altogether fictitious values. At the same time, when apparently money was being made so easily & quickly, it was squandered lavishly. But the reaction came, credit was stopped, land & stocks dropped till they could not be realized at any price, the paper money depreciated to one-third of its nominal value & something approaching a general crash supervened.

An outcry began against the abuses & mismanagement of the Government & public feeling ran very high. A mass meeting was held 10 days ago in Buenos Ayres, & most energetic speeches were delivered, some of the orators making scarcely veiled hints at revolution, in case a thorough reform could not be achieved by pacific methods.

Seeing that public opinion was going to strongly against them the Minister resigned on the evening before the meeting. Unfortunately the President, Juarez Celman, who is a strong partisan, sticks to power, but in the selection of his new cabinet he has been obliged to yield somewhat to popular demand & the appointment of Mr Uriburu as finance minister has given satisfaction.[6]

The immediate effect of the change of ministry, before even it was known what Mr Uriburu's plans were, or whether he had any at all, – merely because of his known honesty & capacity – was that in two days the paper currency regained in value 20%; – an occurrence unparalleled, it is said, in any country.

The situation has continued to improve during the last few days, & there is a general hope, almost amounting to a belief, that the worst is over & that the improvement will be lasting.

I am afraid I have tired you with Change gossip, but my excuse is that the Gold premium is uppermost in people's thoughts & forms the sole topic of conversation today in Buenos Ayres.

---

4. For Eduard Hirschberg, see Index of People. His wife, Selma, was pregnant with their 3rd child who was born 2 ½ months later in Badenweiler (a spa resort in southern Germany). The son was Frederick Rudolf (b 4th June 1890, d 15 December 1963 Argentina).
5. Edward Hirschberg, initially represented I. J. Weinberg in Dundee during his absence, then established himself in Manchester, and finally established a successful business in Buenos Aires for Philip Goldschmidt (ref Isaac Julius Weinberg memoir, http://dx.doi.org/10.17613/ch97-0r17)
6. Miguel Ángel Juárez Celman (b 29th September 1844, d 14th April 1909) was an Argentine lawyer and politician. President of the Nation from October 12, 1886 until his resignation on August 6, 1890.

<u>28th</u> Mr Hirschberg left today for Montevideo where he will join the homeward steamer in 3 / 4 days. He has promised to send a line to the Pater to say he left me well.

¼ to 12, – about 3 o'clock with you, – you will all be snoring – beg pardon, – breathing softly, wrapped in gentle slumber – as I should be, instead of burning the midnight tallow, which will be charged to me in the bill as bougie 25 cents, & in the present unfavorable state of my bougie-t, – I should say budget, – I can't tallow it, – I mean I candle low it – no, – I can't allow it.

Good night

Best love

Jack

13. Letter from Buenos Aires, 3rd-5th May 1890

18900403 See an image of the original letter, http://dx.doi.org/10.17613/1rwc-xk85

N⁰ 5 Buenos Ayres   <u>5th May 90</u>
per "Bresil"

2nd May

My Dear Mother,

As the date becomes to our thinking more summerlike the weather here becomes colder, wetter, & more stormy. May in Buenos Ayres corresponds with November at home, & y'day, May-day, instead of being mild & bright was the first winter's day we have had. Last night a severe storm broke the telegraph wires, so we are today without news from the outside world. The high wind further blew the water eastward out of the broad shallow River Plate, leaving many vessels stuck in the mud.

Talking about mud, – I never saw streets so vile as those of this town. They are mostly paved with "square sets" laid on an insufficient foundation, so that the heavy traffic soon breaks them into great heights & hollows. Water & drainage-works were going on all over the town (until the money ran short) & the streets were torn up in all directions. A part of these works remains incomplete in the shape of huge holes, with their adjoining banks of earth. Other holes were filled up, after the pipes had been laid, but the superfluous earth & stones have been left to take care of themselves. So when it rains lovely mud-lakes are formed which passing wheels distribute among the pedestrians with delightful impartiality.

Beside the tramlines there are ruts six to eight inches deep, & particularly pleasant is it if a cab, trying to keep on the metals, drops into the ruts just as you happen to pass. Last night I was besplashed in this way literally up to the eyes – in fact a small shovelful of mud stuck in my eyebrow (proves how adhesive Buenos Ayres mud can be when it likes!). I felt tempted to make "a few cursory observations" on cab wheels & ruts in general, & those ones in particular, but as I was just on the point of entering the premises of the "English Litterary Society" – I didn't.

<u>3rd May</u>

For the small sum of two paper dollars I have the privileges of membership in this society for one month. It has comfortable reading & smoking-rooms in the centre of the town, & its long list of sucsribers comprises almost all the English Residents.[1] The leading English papers & periodicals are taken in & the library is well stocked. Once a week there is a meeting for lectures, or debates, & smoking concerts are given frequently.

A few evenings ago I went to see a French Comedy company here just now, of which the leading stars are Coquelin (ainé), from the Comédie Française, & Mme Judic, both well-known in Paris, – the latter chiefly as a Comic Opera prima donna.[2]

They gave us first a pathetic pretty little piece "La Joie fait Peur", & then a laughable, but very French, farce. The acting

---

1. "English Litterary Society" and "sucsribers" are as written in the letters.
2. Benoît-Constant Coquelin (b 23rd January 1841, d 27th January 1909), known as Coquelin ainé ("Coquelin the Elder"), was a French actor, "one of the greatest theatrical figures of the age" - https://en.wikipedia.org/wiki/Beno%C3%AEt-Constant_Coquelin. "Mme Judic" was Anna Judic (real name Anne-Marie-Louise Damien), a French comedienne (b 18 July 1849, d 15th April 1911) - https://fr.wikipedia.org/wiki/Anna_Judic

was very finished, but the theatre was not well filled; – the prices were too high & Buenos Ayres people are not so lavish with their "pesos" as they were last year.

In spite of the bad times a magnificent Italian Opera Company is due here in a fortnight, comprising Tamagno, Maurel, the "maestro" Mancinelli, & other notabilities. The prices are exorbitant & I am afraid the enterprise will not be very successful. Last year this Comp^{y} might have asked & obtained what prices they liked, "But, O the heavy change" which makes people more careful of their small change.

But there really is no <u>small</u> change here; the smallest coin, or rather bank-note, is 5 cents. The usual tram-fare is 8 cents & if you give the conductor a 10 cent note, he hands you a 2 cent postage-stamp by way of change!

The gold-premium is still the absorbing topic of conversation. It is now falling delightfully, – that is people are regaining confidence in the paper money of the country. About 3 weeks ago the premium was 215 today it was 124, & no doubt it will have jumped somewhere else by the time this reaches you. So long as such fluctuations are possible no business will be satisfactorily or legitimately conducted, for the paper is the national currency & how can a man know at what price to sell his goods when, in a few weeks' time, the gold with which he has to pay for them may cost him 30% dearer or cheaper.

<u>4th</u> By end of next week I hope to see my way clearly & to be able to send a telegram to Dundee about my movements. I shall go up to Rosario for a week or so, then possibly across to Montevideo, & after that if things continue to improve as rapidly as they have done in the last 3 weeks, I may come back to Buenos Ayres to try to take a few orders.

I hope to have letters from your tomorrow.

Best love to all

Jack

14. Letter from Buenos Aires, 8th-14th May 1890

18900508 See an image of the original letter, http://dx.doi.org/10.17613/as23-gn59

N.º 6   Buenos Ayres   14th May 1890

<u>8th May</u>

My dear Mother,

My last letter went by the French Mail S. "Brésil" on the 5th.

Today came your few lines from Portrush, 6th April, a little more than a month on the way. By the same post I had a letter, dated 8th, from Dundee, in a post-script to which they mention that they have just had a wire announcing the arrival at Montevideo of the "Coleridge".

It seems much more than a month since I arrived. I sincerely hope that in less than another month I shall have said farewell to Buenos Ayres.

I am very glad you went to Portrush & had a pleasant couple of days at Easter, favoured with bright weather. The fresh sea-breezes & the rest, though short, ought to do you & the Pater good. It is not strange that so many people take advantage of the cheap rates to spend a Friday till Monday holiday at Portrush.

I must leave the continuation of this letter till a more convenient season. Dinner has begun downstairs, & so has a band of 3 or 4 musicians who are playing Fra Diavolo most energetically,[1] in the open patio, to say nothing of a man in the next room who has just wound up for the sixth time consecutively a one-tuned musical box; – there it goes – "Air sung by Jenny Lind" I think my old musical primer called it – ;[2] the spring is not quite strong enough to roll off the whole air at one winding; – it begins "allegro vivace", soon slacks to "allegro", & gradually calms down to "andante" & all at once stops short in the middle of a bar; – most provoking, & I can't help listening unconsciously & speculating "now it's going to stop, – no -, well this time, – not yet -, next bar then, – once more – ah, there!" – Click – Click – Click – off it goes again. Well I'm off too –

<u>After dinner</u>. The number of itinerant musicians in Buenos Ayres is astounding. Every evening during dinner we are obliged to let the sound of music creep in our ears from the patio which is taken possession of by fiddlers, harpers, & guitarists. They seem to think that soups, fishes, & rosbif (à l'Anglaise) become the touches of sweet harmony.

In Thackeray's Irish Sketch-book (which I read not long ago & found, on the whole, dull & uninteresting) there is an amusing reference to music during dinner. Thackeray objects to it because, among other reasons, if you have a musical ear you are obliged to eat in time. The soup is served very hot, – the band strikes up a galop or a quick march, & you burn your tongue painfully. Next comes the fish, already cold, & you eat it deliberately to a minuet while the butter congeals on the plate; – & so on.

---

1. Fra Diavolo (or The Inn of Terracina) is a comic opera in three acts by the French composer Daniel Auber, from a libretto by Auber's regular collaborator Eugène Scribe: https://en.wikipedia.org/wiki/Fra_Diavolo_(opera)
2. Johanna Maria "Jenny" Lind (b 6th October 1820, d 2nd November 1887) was a Swedish opera singer, often called the "Swedish Nightingale": https://en.wikipedia.org/wiki/Jenny_Lind

An Agricultural Exhibition is now being held in the fine Park at Palermo, the best quarter of Buenos Ayres.[3] I took a walk through it the other day, but prize horses & oxen do not interest me. There was a large collection of wools from "estancias" or sheep ranches all over the country, & one section contained an exhibit of ramie from its natural state through all the stage of scutching, spinning, weaving & printing.[4] Some people think that this fibre has a great future.

Cheese & butter were well represented, & in the way of fruits there were some magnificent pears, peaches & apples. Tinned tongues & preserved meat were there on behalf of that important national industry, & a room full of huge hides to prove that "there is nothing like leather". From Paraguay came a snake-skin measuring fully twenty feet long by two feet across (when laid flat). The original owner must have been a pleasant & playful creature to meet when wriggling through its native woods! There was grain of all kinds to show the fatness of the land, & one from the mines far back in the cordillera.

Altogether the Exhibition proved the immense resources of the country. With its fine climate & splendid waterways navigable for hundreds of miles, the Argentine Republic must have a great future.

The people are a mixture of all nationalities, Spaniards, Italians predominating, & the fusion ought ultimately to produce a fine race, if at first they seem rather a mongrel lot.

13th May

No wonder lawyers are in such bad repute all the world over; what an aggravating set they are to have anything to do with. I expected to finish an affair this afternoon about which endless consultations have been held; and there at the last moment up crops a legal quibble to cause further expense & loss of time. I dare say Spanish & Spanish American lawyers are not fair specimens of the profession generally, but in any case, the less one requires their assistance the better. I shall have a wholesome dislike for lawyers as long as I live, if I beat Methuselah's record.

I have been exchanging a good many telegrams with Dundee during the last few days, which little amusement costs on the average some £3 a message. If people had always to economize their words as carefully as they are obliged to do when they cost 7/- or 8/- each there would be much less twaddle spoken & written.

The application of the Cable Company's tariff in the House of Commons, for instance, would be more effective than any method of cloture yet proposed.

A few evenings ago I was fortunate enough to see Coquelin & Mme. Juvic in "Tartuffe", a high-class treat. Afterwards Mme. Juvic sang some little "descriptive" songs inimitably. One was "Je suis chatouilleuse" which may be freely translated "Don't tickle me, I pray." The laughing chorus was so natural & so irresistibly infectious that the audience was fairly convulsed with laughter.

14th May

No more by this mail. I have ever so much to do today, & I shall have to do things in a hurry, which, it is perhaps scarcely necessary to assure you, I do not like.

Best love

Jack

---

3. Parque Tres de Febrero, popularly known as Bosques de Palermo (Palermo Woods), is an urban park of approximately 400 hectares (about 989 acres) located in the neighbourhood of Palermo in Buenos Aires: https://en.wikipedia.org/wiki/Parque_Tres_de_Febrero
4. Ramie is one of the oldest fiber crops, having been used for at least 6,000 years, and is principally used for fabric production: https://en.wikipedia.org/wiki/Ramie

15. Letter from Buenos Aires, 18th-27th May 1890

18900518 See an image of the original letter, http://dx.doi.org/10.17613/mhpn-h916

N° 7 Buenos Ayres   27th May 1890
Royal Mail "Thames"
<u>18th May</u>

My dear Mother,

Since posting my last letter 4 days ago I recvd. your welcome letter of 14th last month, telling me that you had just heard of the arrival at Montevideo of the "Coleridge". Before closing this letter I hope to be able to inform you of the close of one of the principal <u>diplomatic</u> affairs I came here to arrange, so that I shall soon be able to say good-bye to Buenos Ayres, & shall do so with a light heart. I wish I were at home just now to take part in your picnics & to enjoy the summer.

Has G.Y. started a bicycle? You say he rode to Clandeboye on one, & I read the sentence over again to see if I had rightly understood it.[1]

Bertie Weinberg seems to have seen & done so much as he possibly could in the time ...(inkblot) & I have no doubt he enjoyed himself.

I am sorry you have not sent me Harry Fuhr's address. I should have written to him & perhaps might have seen him here or at Rosario. I am glad he has got a good berth & have no doubt he will do well.[2]

Victor Kamcke will find an under engineer's lives on board ship cast in anything but pleasant places, but he is a fine fellow & won't mind hard work & rough quarters.[3]

You don't say in your last two letters what news you have from Addie.[4]

We have it very cold for the last week, but clear & bright during the day; any rain there is falls at night. The cold bath makes me tingle. I step into it the minute I get out of bed, & the first spongeful of cold water I squeeze down the back of my neck makes me gasp, I can tell you.

1. "G.Y." refers to George Young Kinnaird (see Index to People). The Clandeboye Estate is a country estate located in Bangor, County Down, Northern Ireland, 12 miles (19 km) outside Belfast. https://en.wikipedia.org/wiki/Clandeboye_Estate
2. Harry Fuhr (see Index to People): Harry Augustus Fuhr b 17 May 1868 in Belfast, died 1942 King William's Town, Cape Colony, South Africa. Father Ernest Augustus Fuhr, Mother Dorothea Hannay (1836-1894). He was a civil engineer – and although no record of this, he was likely involved with the railway in Argentina / Rosario. In "List of Associate Members of The Institution of Civil Engineers" in 1900. https://www.forgottenbooks.com/en/download/CharterSupplementalChartersbyLawsandListofMembersoftheInstitutionofCivilEngineer_10672245.pdf
3. (William) Victor Rung Kamcke b ~1863. Son of a flax and linen merchant in Belfast - ended up being a missionary in Bengal, married Mabel Eliza Lloyd in Lichfield on 10th April 1902 (Marriage notice in *The Belfast Newsletter* 12 April 1902). She also became a missionary in Bengal. Victor's parents were William Roderick Kamcke (b 1825 in Danzig) and Helene Emilie Rung (also born in Danzig, where they were married on 28th July 1861, according to a marriage notice in *The Belfast Newsletter* on 3rd August 1861). William Kamcke arrived in Belfast on the 28th June 1848 as an "apprentice to a merchant" and established "Kamcke, W.R., & Co., flax, linen yarn, and linen merchants." He died in Belfast 27th November 1896.
4. Addie is JMcC's brother, Ferdinand Adolf – see Index to People). In 1890 he was 25 years old and doing business in New York.

21st May

Last night was the "premiere" of the Opera; "Othello" with Tamagno & Maurel, Gabbi, & Mancinelli as conductor of the orchestra. I was very much tempted to go, but didn't. £2 for a stall in the pit is too exorbitant, but it would have been a great treat.

Two days ago the principal part of the affair, to which I referred at the beginning of this letter, was closed by the signing, in solemn state before a notary, of a mortgage & other documents; – a great relief to my mind as the affair has been very troublesome all through. The rest of it has to be done in Rosario, where I expect to go this week.

A Northern Whig came the other day containing the announcement of Dora Boas's marriage, & Mr Goschen's speech in presenting the Budget.[56] When you have an opportunity please convey my congratulations to Mrs Catz & Mr Goschen.

Mr Goschen's figures showing the enormous increase in the consumption of rum & other spirits as the immediate consequence of improved trade & higher wages are very curious. He says they impose on the Government the obligation of dealing with the matter, which I suppose means the speedy triumph of local option & other temperance measures. Everyone who cares for the real good of the country must hope so.

25th May

Your welcome letter of 21st April, also chatty letters from Emma & Olga[7], came the other day. I am very sorry to hear of Kolkenbeck's illness, & I trust he is meanwhile better[8]. Madrid is a nasty place owing to the sudden & great changes of temperature, & it is very easy to take cold there. One has to be very careful. Inflammation of the lungs is probably more prevalent in Madrid than in any other city in Europe, on account of the cold winds from the Sierra Guadarama after the hot days, & the same cause might easily bring on an attack of rheumatic fever.

We are having very cold weather here & I long for a good fire with sparkling logs & a comfortable armchair in front of it. No open fires & no armchairs in Buenos Ayres Hotels!

Today, the 25th May, is the anniversary of the achievement of Argentine Independence in 1810 & consequently a great holiday. The whole town is gay with the national flags, two light blue stripes enclosing a white one. Last night & tonight the government buildings, clubs, etc. have been illuminated, the favorite device being an arrangement of blue & white lights, – the national colours; – the effect is very picturesque.

Today the President, ministers, Staff officers, consular corps, & other personages attended service in the Cathedral where a Te Deum was sung. The square in which the Cathedral & Government House stand, was lined with troops, & the regimental bands played the national anthem as the President & company walked from one to the other. It was a very imposing sight. I had a good view from a window over-looking the square. This "Plaza de Victoria", as it is called, was gaily decorated with flags, & the monument in the centre, commemorating the event celebrated today, was covered with flowers.

27th May

I had letters y'day. from Dundee dated 2nd May; they came by French mail. I hoped to have had one from you but it has probably come by another route. The French steamers of the messagerie maritimes are the most rapid mails for Buenos Ayres. Best love to all. Jack

5. Dora Boas (see Index to People). Dora Rosetta Boas was born 30th March 1865 in Antrim. Her parents were Hermann Boas and Caroline nee Spiers. She was married in Groningen on 12th February 1891 to Bernard Israel Catz (b ~1857 Groningen). His parents were Israel Catz and Jannetje née van Aalten. Hermann Boas (b ~1828 Germany) and Caroline Boas (née Caroline Spiers, b ~1840 Holland) are shown in the 1901 Census living in Windsor Park, Belfast. Dora's brother (Hermann and Caroline's son) was Frederick Samuel Boas (see Index to People) whose disappointing play is referred to in an earlier letter.

6. Mr Goschen: George Joachim Goschen was British Chancellor of the Exchequer 1886-1892: https://en.wikipedia.org/wiki/George_Goschen,_1st_Viscount_Goschen. Budget dated 18th April 1890.

7. His sisters.

8. See Index to People: Refers either to Hermann Kölkenbeck or one of his sons, Eduard or Alfred. They were merchants based in Belfast.

16. Letter from Buenos Aires, 1st June 1890

18900601 See an image of the original letter, http://dx.doi.org/10.17613/6f9w-c288

N<u>o</u> 9[1] Buenos Ayres posted 3rd June

<u>1st June 1890</u>

My dear Mother,

Eight letters & one postcard on the way already, so I suppose I shall soon begin to hear of your having received some of them. In your last, of 28th Apl. you write that none have yet arrived.

I am very sorry not to have seen Wheeler of Guayaquil.[2] He is a very good fellow & we spent many evenings together in Guayaquil playing chess, supporting ourselves the while under the mental strain, by drinking a glass of some rare old port he had picked up by good luck.

I would have been glad if you had asked him to dinner or something, & I would have left word with you to that effect if I had known he was coming to Belfast.

I hope Aunt Martha is better.[3] Give her my love.

You having the heiresses as neighbours is evidently owing to Julie's dancing, as he wrote me once, with £60,000 in one evg., & making a favorable impression.[4] Let him go in & win. The embroidery department, with Mr Hicks's lead, is evidently the one marked to set the example to the long list of bachelors in Moore & Weinberg's.

The girls (unless some old fossil of a pre-Raphaelite professor takes pity on Olga) & myself are evidently doomed to grow, live, & die in single blessedness.[5]

About Addie I am not sure; I have not yet quite recovered from the shock to my nervous system occasioned, on my first entering his lodgings, by hearing a voice from the next room ask me, in a musical treble, & accompanying the enquiry with an endearing epithet of what might be called a pastoral character, whether it was really I, – and, – before I had regained sufficient composure to assure the affectionate enquirer of my identity, – hearing my younger brother's complacent & sprightly reply "Yes, dear!"[6]

---

1. Labelled No. 9 by JMcC – he also notes that "Eight letters & one postcard on the way already" – but we do not have the No 8 – presumed the postcard.
2. I wonder at what stage JMcC was in Ecuador? Mr Wheeler not identified so far. https://en.wikipedia.org/wiki/Guayaquil
3. This is Martha McCaldin (b 1808, d 23 Dec 1897). She was JMcC's great-aunt, his mother Jane's Aunt - sister of her mother Ann Isabella McCully (née McCaldin), the granny who lived with them at Lennoxvale.
4. "Julie" this is the nickname of his brother Julius who was 17 ½ at the time (see Index of People). These neighbours, the Blacks, have been mentioned before in association with Julie (who danced with "£60,000" and obviously impressed!) Who knows – if it had not been for his premature death he may well have married in there.
5. Very sad perspective of the fate of himself and "the girls" on the marriage market - although he was correct regarding his sisters Annie and Emma. Olga married "late" at the age of 29 to Claude Hardy, a man 13 years older than her (although not quite an "old fossil of a pre-Raphaelite professor")
6. Wonderful description of his younger brother's debauchedness (to his mum!!). I assume this is Addie in New York – we have a description of his life there from JMcC's later visit (and the "pretty young widow") – but can't find anything about him in NY in early 1890. I wonder if JMcC returned for the West Indies via New York after January 1890 (unfortunately we do not have any letters following on from the last one from Curaçao dated 24 Jan 1890).

I meant to have told you, in this letter, about some choice little bits of English as she is spoke by a young German at our table, but this must wait till the next letter, for my candle (charged at 1/3 in the bill!) is burning low, & besides I must be up early to-morrow to prepare for my trip to Rosario.

For tomorrow, 3rd June, I am off to Rosario de Santa Fé, where I hope to finish my business in a few days, returning to spend another very few in Buenos Ayres. Then I shall joyfully bid farewell to the Argentine (It won't be "dreful sorry Argentine!") & take me to the other side of the Silver Plate; – which expression is tautological, but that matters little since it affords me the opportunity of remarking wittily, with regard to the whole district, that when you rub the surface glitter off this Silver Plate you find that its solid foundation is really our Britannia metal.

When I leave Buenos Ayres, & I hope you will have news, from Dundee, of my having done so before this letter reaches you, I shall consider that I have started homeward, though on the way, I shall have to call at a few of the principal towns to find out how the intelligent natives are off for coffee bags (& other necessaries) & pocket handkerchiefs (& other luxuries).[7]

Best love to all

Jack

---

7. Presuming the "necessary" jute coffee bags from Dundee, and the "luxury" linen handkerchiefs from Belfast. Jute sacs were often used for transporting coffee.

17. Letter from Buenos Aires, 9th June 1890

18900609 See an image of the original letter, http://dx.doi.org/10.17613/m261-k557

Letter written on 3 sheets, 1st and 3rd headed paper:

1st sheet:

MEILI & ROESLI[1]

BUENOS AIRES

Casilla del Correo No. 137(further illegible)

Para Telegrammes

MEILI, BUENOS AIRES

3rd sheet:

MOORE & WEINBERG

BELFAST

AND

DUNDEE

Address Telegrams,

"WEINBERG".

1. See Index to People. Meili & Roesli are listed as "commission merchants" in Buenos Aires in the *International Bureau of the American Republics Argentina Handbook* of 1894: "Manufacture of bags and sacks. This industry, owing largely to the spread of agriculture, has increased to such an extent that from 30,000 to 50,000 of sacks are now sold annually (according to the year and the crops) in the country. The five principal factories are capable of producing more than 100,000 sacks. The importation of manufactured sacks is thus rendered impossible. The five factories are as follows [in order of output]: La Primitiva, G. A. Sere & Co, Meili & Roesli, O. Nordtmeyer & Co., Salina & Co."

My dear Mother,

For the last three days I have been in Rosario de Santa Fé, the saintly Apostolic-Roman-Catholic name – Rosary of the Holy Faith – of the capital of the Province of Santa Fé, the second department, in importance, of the Argentine Republic. We left Buenos Ayres (Roesli[2] & I) by the mid-day train, & arrived at Rosario towards eight. The country we passed through is perfectly flat, the immense plains stretching as far as the eye can reach, like a calm sea; in fact towards the horizon, especially in the dusk of the evening (poetic "gloaming") they faded into a grey-blue (Alsatian-mountain) colour that made me think the Atlantic or the Rio de la Plata must be there, until I remembered that both were in a quite opposite direction. Coming from the northern hemisphere one is confused as to the points of the compass by the sun being due north, instead of due south, at noon. Scarcely a tree is to be seen, the only vegetation being a kind of coarse grass, & in the swampy places a low rush or cane with tangled roots. Only a small part of the land is cultivated, & as it is now mid-winter here the crops are gathered in & only the dry maize-stalks are left. These were being burned right & left as we passed, & in the evening the bright lines of flame on all sides had a striking effect. Immense herds of cattle & sheep (flocks of sheep I suppose I should say) were grazing on the plains. We saw numbers of wild-duck, partridge, snipe & other birds, & in the distance I think I saw, but I am not sure of it, some ostriches.

Rosario itself is a new & uninteresting town with ill-paved perfectly straight streets, crossing each other at right angles & dividing the town into regular blocks, as at Buenos Ayres. The River Paraná, which, with the other inflowing rivers, forms at its estuary the Rio de la Plata, is here 32 miles wide, & large steamers come up to Rosario.[3]

One of my fellow passengers on the "Coleridge" was a Miss Morley whose brother is in the London Bank at Rosario. I made the acquaintance of the latter, a very nice fellow, when he came to meet his sister on her arrival. I saw him again at Rosario & we lunched together & on Sunday afternoon he took me for a row in a light pleasure-boat to an island about a mile out in the River. I enjoyed the exercise & the outing very much, as also the tea we had at his house on our return.

I came back to Buenos Ayres by the night train & had a bunk in a sleeping car; it was very cold & I did not sleep very well, though I had my rug. I am going to make up for it tonight & to that effect I shall not write any more now. Though there is no frost at nights the thermometer must go down to almost freezing point, & there is no comfortable fire in my room, – not even a grate to make one in; so the warmest & snuggest place is bed.

Besides the only thing else of interest that I have to mention is that I went to the Senate some days ago & heard the finance minister, Mr Uriburro, make a remarkable speech about some secret issues of National Bank-notes which have created considerable alarm among the public. The news of today is that this minister being unable to carry out his reforms as he wished, has sent in his resignation, with the immediate result of sending up the gold-premium 25 points at one jump, & spreading consternation among commercial circles. We shall see what tomorrow will bring forth.

Best love to all.

Jack

---

2. Eugen Roesli-Bidermann (see Index to People)

3. The Paraná River (Spanish: Río Paraná, Portuguese: Rio Paraná, Guarani: Ysyry Parana) is a river in south Central South America, running through Brazil, Paraguay, and Argentina for some 4,880 kilometres (3,030 mi). It is second in length only to the Amazon River among South American rivers. The name Paraná is an abbreviation of the phrase "para rehe onáva", which comes from the Tupi language and means "like the sea" (that is, "as big as the sea"). https://en.wikipedia.org/wiki/Paran%C3%A1_River

18. Letter from Buenos Aires, 15th June 1890

18900615 See an image of the original letter, http://dx.doi.org/10.17613/nhtf-7p94

Buenos Ayres 1890
15th June.

My dear Mother,

My last letter went by "Britannia", a week ago.

Y'day., after a somewhat long interval, we had a mail from England, bringing your welcome letters of 8th & 12th May, also one dated 27th Apl. from Annie[1].

Em. seems to have exhausted herself baking so many delightful cakes & tarts, & puddings, during the visit of the Weinbergs. I depend upon you all, but I particularly rely on Jim, to persuade her not to tax her strength by making any more goodies for the present, but to reserve all her energies till I come home.[2]

I was very glad to get Harry Fuhr's long & interesting letter & to hear he is doing so well.[3]

He has a first-rate chance. The place he is working at is some 200 miles, I think, South of Buenos Ayres & altogether out of my way so I shall not see him, but I intend writing him a line this afternoon.

What you write about Miss Higginbotham is very sad, but perhaps it may turn out not to be really the case.[4]

I finished y'day a long letter to Addie[5], but I don't know anything about the mails to New York & he may not have it for a month or six weeks. The letter may have to go via England.

You will have heard from Dundee that I sent them a telegram last week informing them that I intended leaving for Montevideo in a week. I mean to push on quickly now.

Y'day. evg. I went with a young fellow called Ferguson, a fellow passenger by the "Coleridge" & now employed as engineer on the drainage works, to his lodgings; he has a room in a comfortable house owned by a Scotch family. We were asked by the Paterfamilias to join the family circle in the drawing-room which we gladly did, the circle consisting of the Father, Mother, three grown-up daughters & a number of small fry; – there were also three or four friends. The piano was put into the corner, the room cleared & we had a lively little dance. Towards the end of the evg. I found out that one of the young ladies present, a Miss Petulla, was a Dundee girl, & of course knew a lot of Dundee people. She was with her sister-in-law Mrs Petulla, & has come out to the Plate for a two months' holiday. I think I shall call at their house & cultivate their acquaintance a little, as they seem very pleasant people. Only as I purpose leaving in a week, I shall not see much of them here, but I may possibly meet Miss Petulla again in Dundee.[6]

1. His sister Anne Isabella who is 23.
2. Em (his sister Emma) is 21 ½. Jim (brother James Moore) is 15 ½.
3. Harry Fuhr again (see Index of People) – a registered Associate Members of the Institution of Civil Engineers in 1900 when he was living in the "Cape Colony" in South Africa – he was elected Member in 1893.
4. Miss Higginbotham, identity uncertain. There was a Miss Mary Louisa Higinbotham who died in Belfast in 1892 age 30, at 46 Wellington Park (7 mins walk from Lennoxvale). Her father Granby was a Bank Director.
5. His brother Ferdinand Adolphus who was a "commission agent" in New York at the time
6. Miss "Petulla". See Index to People. There were no Petullas in Dundee – but plenty of Patullos. A single lady (Scotchwoman) Catherine Patullo, aged 32, sailed back to Southampton from Buenos Aires arriving 5th August 1890. I suspect it is she.

<u>15th June</u>, afternoon. Have just received a further batch of letters, among which yours of 19th May, & one from Em., cheeky as usual.

Geo.Y. says he was appealed to by Uncle Addie & Father to say which was the better-looking, & found the position awkward.[7] It was a young man called Paris was it not? who was once upon a time called upon to decide a similar question for three professional beauties.

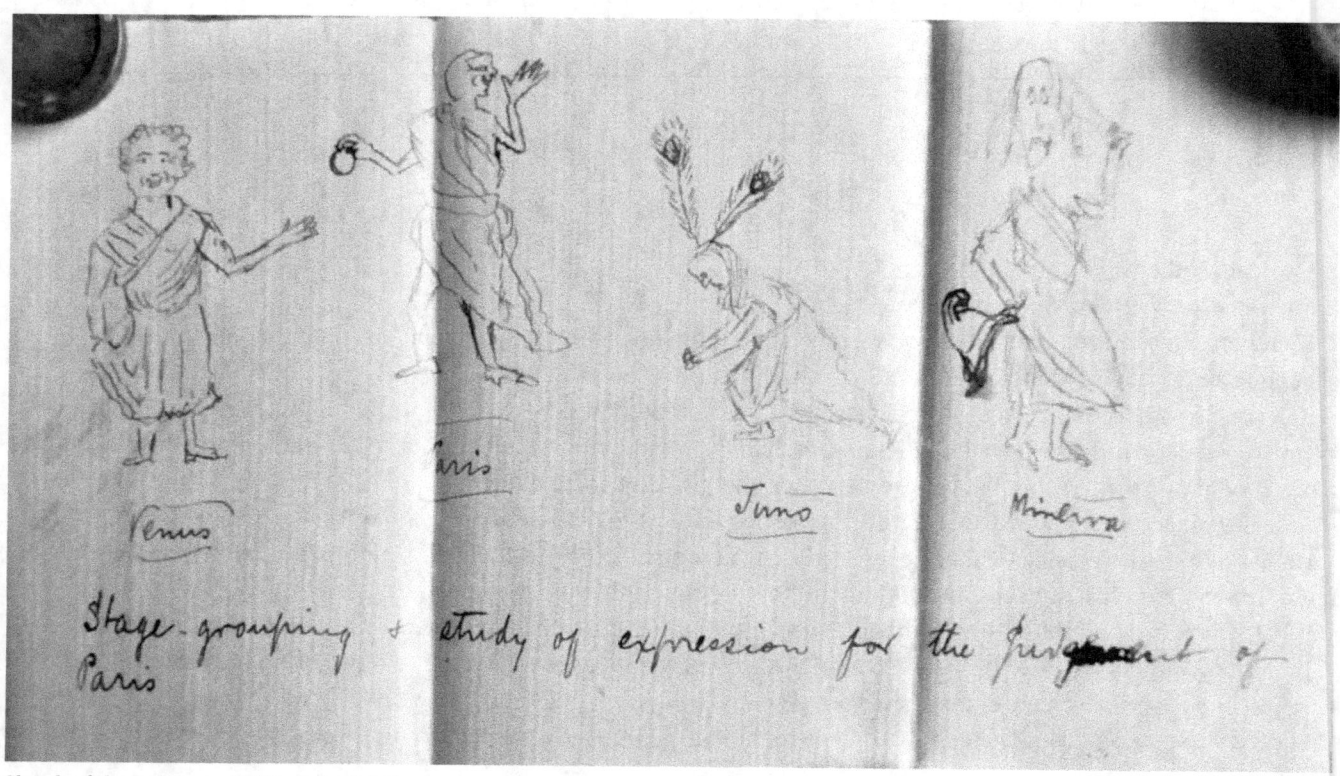

Sketch of the Judgement of Paris by JMcC

I offer a valuable suggestion for the next tableaux in the Ulster Hall, Geo.Y. & say, the three Miss (Whitey) Browns, as Paris, Venus, Minerva, & Juno (were these the claimants?) respectively, all in the orthodox costume of heathen gods & goddesses. Sketch herewith. The drapery is not quite right, but that is a detail. And if it wasn't Venus, Juno, & Minerva, why it must have been other three attractive but vain young women.

I hope your fears of being turned out of the house are unfounded. When I have realized part of the half million sterling coming to me from a silver & lead mine, of which I am part-proprietor, I may make Musgrave an offer for the house myself[8] : – please ask him to wait! My mine is in the Cordillera, & my share cost me £20.

How is it you are not keeping the tennis-court in order? Are the youngsters becoming too lazy to play? And the exercise of lawn-mowing in the afternoons is first-rate for you!

7. Geo. Y. – Presumably George Young Kinnaird. JMcC usually refers to him as G.Y.K. Uncle Addie is the never really mentioned brother of Julius – registered as "Adolf Löwenthal" at birth in Ludwigslust in 1833 – and later known as "the merchant Ferdinand Adolph Loewenthal – residing at 205 Adelaide Road," after marrying Caroline Goldschmidt (of Brunswick), with whose relatives he was in business – and one of whom lived at 209 Adelaide Road. See Index to People.

8. Presumably Henry Musgrave (b 1827, d 2 January 1922), DL, a Northern Irish businessman and philanthropist. He is perhaps best remembered for Musgrave Park in Belfast which he donated to the city. His portrait hangs in the Examination Hall of Queen's University Belfast. https://en.wikipedia.org/wiki/Henry_Musgrave

I have nothing of special interest to tell you this week. The alarm caused by the change of ministry has subsided; they have borrowed more money in London, five millions meanwhile, which ought to help them to pay their way for a little while, but unless they radically mend their ways, turn honest & economize, they will only sink deeper into the mire.

Last week their paper currency depreciated, & recoiled again, 15%, these fluctuations make legitimate business impossible.

The 19th-century Italian operatic tenor Francesco Tamagno (1850-1905). A photograph by Guilio Rossi.

One evg. I went to the Opera, with (comparative) economy taking a ticket for the 4th balcony, or "gods". The Opera was "The Huguenottes" & the principal singers Tamagno, Gabbi, Dalty, Stahl, & Kaschmann. Tamagno's tremendous voice overpowered all others, but the whole performance was magnificent.[9]

The last mail brought me also a letter from G.Y.K. I am glad to hear he is busy. He has a large sum to pay me for commission on those West Indian collar orders.

There is no immediate prospect of an unoccupied wet Sunday so tell him not to expect a letter from me for some time & meanwhile give him my fondest love.

By the way this Sunday is particularly wet & uncomfortable (but not unoccupied) – unfortunately there is no fireplace in my room or I should treat myself to a snug fire, as Messrs Moore & Weinberg's minister plenipotentiary is expected to take care of himself, & will not disappoint expectations formed of him.

Such an entertainment would be, as our German friend said y'day at dinner "very instructious", & at the same time delightful.

But just now I must think of something else than "instructious" tableaus; & by the way of entertainment I have half a dozen letters from Dundee to digest.

So bye-bye.

Best love

Jack

9. *Les Huguenots* is a French opera by Giacomo Meyerbeer and is one of the most popular and spectacular examples of grand opera. In five acts, to a libretto by Eugène Scribe and Émile Deschamps, it premiered in Paris in 1836. https://en.wikipedia.org/wiki/Les_Huguenots. Francesco Tamagno was an Italian operatic tenor - the first to sing Othello in Verdi's opera of the same name (a 1905 recorded clip is available: https://archive.org/details/niunmitema1903). Giuseppe Kaschmann was a noted Austrian baritone (born in Croatia), Zina Dalty was a soprano from Madrid, and Amalie Stahl was an Austrian alto. These were top stars of the day.

19. Letter from Buenos Aires, 18th June 1890

18900618 See an image of the original letter, http://dx.doi.org/10.17613/jxm6-jm41

Nº 12   Buenos Ayres   1890

<u>18th June</u>

My dear Mother,

I think I may claim to be a fairly diligent correspondent, having sent you eleven letters in two months.

My last went on the 15th, but by a slow steamer, whereas I mean to send this by a quick boat on the 20th, & it will probably reach you as soon as the first.

I have just come (11 p.m.) from an auction of pictures. The works offered formed a very mixed collection, the only well-known painting being Falero's "L'Etoile Double", which was awarded a prize in the Paris Salon of '86. It was knocked down for £180, a fair price considering the times.[1] A fellow who was with me, Ferguson by name, by my advice bought a landscape in oils for £8 & a little water-colour sketch for 30/-, & as far as I can judge, he got them exceedingly cheap; they are worth three times the money.

He is very proud of his purchase & he will derive at least £10 worth of pleasure from having these pictures in his room during the three years he intends remaining here, even if he should ultimately not be able to sell them at a profit. They are both really pretty. The oil-painting represents the evening sun shining from behind a bank of low clouds & lighting up a stretch of calm sea winding into a level beach of yellow sand. The water-colour is a sloping bank with golden corn & a few overhanging trees whose early Autumn tints are reflected in a pool of transparent water; – a "truly rural" subject like the "meadow with cows & sheep & a river" that Uncle Addie proposed to buy for the silver wedding.[2]

There were some fearful daubs sold. In one the most conspicuous object was a mill-chimney! Another represented the back-view of a serenading cavalier. Someone present suggested to turn the picture round so that we might see the man's face.

Last night I dined at the house of a Mr Agrelo, one of Dundee's customers, a Portuguese by birth but an Argentine through having lived 25 years in this Republic.

His house is furnished with gilt-backed chairs, many mirrors, & coloured plaster busts of Portuguese worthies. His wife is a pleasant, good looking, easy going, native lady, with a healthy appetite, – very fond of her two children, a spoilt youngster of eight & a lively little girl of five.

The dinner must have consisted of at least a dozen courses, & as I was the only guest & the feast had been prepared in my honour, I had to eat of all, so that at the end I was considerably "crowded".

As a special treat, & as the crowning glory of the dinner, there was the "plato ingles" (English dish) of fried ham & eggs!

I could scarcely suppress a smile when I saw this appear, but at the same time I was pleased at the proof of their thoughtful kindness in wishing to give me what they considered a genuine English dinner dish, in case the others should not be to my taste. I am quite sure they consulted beforehand what kind of viands "un ingles" would be likely to

---

1. Falero "L'etoile double" painted by Luis Ricardo Falero in 1881. Not to everyone's liking. https://en.wikipedia.org/wiki/Luis_Ricardo_Falero
2. Uncle Addie (Julius' brother Adolf – later to be known as Ferdinand Adolph) - and whose silver wedding? Possibly Jane and Julius' (25th wedding anniversary would have been in 1886)

appreciate, & that "fried ham & eggs" came to them as an entirely happy inspiration, as also the subsequent (native) tea & milk.

<u>19th June</u> Roesli has been in bed for the last few days with influenza or something of that sort; he is better now, but his absence from the office will delay my leaving for a day or two. Nevertheless I may be off now any day.

You will be relieved to learn that my health (notwithstanding Mr Agrelo's dozen courses) continues excellent, & my spirits, as usual, buoyant, my only ailment being a strong disinclination to get out of bed these cold mornings.

I have little to write about except myself & my doings, & six pages are enough for to-day of even this interesting subject, so I shall say good night & seek the grateful warmth of my blankets & travelling rug. At this hour (midnight – 3 p.m. with you) Lennoxvale is wrapped in slumber – all silent save, perhaps, for a few rhymical snores. Buenas noches.

Best love to all

Jack

20. Letter from Montevideo, 30th June-3rd July 1890

18900630 See an image of the original letter, http://dx.doi.org/10.17613/3tr6-5t93

12   Montevideo   30th June 1890

My dear Mother,

At last I am able to head my letters from some other place than Buenos Ayres, which fact is sufficient to bring about a devoutly thankful frame of mind.

I left y'day. afternoon about five o'clock, being accompanied to the steamer by Malcolm, Douglas, & Fergusson, three fellows whose names I have mentioned in previous letters, who came to bid me an affecting farewell. As the ropes were being hauled in we exchanged parting volleys of chaff between the wharf & the deck, causing considerable amusement to a sandy haired English workman close by, & then they enviously watched as the steamer carried me away from Buenos Ayres.

The river boats that ply between Buenos Ayres & Montevideo belong to an English Company.[1] They are large, comfortable, & tastefully fitted, not unlike those Clyde steamers on which we had such a jolly time about a year ago.[2]

I arrived at Montevideo at day light next morning & now I have a comfortable room in the Hotel des Pyramides, looking out on a fine Square.[3] From the flat roof of the Hotel, one of the highest points in the town, there is a magnificent view of the harbour & the outer river.

A turn of the century colour picture of the Pyramides Hotel with a horse-drawn carriage waiting outside.

1. The river trip from Bueneos Aires to Montevideo across the Rio de la Plata - nearly 200 km as the crow flies
2. https://en.wikipedia.org/wiki/Clyde_steamer and https://electricscotland.com/history/articles/clydesteamers.pdf. Perhaps they had an outing on the "Lord of the Isles", a particularly celebrated "ideal saloon excursion steamer."
3. The "Gran Hotel Pyramides" was famously elegant hotel. The cafe and restaurant were located on the ground floor. At the end of the 19th century, it was a male custom to stop at the Café de las Pyramides to sit at a table near the windows and from there to contemplate the ladies' calves getting on the tram, which stopped at the corner of Ituzaingó and Sarandi. https://montevideoantiguo.net/index.php/presentes/hotel-pyramides.htm

It is a relief to be away from the vile smells of Buenos Ayres; – the air here seems fresher & more invigorating.

The town is much more picturesque, rather hilly than otherwise, whereas Buenos Ayres is a stretch of dead flatness, & the latter place is cut up by its narrow regular streets into monotonous blocks, while Montevideo is pleasantly varied.

<u>3rd July</u>. I shall likely, barring unforeseen accidents, take a steamer for Brazil in about a week, & then I shall be fairly on my way home.

The weather here for the last few days has been delightfully warm & bright, enabling me to shake off a cold I had brought with me from Buenos Ayres.

Business in Montevideo is at a standstill – as complex as that of Buenos Ayres. The two towns are so closely connected commercially, many firms having houses in both places, that if business in one is bad the other suffers too. It is true Uruguay is so far ahead of the Argentine that it has a gold currency & so it is not constantly in a state of feverish excitement over a fluctuating premium. But there is a want of confidence & credit all round, beginning with the Banks, & the money is not circulating.

The wind is rising & I think we shall have another "pampero" tonight.[4] There are still traces, all round the bay, of the work of the last "pampero", in the shape of hulls on their beams' ends, broken spars, & so on. This Southwesterly gale does tremendous mischief here every time it comes. Its force is irresistible, & the shipping in the bay is quite un-protected. The storm springs up too with very brief warning.

The latest telegrams from England bring news as to the difficulties of the Salisbury cabinet & the probabilities of its speedy fall.[5] Prepare yourselves for Home-Rule. If I am appointed Chancellor of the Irish Exchequer, wire me at once.

I have not had letters from you for a long time. I hope some will come soon.

With best love.

Jack

4. The pampero is a burst of cold polar air from the west, southwest or south on the pampas in the south of Brazil, Argentina, Uruguay, Paraguay and Bolivia. https://en.wikipedia.org/wiki/Pampero_(wind)
5. https://en.wikipedia.org/wiki/Second_Salisbury_ministry

21. Letter from Santos, 14th July 1890

18900714 See an image of the original letter, http://dx.doi.org/10.17613/h2rp-ww71

Nº 14   Santos, Brazil
14th July 1890

My dear Mother,

You will see by the heading that I have left the Plate behind & that I am now at Santos, homeward bound.

Before leaving Montevideo I was glad to receive your two welcome letters of 25th May & 3rd June, – dates somewhat old to be acknowledging on the 14th July, but I hope to have later news at Rio.

I am pleased that you were interested in gold premium explanations; I was afraid you would be rather bored by them.

So you are still supported by the House of Commons on Sundays after Church, when Corryolanus is not occupied in shaping the destiny of the nation.

I send my congratulations to Julie on the acquisition of a tail-coat; but this new dignity is rather a reminder that we are all getting awfully old – a melancholy reflection.[1] As the American poet sings – "Listen to my tail of woe!"

Annie seems to be having a good time in Paris, to judge from her letters.[2]

No doubt you are relieved to have house cleaning over. That my davenport was respected in the general war on harmless dust was perhaps owing rather to your not having the key to it than to a consideration for the private nature of its contents.[3] People out in this part of the world are not so fastidious about a little matter in the wrong place, & if cleanliness is next to godliness they are in a very bad way.

By the time James will have finished his Intermediate Exams I hope I shall be home in time to celebrate his triumph.[4]

The 12th of glorious pious & immortal memory is also over – I hope without very many killed & wounded.[5]

I came up from Montevideo by the Royal Mail Steamer "La Plata".[6] When I went on board I stared very hard at one of the officers whose face seemed quite familiar to me, & he returned my gaze. I said to a passenger "That must be brother of Captain Milner of the "Avon" – one of the West Indian boats, but on asking one of the stewards I was told that it was Captain Milner himself, with whom I had made two short but very jolly voyages along the coast of Venezuela on my first trip to the West Indies. He remembered me perfectly when I spoke to him, & invited me into his cabin to take a liqueur. We had a long conversation & altogether he was very civil. He had been promoted a short time before to the "La Plata", a regular passenger & mail packet, from the "Avon", which is only a cargo-boat.

---

1. Julius Jnr acquisition of a tail coat age 17 ½ (b 17 December 1872)
2. Annie, in Paris age 23 (b 24 April 1867): what is she doing there? And with whom is she staying - possibly Clara Iklé and her family?
3. A davenport is a type of desk, a piece of furniture with a writing surface and usually drawers or other compartments
4. His brother Jim (James Moore b 19 November 1874) – will be just under 16 by the time JMcC gets home
5. Twelfth of July = the Glorious Twelfth / Orangemen's Day. In Ulster, where about half the population is from a Protestant background and half from a Catholic background, the Twelfth has been accompanied by violence since its beginning. https://en.wikipedia.org/wiki/The_Twelfth
6. There are several Royal Mail Ships called "La Plata" but none are recorded as in service in 1890. The only ship "La Plata" in service in the region in 1890 was actually a "Messageries Maritimes" ship. It was in service from 1889-1903.

Another passenger by the steamer was the Miss Petullo whom I mentioned having met at Buenos-Ayres. I think I told you she was from Broughty Ferry & knew many Dundee people.[7]

Curious to say she was at a dance at Fernbrae which took place while I was there. It was on a 19th Jany. either two or three years ago & was given in honour of Fred Weinberg's coming of age.[8] I did not remember having met her, nor was her memory any better or more flattering than mine, but I have a distant recollection of the date of the month from a New Year's card that I sent Fred Weinberg, & also of having enjoyed myself very much at it. Miss Petullo played a very good game of whist & we also entertained each other in the afternoons with reversi & backgammon.[9] She is a little woman, no longer very young nor beautiful, but an interesting conversationalist, appreciating fun, & altogether very nice.[10]

The other passengers were also a very pleasant set & I was sorry to leave the ship. Several of them civilly expressed their regret that I was not continuing the voyage with them – one of them rather magnanimously, as I am afraid I was a little rude to him on his maintaining that one way of playing whist was as good as another, & that there was no advantage in informing your partner as to your hand for you conveyed the same information to your opponents.

The run from Montevideo to Santos lasted from Wednesday afternoon till Sunday morning. The sea was perfectly calm & the weather became at once warm & delightful.

Today, Monday, is a holiday, being the anniversary of the Declaration of the Republic in France, or the taking of the Bastille, or something of that sort. The Brazilians in the flush of their recently asserted political liberty feel called upon to celebrate not only their own, but also everyone else's independence.

Santos is a small town with narrow streets & insignificant houses, but the situation is fine. It is on an island or delta & has a good harbour formed by the widening of the river some four or five miles from its mouth, at the apex of the delta. The country all round is mountainous, with dense tropical vegetation, & exceedingly picturesque. I find it particularly beautiful, after having spent two months in Buenos Ayres with its perfectly flat surroundings devoid of trees. I don't think I shall remain here more than a couple of days, & I shall probably go to Rio overland, by way of San Paulo where I may spend a few days.

The Dundee letters seem to catch the mails better than the Belfast ones. I found here a very nice letter from Mrs Weinberg, dated 19th June. She says Emma & Olga are to pay them a visit end of July at Kingnossie, & to return with them to Dundee.[11] I must write to Addie some day soon for his birthday.[12] One must look ahead so far when letters have to be sent from the Southern Hemisphere. I hope the cider & the shower-baths (which was to blame?) have not further disagreed with the Pater. I think the Pilsener that Dr Whittla recommends is safer[13]. On receipt of this I think you had better write to Pernambuco Bahia c/o Mr John Eggers, Caixa 114 (Brazil) unless you hear to the contrary by my telegrams to Dundee.[14]

If I should have left Bahia the letters will follow me to Pernambuco, or better still, to Belfast.

Best love.

Jack

7. Miss Petullo: see Index to People

8. "Fred's coming of age dance at Fernbrae" was in honour of Frederick Simon Weinberg (b 5 August 1865) – so age 21 in 1886. However, the party was on 19 January – must have been "three years ago" when he writes, i.e. in 1887 when Fred was 21 ½.

9. Reversi is a strategy board game for two players, played on an 8×8 uncheckered board. It was invented in 1883. The game gained considerable popularity in England at the end of the nineteenth century. https://en.wikipedia.org/wiki/Reversi

10. Miss Petullo "no longer very young nor beautiful". If she is the Catherine Patullo on the passenger list returning from Buenos Aries arriving in Southampton on 5 August 1890 – she is about 6 years older than him

11. Could only find a Kingussie - a small town in the Badenoch and Strathspey ward of the Highland council area of Scotland. https://en.wikipedia.org/wiki/Kingussie

12. Addie's 25th birthday (born 23 August 1865)

13. Sir William Whitla (see Index to People)

14. John C Eggers (see Index to People)

A painting of the port of Santos in the early 1900s by the Brazilian artist Benedito Calixto de Jesus (1853–1927).

22. Letter from São Paulo and Rio de Janeiro, 24th and 27th July 1890

18900724 See an image of the original letter here, http://dx.doi.org/10.17613/rt7t-dn61

N.º 15   São Paulo, Brazil
24th July 1890
Rio de Janeiro 27th

My dear Mother,

My last was from Santos, which place I left on the 18th, the journey by rail to São Paulo takes only three hours & a half, & yet it is worth while coming from England to Brazil to make it.

São Paulo lies some 3000 feet above the sea level on a plateau, or rather in a shallow basin among the hills. The train, after leaving Santos, winds for some little distance along the river, & then stops as if to take breath for the climb up the mountain range. Here we leave the engine behind; the train is divided into two parts, & part one, after being attached to a special break van with a powerful vice over each rail, is hooked to the end of a wire rope that comes down on small wheels in the middle of the track, & is pulled quickly up a long & dizzily steep incline, disappearing round a curve. Midway there is a siding where the half of our train passes the half of the return train. Then our turn in the second half comes; we are hooked to the wire rope, provided with a break van, the wire tightens & up we go.

I assure you that the ride is not one to be recommended to nervous people. On such an incline it looks as if no break could possibly be of the slightest use; the wire rope seems terribly slender & if it should snap...!

Half-way up we pass the remainder of the return train, & at the top there is a level platform where we are unhooked & we take breath again. Here there is an engine house & a powerful fixed engine with large drum wheels round which the wire-rope passes, one end of the rope being fastened to the ascending & one to the descending carriages, the weight of the one counterbalancing that of the other. This is only the beginning of the climb; there are three other such stages, one after the other, before we say good-bye to the wire ropes & are taken charge of by a new locomotive on the higher level.[1]

When we started from Santos at 4 in the afternoon the air was very warm, almost sultry. Up above we could see the evening clouds slowly gathering round the hill-tops. As we rose the air became cooler, the clouds seemed to change slowly into mist, gradually thinner & thinner as we approached & passed through it & when we came into the clear air

---

1. The cable train journey from Santos to Sao Paulo: In 1859, a group of people led by the Barão de Mauá convinced the Brazilian government that it was important to construct a railroad connecting São Paulo to the seaport at Santos. The main purpose of the project was the transport of the coffee grown on the inland plateau to the Atlantic coast for export. The biggest difficulty was the task to overcome the steep east slope of the 800-meter high Serra do Mar, which was considered to be nearly impracticable. The São Paulo Railway consists of three parts: 1. The 20 km (12 mi) long adhesion railway at the coast from Santos to Piassaguera near Cubatão 2. The 8 km (5 mi) long steep grade from Piassaguera to Paranapiacaba 3. The adhesion railway on the plateau from Paranapiacaba via São Paulo to Jundiaí. The first system used to climb the steep grade between Piassaguera and Paranapiacaba was a four-section cable railway with stationary steam engines, in use from 1867 till 1970. At each section, the wagons were attached to a steel wire rope with the help of a specially fitted brake van. JMcC talks of "break vans". https://en.wikipedia.org/wiki/S%C3%A3o_Paulo_Railway_Company

above the mist seemed to change into cloud again, spreading out, in the evening light, like a grey-white sea, through which the higher peaks & mounds rose like little islands.

A few yards distant, on either side of the line, the impenetrably dense vegetation began, spreading all over the hills in an unbroken covering. Trees, every branch & every fork of which formed a resting place for innumerable parasites, while festoons of climbing plants bound them together like tangled cords; many varieties of palms, with a thick under growth of fern, cactus, aloes & spear-like grasses of all kinds, every here & there a little mountain cascade tumbling down to join the river which wound through the plain far below, the whole landscape varied in light & shadow; – all formed a scene which no description can convey any idea of.

From São Paulo to Rio, a thirteen hours' journey, the country is also very fine, but not so wild as that between the former place & Santos. About three hours before reaching Rio, when the line begins to descend there are some beautiful panoramas: – deep winding valleys & beyond successive ranges of hills, each one less distinct than the one before it, – the nearest dark green, the furthest dim purple.

This part of the country is the most thickly populated & the best cultivated. The white cottages dotted over the hills, look very picturesque in among the trees. On the plantations, the deep-green coffee trees or shrubs, standing on an average, about two yards high, are planted at regular intervals, & the ground about them kept free from weeds. The crop is now being gathered in. There are also vines, orange tree, & bananas; – in fact soil & sun between them will produce anything.

Both in Santos & São Paulo I had a very good time. At the former place, Mr Lange, of the firm of Lion & Co, who act as agents for Dundee, came in a small boat to the steamer to receive me & had a room prepared for me at his house, but I missed him & went to the hotel.[2] He introduced me to the German Club, a very nice place, where they have excellent German beer & sandwiches & we spent the evenings there very pleasantly, playing whist.

In São Paulo I also met with much kindness from Mr Lion. He had a cousin from Hamburg staying with him for a few days & was entertaining him, so I came in for two bachelors' dinner parties & some delightful drives in the country.

At one of the dinners I became quite chummy with a nice old gentleman, Senhor Commendador Antonio Manoel Alves, grandfather-in-law to Mr Lion (who is married to a Brazilian lady). The Commendador gave me his card & promised to send me some tobacco of his own cultivation.

At São Paulo I received, via Montevideo & Rio, your welcome letters of 9th, 16th, & 23rd June, & I was very glad to have your news.

I also have to send my thanks for another letter from Annie, who is having, as I expected she would, a first rate time at Paris, & a very amusing letter from Olga. – "Sauntering sneer" & "copious smile" are lovely, the first is about the best thing of the kind I have heard.

You seem to have had a very jolly tennis-&-high-tea party. I wish I had been there; I should enjoy something of that kind very much now.

So Dora Sinton is off to Switzerland; what a jolly trip we had to Scotland about this time last year![3] I am afraid it will be too late for another one this year. However we shall see.

I arrived at Rio on the evg. of the 25th. I had to rise at 4.30 to catch the 6 o'clock train, an uncomfortable start.

I am staying at the Hôtel des Etrangers, very comfortable. Mr Martin Ree is at the same hotel & I saw him the evg. I arrived. Poor man, he has had a very bad accident. He was in the country & must have exposed himself to the sun, took some kind of attack or became dizzy & fell heavily, breaking his jaw on both sides. He is now rather better and goes out to the garden, but his head is all bandaged up & he can only speak slowly & with difficulty. His nephew is here & fortunately he has many friends to look after him.

He purposes going soon North to Bahia & Pernambuco & later in the year down to Buenos Ayres.

2. I cannot find anything about Lion & Co, nor Mr Lange, nor Mr Lion. There was however a Ludwig Loewe & Co in Brazil, German importer of firearms
3. Dora Sinton: see Index to People

I expect to be here for about a fortnight & shall then go on to Bahia & Pernambuco, & home. I shall postpone till my next any description of Rio, for it deserves a letter to itself.

The last telegrams announce a revolution in Buenos Ayres.[4] I hope it may be speedily successful. If so it is about the best thing that could happen. Further news will be anxiously awaited by all interested in the Argentine Republic. The present (or late?) Government is utterly corrupt & incapable, & almost any change would be an improvement. It is only a pity of the poor wretches of soldiers who are obliged by their officers & political leaders to shoot one another down.

I must stop now. It is already past the breakfast hour & I am very hungry – my appetite is still reassuring, & my general condition eminently satisfactory. I hope you can all say the same of yourselves.

Best love to all

Jack

4. "Revolution of the Park" in Buenos Aires, 26th-29th July 1890. Crushed by the government – president Miguel Juárez Celman resigns.

23. Letter from Rio de Janeiro, 10th August 1890

18900810 See an image of the original letter, http://dx.doi.org/10.17613/mfyq-k965

Nº 16   Rio de Janeiro
10th August 1890

My dear Mother,

I have been writing all day & feel about written out, but I don't want to let this mail go without a few lines from me. Since my last letter of about a fortnight ago (a longer interval than usual) I had your welcome weeklies of 30 June & 7 July. I hoped to have had a later one but I suppose it has gone to Bahia or Pernambuco.

So Fred Boas has announced his engagement! Is the marriage to take place soon?[1]

You say you had a pleasant (small) family picnic at Newcastle, though I suppose to mention that now is like referring to ancient history; – you should make those little excursions oftener.

Em & Olga will now be at Kingussie or whatever that place is with the heathen name, & Annie very likely at home. The girls are having a good summer.[2]

I hope your troublesome cough has gone.[3] It would go very soon if you had a little of this sunshine here – the warm air just subdued to pleasant temperature by the cool afternoon breezes from the sea.

Mr Ree is much better, & now goes to town daily to look after his business; he still wears a bandage round his chin, but he can speak without difficulty & is quite another man from when I saw him first. We played a game of whist the other night – the first he has played since he left Belfast he told me. He had a letter from Mrs Ree who mentioned that Annie had just left Paris.

Last week I presented Mr Gotto's letter to his brother who received me very kindly.[4] He is managing engineer of the City Improvement Coy who have charge of the town drainage. He took me for a sail among the islands of the Bay, on the Coy's steam-launch. The famous Bay of Rio is said to be, after Sidney, the finest natural harbour in the World. It has a narrow entrance, with a great depth of water, & opens out into a wide lake sending its quiet little bays of blue water in among the high hills by which it is surrounded.

It is said to have a coastline of more than 100 miles, & scattered over its surface are some 300 islands, large & small, many of these studded with pretty summer residences shaded by palm-trees. You can perhaps form some faint idea of what a sail among these islands is! The hills all round rise steeply in the most fantastic shapes. One pinnacle of rock is called the Finger of God; another huge mountain - rock rising bleakly & precipitously at the entrance to the Bay is called the Sugarloaf; the other heights are mostly known by Indian names.

The City Improvement Coy. have a little island of their own for the manufacture of lime from oyster-shell & coral.

1. Frederick Samuel Boas (b Belfast 1862, d 1957) married Henrietta O'Brien Owen (the same age as him) in Oxford in 1892. He had matriculated from Balliol College in 1881. https://en.wikipedia.org/wiki/Frederick_S._Boas
2. Kingussie - a small town in the Badenoch and Strathspey ward of the Highland council area of Scotland.
3. Jane's death certificate says she died in 1901 age 65 of Tuberculosis of the Bladder (could have been many another thing) – but could she have had "consumption"?
4. Mr Arthur Charles Gotto who lived with his wife Margaret on the Malone Road in Belfast. He was the brother of Percy Murly Gotto, civil engineer b 18 April 1859, Rio de Janeiro. This refers to a letter of introduction to Percy Murly Gotto from Arthur Charles Gotto of Belfast. See Index to People.

Their man in charge, Mr Holliday, lives like Robinson Crusoe, – monarch of all he surveys, except that he has his wife (who looks like the real ruler) & a snug little house. But he is absolute master of the darkeys under him, & acts not only as their employer, but also as their guide, philosopher, & friend – banker & all the rest of it.

He has a youngster of five years, who wore, when we landed, but the meagerest of blouses, with the tails flapping in the breeze. This boy paddles (literally) his own canoe – a flat-bottomed little cockleshell – all about the island, in the most independent fashion.

Nervous mothers please note!

Mrs Holliday gave us a very nice cup of tea & some bread & butter & then showed us with pride over her island. They have a spring of the clearest water, a garden that produces everything from pineapples & mangoes to carrots & turnips, & a fish-pond with oysters growing thick all round the walls. What a place for a lonely eremite, if only the spring ran Guinness's XX![5] In the garden there was a green pepper plant which excited my curiosity & I bit a berry in two & then ————— looked round for an iceberg to chew.

Next time I am told that green pepper is hot I shall take my informant's word for it.

On our return from the island Mr Gotto took me home with him to dinner. Mrs Gotto received us. She is young and pretty and makes a very pleasant hostess.[6] They live, together with her brother, a Mr Osborne, in a nice little house on a hill fronting the entrance to the harbour. Mrs Gotto is a great stamp-collector & has an excellent collection. If Julie or Olga would send out some good exchange stamps to Mr or Mrs G. address City Improvement Coy, Rua Santa Luzia, Rio de Janeiro, Brazil, they would likely get some good old Brazilian stamps in exchange.

Mr Gotto has asked me to dine again with them & go afterwards to a dance at an English family's, some evg. this next week, – he is to let me know.

I meant to write a "few lines" & I find myself on page 3 (my last half-sheet, & the candle burns low. I have not written all I meant to write but other things have crept in, & what has been crowded out must wait for the next-train).

But I must tell you in any case of my bitterest grievance – the latest injustice to Ireland; – listen to my tale of woe: I have been asked to a ball tomorrow night & this morning I woke up with a conspicuous, & obnoxious, & shining, & altogether ridiculous little red spot right on the tip of my nose!!

With love,

Your woebegone & red-tipped-nosed

Jack

5. "Originally brewed as the XX version of Guinness' Porter, Guinness Original is a direct descendant of our archival recipes, based on a beer first brewed in 1821, when Arthur Guinness II set down precise instructions for brewing his Superior Porter." https://www.guinness.com/en-gb/our-beers/guinness-original/

6. This refers to Percy Murly Gotto (b Apr-June 1859, d 20th July 1935 in Stockbridge) who was a civil engineer and directed the Rio de Janeiro City Improvements Company founded in 1862 by his father Edward Gotto (see Index to People). Percy M Gotto was married in London to Jane T Gotto on 15 December 1888. Jane Tulloch Fiddes Murly Gotto (nee Laing) (b Glasgow ~ 1862, d 1934 in Romsey, Hants). Their wedding had been announced in The Belfast Newsletter of 20th December 1888. She was 28 at the time (and pretty!)

24. Letter from Rio de Janeiro, 17th August 1890

18900817 See an image of the original letter, http://dx.doi.org/10.17613/xnrr-2p51

Nº 17
Rio de Janeiro
17th August 1890

My dear Mother,

No home letters since I wrote you last week – they must have gone further north. I am making a longer stay here than I anticipated; Rio is a big place & the Brazilians are fearfully procrastinating: they never keep an appointment except by accident & they are still fonder than the Spaniards of "tomorrow"; the phrase most often used is "tenha paciencia" & really one requires an inexhaustible fund of the monumental virtue.

On Thursday I dined at the Gottos' & afterwards drove with them to a dance given by friends of theirs, Mr & Mrs McKinnel, at a kind of private hotel in Botafogo – one of the outskirts of the town. The garden of the hotel was illuminated by Chinese lanterns, hung between the palm trees with pretty effect; the ballroom was decorated with fern & palm leaves & the English, American, & Brazilian flags. Mr McKinnel is English & Mrs is American – an excellent hostess, looking as if she were especially pleased to see each particular guest there.

There were some 50 or 60 people – not very many pretty faces; – one of the prettiest girls was a Miss Lee, daughter of the American minister (chargé d'affaires, not parson), very lively & original & not by any means conventional.[1]

Among the young married ladies Mrs Gotto was quite the nicest looking! There was a substantial cold supper, during which the fun ran high & all evening there were ices & other refreshments.

Altogether it was a very pleasant & successful evening.

I had a card for a dance at the German Club last night, but did not feel in the humour to go.

Some evenings ago I visited the Botanic Garden which is a few miles out of town. It is beautifully kept & is a most interesting place, even to me who know nothing whatever about botany. What strikes one most is the long avenues of regularly planted & equal sized palms like smooth polished columns. There are pretty fountains & a little stream running through clumps of bamboos whose clustered canes rising in solid circles curve outwards gracefully & symmetrically till they join overhead, forming intersecting vaults[2], & reminding one of the crypt of some old cathedral: Glasgow for instance which you would not admit that you enjoyed in spite of the violent fit of sneezing that obliged you reluctantly to leave its damp delightfulness.

Mr Ree is now almost himself again. He has taken off the bandages & he goes to town daily to look after his business. His face is still somewhat swollen on one side.[3]

I expect to leave Rio about the end of this week, & when you get this letter I shall be looking up the sailing lists to see what steamer will suit to carry me home.

---

1. The Gottos – Percy and the nice looking young Jane - were described in the previous letter. No trace of these McKinnels in Rio – although I think he may also have been an engineer. Sounds like Mrs McK was very effusive in her welcoming of the guests to her ball. Miss Lee was the daughter of James Fenner Lee, US chargé d'affaires (b 13th February 1827, d 23rd April 1892): https://history.state.gov/historicaldocuments/frus1890/d15
2. Marvelous description of the Botanical Gardens. https://en.wikipedia.org/wiki/Rio_de_Janeiro_Botanical_Garden
3. Mr Ree, whose identity is uncertain, but is known to Jane and Julius, is amazingly recovering from his bilateral mandibular fractures.

I hope the fine weather has come meanwhile & that you have got rid of your cough & are feeling better, & that the Pater is all right.

Best love to all.

Jack

Rio de Janeiro Botanical Gardens with Mt Corcovado in the background. From Glimpses of the World: A Portfolio of Photographs of the Works of God and Man, by John L. Stoddard (New York, 1899), p. 499. https://hdl.handle.net/2027/mdp.39015077530429

25. Letter from Rio de Janeiro, 27th August 1890

18900827 See an image of the original letter, http://dx.doi.org/10.17613/cdk9-na77

On headed notepaper:
SHIFFMANN & MEYER
RIO DE JANEIRO
E
HAMBURGO
ENDEREÇO TELEGRAPHICO
"SCHIFMAST"

Por...

Rio de Janeiro,..27th de August..de 1890
Caixa 117

My dear Mother,

I wrote you by the "Iberia" which sailed two days ago. I am now sitting in the office waiting for a customer who said he would come at 11 & as he is not likely to turn up before 12, if at all, I may as well employ the time in inking a sheet of Messrs. Schiffmann & Meyer's letter paper.[1]

I expect the Pater will by this time be about starting for his Russian trip, & wishing he could stay at home. I hope things will go well with him & that his trip will be a short one. I would rather he could make a yearly holiday tour than a business one.[2]

The rain is falling steadily & rather dismally today; still the plants & trees in the public squares look fresher, & the hills cooler, & one can do without grumbling with one wet day in a fortnight.

Telegrams announce great want in Ireland owing to the drought, the wet spring seems to have been followed by a dry summer.

Mr Ree is now quite well again & no longer takes his meals in the sitting-room, but comes to the dining room, where we have a small table for ourselves. He often asks if I have news from you, & the other evg. drank to the good health of you & the Pater in a glass of Burgundy. He tells me he frequently goes to Leeds or Manchester. I told him he might very well come across the channel & pay us a visit.

Last week I was out almost every evg. On Wed. a Mr Salomon, stockbroker, to whom I had been introduced, took me to see his pictures & afterwards gave me a very good dinner. On Thursday I dined again at Gottos & went with them to the theatre to see Coquelin. On Friday I dined with a Mr Lucius, an American German & a very nice fellow, at a boarding house where he lives with half a dozen young Englishmen, he being President at the dinner table etc. & after dinner we took a long walk over the hills.[3] It was a bright moonlight night & the way wound far above the town, beyond the pretty

---

1. I imagine these are yet German commercial agents – but can find no information on them
2. "The Pater's annual trip to Russia" – where did he go/ how/ and who did he trade what with. It looks like Russia was an important source of flax for the manufacture of linen in Ireland. Was that what his trips were about? In the late 19th and early 20th centuries, linen was very significant to Russia and its economy. At one time it was the country's greatest export item and Russia produced about 80% of the world's fiber flax crop. Or was Russia just another market for the products that Moore & Weinberg produced, as implied by Isaac Weinberg's self-published autobiography (http://dx.doi.org/10.17613/ch97-0r17)? https://en.wikipedia.org/wiki/Linen#Modern_history
3. Could not identify Mr Salomon the stockbroker, nor Mr Lucius the American German.

suburb of Larangeiras & Santa Theresa (I think Larangeiras means "orange grove").[4] The bright lights of Rio at our feet, & the Bay with the distant hills in the "moonbeams misty light" formed a lovely scene.

View of Rio de Janeiro's harbour in 1899, seen from above Laranjeiras. Taken by Pedro Correa do Lago.

On Saturday evg. I was at a ball given by the English Cricket Club, a very successful affair; – string band between the two dancing rooms, a "full house" with many pretty dresses & dressed.[5]

On Sunday I wrote letters all day. I have contributed generously to the Postal Revenue of Rio, but I don't want to send many more letters from here. In a few days I hope to be off to Bahia; – thence Pernambuco & home.

Best love to all.

Jack

4. Laranjeiras (Portuguese: orange trees) is an upper-middle-class neighborhood located in the South Zone of Rio de Janeiro. https://en.wikipedia.org/wiki/Laranjeiras
5. English cricket club in Rio de Janeiro: Cricket in Brazil began in the mid-1800s in Rio de Janeiro, during a period when a portion of the city's population was British or of British descent. By the early 1860s, a number of cricket clubs were in operation, including the British CC, Artisan Amateurs CC, Rio British CC, Anglo-Brazilian CC and the British and American Club. In 1872, George Cox formed the Rio Cricket Club, which soon began using the field as its home. In the early 1880s, George's son Oscar organized Brazil's first football games on this same ground. In 1889, Brazil became a Republic and Princess Isabel was forced to move from her residence. The cricket ground was taken over by the new government, and although the sport was allowed to continue for a time, a permanent facility was now required. https://en.wikipedia.org/wiki/Brazilian_Cricket_Association

26. Letter from Rio de Janeiro, 31st August to 8th September 1890

18900831 See an image of the original letter, http://dx.doi.org/10.17613/pzjp-k009

Nº 18
Rio de Janeiro.
31st Aug. 1890

My dear Mother,

I wrote you a few lines the other day from the office. This will be the last letter that I shall date from Rio & before it leaves for England I hope to be in Bahia. I have had to stay here longer than I anticipated, but I don't think Bahia will detain me & once in Pernambuco I shall fix my steamer & go with it, leaving the untaken orders for somebody else.

I have been very quiet this week, spending most of the evgs. in the hotel, writing or reading. I dined once more with Mr Lucius, & after dinner the young Englishmen boarding at the same house entertained us with a varied vocal & instrumental concert, ranging from Wagner to Gilbert & Sullivan, – very pleasant it was; I had not heard any music for a long time.

Last night I called at Gottos & found Mr & Mrs G. deep in stamps & albums. But what is interesting Mr G most just now is a picture, said to be a genuine Murillo, which he is trying to buy from an old native. They say the picture represents some saint or other, & the old gentleman is unwilling to part with it, not because he likes it, but because he has a vague idea that it is a valuable picture. He said to Mr Gotto "They say it's by some fellow called Murillo, or something like that, but I don't know; – I like the landscapes better."

I hope to have a look at it tomorrow.

S.S. "Finance" 5th Sept.

Northward bound once more! I left Rio on the 3rd, having had altogether a very pleasant stay there; still I was glad to say goodbye to it & to make for Bahia, my last port but one.

On Monday evg. I dined for the last time at Gottos' who crowned their many kindnesses by giving me an excellent farewell dinner. They have a first rate cook – no small blessing in a place like Rio where it is extremely difficult to find good servants, & having found them, to keep them. Mrs Gotto complains that as soon as she has trained a servant to orderly & clean ways, the servant takes another place, for preference & higher wages are always given to those who have been in English houses. The last maid they had was a "breaker", & one day Mr G had to beseech her "by the love of all the saints" to leave – to leave at once, & by the back door, for if she were to go by the front door, she would break something on the way!

The next day I met Mr Gotto by appointment & we went to see the celebrated Murillo. I must say I was not very much surprised to find that the picture was a copy, – a good copy, of a well-known Murillo: it represents a dirty little beggar boy looking inside his shirt for – well perhaps for a lost stud.

The old gentleman – a "Commendador" – maintained that the picture was a genuine Murillo, & Mr Gotto let him down gently by suggesting that perhaps this was the original & the other one the copy.

From Rio to Bahia is a three days' sail. Yesterday we had a head wind & the vessel pitched rather, & as I could not write, nor walk, nor sit comfortably, I lay in my bunk & read Ruskin on the Relation of Art to Morals, & was much edified thereby. A little Ruskin at a time is conducive to meditation, & I can always meditate best with my eyes closed, as Addie used to do over the preparation of his lessons.

Bahia 8th Sept   Have just recvd. pleasant letters from Father – the last of 18th Aug. before starting for Russia – but yours have gone to Pernambuco. In future I must give you a copying-press or books specially prepared with carbon paper, so that you may send me duplicates of your letters to different places. We might screw the copying-press on the top of your Davenport.[1]

I have not seen anyone here yet except the agent. Today is a holiday & I shall employ it in advancing a stage further my never-ending correspondence.

If I can manage it I shall write you a few lines again by the "Clyde" Royal Mail, due in 2/3 days.

With best love

Jack

---

1. What exactly is a letter copying press? Apparently, back in the 1800s these 'book presses' were used for making copies of letters into blank books. A copying book, which sounds to be a blank book filled with thin tissue paper, was used inside of these machines. Once a letter was freshly written, it was sandwiched inside the book. An oiled sheet sat atop a blank page, while the fresh letter sat under it, and another oiled sheet below the fresh letter. The tissue paper was dampened to encourage the ink to transfer onto the tissue paper when the book was being pressed. Of course, we know when printing, everything prints backwards. This was the reason the paper was made from tissue, so the ink could easily be seen from the other side! It might seem tedious today, but this was before the invention of carbon paper, so having such a device around saved more time than having to write everything out a second, third or fourth time: https://lakemichiganbookpress.com/blogs/news/what-is-the-difference-between-a-book-press-and-a-copying-press

27. Letter from Bahia, 13th September 1890

18900913 See an image of the original letter, http://dx.doi.org/10.17613/f5d6-be88

On headed notepaper.
JOHN EGGERS
Caixa 114
Telegrammes
ATLANTIC-BAHIA.

Bahia, 13th Sept. 1890

My dear Mother,

8 a.m. – in the office – waiting for a blooming "Portuguese", who promised solemnly to be punctual, & who is now probably drinking coffee & smoking cigarettes, oblivious of his appointment, reading the newspaper or settling the affairs of the Republic, with half a dozen patriots like himself, who – not holding any public office themselves – are fully convinced that the Government is made up of rogues & swindlers. Tomorrow he will tell me he was fearfully busy, had not a moment to spare, – infinitely distressed at having inconvenienced me, & so on & so on. At first this kind of thing used to irritate me, but now I take it calmly in my old age, having altered my way of looking at it with the "years that bring the philosophic mind", as the poet says.[1]

São-Salvador-da-Bahia-de-todo-os-Santos is the name of this town, – that is what they call it "for short", on week-days, – what its full Sunday name is I don't know, I shall find out & learn it by heart when I have an hour or two to spare.[2] It is built in two storeys (the town, not the name of it) so to speak. By the way: my dictionary says stories – I thought it was -eys in this sense. There are about three streets parallel with the sea, on the lower level, behind which rises a steep bluff, almost a cliff, from a hundred to a hundred and fifty feet high – the rest of the town is on this higher level.

At one place there is a steep winding road cut in the face of this bluff, but it is little fancied by pedestrians, especially coming up, on account of the incline. There are two other ways of going from the lower to the higher town, or vice versa. One is by a steam elevator or hoist; as it carries you quickly up you look down through the narrow windows to the roofs of the houses at a dizzy distance below.[3] The other is a double line of railroad, at an angle of 45 degrees, with carriages drawn up & let down by a steel cable.

The view from the top is very fine: – the blue bay stretching out for many miles, the distant hills on the far side lost in mist, the green island at the mouth of the bay, & the shipping; – I have bought photographs both of Rio & of this place, but they do not give any just idea of the scene, the life & the colour that the bright sun gives are wanting.

---

1. "years that bring the philosophic mind." From "Splendour in the grass" by William Wordsworth
2. Salvador (English: Savior), also known as São Salvador da Bahia de Todos os Santos (English: Holy Savior of the Bay of All Saints), is the capital of the Brazilian state of Bahia.
3. In 1873, Brazil's first elevator, the powerful hydraulic Elevador Lacerda, was constructed to connect the city's upper and lower towns. The Jesuits installed the first manual rope-and-pulley elevator around 1610 to transport goods and passengers from the port to the settlement. In 1868 an iron structure with clanking steam elevators was inaugurated, replaced by an electric system in 1928. https://en.wikipedia.org/wiki/Salvador,_Bahia and https://en.wikipedia.org/wiki/Elevador_Lacerda.

Panorama of Salvador, the capital of Bahia, in 1870, taken by the Swiss photographer Guilherme Gaensly (1843-1928).

I purpose going on to Pernambuco this week, & shall perhaps take the royal Mail "S.S. Magdalena" home. I believe she sails from Rio abt 6th prox. say 10th from Pernambuco, & abt. 24th in England, but I don't know the exact dates.

At all events I shall write you many more letters.

Best love

Jack

16th Sept. per German Steamer "Argentina" via Lisbon.

28. Letter from Pernambuco, 30th September 1890

18900930 See an image of the original letter, http://dx.doi.org/10.17613/1qge-ex56

Pernambuco   30th Sept.   1890

My dear Mother,

This is the last of my letters on <u>this</u> journey, I am glad to say, & it will arrive only some ten days before myself.

I need scarcely say that I was tolerably cheerful at find myself at last in Pernambuco, the end of my visiting-list, & also at having there all your home news, which had been accumulating for some time.

I recvd. here four of your welcome weekly letters, from 14th July (very long ago) till 4th Aug. (from Oban). Then there is a blank till your P.C. of 2nd Sept. – I am afraid some Aug. letters must have gone astray or else they are coming by this next Royal Mail & have been delayed by the Southampton strikes.[1]

The meeting at the Perth station must have been very funny. The letter-paper of the Station Hotel, with the view, took me back to Oban again.

I am very glad Jim did so well at the Interm.[2] It was hard lines his not getting an exhibition though coming so near it. The Board seems to be running short of money. You say Jim took honours in everything, so he must have done better in Latin than you had thought. His marks are first rate.

The natural harbour of Recife around 1890. Photograph by F. Labadie of 14 Rua do Barão da Victoria, Pernambuco.

Anyone coming to Pernambuco must be very much struck by the curious natural harbour. It is formed by a coral reef, like a submarine wall, running parallel with the coast, & leaving a channel of about 20 yards wide of deep smooth water inside. Outside, the sea is generally very rough, & landing by small boats from such steamers as do not come inside the reef – The Royal Mail for instance, which has little or no cargo to take from this place, – is no pleasant matter, nor cheap either, the usual charge being about £2.

Fortunately I was able to come up from Bahia by a national steamer which entered the harbour; & now sailing under

1. The 1890 Southampton Dock strike took place in Southampton, England, September, 1890. https://en.wikipedia.org/wiki/Southampton_Dock_strike_of_1890
2. Jim's Intermediate Exams: He was just short of his 16th birthday (b 19th November 1874)

the Brazilian flag one has the further advantage of being allowed to take one's luggage to the hotel without examination by the Brazilian customhouse officers, the most troublesome & inquisitive of all such officials in the world. The steamer was, of course, horribly dirty, (the tablecloth was "a caution to snakes"!), but as the voyage is only 36 hours it did not matter very much.

Pernambuco is perhaps the most European-looking of Brazilian towns; – though, correctly speaking, Recife is the name of the town, & Pernambuco of the province. A broad river winds, like an S, through Recife, & four or five fine iron & stone bridges cross it. The streets are well paved & clean, & though there is nothing remarkable about the houses, still the place has a general air of prosperity.

The staple product of this part of Brazil is cane-sugar, but coffee, cotton, tobacco, & hides are also exported, which information will be found very interesting & instructive by anyone with a mind properly trained on the lines of "Sullivan's Generalized for Beginners".

There is a fairly large English colony & I have made already a number of very pleasant acquaintances. The telegraph house, where the men of the Cable Company live, is one of the jolliest & best houses in Pernambuco.[3] They have a fine ball-room, a billiard-room, a tennis-court, & a nice garden. I had some tennis there the other day & a game of whist one evening.

Last night I dined with a fellow called Smethurst, manager of a large English firm here, at a pleasant English boarding house where he lives, & after dinner we had a rubber in which the English parson took a hand, – & a very good player he is. The English clergyman abroad is always called "the parson". This Rev. gentleman is of the muscular kind, & though he weighs fifteen stone, if an ounce, you should see him play tennis, sending the balls over like a sportsman.

I am sorry I must cut my letter short for I could spin it out to some length, but the "Trent" is there already & the mail will close soon, so I shall tell you the rest viva voce.

Best love,

Jack

---

3. The Cable Company. A HUGE feat to link up practically the whole world. The "fellows" in Recife must have been working for The Western and Brazilian Telegraph Company. https://atlantic-cable.com/CableCos/CandW/EATC/index.htm

29. Letter from aboard the SS Magdalena sailing from Brazil to Southampton, 19th October 1890

18901019 See an image of the original letter, http://dx.doi.org/10.17613/c5pt-8h20

S.S. Magdalena
Sunday 19th Oct. 1890

My dear Mother,

We are now drawing near Lisbon, so I want to have a short letter ready to send to you overland.

We have had a splendid voyage so far – perfectly calm the whole way – the heat was not so oppressive crossing the line this time as on the outward trip.

I think I wrote you that I was having a good time in Pernambuco. I found it quite the pleasantest place, in a social way, on this coast, there is a large English colony, & strange to say, it is not split up into cliques, as is mostly the case with English people living abroad. There are several boarding houses, where the unmarried men live, & these, as well as the better houses of the English families, have tennis-courts in their grounds. There is also a club with two good courts, & people play every afternoon. They can rely on the weather in Pernambuco, & as they can practise all the year round, they are mostly capital players. Mr Midgely, the "parson", whom I mentioned before, is a very energetic player, & holds his own well against the younger men. I went one afternoon to his boarding house & had about an hour & a half good tennis.

One invitation I had that rather surprised me. It was from Mr Bilton, the manager of the London & Brazilian Bank, to dinner & whist, to meet Mr Midgely to whom I fancy I was indebted for the invite. It was a very pleasant evg. indeed.[1]

Mr Bilton is a very nice man, & Mrs B. is handsome woman & capital hostess, her only failing being that she always calls Mr. B. "Hubby". They have a comfortable house some miles out of town alongside the railway.

The "Magdalena" is one of the Company's newest boats, – steams 14 knots, is very steady & comfortable. She is almost full up but with my usual good luck, I have a cabin to myself. A Brazilian was put in with me, but I got round the purser, & had the native "shunted".[2]

The voyage has been uneventful, – leaving Pernambuco on Saturday 11th we passed next day Fernando Noronha, an island used by Brazil as a penal station. An odd rock towers up towards on end like a lighthouse.[3] On the following Thursday we arrived at St Vincent of the Cape de Verde Islands, & coaled, but all the Portuguese settlements quarantine vessels from Brazil 10 months in the year, so we were not able to go ashore.[4] After the heavy rains a slight carpet of green

---

1. Mr Bilton (see Index to People): Mr W H Bilton – the "hubby" of Mrs B – they were both on the passenger list travelling from Southampton to Pernambuco in May 1897.

2. The SS Magdalena was indeed a very new steamer. Ship Name: Magdalena. Years in service: 1889-1921. Funnels: 2. Masts: 3. Shipping Line: Royal Mail (British).

3. Fernando de Noronha was an archipelago in the Atlantic Ocean, part of the State of Pernambuco. In the late 18th century, the first prisoners were sent to Fernando de Noronha. A prison was built. In 1897 the government of the state of Pernambuco took possession of the prison. Between 1938 and 1945, Fernando de Noronha was a political prison: https://en.wikipedia.org/wiki/Fernando_de_Noronha

4. https://en.wikipedia.org/wiki/S%C3%A3o_Vicente,_Cape_Verde

covered the valleys so that the jagged masses of lava did not present the same barren appearance as when we passed south.

Early on Sunday morning we sighted Palma, the most westerly of the Canaries, but heavy masses of cloud hanging over the island prevented us from having a glimpse of the Peak of Teneriffe, lying some 40 or 50 miles to the eastward.

On the way we have had lots of companions in the shape of whales, flying-fish, dolphins, & Portuguese-men-of-war. One flying-fish came in at a porthole & lit in a cabin. Another skimmed past the chief engineer's nose as he was standing on deck one night, rather startling him.

The passengers are all "nobodies", – the only one who has any claim to be considered a "somebody" is an Argentine politician, going on a financial mission to Europe. In that happy Republic, when the President wants to provide for any of his friends & has not an office disposable, or when he wants to get rid of a troublesome supporter, he sends him on a financial mission to Europe, that being understood as a six-months' holiday at the expense of the state.

Notwithstanding their insignificance the passengers are, on the whole, a very pleasant set. There are one or two families, a crowd of young men, but no pretty girls. By way of amusement we have had whist daily, of course, & some chess. A Christy Minstrel Troupe was organized & gave a very presentable performance.

The crew got up a rival show, & rather eclipsed the passengers' entertainment. There is a huge young Brazilian girl (age 14, weight about as many stones) hammering on the pianofifty, as our Christy "Bones" called it, just over my head, & I must run away. I think we shall be in Southampton on Friday – home Sunday!

Best love

Jack

PART III

THE LETTERS: NEW YORK, CURAÇAO, COLOMBIA, VENEZUELA, 1891

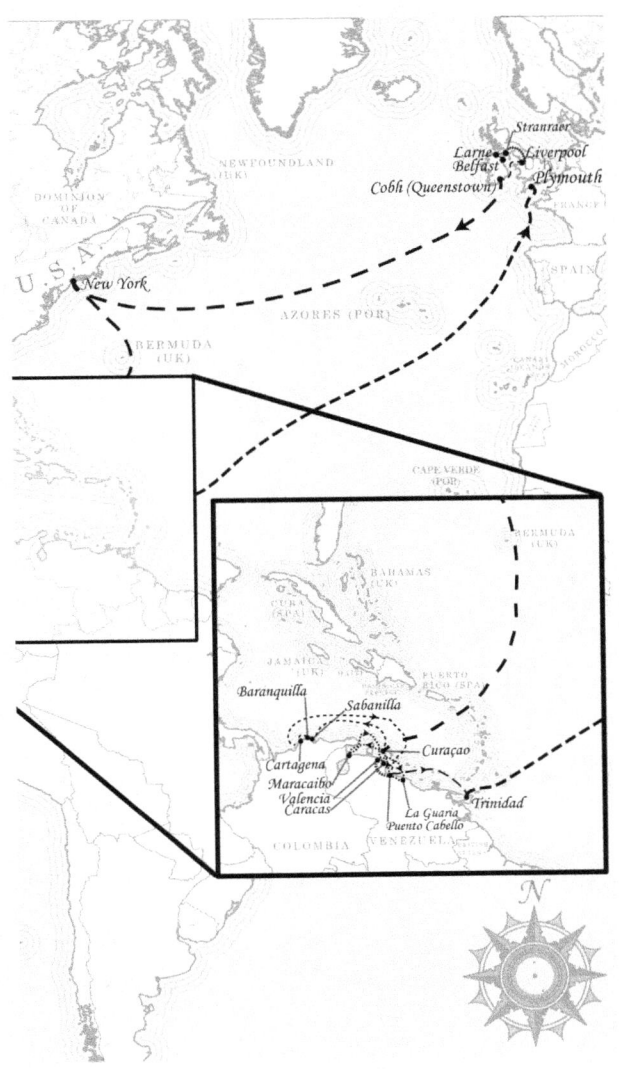

Map of the 1891 voyage by John McCaldin Loewenthal, showing the places mentioned in the letter and an approximate route for his travels which included stops in New York, Curaçao, Colombia, and Venezuela. A high-res version is available online: https://doi.org/10.17613/ 1wfx-1z82 (Original map by Thomas Bachrach)

30. Letter on board RMS "Germanic" sailing from Liverpool to Queenstown, 14th January 1891

18910114 See an image of the original letter, http://dx.doi.org/10.17613/yhef-p745

White Star Shipping Line Letterhead: R.M.S."GERMANIC"

R.M.S."GERMANIC"

Wed. 14th Jan 1891

My dear Mother

You will have had particulars of the great leave-taking at the Northern Counties Railway, when Geo Y. & Mr Wise turned up, & Emma felt so melancholy that she made puns.[1]

We ran down to Larne in ¾ of an hour; meanwhile the wind had risen & the boat danced about in a lively fashion, but she was fast & crossed in little over two hours. I had a comfortable carriage all to myself, & foot-warmers, as far as Wigan where I had to change. I slept very well – had just one wink from Carlisle to Preston, thanks probably to a sausage roll fearlessly eaten at former place, – before that I had tried the plumcake (just to see if it would keep!) & found it excellent.

Owing to delay at Stranraer it was 4.30 when I arrived at Liverpool. There is fortunately a fine hotel at the terminus. I turned in & slept soundly till 9. Had breakfast of am hand heggs & a cup of kaw[fee], & strolled down to take ticket at White Star Co's office. After that I called on young Boxwell, fellow-passenger from Pernambuco by the "Magdalena" & had a chat with him.[2]

I then drove down to the Germanic which was lying in the Alexandra dock, about 5 miles from Hotel, & once safe on board with all luggage I wired you.[3]

1. The Sligo, Leitrim and Northern Counties Railway (SL&NCR) was a privately-owned railway in counties Cavan, Fermanagh, Leitrim and Sligo in north-west Ireland. It consisted of one main line, with no branch lines: https://en.wikipedia.org/wiki/Sligo,_Leitrim_and_Northern_Counties_Railway. "Geo Y" is George Young Kinnaird (see Index to People). "Mr Wise" is unidentified. "Emma" is his sister Emma Loewenthal.
2. I think this is one of 2 nephews of John Harvey Boxwell (b~1845), who lives in Pernambuco; either John Harvey Boxwell Jr (b~1868) or Willam E.G. Boxwell (b~1870), both of which were "Cotton and Sugar Merchants". See Index to People
3. S.S. Germanic, White Star Line, was built 1874 in Belfast by Harland & Wolff. It was launched 15 July 1874. 20th May 1875 was its maiden voyage (Liverpool-Queenstown-New York). This voyage of JMcC recorded as arriving New York on the 23rd January 1891. https://en.wikipedia.org/wiki/SS_Germanic_(1874) and http://www.norwayheritage.com/p_ship.asp?sh=germc

There are abt. 100 passengers on board; no other Belfast people than Weir & young Russell.[4] I am in a cabin amid ships with a Canadian, a decent fellow, but I think I shall get a cabin to myself after leaving Queenstown.[5]

We left the dock punctually at noon, & we have had a fine clear afternoon for our run down channel, & very little sea.

My address by next White Star boat, Tuesday next, or, via Queenstown, Wednesday morning, is c/o J.D. Smyth, after that <u>Barranquilla</u>, <u>Colombia</u> S.A. c/o Messrs. Aepli, Eberbach & Co. until further advice.[6]

Tell Julie to keep at the Spanish, & to write me in Spanish, he can do a little at a letter every evening or so, & when he does not know how to say anything to jot it down in English.[7]

Lights being put out – 11 o'clock.   Best love

Jack

over

————

In pencil

Queenstown

Friday 9 a.m.

Beautiful morning bright & clear, the tender with mails not due till one o'clock.

If we have only weather like this all way across.

Goodbye

Jack

4. Unidentified

5. Queenstown = Cobh, Co. Cork. He had to travel from Belfast to Stranraer to Liverpool to catch the ocean liner to New York via Co. Cork!

6. See Index to People. Aepli, Eberbach & Co, in Barranquilla, Colombia, were "Importers and Exporters and General Merchants" (from *Colombia, a Handbook* published by International Bureau of American Republics 1892). From an article on "Hanseatic Barranquilla" - "The tobacco boom that Colombia had, more specifically Carmen de Bolívar, starting in the 1850s, prompted the arrival of German commercial houses and shipping agencies to Barranquilla. In addition, at the same time, there was a reduction in shipping rates for some European companies, which meant a boost to trade and migration from Germany. In the last decades of the last century, the German firms with the highest economic activity in Barranquilla were, among others, those of J. Helm, O. Berne, Hoenisberg & Wessels, Müller & Siefken, Hollman & Merkel, Aepli & Eberbach and Gieseken & Held." See also "The German Barranquilla Colony" by Enrique Yidi Daccarett: http://www.scielo.org.co/scielo.php?script=sci_arttext&pid=S1794-88862013000100014

7. Julie is his younger brother Julius (see Index to People)

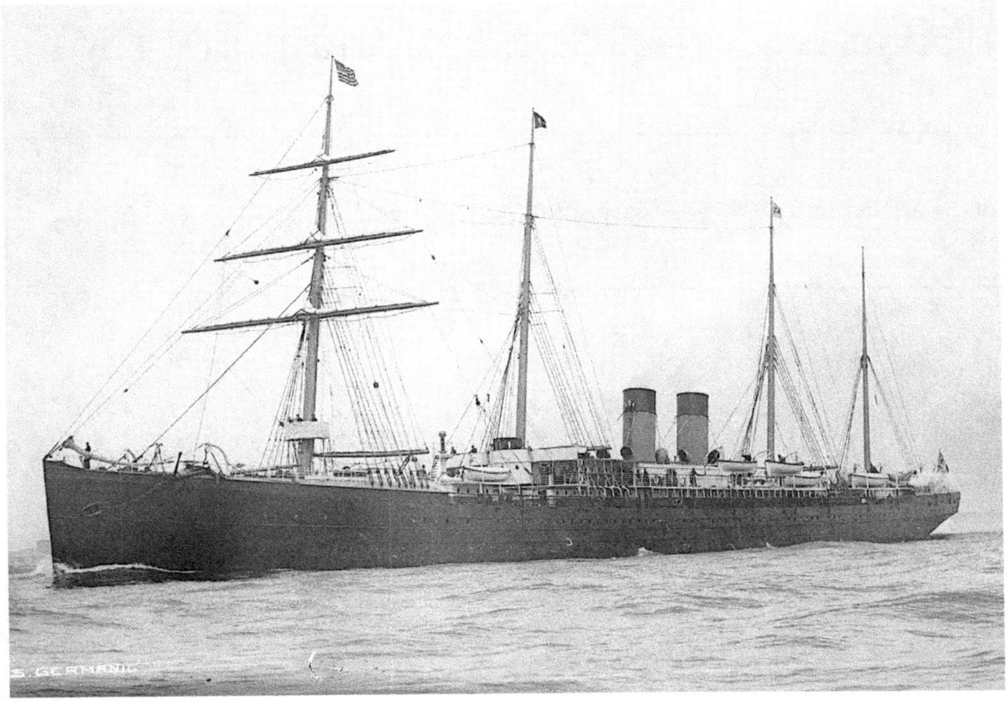

The RMS Germanic ca. 1890–1900

31. Letter on arrival to New York, 22nd January 1891

18910122 See an image of the original letter, http://dx.doi.org/10.17613/jj7w-ps36

Penultimate page on headed notepaper:

JAMES D. SMYTH,   Cable Address: "EQUINE, NEW YORK"

Manufacturers' Agent.   335, Broadway,

New York,.............................**18**.............

N⁰ 1

S.S. "Germanic"   22nd Jany.   1891

My dear Mother,

Our voyage is nearly over; we are within a couple of hundred miles of New York & most of the passengers are on the look-out for the pilot-boat & for a sight of the islands to the north.

We shall be up to "Quarantine" tonight & on shore early tomorrow. We have had a capital run across, & if we had not run into a gale on Wednesday the officers say we should have beaten the ship's record.

The day at Queenstown was glorious, – bright warm sun, more like June than January. We almost all went ashore & walked through the town & along the road overlooking the harbour & the beautiful bay or river that winds towards Cork. Young Weir & I also visited a fine Roman Catholic church which is being built on a prominent height in the middle of the town, & Weir listened respectfully while, fresh from "Stones of Venice", I improved the occasion. After that we had a game of billiards which I had the satisfaction of winning like a worthy chip of the old block. At one o'clock the Dublin train came in bringing a few passengers & a tremendous pile of mail-bags; the latter filled about half the tender. Towards three o'clock we sailed out of the harbour, about an hour behind the Inman liner "City of Berlin", which we passed on the following day.[1] The fine weather came with us & the first four days we made splendid runs, – one day as much as 395 knots, which is very high for the "Germanic". Off the Newfoundland Banks we ran into a dense fog that generally hangs over this part of the ocean; it is caused by the Gulf Stream.[2] The fog lasted the greater part of two days during which the fog-horn's mellow music filled the air. Strong head winds & heavy seas delayed us considerably during the last three days & spoiled the prospect we had of arriving on the Thursday evg., but altogether we were lucky in having a remarkably fine trip for this time of year. We did not slow down in the fog, & only once we stopped to make sure of the whereabouts of another steamer which seemed, from her fog-horn to be uncomfortably near.

At first I had a fair, but rather small cabin along with a young Canadian, but being somewhat crowded with all our bags, I spoke to the Purser, a very affable obliging man, & he moved me into another cabin twice as large, in fact one of the finest on the ship. My mate in it was a Mexican-Englishman who arranged all his belongings in most tidy fashion & gave no trouble. I felt in capital form the whole voyage; – had my salt water bath every morning, stowed away a startling amount of porridge & real <u>cream</u> as an appetising introduction to breakfast, & fed formidably at frequent intervals from

---

1. City of Berlin was a British ocean liner that won the Blue Riband for the Inman Line in 1875 as the fastest liner on the Atlantic: https://en.wikipedia.org/wiki/SS_City_of_Berlin

2. The Grand Banks of Newfoundland are a series of underwater plateaus south-east of the island of Newfoundland on the North American continental shelf: https://en.wikipedia.org/wiki/Grand_Banks_of_Newfoundland

that meal till ten o'clock at night, when our whist party used to "supper" on tea & anchovy toast. Starvation was staved off between lunch & dinner by slices of that excellent plumcake, of which I have still rather more than half left for Addie, & by pieces of the very good toffy that I have to thank Annie for. By the way it was a capital idea to cut it up into little squares.

There were not many passengers, – I think about a hundred, & no notabilities among them except Donoghue the champion skater; – though perhaps you are as shamefully ignorant of his existence as I was.[3] Of ladies there were only about half a dozen, & none pretty, but among the men were some very nice fellows. "The parson", a Rev. Mr. Johnston from Bundoran was very popular, – always genial, good at a song or a story, & a keen whist player. He & I took the lead (not the American lead because not fourth-best: make a note) at the latter, & our table was completed by a Mr Muirhead, a Glasgow solicitor, & a rancher from Texas, Mr Creswell, both good fellows.[4] The whist form was not A1, but we had plenty of fun over our games.

The "Germanic" took her pilot on board at midnight on Thursday-Friday, & sent up her signal rocket showing two white stars so that no doubt her arrival will have been published on this (Friday) afternoon's papers in England. About two we anchored at Quarantine, & "passing the doctor" at day break, we went into dock between nine & ten.

As the steamer approached the wharf I looked out in vain for Addie, & I was reflecting what I should do if he failed to turn up, when just at the last moment he came up smiling, exactly as when I landed from the West Indies.[5] He is looking & feeling very well indeed, the only change in his personal appearance is that he has discarded the blue glasses! I feel bound to report this fact forthwith, remembering your farewell charge to me to pulverize them; so you may ask in your neighbours to rejoice with you, & sup on oysters. At the same time you must not sup too liberally, for he has replaced the blue glasses with plain ones. I asked him if they magnified much, & he answered smiling & with hesitation "Well —– not very much", & on closer examination I found they were two bits of plain glass. But at last I have got at the reason of his wearing them. In confidence & in the dead darkness of night he acknowledged that without them he did not feel "quite dressed", but was self conscious & timid, whereas with the glasses on this nose he was self-possessed & bold as a lion, & felt that he had all his clothes on.

We passed the customs examination, thanks to Addie's experience, without much trouble, & expressed the luggage, part to Brooklyn, & part to the "Red D" line.[6] We then had a rest in his office,[7] some lunch, & a walk through town, left a card at Adam Jenkins's hotel, & paid Walter Portheim a visit.[8] The latter is very well, & hard at work, though the business season has scarcely opened yet.

In the afternoon we went out to Addie's digs in Brooklyn. The house is a nice three-storey one in a quiet side street;

---

3. Joseph F. Donoghue (b February 11, 1871, d April 1, 1921) was an American speed skater. He became the speed skating World Champion in 1891 and was a member of the Manhattan Athletic Club: https://en.wikipedia.org/wiki/Joe_Donoghue

4. The rancher from Texas was possibly Henry Whiteside (Hank) Cresswell, range cattleman in the Texas Panhandle, the son of John Cresswell. He was born at Fairfield House, Lancashire, England, in 1830. In 1877 he formed the Cresswell Land and Cattle Company with the brothers J. A. and M. D. Thatcher and O. H. P. Baxter. That same year Cresswell established his Bar CC headquarters in Ochiltree County, Texas, with a foundation herd he drove south from Colorado. As his acreage and cattle expanded, he became a favorite among ranchers and their families throughout the upper Panhandle: https://www.tshaonline.org/handbook/entries/cresswell-henry-whiteside

5. That was on 13th February 1890.

6. The Atlantic and Caribbean Steam Navigation Co. / Red "D" Line was founded in 1881 and was a successor to Boulton, Bliss and Dallett & Co. who operated services to Venezuela. Commonly known as the Red "D" Line as they flew a white house flag with a large red D in the center. Passenger services operated between New York, San Juan, Curacao, La Guaira and Puerto Cabello and returned to New York via Curacao and San Juan. Another service operated to Mayaguez, La Guaira, Curacao and Maracaibo. The company and its services were taken over by the Grace Line in 1937: http://www.theshipslist.com/ships/lines/redd.shtml

7. Who did Addie work for and where was his office? On the passenger list when he returns to England in June 1891 he is listed as "Com Agent" – probably Commission Agent.

8. Adam (Primrose) Jenkins was from Antrim, Ireland, (b ~ 1866, arrived NY on the "Celtic" on 17 Jan 1891). He was a linen merchant (See Index to People). Walter Portheim is on the arriving passenger list into NY on 5th Jan 1891 as a "merchant", b~1861. Probably US citizen. Nothing else known.

opposite is a church with some ground about it over which Addie's window looks. His room, "a fine room, a **large** room" (without joking), is on the second floor, & is bright & cheerful, & tastefully decorated. The wash-stand is fixed in a little recess in the wall, & has hot & cold water taps fixed over it, the mantel-board is decorated with photographs, & on the toilet-table are an amber satin & lace cover & pin-cushion to match, presents from two of his numerous lady friends, while a handkerchief sachet, the gift of a third, stands on a little table.

So much for his room; I must ungallantly leave till next letter, Mrs Bridge, the pretty young widow, I mean the young & pretty widow; besides by that time I shall have more to say about her. As "Goldie" (aged 5) observes "I know who you are, but we aint acquainted yet".[9]

Best love to all,

Jack

I have told Addie about Troy marking ink,[10] as desired by G.Y.K.[11]

Letters c/o Sñres. Aepli Eberbach & Co

Barranquilla

Colombia   S.A.

by Royal Mail, if you just catch it, otherwise via New York

9. Goldie is Mrs Bridge's daughter.
10. I think this must refer to the collar and cuff-making industry in Troy, NY: https://en.wikipedia.org/wiki/Troy,_New_York and https://www.albany.edu/history/Troy-Cohoes/ The one large-scale industry that survived into the 20th century was collar- and cuff-making. Beginning with the detachable collar, supposedly invented by a Troy woman, Hannah Montague, in 1827, the collar industry grew steadily and eventually included over 20 factories manufacturing collars, cuffs, and shirts in Troy.
11. G.Y.K. is George Young Kinnaird (see Index to People).

32. Letter from New York, 29th January 1891

18910129 See an image of the original letter, http://dx.doi.org/10.17613/x4cd-v709

Nº 2   New York

29th Jany. 1891

My dear Mother,

I sent you a long letter last Sat'day (Nº 1) by the "Gallia", – & I wrote since to Father by the "Germanic". Addie had arranged such a continuous round of dissipation for me that I had no time to write to you by the last mentioned boat.

I shall try to give you some account of our doings beginning with last night's gaiety, partly because it is still fresh & partly as no doubt it will interest you more than anything else; – that is James Black's wedding.

Addie had received his invitation some ten days ago. I did not call on Black as I did not wish to seem as if I were fishing, but he heard of my arrival from Tom Wallace & at once sent me cards which I enclose, to show you "how to do it".

Park Avenue near E 55th Street, New York, in 1901. Nearby 65 East 55th Street, now a skyscaper. (447-449 Fourth Avenue, Manhattan.)

We did not go to the church but turned up towards nine at 65 East 55th Street. The house is one of a terrace in a very good part of New York. A carpet covered the steps, with a canopy overtied, leading into a small hall.[1] Adam Jenkins, acting as usher, took us up to the end of a small reception room where the bride & groom stood, supported by bride's

---

1. If you look on Street View on Google maps it is now in the heart of skyscraper Manhattan – and the home of "Park Avenue Tower" – rather hideous. Certainly nothing like the genteel terrace with carpeted stairs leading to the entrance!

maids & groom's men, to receive congratulations. The bride looked very pretty; she is of medium height, neither dark nor fair, & with that brightness of expression & thin-ness of face which are, it seems to me, typical of American women. It is with trembling that I attempt any description of dresses but as I know I should not be forgiven if I passed over in silence as important a matter, I took a few mental notes for your specific edification, & here I plunge.

The wedding garment was of white brocaded silk or satin covered with tulle, with a long square train; the veil was of white tulle fastened like a cap on the top of the head & flowing down the back. There was lace somewhere about the front, & the general effect of the picture was very good. The tulle softened the outlines & gave "atmosphere", while the background of green palm-leave, and the light falling on the foreground & middle distance showed up the central figures to advantage.

The bride carried a large bouquet of lillies of the valley, & the groom wore a button hole of the same flower, while the bride's maids had magnificent bouquets of Marechal Neill roses.[2]

There were, I think, six bride's maids. One, a Miss Pulman, related to the Belfast people of that ilk, a pretty & very lively girl who reads Emerson but does not quite "grasp" some of his ideas, wore a white white Cachemire dress. She said she had made a bet with a gentleman that she herself would not be married within two years, & I advised her to hedge at once.

Two Miss Peacocks wore amber satin, – the upper part made sash-ways with white muslin. One lady had a handsome dress of pink satin with white ostrich feather trimming. Knowing what a <u>Medici</u> collar was, & thinking it would be a good word to bring into my description, I looked out for that rig, but I only noticed one built that way.[3] There were all kinds of colours, from mauve & green to crimson, & the most marked characteristic of the dresses all round, was their "strikingness". There was no sameness, but lots of originality.

Now I have given you three pages on dress & for exhaustive, precise, & graphic description I take the Huntley Palmer; in fact I have shown what a letter from "our own lady correspondent" **ought** to be.

The floral decorations were very profuse. The stair-rail was covered with evergreens bound with pink ribbon, palm-fern leaves covered the walls. Over the entrance to the reception room was a bell of white flowers, mostly large lillies; on one wall the initials B & R were interlaced in white & red roses, & a medallion of the same flowers in concentrate rings hung on the wall behind the happy pair.

A band in the hall discourses sweet music at intervals; there was some kind of supper down below in the basement but as the crowd was thick I did not think it worth the crush to go down. The presents were displayed in a room upstairs & were, of course, numerous & costly, – excuse the startling novelty of the remark.

James Black's brother, – Tom is his name, I think, – was very attentive throughout, introducing & asking people to go down to supper. Jack Savage was there in great form, also two Steins who enquired politely as to the well being of all the members of the family.

The couple left about midnight for the Southern States where they mean to spend their honey-moon, returning to New York for March & sailing in April for Belfast.

Mrs Russell seems a nice kindly elderly or rather middle aged lady; – I did not see anything of the other members of the family.[4]

<u>Friday 30th</u> Y'day afternoon I learnt of an alteration in the sailings of the Red D Line, which suddenly changes my plans. The last steamer that left broke her steaming gear the day after starting & had to return to New York, & my boat,

---

2. The Maréchal Niel is a yellow climbing rose introduced in 1864.

3. A Medici collar is a fan-shaped collar that comes up dramatically behind the head. Originally an Elizabeth style, the general shape again became fashionable in the 18th century.

4. The identity of all mentioned individuals is uncertain. Many had Belfast connections at this very posh Black wedding. Tom Wallace probably Thomas Parker Wallace (see Index to People); James Black may be part of the Black family of the "heiresses" across the way from the Loewenthals in Belfast, perhaps their brother?; Adam Jenkins, acting as usher, most likely Adam Primrose Jenkins b~1865 Belfast (see Index to People); Tom (he thinks) Black, James Black's brother; Mrs Russell, probably the mother of the American bride ("the initials B & R were interlaced in white & red roses").

the "Philadelphia", sails tomorrow 31st, instead of Wednesday 4th, the other steamer will leave on the latter date. I have decided to sail tomorrow as the four days' earlier arrival will suit me very well in the way of business, though the change upsets our pleasure arrangements & we shall have to cancel several engagements.

The actor Richard Mansfield as Beau Brummel

To re-commence at the beginning, on Friday evg. Addie took me to see Mansfield, a rising American actor, in "Beau Brummel".[5] I enjoyed the performance thoroughly; the acting was capital, & the play, which is founded on fact, interesting throughout, & very amusing in parts, though quite sad at the end, where the poor Beau dies in poverty & neglect, though still keeping up, in his semi-madness, the artificial etiquette & the elaborate compliments of his old life as leader of fashion & tone at the court.

On Saturday we called on Tom Wallace.[6]

Must close this letter now in haste for tomorrow's mail. Am now playing of billiards with Tom Wallace who sends his kind regards.

Addie writes by next mail due here a couple of days after this.

Best love

Jack

(the last lines scribbled untidily in pencil!)

5. *Beau Brummel: A Play in Four Acts* written for Richard Mansfield by Clyde Fitch: https://en.wikipedia.org/wiki/Richard_Mansfield. Mansfield was born in Berlin and spent his early childhood on Heligoland, Germany, an island in the North Sea, then under British rule. His parents were Erminia Rudersdorff (1822–1882), a Russian-born operatic soprano, and Maurice Mansfield (d 1861), a British London-based wine merchant. His grandfather was the violinist Joseph Rudersdorff. Mansfield was educated at Derby School, in Derby, England, where he studied painting in London. His mother took him to America, where she was performing, but he returned to England at age 20. Finding that he could not make a living as a painter, he gained some success as a drawing-room entertainer, eventually moving into acting.

6. See Index to People. Probably Thomas Parker Wallace, commission merchant b 1846, married in Belfast.

33. Letter from Curaçao, 4th February 1891

18910204 See an image of the original letter, http://dx.doi.org/10.17613/mww8-tc17

No 3   S.S. "Philadelphia"

4th Feby. 1891

My dear Mother,

My first letter was posted in N. York 24th Jany. My second, mailed 31st was broken off short owing to the sudden change in my day of sailing & I had only time to add a few words in pencil, while spending the evg. with Tom Wallace, & give the letter to Addie to post by the steamer leaving early next morning.

I think I had only managed to describe Black's wedding & "Beau Brummel" & was about to tell you about Tom Wallace when the abrupt stop came, so I shall begin where I left off.[1] Wallace[2] received us in a very friendly way when we called at his office, made kind enquiries about you all, & asked us to dinner at the Manhattan Athletic Club for the following evg.[3] This Club is the finest of its kind in the world. In the basement they have a swimming bath with the water warmed to a pleasant temperature, further shooting galleries for rifle & pistol practice, shovel-board & first rate skittle alleys. On the ground-floor is the billiard-room with twelve tables, a luncheon room & café, & a reception room, besides the offices. On the first storey there is a large theatre for amateur theatricals, card-rooms, smoking room & library. In the centre of the building & reaching up through the next two floors is the magnificent gymnasium, said to be undoubtedly the finest & most complete in the world. In addition to the usual fittings in the way of bars, horses, clubs, & dumbells, they have the mast & tackle of a yacht to teach sailing, the sliding seats & model oars of an outrigger for oarsmen, suspended footballs for boxers to punch & dodge on the return, & all kinds of ingenious machines for exercising every muscle in the body. In a gallery round the wall there is a running course, floored with padded canvas & sloped at the corners, for those who wish to train for races. This gymnasium rises through the middle of the third floor, on one side of which is the dining room, where we sat down after inspecting the building. Wallace gave us a first rate dinner, beginning with a Manhattan cocktail (they do make them in nice in New York), blue-point oysters & chablis & turtle-soup, then crab farcie, terrapin, which is a kind of small land-turtle, & a great delicacy & special New York dish, & roast chicken, with Pommery sec frappé, coffee, Chartreuse, & a good cigar.[4] He did the thing really well & was very nice about it. After dinner we, – that is Wallace & I, played billiards, while Addie looked on. We played on a French table & Wallace beat me easily, which of course proves that he is a fist class player. He said to mention to Father that he had been practising the English game a little, & would not be afraid to meet him next time at the Reform Club, as he had made a break of seventy-odd the other day.

1. A frivolous time in New York with Addie, JMcC's next brother down (Ferdinand Adolph Loewenthal b 1865, named after his uncle, Julius' brother, see Index to People). He was an unusual and rather unreliable character all his life. At the time of this letter Addie was aged 25 and JMcC nearly 27. As to Addie's work in NYC: I believe he was a "commission agent."
2. Tom Wallace sounds like a Belfast man, possibly a friend of Julius Sr. Probably Thomas Parker Wallace (b 8th June, 1846 Irvine, Ayrshire) who was married in Belfast to Jane Anderson (b 29th June, 1868). He arrived in the US in 1868 and worked as a Commission Merchant. He became a naturalized US citizen in 1874. Lived in Brooklyn in 1930 and died there in 1931. See Index to People.
3. The Manhattan Athletic Club was an athletic club in Manhattan, New York City. It was founded in November 1877. https://en.wikipedia.org/wiki/Manhattan_Athletic_Club
4. Pommery sec frappé = the practice of drinking it very cold (frappé) at the end of the meal.

The following evening Addie had tickets for the Opera so we went to hear *Lohengrin*. I had not heard that Opera before, & I don't think I found it much heavier than I expected to. Most of the singers were good, but the tenor was feeble. The orchestra was very fine. The Metropolitan Opera House is a tremendous building, but not a pretty one. There was an exhibition of diamonds in the boxes that I have never seen anything to equal; – they must have represented not a few hundreds of thousands of the almighty dollar.

6th Feby. Addie had written to his friends the Chappells saying we would call the evening after that, & promptly received a reply that we were to go there for dinner. They live at the other end of Brooklyn from Addie, in a comfortably furnished house, & are very good friends of his. We met with a very cordial reception & had a quite a jolly evening. Mrs Chappell is a lively little woman, full of fun & always in good spirits; Mr C. is considerably older than his better half & more serious, though he became quite brisk over a game of whist after dinner. Millie, the only child, is a nice girl of thirteen or fourteen, more grown-up than I had expected & I was somewhat taken aback to see Addie kiss her in a fatherly manner.[5]

Some of their friends came in after dinner, – among them Mrs Simmelkiaer, the widow who offered to give Addie music lessons, – tall, thin, sprightly, & a little sentimental, but very nice withal. She wanted us to spend an evening with her, even proposing to arrange a little dance, but we had none disengaged, so she kindly asked us to luncheon next day, inviting Mrs Chappell to meet us. Addie was busy in town but I accepted & was treated to nice little lunch, & allowed to smoke after it. In the afternoon the two ladies drove me over the famous Brooklyn Cemetery, Greenwood, an immense place with its beautifully undulating grounds covered that morning with snow & its many little lakes frozen over.[6] Our driver & guide pointed out all the famous tombs & rattled through the list heedless of interruption or query. In one place a noted "dance-shuse" was buried, in another an actor celebrated for his rendering of "Othelio", he discoursed learnedly on symbols taken from the ancient "my-thology", & on driving out quoted a stanza from Gray's Elegy. When his back was turned Mrs Chappell wound him up with an imaginary handle, & I am afraid altogether we were not as solemn as we ought to have been.

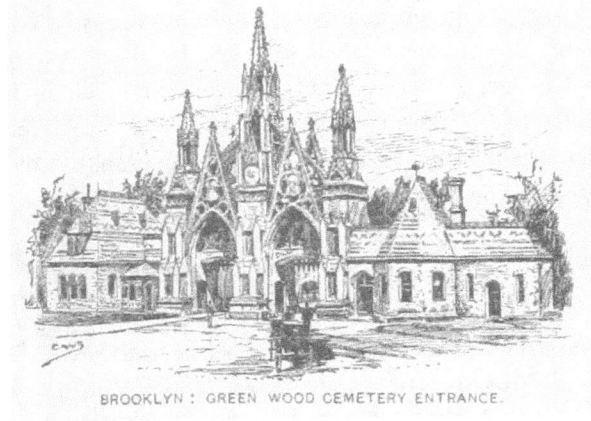

BROOKLYN : GREEN WOOD CEMETERY ENTRANCE.

Green Wood Cemetery in Brooklyn, NY, in 1891. From King's Handbook of the United States, by M. F. Sweetser.

The monuments were mostly heavy & ostentatious, their greatest praise being that they had cost so many thousand dollars. I noticed only one quiet tasteful tombstone enclosing a white marble medallion with a young girl's head exquisitely carved by some Italian sculptor.

The mention of the snow on the ground reminds me that I have not said anything about the great snow-storm of Saturday night & Sunday morning. There was a fall equivalent to nine inches of dry snow; it had been preceded by rain which made it

5. Mr & Mrs J.H. Chappell are noted in the Brooklyn Daily Eagle (18th February 1891) as hosting a 25th wedding anniversary of friends at their house on Rockaway Avenue. See Index to People.

6. Green-Wood Cemetery in Brooklyn was founded in 1838 and is now a National Historic Landmark. Green-Wood was one of the first rural cemeteries in America. By the early 1860s, it had earned an international reputation for its magnificent beauty and became the prestigious place to be buried, attracting 500,000 visitors a year, second only to Niagara Falls as the nation's greatest tourist attraction. Crowds flocked there to enjoy family outings, carriage rides, and sculpture viewing in the finest of first generation American landscapes. Green-Wood's popularity helped inspire the creation of public parks, including New York City's Central and Prospect Parks: https://www.green-wood.com/about-history/

adhere to the telephone & electric light wires causing a breakdown in these unequalled even during the famous blizzard of some years ago. [7]

Fortunately there were no lives lost, but there was great damage to houses & streets through the falling telegraph-poles, while for several days the wires lay tangled about in all directions, & for two nights many of the streets were in darkness as the electric current could not be turned on with safety.

Thursday evg. we spent at Addie's lodgings, Mrs Bridge having invited two of her lady friends, & the other lodger, General Gates, her god-father & protector, for the occasion. We played some very bad whist & then some noisy euchre, winding up with sandwiches & beer in the small hours of the morning, having enjoyed ourselves well.

On Friday evg. we were again invited to dinner by Wallace, who was really very kind to us; he wd. not let us breakfast him or make him any return, saying we could do that in Belfast. I hope to have an opportunity of doing so some day. This time he gave us a table-d'hôte dinner at a nice restaurant up-town in the neighbourhood of the big hotels, very good indeed & less expensive I am glad to say than the order dinner at the Club. After dinner we had a game of billiards, during which I scrawled a pencil-note at the foot of my last letter to you & gave it to Addie to post.

La Carmencita, painted by John Singer Sargent in 1890

Later in the evg. I went alone, as Addie did not care to accompany me, to a subscription ball, given in the Madison Square Hall, a huge place like the Hippodrome at Paris or the Tournament Hall at Islington, but with a splendid dancing floor. They say there were ten thousand people there; that may be an exaggeration, but there certainly were fully five thousand & the Hall was not crowded, though I have never been in a crush like that at the entrance. It was a Spanish ball given for the benefit of Carmencita, a danseuse who has taken New York by storm. [8] There was first a procession round the hall, Carmencita riding on a triumphal car, after which she danced some Spanish dances on a raised platform. The general dancing then began, to the alternate music of two large bands, & was kept up till a late hour in the morning. Mrs Bridge & some of her friends were there, & I also met a young fellow from Curaçao whom I knew very well.

Next morning I packed & took my things on board the "Philadelphia", & in the afternoon we met, by appointment, Mrs Chappell, Millie, & Mrs Simmelkiaer & took them to a wax-works exhibition & concert, where we had to leave them in about an hour as the steamer was to sail at five. [9] Addie went round to his office to fetch Ruskin's "Modern Painters", which I had bought in a nice American edition, but did not turn up in time, for as soon as I was on board the steamer sailed out of the dock,

7. A four-day blizzard that hit late in the winter of 1888 threw New York City into chaos and killed more than 200 people. The March 11th–14th storm brought 21 inches of snow to the city and pummeled New Jersey, Massachusetts and Connecticut as well. Accumulation and winds blowing more than 70 miles per hour stopped taxis and horse-drawn carriage operations and caused to a locomotive to derail, leaving passengers stranded on elevated tracks in freezing cars: https://www.nydailynews.com/new-york/5-snowiest-blizzards-new-york-city-history-article-1.2507123

8. Carmen Dauset Moreno, better known as Carmencita (b Almería 1868, d 1910) was a Spanish dancer living in the United States. She performed at Madison Square Gardens in New York at the end of January 1891, before some 8000 people, obtaining great success with her flamenco dance. She received so many job offers there that she decided to stay and live in the United States, acting non-stop, sometimes dressed as a man, and acting as a model for great painters and even for advertisements. During the following years, Carmencita performed in many large American cities. She appeared at the Music Hall in Koster and Bial in November and early December 1894 before selling her properties in the United States and returning to Europe, although she continued to tour. She performed at the Palace Theater in February 1895 and periodically at the Théâtre des Nouveautés in Paris. She is best known for her role in a short documentary of the same name and for having her portrait painted by such notable artists as John Singer Sargent, William Merritt Chase, and James Beckworth.

9. Mrs Simmelkiaer, the widow who offered to give Addie music lessons, is recorded in the Brooklyn Daily Eagle (26th May 1915) as contributing to "an entertaining evening" at the Laurier Musical Club.

though it was still ten minutes before the advertised hour, but the evg. was wet & foggy & the Captain wanted to go out of the harbour by day-light.

From the foregoing lengthy list, which I hope has not bored you, you will see that I had a jolly week in New York; Addie did all he could to make my stay pleasant, & would have taken me round all the theatres in the town, I believe, if I had let him. We had intended going to Staten Island to dine with the Finlays on Sunday, & had accepted an invitation to dine at a good Brooklyn Club with a Mr Perego, a business friend of Addie's, on Tuesday, but these & other plans were upset by my sailing on Saturday 1st, instead of the following Wednesday.[10] On the whole I was glad of the change, for one week of New York gaiety is enough at a time & I was ready to go South to work.

O'Flaherty arrived on the Friday, luckily for us two days late, having had a bad passage.[11] Addie will now be hard at work with him.

In the theatre, at "Beau Brummel", we saw Adam Jenkins who said he had been bobbing up & down for half an hour trying to catch my eye, but I looked everywhere except at him.[12] He arranged to call for us & take us to lunch next day, but apparently forgot the engagement, as he did not turn up & did not refer to the matter when we met him afterwards at Black's wedding; – I did not see him since.

Of course we had many walks through the town, saw the New York beauties "mince along in fashion's tide, adown Broadway on the proper side, when the golden sun was setting", looked into the shops, strolled through Central Park, & generally did everything[13]. I got quite used to the Elevated Railroad (called the "El" by the speech sparing Americans) & to the trains pulled quickly & smoothly by endless cable over the great Brooklyn Suspension Bridge. The trams or street-cars are too slow for the great distances, & even the present "El" is not quick enough for the New Yorkers, with whom time is still more money than it is with us, & they are agitating for an accelerated express service of trains. A Yankee, asked why he preferred the "El" to the trams, replied that his insurance policy covered death through accident, but not death from old age.

Addie says perhaps he may take a run over in the Summer, but he is not at all certain yet; I hope he will be able to manage it. He says there is little or nothing doing in July-August.

The "Philadelphia" has had delightful weather from the day after sailing.[14] The first night we had to anchor twelve hours in the fog, but since then all has been fine & clear, & the third day out I put on tennis-flannels. There are only three other passengers, – two young Spaniards who have not left their bunks, nor, I believe, changed their clothes since we started this day week, & a very young lieutenant from the American Navy, called Welles[15], going to visit Venezuela & some of the neighbouring countries as Special Commissioner from the Government on behalf of the "World's Fair" – the great exhibition which is to be held in Chicago in year or two.[16] I have read Westwards-Ho once more, & a couple

10. Joseph O Perego of Brooklyn (b~1860)? Or (more likely) Arthur Wesley Perego, importer, who was on a passenger list arriving NYC on 26th April 1886 from Liverpool (b~1861, US citizen).

11. JMcC says his own departure was brought forward to Saturday 1st – but the 1st February was a Sunday. There is a F. H. C. Flaherty (merchant, aged 48, "US citizen") on the passenger list arriving NYC from Southampton on 30th January 1891.

12. See Index to People. Adam Jenkins. Likely Adam Primrose Jenkins (b 1865 in Belfast) who arrived in NYC on 17th January 1891 on the "Celtic," aged 25, from Ireland. Usher at James Black's wedding

13. From "The Proud Miss MacBride" by John Godrey Sace (1816-1887): "O, TERRIBLY proud was Miss MacBride, The very personification of pride, As she minced along in fashion's tide, Adown Broadway—on the proper side, When the golden sun was setting." More at https://www.bartleby.com/360/9/54.html

14. Built and launched at Glasgow for the Inman Line in 1889, the Philadelphia was originally called the "City of Paris" and sailed the Liverpool - Queenstown - New York route. The ship weighed 10,500 tons, was 527 feet long and could carry 540 1st class passengers, 200 in 2nd class and 100 3rd class passengers. The ship changed name and ownership several more times before going aground off of Cornwall, England. She was refloated and repaired at Belfast and renamed the SS Philadelphia. From 1901 she operated the Southampton - Cherbourg - New York route. In 1914 she was transferred to the Liverpool - New York service: https://www.burgumfamily.co.uk/ref_sh_philadelphia.php

15. Lieut. Roger Welles U.S.N. (See (Index to People)

16. The World's Columbian Exposition of 1893 was held in Chicago to celebrate the 400th anniversary of Christopher Columbus' arrival in the New World: https://en.wikipedia.org/wiki/World%27s_Columbian_Exposition

of yellow-backs, & have spent the evenings playing whist, the Captain & Purser making up our four. We have played 35 rubbers, & I come out minus 2 points – a result not flattering to my vanity, considering that the two players just named know nothing of the game, & the other not very much. However the outcome was very even all round, Welles winning 13 points which the other three of us lost among us. We had good fun over it, & many a laugh at some of the Captain's brilliant strokes, when an ace or a king would turn up in his hand in the most unexpected manner, with lots of joking about the call for trumps, constant penalties for leads out of turn. We always had an interval about 10.30 for sandwiches & beer & then resumed business until 12.

Curaçao <u>9th Feby.</u> Just landed. I shall now close this letter which is long enough to try your patience, but those I shall write on shore won't be as long. Best love to all

Jack

34. Letter from Barranquilla, 14th February 1891

18910214 See an image of the original letter, http://dx.doi.org/10.17613/qwy3-a682

Nº 4

Barranquilla,   14th Feby. 1891[1]

My dear Mother,

My last letter was dated 9th inst. & posted in Curaçao. I mention it in proper business-like fashion so that you may know whether any of my valuable communications have gone astray. – an eventual loss that would be much bemoaned by your appreciative selves though possibly not realised by an undiscerning posterity.

Valentine's day – but none of the giddy thoughtless creatures have sent me a valentine

> "Ah" say the girls I left behind
> "He's gone out to the tropics
> "That place, you know, where you may find
> "Immense & microscopic s-
> "-orts of every insect kind,
> "Wriggl-ic, – crawl-ic, hop-pic, s-
> "-o out of sight is out of mind,
> "Let's talk of other topics."

If I had time I would write you some pretty verses for the 17th March, "while I'm in the way of carvin'" as Tommy would say, but not having hired the horse of the Muses I must send by Royal Mail or Mail Pegasus, & in prose, my best wishes for many happy returns of the day; for the steamer sails to-morrow, & to produce any dapper couplets worthy of the occasion I should have to sit up all night with my head in a tub of warm water, & a cold bandage round my feet.[2]

I was warmly received by old Curaçao friends & I have been promised entertainment on my return. Before leaving I received from New York my waterproof & the five volumes of Modern Painters, left behind owing to the early sailing of the "Philadelphia". I am very pleased with my purchase & am already half way through the first volume.

I met some old friends in the officers of the steamer that brought me down to Savanilla[3] – the port for this place – for by a curious chance it was the "Australian", the boat on which I spent a week very pleasantly last year, between Trinidad & Curaçao, when I met the young engineer, Copperthwaite, whose name you may remember.[4]

1. Barranquilla lies strategically next to the delta of the Magdalena River, 7.5 kilometres (4.7 miles) [originally 25 kilometres (16 miles) before rapid urban growth] from its mouth at the Caribbean Sea, serving as a port for river and maritime transportation within Colombia: https://en.wikipedia.org/wiki/Barranquilla
2. Jane's 55th Birthday on 17 March
3. Sabanilla is a district of the municipality of Puerto Colombia. During the 19th century it was an important commercial port through which products from the interior of the country went abroad, which is why the province of Sabanilla was formed around it: https://es.wikipedia.org/wiki/Sabanilla_(Colombia)
4. He mentioned Copperthwaite the year before when he was on ship between Trinidad and Curaçao, going to Columbia. He worked in Mexico in charge of railway works. This is William Charles Coppertwhaite – civil engineer – b 7 March 1861. Membership of Institution of Civil Engineers recorded 2nd April 1896 and married Alice Hobroyd in Mexico City on 22nd April 1889. See Index to People

On landing one of the first people I saw was my old acquaintance, Colonel Pellet, of New York, proprietor & editor of "The Shipping List", in which, on my first visit to Barranquilla, he <u>cordially extended</u> to me the <u>freedom of the City</u>.

It is welcome Sunday today, & I can be as lazy as I like. I have had my bath & my coffee, & I am now not obliged to dress & feel hot & uncomfortable, but can sit in my many coloured garments, write, & smoke the while, windows & doors open, but the venetian shutters closed, to keep out the sun on the one side, & the curious stares of the chocolate-complexioned natives on the other. There is not much superfluous luxury in the furniture; – two trestle beds (one I use as a stand for my portmanteau), being six feet of brown canvas stretched between two parallel bars, supported on cross legs at the ends, two sheets, two pillows, & a mosquito curtain overhead; the most comfortable kind of bed in these hot countries when one is used to it, though rather hard at first. I have a little table, three feet by one & a half, & two straw chairs – one a rocker which I stole from the sitting room. There is a small tripod wooden wash stand with a metal basin, & beside it a tin pail. The walls are of unplaned planks, whitewashed, & rise to about eight feet, leaving some four feet of unwalled space to the bare beams of the roof, thus ensuring a free circulation of air, & offering facilities for conversation with the other inmates of the hotel. At the same time this through communication has its trifling disadvantages; one cannot have undisturbed rest till all one's neighbours have retired, usually in the small hours of the morning, sometimes not even then, – last night, for instance, I had to sing out to an unknown neighbour on the right to stop snoring.

One wall has six wooden pegs for clothes & a mirror eight inches by six, &, voilà, I have completed the "Voyage autour de ma Chambre", describing every article in it. Stay, there is a large shell to hold back the door, & a much used straw mat before the bed.

The bare-footed, unkempt, dusky valet-de-chambre has just been to settle the room, but has limited himself to emptying the india-rubber bath by the simple process of dropping its contents over the balcony on the street below. "Catalino!" I said, (that is his name, – anything less than four syllables would be too mean) "you might at least have called out "Agua va". The old Spaniards used to do so in similar cases, as Julie will find in Gil Blas. "It's Carnival" was his laconic reply, meaning that if he did douse anyone the Season would excuse the deed.

My previous letters were so long that I am not going to exceed the four pages this time. You can still address to Curaçao, via New York, c/o Rivas Fensohn & Co. Should I have left, they will forward letters.[5]

Best love to all

Jack

---

5. Rivas Fensohn & Co was a trading company in Curaçao that issued private paper money in 1893 in denominations of 25 cents, 50 cents, 1 guilder and 2½ guilders. They were listed as Lloyd's Agents in Puerto Cabello, Venezuela. See Index to People

35. Letter from Barranquilla, 21st February 1891

N.º 5   Barranquilla

French Packet   21st Feby. 1891

My dear Mother,

The French steamer passes tomorrow, & though I have nothing to write about & am not quite in the mood for writing about nothing, still mails are so far between & irregular that I like to send at least a few words by each, if merely to let you know that I am alright.

I have not had any letters from you meanwhile, so some ought to come soon.

A few days ago young Clark, traveller for York St., arrived from Cuba.[1] He witnessed a startling occurrence in Havana just before leaving. Some six highway robbers trying to escape from the country had taken passage by his steamer. The police were on their back & came, in plain clothes, on board the steamer to arrest them, when a pitched battle took place. The robbers were armed with two revolvers each, & fought to the last, but five of them were shot dead on the spot & the sixth was taken prisoner. Clark was standing on deck at the time & dare not stir, for the bullets were flying all round & the safest thing was to stand still. One man fell within five yards of him. Two jumped into a boat that had come off with some passengers & made the boatman pull away, but they were followed by a gunboat with which they exchanged fire till they were killed & the boatman was shot in the arm. They say adventures are to the venturous; – be that as it may, having such a thrilling story to tell gives Clark quite an advantage in the way of business over me to whom nothing exciting ever happens.

A Mr Taylor, from Dundee, is here too, a very nice fellow.[2] We had a little whist the other evening; – my points so far, since the beginning of the year, are slightly to the good. I am keeping a record to test the rest of my play.

Last night was a perfect tropical night. Warm but not oppressive, a faint breeze coming in from the sea, glorious full moon turning all colours into bright white or intense black; – we sat on the balcony of a quiet restaurant outside the town & lazily watched the winding Magdalena which flows slowly through the plain till it loses itself in the soft haze of the horizon. Everything seemed so still & quiet & yet the air was full of the humming of insects & the odd notes of strange birds. Inside the room friend Twose was at the piano playing softly snatches from Songs without Words & other dreamy music, while, to complete the poetry of the picture, I sat in a low rocking chair, with my feet on the balcony rail, & smoked, refreshing myself at intervals with an iced blend of ginger ale & lager beer.[3]

Pity the sorrows of a poor bag-man. Jack

---

1. Clark(e): see Index to People. He probably represents the "York Street Flax Spinning Company".
2. See Index to People.
3. Probably Robert Warren Twose (b 1858 Exeter, d between 1926-1930 Panama). Found on passenger list from Southampton to Savanilla in 1893. Involved with late 19th Century transportation modernization (rail and river boats on the Magdalena) in Colombia. See article by Hernán Horna in the *Journal of Latin American Studies*, 1982: 14(1), 33-54. https://www.jstor.org/stable/155726

36. Letter from Barranquilla, 1st March 1891

18910301 See an image of the original letter, http://dx.doi.org/10.17613/mqz7-pc39

N<u>o</u> 6

Royal Mail   Barranquilla 1st March 1891

My dear Mother,

I wrote on the 13th Feb (N<u>o</u> 4) by Royal mail, & on the 21st by French Packet.

Y'day I received your welcome letters of 26th Jany & 1st Feby, & as it was my birthday, for want of a 29th, I was particularly glad to have your home news. The day before, I had a letter from Addie & also letters & cards from Mrs Chappell & Mrs Simmelkiaer, – very kind of them to remember.[1] I am sorry to have missed Mrs H. Brown's dance, particularly as it took place on such a memorable date as the 28th. I made the occasion festive by giving a little dinner. We were four, – Taylor of Dundee, Clark from Belfast, & a fellow from Manchester living here, called Pearce.[2] I have moved into a larger room & I persuaded the old landlady to let us have dinner in it, being so much snugger & nicer than at the long common table. We had a little round table, with a clean cloth!, & two side-tables for fruit etc. & copper faced, bare-footed, four-feet-high Blas to wait on us. I asked him to get some flowers, so he came in triumphantly with two long-stalked, big-leaved, artificial plants, – fearful things – the leaves streaked white & green, & on the stalk a ticket with the price. I would not let him put them on the table, but he insisted on leaving them on the side-board & was quite delighted with the effect.

In the morning I interviewed & tipped Pachita, the black cook, praised her powers, & asked her to excel herself, & she really did very well. We had macaroni soup, boiled fish, roast beef, fowl, tongue (solid you see) salad, tomatoes, tart, preserves, oranges & papaya, a kind of melon; – wines claret & iced Heidsieck sec (don't be alarmed – only one bottle of each), coffee & cigars. As it was the birthday of your eldest son I wanted to give him an entertainment befitting the occasion.

Thanks to Julie for his second Spanish letter. It is not as good as the first though. I have a letter ready to post to him.

Addie writes that he has been able to open a fair number of new accounts with O'Flaherty. I hope he will get commission on them.[3]

I am now waiting for a steamer to take me to Cartagena.[4] The worst of travelling on this coast is that one must often lose time owing to the irregularity of the few vessels that come round. I hope to be back in Curaçao about 15th March.

This is Sunday evg. & very likely just about the time I am writing to you, you will be writing to me.

We have some new neighbours in the hotel; among them a family with three small children that howl night & day. "Why doesn't someone drown those children?" is a question put every morning at breakfast & every evening at dinner.

---

1. Mrs Simmelkiaer and The Chappells were friends of Addie's in NYC (see Index to people). Mrs Simmelkiaer was the widow who offered to give Addie music lessons in January 1891.

2. Clark from Belfast (worked for "York Street") and Taylor from Dundee were both mentioned in the last letter. See Index to People for both

3. Addie – brother Ferdinand Adolphus – who is a commission agent in NYC. O'Flaherty, probably Francis Hale Hill O'Flaherty (b~1848 Belfast) linen merchant in Belfast. In the 1901 Census living in Eglantine Avenue (same as Elizabeth Kinnaird).

4. Cartagena is about 130 km south of Barranquilla: https://en.wikipedia.org/wiki/Cartagena,_Colombia

My snoring friend has been put in the background by a more recent arrival, & now he is simply "not in it". It is very funny now to hear N⁰ 1 complain that N⁰ 2 prevents him from sleeping.

I have just been reading a book of Burnand's, – on the whole tedious, but with "happy thoughts" here & there.[5] Apropos of nautical ballads he says that "the words do not always realize the deferred expectations of a lifetime" & then two lines from "The Saucy Arethusa"

"On deck five hundred men did dance,
The stoutest they could get in France

about this he remarks

"What possible glory could there be in taking prisoners & crew of five hundred dancing French Daniel Lamberts?[6] Notoriously, when a Frenchman is stout he goes to twenty-two stone in a very short time, & if these were the stoutest they could get in France, i.e. the very fat of the land, so to speak, – what a helpless set they must have been, except for dancing, by way of exercise, just to keep it down a bit! And what accommodation they must have had on board that vessel. Fancy five hundred of the stoutest Frenchmen in five hundred hammocks"!

I have also been reading a pretty story called "Not like other Girls", simple & interesting. Towards the end it is amusing to see how the husbands are imported wholesale to provide for all the unattached spinsters.

Best love to all

Jack

5. Sir Francis Cowley Burnand (b 29th November 1836, d 21 April 1917), usually known as F. C. Burnand, was an English comic writer and prolific playwright, best known today as the librettist of Arthur Sullivan's opera Cox and Box: https://en.wikipedia.org/wiki/F._C._Burnand#1870s:_prolific_author
6. Daniel Lambert (b 13 March 1770, d 21 June 1809) was a gaol keeper and animal breeder from Leicester, England, famous for his unusually large size: https://en.wikipedia.org/wiki/Daniel_Lambert

37. Letter from Cartagena, 10th March 1891

18910310 See an image of the original letter, http://dx.doi.org/10.17613/85ry-f969

Nº 7 Cartagena,   Colombia
10th March 1891

My dear Mother,

My list tells me that I posted Nº 6 to you on the 1st inst by French Mail from Barranquilla.

I had to wait several days for a steamer to bring me here; finally a German boat came along, & though she was supposed to carry cargo only I could wait no longer. The food on board was neither varied nor plentiful but my fellow passenger, Clark, & myself, were not very exacting & we went for the ham, sausage, & blackbread, passed the sauerkraut, & consoled ourselves with deep draughts of excellent lager-beer, made deliciously cool by the ingenious plan of hanging the bottles in a damp canvas bag exposed to the breeze on deck, the evaporation having he same effect as if the bottles had been on ice for hours.

Cartagena is my Western limit & now I turn my face eastward, unlike "the youth who daily farther from the east must travel."[1] On the 15th I hope to take the French steamer to Puerto Cabello, as there won't be a direct boat for Curaçao for some time, but there is frequent communication between the two places mentioned.

Cartagena, Columbia, 1893. A partial view of the habour. Photographer, Clímaco Calderón (1852-1913).

---

1. Quote from William Wordsworth's Ode: Intimations of Immortality from Recollections of Early Childhood: "The youth, who daily farther from the east Must travel, still is Nature's priest"

Cartagena is a curious old town. It is really an island, having the sea on one side& the harbour on the other, while a narrow passage between these is spanned by a drawbridge.[2] All round the town are massive walls, built by the old Spaniards in the days of Indian slave labour. These walls measure from thirty to forty feet high & as much across; – I paced one part last night where the rampart was sixty feet across. The masonry is splendid – large blocks of stone bound as in a solid mass by mortar that they say cannot be made to-day. It is supposed that it was mixed with white of eggs, but that I venture to doubt. There are forts on the heights at the back of the town & at the entrance to the harbour, &, before the days of modern artillery, the place was practically impregnable. It has seen many a fight from the days of Drake & Captain Amyas Leigh down, & is still the spot where the victory is decided for one party or another during the periodical revolutions.[3]

To-day it is a hot place, a hungry place, & a dusty place, & generally – a most delightful place to leave behind. I have managed to scribble these few lines in haste, to take advantage of the quick mail by N.Orleans & N.York. I don't know exactly when the next opportunity will be.

Best love

Jack.

Curaçao via N. York. Rivas Fensohn & Co[4] who will forward.

---

2. During the colonial period, a drawbridge was raised at the foot of the channel of San Anastasio, which linked the walled city to the legendary Getsemani neighbourhood. https://en.wikipedia.org/wiki/Puerta_del_Reloj,_Cartagena. Once a district characterized by crime, Getsemani, just south of the ancient walled fortress, has become "Cartagena's hippest neighborhood and one of Latin America's newest hotspots" https://en.wikipedia.org/wiki/Cartagena,_Colombia#1811_to_the_21st_century

3. Captain Amyas Leigh Refers to the Character in Westward Ho!, the 1855 historical novel by Charles Kingsley, based on the experiences of Elizabethan privateer Amyas Preston (Amyas Leigh in the novel), who sets sail with Francis Drake, Walter Raleigh and other privateers to the New World, namely the Preston Somers Expedition and Raleigh's El Dorado Expedition where they battle with the Spanish. https://en.wikipedia.org/wiki/Westward_Ho!_(novel)

4. See Index to People

38. Letter from Puerto Cabello, 20th March 1891

18910320 See an image of the original letter, http://dx.doi.org/10.17613/ytc2-wq93

Nº 8   Puerto Cabello, Venezuela
via N.York   20th March 1891.

My dear Mother,

Let me see, – I think I have a good many things to write about this time, though I have no very startling news to communicate.

In the first place, for the last ten days or so I have been working hard. George Y. would probably remark that this, in itself, is most startling news, but then he has always held most mistaken views as to my laboriousness, & because of the unvarying cheerfulness with which I always mopped "the sweat of my brow", he absurdly maintained that the lines had fallen to me in exceptionally pleasant places, instead of advising, as he should have done, the indolent youth of the rising generation to consider my ways & those of the ant.[1]

In my last I wrote you about the German steamer that brought us, – Clark & myself, to Cartagena. I have always to think how far I came in my last report, so as to know where to begin.

The special reasons for my exerting myself in Cartagena were firstly, the presence of the other philanthropist Clark, who is inspired with the same benevolent & disinterested desire as myself to forward the cause of civilisation by supplying the natives with Belfast linens, & secondly, the fact that a return steamer which I had to catch was coming along in one week.

This boat was guaranteed not to leave before noon on Sunday last & for that morning a riding excursion was arranged by some young men whose acquaintance we had made. We were to start at 5.30 & ride up a hill about a thousand feet high, overlooking the town & from this point of vantage we were to see the sun rise. Clark came hammering at my door at five, & as I had been up till after twelve the night before – first playing scat, – & afterwards writing letters, I would willingly have obliged any Richard III who might at that moment have offered a good bargain for a mount. Mine would have been, with something more than Spanish politeness, "very much at his disposal", & the sun might have risen without my assistance.

As it was, the other boys did not turn up till half past six & I spent the interval between writing more letters & blessing Clark for his childlike faith in Colombian punctuality on the altar of which faith he had offered me up a growling victim. I might have asked him, with withering sarcasm, if he was under the impression that I was to be Queen of the May, but these happy thoughts always come too late!

Finally we started, five of us, trotted through the town & out into the country. At the foot of the Popa, the-to-be-conquered-hill,[2] we took coffee with biscuits of the flint age and butter, – none of your modern stuff but from a tin brought over by the hardy Norsemen, reverenced as a relic by Columbus, & handed down from Father to Son, to be produced only on occasions of peculiar solemnity.

By the time we topped the mountain the dappled dawn was past & the sun was high in the sky; – still there was some

---

1. George Y. = George Young Kinnaird (b~1857, d 6th January 1921) (see Index to people). George Kinnaird & Co, linen merchants, Belfast; also collar & cuff manufacturers). Father of Elizabeth Kinnaird (b~1895).
2. The top of the La Popa hill, which gets its name based on its shape similar to that of a poop deck, offers the best view of Cartagena.

satisfaction in the thought that Clark was after all not there to see him rise. That was consolation enough for missing it myself, & besides, you know, I am <u>blasé</u> in the matter of sunrises.

During the early part of the ride my charger persisted in screwing his mouth round, like a contortionist, trying to catch the side of the bit in his teeth. Not being familiar with the "ways" of horses, I was not sure what the result might be in our relative positions if he succeeded in chewing the coveted morsel, so I as persistently pulled it out of reach, whereupon ensued a pump-handle-like movement of his head – pretty but uncomfortable. After a little I let him have his own way & then we got on most harmoniously. When we passed a group of ladies I rode with "the easy grace that only comes with long experience", as Mark Twain says about the putting on of gloves, – absorbed in the beauty of the scenery, one hand carelessly resting on the thigh, trying to seem as if I felt, in the saddle, like Brier Rabbit in the briar-patch into which his enemy, Brier Fox, had chucked him: – "Born & bred in a briar-patch, Brier Fox!– Born & bred in it!"

Clark was not so fortunate. He rode a spirited horse, & on the way home, it refused to cross the tram-rails, & in consequence got mixed up with the wheels of a carriage. He jumped off, mounted again, & then the horse reared, falling back, but fortunately clear of Clark who was pitched well out the saddle on the road, where he lit on his head. He might have been severely injured, but luckily, as he proved, his head is a hard one, & escaped with a newly developed bump. He then changed horses with another man & we reached home without further mishap, at about ten o'clock.

That was on Saturday last. Since Thursday I have been able to sit down without much discomfort.

On the way to the Hotel I called at the agency of the steamer; it had not yet arrived, & would not, in any case, – so the agent assured me – leave till the following morning, so I had plenty of time to finish my correspondence comfortably & pack my trunks, besides having a good rest! But at exactly one o'clock, while I was enjoying an after-lunch cigar, & playing a game of chess with Clark I was informed by telephone that the steamer was in, & was to leave again at two! My trunks were all unpacked, the Hotel was on the outskirts of the town, & the steamer was anchored out in the bay; – & I had just one hour to pack everything & get there. For once in my life I was under the disagreeable necessity of being in a hurry. I sent Clark into town to arrange about a boat & to bring a cart with him for the baggage. I asked another man called Behrens, from Manchester, to get my bill, add it up, & pay it, – & I gave him my pocket-book for the purpose: – a touching proof of confidence, seeing it was full of banknotes (true, they were Colombian notes, & worth altogether about three pounds). Knowing exactly where everything had to go, I had all packed by the time the cart was at the door, – the donkey obligingly would go, – the boat skimmed quickly out before a strong breeze, – & at two precisely I was on board the Fernando de Lesseps.[3]

I would here remark that, no matter how great your haste, never fail to check the addition of your hotel bill, or get someone else to do it; – in fact, the greater your haste the more absolute necessity for this precaution. This time the sum was only three dollars too much. Nevertheless I cannot complain of high charges, the rate per day being 3/9 for board & lodging, & the whole account for nine days, amounting, with extras, to £ 2-4-5, – not much compared with Scotch Hotel-bills in tourist times, but quite enough for the accommodation given!

The Fernando de Lesseps is a French boat, & during the two days & a half to Puerto Cabello I had an opportunity of showing how thoroughly I was "insthructed in the game of parlez-voo'"

Wednesday till Saturday were spent in Puerto Cabello & on Sunday morning I landed once more in Curaçao, where I now finish this letter.

As on a previous occasion, I was hospitably entertained, in the former place, by a German gentleman, a Mr Gruen, who does business with Dundee. He has a fine house, with a verandah shaded by vines & a garden bright with roses & tropical plants, in a little village beautifully situated among the hills, some five miles out of "The Port", as the town proper is called.

We drove out to this village, San Esteban, in the afternoon about five, &, after an excellent dinner, a good night's

3. The Ferdinand de Lesseps was a French Line steamship built 1875 at Glasgow by A. & J. Inglis, originally as the "Stad Haarlem" for the Royal Netherlands.

rest, a bath in the river, & an early breakfast of coffee & eggs, we drove into town again, much refreshed, the following morning.[4]

In my Puerto Cabello Hotel bill here is the following item: 1 sanguidié 12 cents. Not a bad shot at "sandwich", that, phonetically – it might have been wider of the mark.

I expected to find letters from you here in Curaçao, but there are none so far. The New York steamer is due today, & "hopingly" (to adapt a word from the German) brings something.[5]

Best love to all

Jack

Curaçao   23rd Mar. 1891

4. San Esteban is a picturesque town located fifteen minutes from Puerto Cabello, with a much cooler climate, which is why, in past centuries, prosperous merchants were established, most of them of foreign origin. There are still vestiges of a formidable architecture of its impressive mansions, among them, it is worth highlighting the one built by the engineer Muñoz Tebar for the wealthy Dane Julio Sturup, later acquired by General Vicencio Perez Soto and today turned into a Museum.
5. The German word is "hoffentlich."

39. Letter from Curaçao, 3rd April 1891

18910403 See an image of the original letter, http://dx.doi.org/10.17613/18xk-vk67

Nº 9 Curaçao 3rd April 1891

My dear Mother,

The day after posting my last letter to you I received your three welcome weeklies of 16th & 22nd Feby. & 2nd March, with account of Dora Sinton's visit, your amusements during same, etc.[1] I congratulate you on the acquisition of the secretaire.[2]

I have done a fair business here in Curaçao & in addition have had a good time. One of my friends, Mr van Kleunen, gave a dance in my honour & we separated at 4 o'clock in the morning.[3] It was very jolly indeed. I had lots of nice things said to me, had my health proposed, & so on. The girls here know how to dance; – no pain in the arm next day like what one has at home, after careering round with a few heavy-weights!

I was introduced to a middle-aged married lady, weight about 15 stone, but with sprightly youthful aspirations. I did not ask her to dance, not being able to go round even half of the younger ladies present. Next day her husband, a jolly fellow whom I know very well, told me the following dialogue had taken place on the way home.

– "So that's what you call a nice young man!" –
– "Yes, one of the nicest young men I have met in the West Indies" –
– "Well, I don't think so at all; – he never asked me to dance!"

Before going to the dance I was one of four guests (& I had the seat of honour) at a very pleasant dinner-party at Mr Fensohn's, to celebrate his birthday.[4] The six or eight excellent courses (the invitation was for 6 o'c. & we rose from table at 9) prepared me for the subsequent exertions.

I had already spent an evening at Mr Fensohn's delightful house, playing whist & scat, & he has arranged another whist party for tomorrow evg.

Further I have paid several visits at different houses, & have been asked to pay more, so that I can always spend the spare time agreeably enough in Curaçao. Today a Mr Bethencourt, one of the most cultured of the Venezuelans living here, made me a present of a nice book.[5]

1. Dora Sinton (see Index to people)
2. a secretary desk,https://en.wikipedia.org/wiki/Secretary_desk
3. Mr van Kleunen (see Index to People) was probably Jacob van Kleunen ('merchant'), a Dutch citizen from Curaçao (b 27th November 1859, m 31st August 1881 in Curaçao to Margaretha Louisa Moors, d Curaçao 25th October 1912).
4. Mr Fensohn could have been Emil Fensohn born in Hamburg ~1849, a merchant, or Carl Fensohn (b 20th September 1850 in Hamburg, d 1st June 1942 in Curaçao). Carl was the German Consul in Curaçao, "acting as agent for the Red D Line and who as such was one of the leading business men on the island" (see Index to People) https://udspace.udel.edu/bitstream/handle/19716/7896/mss0109_1930-00.pdf. He was a secret German agent during WWII. He married Marianna Léonore Esteva (b 24th January 1862 in Paris) on 23rd February 1881 in Curaçao.
5. Pascual Telesforo Bethencourt (b ~1854 Bejuma, Venezuela; m Maria Aurelia van der Wall Arneman; d 31st October 1918 Curaçao), OR his brother, Rafael Minguel Felipe Bethencourt (b 1st February 1848 Bejuma, Venezuela; m Maria Aleida Prince; d 11th February 1901 Curaçao).

I have already spent some 4/- in postage of letters by this mail, so you may imagine I am about written out. I should like to write to Father, Addie, & Julie, but I really can't manage it. But I have sent a few lines with birthday wishes to Annie.[6]

I wrote part of this last night after 12, & this morning I was up shortly after 6. The mornings are so delightful – warm & fresh at the same time – that it does not require an effort to rise early. As a rule I wander about a little in pyjamas, lean out of the window that overlooks the picturesque little harbour, & watch the steamers passing in not 50 yards away, as soon as it is daylight. By the way you have no idea what a useful present I find your field glasses. I can make out every face on the steamers, & can distinguish people in their houses on the other side of the harbour.

Two captains, two first mates, & several officers of minor degree, not to mention a crowd of civilians, have already praised the glasses highly.

I breakfasted on board one of the steamers in port on Monday last, at the invitation of my old acquaintances, the Captain & the Chief engineer, & with the kind permission of Thomas, the black steward. We had excellent fare – one of the items being a large & tender steak with two fried eggs on the top, for each person.

The "Philadelphia" which brought me down from New York arrived again this morning. I intend going on board bye & bye to see Captain Chambers, & I expect he will invite me to dinner.

At the request of numerous friends & admirers – inverted commas – I am seriously thinking of getting photographed – note of exclamation – this is an appreciative public, quick to discern modest merit – small italics -. The local artist has, among his stock-in-trade a boat, with two oars, & realistic waves, not to mention a sailor hat, – quite a "cocky" hat, as Dora Sinton would say. I have seen this boat, oars, waves, & hat in half the albums of Curaçao, & I think if I were to be taken standing up in the boat, regardless of the realistic waves, leaning carelessly on an oar, & waving the cocky sailor-hat towards the shipwrecked & anguish-torn photographer, as if declaiming

"Fear not but trust in Dollinger and he will bring you through" – the result would be effective – very![7]

Two o'clock, post-time, must shut up the camara. The picture will shortly be on view at Rodman's, admission sixpence, ladies free.

Love to all

Jack

Letters
Boggio Yanes & Monteverde[8]
Valencia
Venezuela
via N.York

6. Her 24th birthday (b 24 April 1867)

7. "Fear not, but lean on Dollinger, And he will fetch you through." From "The Aged Pilot Man" by Mark Twain: https://poets.org/poem/aged-pilot-man

8. Boggio, Yanes & Monteverde is listed as selling "dry goods, wholesale" in Valencia, Venezuela, in the *International Bureau of the American Republics*, 1892.

40. Letter from Curaçao, 12th April 1891

18910412 See an image of the original letter, http://dx.doi.org/10.17613/tg43-5n26

Nº 10   Curaçao 12th April 91
via New York

My dear Mother,

Once more I write you from Curaçao but this will likely be the last letter for some time from this little Dutch Island.

After posting my Nº 9. 3rd inst., I received your welcome letters of 9th & 16th Mar. When the New York mail arrives the P.O. officials require almost a whole day to sort & deliver it with the result that the homeward-bound steamer leaves before we get our letters, a system, – or want of system -, that would be speedily remedied in more civilised regions, as it entails the loss of 10 days in the exchange of correspondence with the States & Europe.

How do you get along with your "Edge-Hill" neighbours?

The Pond is a funny idea; surely a tennis-court would have been more to the purpose.

Just now your letter of 9th Feby. has been forwarded to me, having gone round by Barranquilla, & Cartagena. It contained enclosures from Emma, Olga & Jim with birthday wishes, for which, though they come rather late I am none the less grateful. I see I was wrong in blaming Emma, as I did in a recent letter, for not writing to me & I now humbly apologise.

There is now no blank in your weekly news from 26th Jany till 1th March.

Last week I was down in Maracaibo & just returned this morning. It was frizzingly hot there – it is the hottest place along the coast.[1] You know it was from Maracaibo that the wicked man came who died, went below & finding it chilly, sent back for his blankets.

I had made the same trip, two years before, on the S.S. "Merida", then called the "Maracaibo", & Captain Laksy, Chief-engineer Meyer, & Black Steward & factotum Thomas, were old friends of mine, so both on the downward & upward trip I was the distinguished passenger. The best cabin & the seat next to the Captain were given to me, & I had the run of the Captain's room. When Captain Laksy did not come to table, I was installed in his place by Thomas, so that the other twenty-five passengers looked upon me as a personage of some importance.

The run from Curaçao to Maracaibo takes about twenty-eight hours, & the return trip some six hours more owing to the stiff easterly winds & strong current. Leaving the island we make for the isthmus peninsula of Paranaguá, which is inhabited only by wild Indians among whom white men do not venture.[2] A curious phenomenon is to be seen here. At night, all the year round, there is a continuous play of brilliant sheet lightening over the interior of the peninsula. So regular & unremitting is this that it serves as a guide to passing vessels & is known as the "Lighthouse of Zulia". It is to be seen from many miles away all round, & yet when people approach the spot from where it seems to originate, it disappears.[3] Several explanations have been offered of this interesting phenomenon, – one that there are large oil-springs & coal beds in the vicinity giving off natural gas which ignites in spontaneous flashes, – another & more plausible

---

1. Maracaibo is the capital of the state of Zulia in northwestern Venezuela. For the lake: https://en.wikipedia.org/wiki/Lake_Maracaibo

2. Actually Paraguaná Peninsula

3. Catatumbo lightning is an atmospheric phenomenon that occurs over the mouth of the Catatumbo River where it empties into Lake Maracaibo in Venezuela. It originates from a mass of storm clouds at an altitude of more than 1 km, and occurs during 140 to 160 nights a year, nine hours per day, and from 16 to 40 times per minute: https://en.wikipedia.org/wiki/Catatumbo_lightning

one that the lightning is the evidence of electrical disturbances caused by the difference of temperature between the warm swampy ground & the cold water of the river Zulia which flows through it.[4] The river, always cool, is said turn ice-cold immediately after sunset, but this is probably a tale of some imaginative traveller, already passed into a popular belief.

Maracaibo lies half-way up the large bay of its own name – more like an inland lake than a bay. The entrance to this bay is a narrow & shallow bar which is constantly shifting, making Maracaibo the most dangerous port in this part of the world. Coming out we drew 10 feet 5in & the lead gave just 11 feet of water on the bar. As a rule the little steamer comes bumping over the sand, but this time we came in beautifully, without touching.

I spent only four days in Maracaibo & I was glad not to have to stay longer, on account of the heat & the bad hotel.

The food was bad & the place was infested with rats that scampered all over my bedroom all night long. I caught two one evening in a trap, & I could count them by the dozen as they ran up & down the walls & shutters & over the table. Add to that a plague of mosquitoes & you can form some idea of the paradise that Maracaibo forms for the passer through.

There is however a large German colony – mostly very nice fellows who live comfortably & well in their houses in the outskirts of the town.

One evening I went out with Mr von Jess[5], dined & slept at his house & returned to town early next morning, riding out & in on horseback, & the day before leaving I lunched with Mr Birtner.[6] Both these gentlemen are partners in the firm of Minlos Breuer & Co, the largest house in Maracaibo.[7] Mr Birtner has a beautiful "Hatico", as these country houses are called, on the shore of the lake. The garden is shaded by palms & tree-ferns & is bright with roses & other flowers, while half a dozen splashing fountains keep the air cool & the leaves green. A picturesque little bathing house stands out over the lake & above it is an American "wind-mill" pump which supplies the fountains & fills the cisterns.

Mrs Birtner is a native lady but Mr B. has trained her up in the way she should go, & she gave us an excellent luncheon, consisting of clear soup, haunch of venison, beefsteak, rice-cakes, delicious melon, mangos, bananas, & oranges, – a very agreeable change from the oily awfulness of the hotel. Before table we sat in the garden under the shade of a fine tree & drank the water or milk of a fresh cocoa-nut that the negro servant had fetched down & split open for us. The dining room is almost "al fresco" – open all round, with a light roof to keep the sun off. Climbing plants & tropical shrubs formed the walls, & bright-feathered birds hopped through the branches waiting for crumbs, while the humming birds sucked the many-coloured flowers. To see it & enjoy it all, even for a short time atoned for all the outside un-pleasantnesses.

Must post this now without waiting for the letters I hope to receive by mail just in.

Best love

Jack

4. Zulia River is a river in Venezuela and Colombia. It is a tributary of the Catatumbo River. The Zulia forms a small part of the international boundary between the two countries.
5. Probably Eduard von Jess (b 7th May 1863 Hamburg; m Ana Julia Lossada Diaz in Maracaibo; d 13th July 1935 Maracaibo) In the early 1900s he was a merchant with Breuer, Möller & Co, Maracaibo, which had split off in 1895 from Minlos, Breuer & Co. founded in 1860. He was also German Consul.
6. Friedrich Wilhelm Birtner (b 3rd February 1854 Bremen; m 15th December 1883 to Flor de Maia Baldo Jara).
7. Minlos, Breuer & Co is described in a research paper about German businesses in Maracaibo found on the Internet (in Spanish): "The Germans had majority control of the import-export trade of the port of Maracaibo. The most powerful German firms in the capital of Zulia were Blohm & Co. installed in this city in 1854 and Minlos, Breuer & Co. founded in 1860." https://de.wikipedia.org/wiki/Emil_Minlos

Casa Breuer, Möller & Cª

Breuer, Möller & Co,
Maracaibo (split off in
1895 from Minlos, Breuer
& Co. founded in 1860)

41. Letter from Caracas, 26th April 1891

18910426 See an image of the original letter, http://dx.doi.org/10.17613/mge6-kp55

Nº 11 Caracas, 26th April 1891

My dear Mother,

To-day I recvd. via New York, your welcome letter of 6th of this month, whereas your prior letters of 23rd & 30th March – counting one for each Monday – have not yet arrived, having been sent no doubt by Royal Mail via Southampton, a very slow & unsatisfactory route. I had also a letter from Addie to-day over which, he writes me, he fell asleep, as of old. He refused an invitation to a dance at Blacks' (this is "old news" to you), but has called there, & he seems still to prefer quiet visits to giddy hops.[1]

I arrived here a week ago & I expect to remain here for at least another ten days. Caracas is a large town & like the puffed out frog in the fable, believes itself to be much larger. People here put up to no end of style; – promising youths of 16 or 17 suffer themselves to be admired on the Promenade on Sunday afternoons resplendent in tailed coats, silk hats & patent-leather shoes. As for the ladies, their costumes are more striking & costly than those displayed in the Bois, if not quite so tasteful nor correct. There is a lot of money, – far too much – , spent here in keeping up outside appearances. To have a box in the theatre & to drive a carriage on Sunday afternoons the Caraqueños pre-eminently defraud their daily cheer.

We had a great whist session last night – Lieut. Welles U.S.N.,[2] whom you know already, Mr de Paulard, Mr Tripp of Trinidad,[3] & myself; – we played no less than nine rubbers with the gratifying result that I came out top score with plus forty-four points – which result was of course owing to the scientific principles of Cavendish rightly applied, & alas perhaps, to some slight extent, to the liberal supply of trumps which fell to my share.[4]

I send these few lines by Royal Mail, but I hope to find time & energy sufficient to prepare a longer letter for the American Steamer, – my favorite route.

Best love, Jack

c/o Smith Bros & Cº Trinidad[5]

---

1. "Blacks" = The couple to whose wedding JMcC and Addie went to in NYC in January 1891 (James Black and American Miss Russel). The groom probably related to the Black "heiresses" next door in Lennoxvale. See Index to People.
2. Roger Welles (b 1862, d 1932), see Index to People. US Naval Officer: https://en.wikipedia.org/wiki/Roger_Welles. In 1891 sent to Venezuela and the Guianas to explore the Orinoco River as U.S. special representative for the World's Columbian Exposition, Chicago, Ill. 1925-1926: Commander, U.S. Naval Forces in Europe (retired from Navy in 1926): https://snaccooperative.org/ark:/99166/w6gt77hq
3. (Albert) Edgar Tripp (b 1847 Kent, d 1921 Trinidad) emigrated to Trinidad in 1870 and established its "Electric Light and Power Company" in 1894. Co-author of *Fauna of Trinidad*.
4. Refers to the book Cavendish on *Whist, The Laws and Principles*, first published in 1862. "Cavendish" was the pen name of Henry Jones (b 1831, d 1899): https://www.gutenberg.org/ebooks/51039. He was a surgeon and general practitioner until 1869 when he became a full-time writer on sports and games. It was the must-have book on whist for a generation: https://www.wopc.co.uk/files/personalities-and-books-of-whist.pdf
5. Smith Bros & Co were traders of "dry goods, furnishing goods and miscellaneous articles" in Port of Spain, Trinidad. From *Reports from the Consuls of the United States 1892: Trade of Trinidad*.

42. Letter from Caracas, 6th May 1891

18910506 See an image of this letter, http://dx.doi.org/10.17613/3vbx-j588

Nᵒ 12   Carácas
6th May 1891

My dear Mother,

In my Nᵒ 11, by last Royal Mail, I promised to write again by following American Steamer leaving today, which promise I have not been able to keep, but there is a French boat leaving tomorrow which will only be a couple of days behind the New York mail, so I shall almost redeem my undertaking. But as it is after 11 p.m. already you must not be surprised if my letter reads sleepily. I have been running about this afternoon, with the thermometer at butter-melting point, & have talked & listened to a lot of "gas" – all in the interests of business.

After dinner I had to pay a visit & relate my travel's history to four pretty girls; – all of which is very fatiguing, though I am not unconscious of the high privilege of having such a fair audience.

Since sending my last I have recvd. your welcome letter of 12th April, but the two March letters are still missing.

Father will remember giving me the address of a young engineer called Bartels, a protégé of Aunt Emma's.[1] On enquiry I found he was working at a place called El Tigrito, distant some four hours' journey by rail & mule from Caracas.[2] I sent him a card, asking him to look me up should he come to the "Capital" during my stay. The following Sunday he came up expressly to call on me, & not finding me at home he waited till Monday. He seemed pleased to see me & paid me a long visit on Monday morning. I asked him to lunch with me & we had quite a long chat, during which he spoke very gratefully & affectionately of Aunt Emma. He seems a nice fellow; – works hard & takes great interest in his profession. He does not put much money to the good at present, but when his contract is ended with the Company, in another year & a half, he hopes to go in for the more lucrative branch of sub-contracting.

He intends sending Aunt Emma some photographs, which he has taken himself, of his surroundings at Tigrito, & he has also promised to send me some before I leave.

I shall be glad if Father will communicate this part of my letter to Aunt Emma.

I also made the acquaintance, the other day, of two young men called Letts, from Chile, who curious to say, are cousins of Prof. Letts.[3]

The reason I was not to be found on Sunday was that I had accepted an invitation to lunch at Mr & Mrs Eraso's country house, a short distance out of town. Mr Luis Eraso is a young man, partner in one of the leading firms here, educated at Oxford or Cambridge – I forget which, though he does not for he wears the arms of his college prominently on his gardening cap. In spite of that & one or two other little weaknesses in the direction of Anglo-mania he is a very nice fellow, & his wife, daughter of a former English minister to Bogotá, is an exceptionally nice woman.[4] There were about a dozen people present, all of whom spoke English; the luncheon was excellent & the conversation interesting, &

1. This is Emma Löwenthal, Julius' older sister in Ludwigslust – never married – born and died there (b 1831, d 1913). There were many Bart(h)els in Ludwigslust. Hard to know who her protégé was and what business he was doing in Venezuela.
2. Probably El Tigrito, Miranda, some 42 km away.
3. Edmund Algert Letts (b 27th August 1852, d 19th February 1918) was Professor of Chemistry at Queens College, Belfast 1879-1917: https://en.wikipedia.org/wiki/E._A._Letts
4. Luis Eraso, Merchant, (b~1855 Caracas, d Caracas 1899). He married Helen Baldock Bunch (b ~ 1855 in NYC).

altogether we spent four hours in the most pleasant manner. The house is large & tastefully furnished & the extensive grounds, – almost a Park – planted to advantage with orange-trees, bamboos, & avenues of mangoes.

After a cup of tea at four o'clock we walked back into town through the cool shade of a fine coffee plantation.

<u>7th May</u> <u>6.15 a.m</u>. I cannot resist noting the hour. You see the first worm runs a poor chance with me. But to be honest, I should still be in bed, had not that relentless ebony porter, Mr Santana, insisted on my turning out to receive a message about those photographs.

I hope to move on in a few days. Please address

c/o Da Costa C$^{\underline{o}}$ Barbados

Best love

Jack

43. Letter from Valencia, Venezuela, 17th May 1891

18910517 See an image of this letter, http://dx.doi.org/10.17613/sygq-xf31

Nº 13   Valencia,   Venezuela

17th May 1891

My dear Mother,

Some time after your letter of 12th April came the belated dispatches of 23rd & 29th March – the missing links of your to-be-relied on welcome weekly chain.

I have just arrived here & as it is Sunday the offices are closed, but tomorrow I hope to receive a fresh mail.

Valencia, Venezuela in 1895. Photograph by John Buchanan (1855-1948).

In Carácas I remained for nearly, – no, fully, three weeks, & I was tired of the place & glad to leave it. It is a fearfully expensive town, & good English sovereigns, which one is accustomed to look upon with a complacent conviction of their lasting solidity melt into nothingness with a slippery rapidity greater than that of the ice cream which threatened to become "all sauce" before its time. One has positively no pleasant sense of possession of them. They jingle once in your pocket & are gone, like a tale that is told, – not a serial story in penny weekly numbers, but short as the tail of Mark Twain's cow, which looked like a "bananer".[1] My room in the hotel cost 16/- a day, washing on the basis of one franc a shirt, cabs six shillings & something a drive or an hour, drinks at Sahara prices.

From La Guayra to Puerto Cabello I travelled with a Spanish Opera Company – a fifth-rate gang & a most unsavoury crowd.[2] I was lucky enough to find a quiet spot & a comfortable deck-chair on the steamer, behind the wheel & as the night was very warm. I did not go below at all, but smoked & slept in my chair alternately.

In Puerto Cabello I spent one evening with my kind friends, the Rodriguez family, & we played whist! Young Mrs Rodriguez had never played before, & my partner, Miss Rodriguez, persistently trumped my best cards, – not eights & nines, but kings & queens, – whereat I smiled & tried to look gratified.[3]

In the train this morning,[4] coming up to Valencia there was a pretty girl sitting opposite to me. At least I thought her pretty until I went out to smoke a cigarette &, coming back, found that she had calmly taken possession of my seat on the shady side of the carriage, leaving me to sit in the sun, & then I discovered that she was positively plain-looking. I offer this anecdote gratis to the Society for the Suppression of Cigarette-smoking. The moral is obvious.

There is not much change in these places since I was here before. Two Presidents have come & gone, the electric light has been introduced, & the proprietress of this hotel has refurnished the bedrooms; – there you have the History of Venezuela for 1889-91 epitomised.

I also noticed, on my way from the railway-station, a new public-house, with a conspicuous signboard in blue to inform the passer-by that this select place of refreshment is the "Restaurante Hight Life".

For primitiveness in domestic architecture the dwellings of the Indians & half-casts in Venezuela take the cake. From the simple hut of banana or palm-leaves there are many grades to the more pretentious mud-walled palace. Across the door of one of the latter I read this notice, in large black letters – "Use no hooks". This was not, as might be imagined by the ignorant an appeal to the higher feelings of an eventual burglar, but simply the original inscription on that door when it was not yet a door but merely the sack-clock covering a bale of English cottons.

I have made my plans to sail by French Steamer of 25th to Trinidad (28th), so I am now within a measurable distance of Plymouth. Fat the calf for killing & take one hour's exercise a day on the tennis-court.

21st May

I am just now having a high old time of it with a Crystal-Palace-firework-& traction-engine tooth-ache. For a couple of hours last night I paced the room like a tiger in the Zoo while perhaps my neighbours thought I was training for the walking championship of Venezuela, or writing poetry! This morning one of those dentist fellows who extract teeth without pain (to themselves) inserted a preparation to kill the nerve & give relief. He said I would soon be all right though the introductory process of nerve-killing might be a little unpleasant. I fancy the preliminary attack on the nerve

---

1. The end of Mark Twain's short story: "The celebrated Jumping Frog of Calaveras County." "At the door I met the sociable Wheeler returning, and he buttonholed me and recommenced: Well, thish-yer Smiley had a yaller one-eyed cow that didn't have no tail, only jest a short stump like a bannanner, and —", "Oh! hang Smiley and his afflicted cow!" I muttered, good-naturedly, and bidding the old gentleman good-day, I departed." http://www.eastoftheweb.com/short-stories/UBooks/CelJum.shtml
2. La Guaira is the capital city of the Venezuelan state of Vargas and the country's main port. It was founded in 1577 as an outlet for Caracas, 30 kilometres (19 mi) to the southeast.
3. The Rodriguez family are mentioned again in a much later letter dated 29th April 1894: "At Puerto Cabello, where our steamer also called, I went to see a Mrs Rodriguez with her son & daughter, who were very kind to me before."
4. The Puerto Cabello and Valencia railway is now defunct. The 55 km railway was constructed in the 1880s to link Valencia, then the country's second city, with the Caribbean port of Puerto Cabello. It closed in the 1950s: https://en.wikipedia.org/wiki/Puerto_Cabello_and_Valencia_railway

must be proceeding satisfactorily for the feeling is distinctly **a – little – unpleas**ant!! I imagine that dentist fellow is now chuckling & rubbing his hands. I should like to hire a competent person to swear for me, – payment by time, – liberal terms to an efficient applicant.

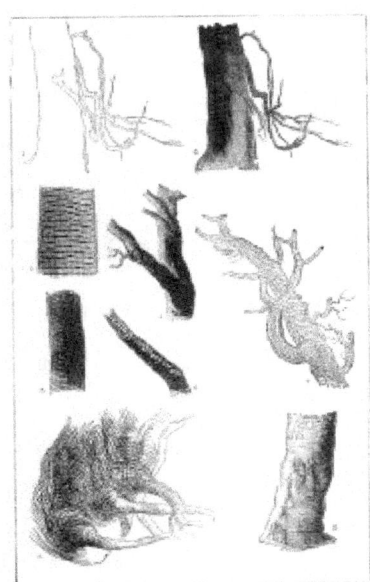

"Drawing of tree-stems" illustration from Modern Painters by John Ruskin, Volume III, 1856.

To distract my attention I tried to read Ruskin "On Truth of Vegetation", but only obtained momentary relief on learning that the trees in Jasper Poussin's pictures were "carrots & parsnips", – "elephant tusks with feathers tied to the end of them", & that a tree of Claude's was "a faithful portrait of a large boa-constrictor, with a handsome tail; the kind of trunk which young ladies at fashionable boarding-schools represent with nosegays at the top of them, by way of forest scenery."[5]

<u>21st May</u>   Later: as the Press Association telegrams say. Nerve is dead. R.I.P. is the fervent prayer of the surviver.

The rainy season is upon us in full force & it is now pouring as if it might never have a chance again. My room overlooks a large square, planted with palms, bamboo, magnolias, & other trees & the splashing of the heavy streams on the leaves makes a pleasant music, while the white light from the electric lamps is reflected in numberless glistening points from the quivering polished surfaces.

One night in Caracas I left the French window open & the rain came in from the balcony in rivers & filtered through the flimsy floor, improvising a shower bath for my neighbour below, the Baron de Wotdyekolim. This was but an earnest of favours to come, for next night while indulging in a little horseplay with Welles (Who shall ask after this "what's in a name?") I kicked over the water-jug, & sent the contents trickling down the opposite wall, over Mr de Wotdyekolim's artistically arranged photographs of professional beauties. He must have felt, in his despair, like Mr Mantalini, when he threatened to become a "damned, damp, miserable body."[6]

> In three days more I'm off to Trinidad.
> When I this letter to begin it had
> Not much, I thought, I to put in it had,
> And so, though thick, but matter thin it had.

What do you think of the rhyme?
Love to all
Jack

---

5. John Ruskin, "Of Truth of Vegetation," from *Modern Painters, Volume 1*, Section VI: https://www.gutenberg.org/files/29907/29907-h/29907-h.htm first published in 1843. Nosegay = a small bunch of flowers, typically one that is sweet-scented.
6. Alfred Mantalini is an idle profligate, husband of Madame Mantalini, in Dickens' *Nicholas Nickleby*. Part 6, Chapter 34, "'Alfred, you cruel, cruel creature,' said Madame Mantalini, sobbing at the dreadful picture. 'She calls me cruel--me--me--who for her sake will become a demd, damp, moist, unpleasant body!' exclaimed Mr Mantalini. 'You know it almost breaks my heart, even to hear you talk of such a thing,' replied Madame Mantalini."

PART IV

THE LETTERS: VOYAGE TO SOUTH AMERICA, 1892-1893

Map of the 1892-1893 voyage by John McCaldin Loewenthal. Note that JMcC refers to Brazilian cities by the names of the states that they are part of. These are shown in parentheses on the map. A high-res version is available online: https://doi.org/10.17613/2njh-xd74 (Original map by Thomas Bachrach)

44. Letter aboard S.S. Trent sailing from Southampton to Lisbon, 15th-18th July 1892

18920715 See an image of this letter, http://dx.doi.org/10.17613/2qz8-s681

N̲o̲ 1
S.S. "Trent"
In the Bay of Biscay oh!
Friday 15th July 1892

My dear Mother,

"Just before the battle" – I mean just starting forth on the deep "where the stormy winds do blow", I wrote you a few lines on a blue card, in pencil, & enclosed same in a white envelope.

I had previously sent a waiter to look for paper, pen & ink; – he brought me an inkstand & a pen but said he could not procure paper, adding significantly that he was not going on with the ship, & that he had the greatest difficulty in finding the inkstand. I gave him 6^d, dived into my own bag for the card & envelope, & found that the pen would not write, & the ink was a thick paste.

> "Oh for a touch of that vanished coin
> Or a word with the cove brought that quill".

The frontage of The Criterion restaurant in 1898.

I enjoyed my evening in London. Edgar & I dined at a nice little restaurant – The Burlington – in Regent St.[1] From a corner window we watched the crowd of people below. We had an excellent dinner for 3/6 each, – much better than what I had at the Criterion for 4/6. The youngster had instructions to pay all, but I w^d not let him.

Corney Grain's entertainment is well worth a visit.[2] First we had a musical farce in one act. A young "photographic artist", who considers himself insulted when called a photographer visits a tiny village & falls in love with the beadle's daughter. The pompous beadle afterwards appears on the scene & scents mischief when the artist declares himself a "roving vagabond" & avows that it was his intention to "take the village pump". The beadle (Corney Grain), fearing violence, beguiles the artist into the stocks by showing him the best seat from which to enjoy the view & inviting him to rest his legs on the board & make himself comfortable. The artist obligingly complies & the beadle shuts down the stocks on him & departs in triumph.

The beadle's son, a "charity boy" under an old bequest in the village comes in & being laughed at on acct. of his charity dress, retaliates by puffing at the artist with a pea-shooter, but is finally bribed to set free the prisoner.

The artist plots vengeance & writes to inform the Beadle that one of the trustees of the charity will come next day to

---

1. This is Edgar Löwenthal (b 1872), JMcC's first cousin (son of Julius' brother Ferdinand Adolphus of 205 Adelaide Road). JMcC refers to him as "the youngster" - in fact 8 years younger than JMcC (b 1864).
2. Richard Corney Grain (26th October 1844-16th March 1895), known by his stage name Corney Grain, was an entertainer and songwriter of the late Victorian era: https://en.wikipedia.org/wiki/Richard_Corney_Grain

inspect the schools. The Beadle is alarmed for his son & daughter are the only scholars, & the regulations provide that the charity shall lapse unless there are at least three boys or three girls on the list.

But he has a happy thought – dresses up his wife (who is a fish wife by reputation) & son as girls in the charity uniform, making with his daughter, three pupils. The artist, disguised as an elderly trustee, enters, & an amusing examination ensues.

Finally the disguise is detected – general forgiveness & finale, – union of artist & beadle's daughter – all photographed in a group.

Some of the songs are capital. The fish-wife's "Will you buy?" with a pretty waltz-chorus, is very taking, but perhaps the best is the trio "Twinkle, twinkle, little Star", sung before the Examiner by the two girl scholars prompted by the Beadle, in this way

Daughter: "Twinkle, twinkle little – "
Beadle (prompts): "Star"
Fishwife as Scholar (passes it on): "Star"
Daughter: "Star"",
"How I wonder what you – – "
Beadle: "Are"
Fishw: "Are"
Daughter: "Are"
& son on.

The second part of the entertainment is Corney Grain's musical sketch "My wife's party", – very funny & sarcastic; – a modern London crush & the people who go to it. The arrangements, the invitations, the arrivals, the people who make a habit of going to half a dozen parties in one evening. Recitation:

"We're going on, we're going on,
For ever & a day".

Song. An English ballad in dialect "Mrs 'Enry 'Awkins", – pronounced vulgar, but when turned into French or German – charming.

It was really one of the cleverest things I have heard for a long time – the translations – (first rate in themselves) sung with the little mannerisms of each country. He must be a first-rate linguist. Then a young lady's song with mandolin accompaniment; – "all young ladies accompany themselves on the mandolin now-a-days." – Skirt dance – so fashionable! Professional lions engaged from music- halls. A sentimental song in Italian.

The mob to get to the supper-room. The candid criticisms of the guests.

Altogether an evening's wholesome fun, much to be recommended.

Next morning I was early at Waterloo Station, but did not recognize anyone. Two fellows said they had seen me before, – one at Pernambuco, one in Buenos Aires, but I have no recollection.

Sat'day   Fortunately the steamer sailed from the dock, so we had no tender. The morning was fine & the channel calm – as was also the Bay y'day; – today there is some wind from the S.W. with "a bit of a sea", but just enough to make things lively & pleasant.

There are some 50-60 passengers. I have spoken to three or four who seem nice enough people, but I don't feel like getting chummy with many of the rest. I have seen only two ladies so far, – not attractive in either appearance or manners. The voyage will be a very quiet one. So much the better. It will give me a chance of writing & doing some work.

I have read two magazines & two shilling shockers already, besides three weekly periodicals.

The "Idler" is a good six-pence worth.[3] The witty-chatty article by Jerome – "Novel notes" is excellent. Discussion in the Author's club on the choice of a heroine. Is she to be good or bad? "Bad, said MacShaugnassy, good heroines are less interesting; no uncertainty about what they'll do." "Not altogether bad" said Jephson. "Bad, with good instincts, the good instincts well under control."

Interesting dissertation on standard of goodness in different nations & at various times. MacShaugnassy puts his feet on the mantelpiece & tilts back his chair to an angle that causes the rest to rivet their attention on it with <u>hopeful interest</u> (!). Says fashionable virtue slumming, "so all our best heroines go slumming". Tells story; – quiet village, – new curate, – bachelor, – private income, – all the unmarried ladies went for him, – he was heard to say w$^{\underline{d}}$ not be attracted by beauty, but by Charity & kindliness to poor, – serious difficulty, – only one poor person in parish - cantankerous old fellow – eleven girls, three old maids, & a widow, wanted to be "good" to him, – fed him on jelly, portwine, chicken, oysters – got so fat couldn't go through his own back door – made them buy his baccy & fetch his beer – they subscribed for harmonium – he didn't want serious music – made them sing "Winked the other eye" with chorus & skirt-dance. Sudden Collapse – curate marries beautiful burlesque actress, & poor man goes to workhouse.

There are several other good articles, notably one by "The American Colonel" on Railroad Travelling, & some humorous notes at the end by the "Idlers".

The Strand Magazine is also good value. Interview with G.A. Sala, full of anecdote.[4] History of Mont Blanc from first ascent in 1786 till today, with an account of some of the accidents that have taken place on it. Fable of American railway porter who dies from vexation because he meets one trunk which he is unable to smash; it is afterwards found the trunk was filled with sandwiches & buns from an English railway refreshment room.

I don't think I shall have any whist. There are some fellows playing whist – of a kind – in the smoke-room, but they don't know the elements. I played three games of chess – won two after hard fight, third was a draw.

The cake is still in the tin; will be produced after Lisbon.

The water is pleasantly warm already. I began with joy my salt-water tub on the first morning.

<u>Lisbon</u>   Monday morning 18th July

We passed Sat'day night in Vigo bay, – went ashore for an hour next morning. Sunday aft'noon we called at Leixoes, new harbour for Oporto with fine breakwater. Made only short stay there to pick up emigrants.

Just arrived at Lisbon. I shall go ashore after breakfast.

I hope some letters will come for me by mid-day mails. Perhaps I shall write from Las Palmas.

Best love to all

Jack

3. *The Idler* was an illustrated monthly magazine published in Great Britain from 1892 to 1911. It was founded by the author Robert Barr, who brought in the humorist Jerome K. Jerome as co-editor, and its contributors included many of the leading writers and illustrators of the time: https://en.wikipedia.org/wiki/The_Idler_(1892%E2%80%931911)

4. George Augustus Henry Fairfield Sala (November 1828–1895) was an author and journalist who wrote extensively for the *Illustrated London News* as G. A. S. and was most famous for his articles and leaders for *The Daily Telegraph*. He founded his own periodical, *Sala's Journal*, and the Savage Club. The former was unsuccessful but the latter still continues: https://en.wikipedia.org/wiki/George_Augustus_Sala

45. Letter on the S.S. Trent from Las Palmas to Pernambuco, 30th July 1892

18920730 See an image of this letter, http://dx.doi.org/10.17613/05jx-m861

S.S.Trent

Pernambuco   30th July 1892

My dear Mother,

From Las Palmas I sent you a few lines some eight days ago. I saw quite a number of old friends there & was gratified at finding myself very kindly remembered. Kölkenbeck was not there, having gone with his wife to Teneriffe.[1] They have lost their baby, & Mrs K. was naturally very much cut up, & in ill health as well, so they went for a change to the other Island.

Rutherford who came out a month ago looks much stronger already, & likes the place.[2] He is working hard at Spanish.

Mr Carlo & his family were surprised to see me. They were very kind to me when I was in Canaries before, so I paid them quite a long visit this time & had a chat about old times.

I saw half a dozen other people & promised, of course, to spend a fortnight in the Canaries, should I pass that way again.

We are having a very quiet time on board. Cricket is the chief amusement. The bat was made by the carpenter out of a piece of heavy wood. The wickets fit into three holes in a square piece of board. The ball, made of twine & waste very tightly rolled, is fastened to a string the other end of which is tied to the rail half way down the deck. So when the ball goes overboard it is not lost. I was lucky enough to make the biggest score the first day & since then I have lived on my reputation.

There are three or four very good fellows on board. One is a man called Whitehorn, a big chap with splendid shoulders, just my age, who has had some tough experiences. He went to a ranche in Australia when he was 17, & he has since had rough & varied adventures in Paraguay, Brazil, & the Argentine. With it all he is a gentleman & he has not gone back. He sits beside me at table & entertains me with bits of his history.

We have some funny whist. One of our players is a Mr Goodwin, a middle-aged but athletic man, who has travelled over most of Europe, – I don't know in what capacity. He plays fairly, but the other two know nothing of the game, & if we don't have whist according to Cavendish, we at all events have some fun. These two fellows play the most extraordinary cards & give the most extraordinary reasons for playing them. Goodwin & I express great admiration for their excellent reasons & deep laid plots, when sometimes it is with the greatest difficulty that we can maintain our gravity.

1. "Kölkenbeck": one of 2 brothers – both merchants and naturalized British subjects, and resident in Belfast. Either: (1) Eduard (Edward) William Emil Kölkenbeck (b June 1865) who was resident in Belfast, 26 Ponsonby Avenue and listed as a "Commercial Traveller." He married Marion Frances Atkin in Frankfurt am Main in 1891 (it is likely to be him as his name appears on the ship manifesto returning to Southampton from Las Palmas in 1896) or (2) Alfred Edward Julius George Kolkenbeck ("Commercial Clerk") born in Germany (b~ 1864). See Index to People.
2. W Rutherford was on the passenger list of "British & Africa Navigation Company Limited" 4th June 1892, sailing from Liverpool to Teneriffe.

Another source of amusement has been the "Trent Gazette", a newspaper published bi-weekly on board. We all contributed articles & a few volunteers did the printing with a type-writer. Some of the items were very good.

It has not been so hot this time, as on previous voyages. One day we had 80° in the shade – that was the highest; – & it usually goes up to about 90° near the line.

The ship dances about considerably, & without reasonable cause, for we have had nothing but fair N.E. & S.E. trade-winds & very little sea. I have been able to keep the porthole in my cabin open almost the whole time – a very great matter when the thermometer stands at 80°.

The plum-cake is first rate. Several passengers privileged to taste it have spoken & proved their appreciation & the cake is now almost done.

I find the pipe G.Y.K. gave me, & your capacious tobacco-pouch very useful & comforting.[3]

On landing to-morrow at Pernambuco I suppose we shall have some political & other news from England by cable. All we heard at Las Palmas was that Gladstone had a majority of 42.[4]

From Buenos-Ayres I shall write on thinner paper. The postage on this w$\underline{^d}$ be too expensive if I had matter sufficient to fill a longer letter than this uninteresting communication.

The main object of this is, however, to tell you it leaves me well, "hoping as how it will find you all the same".

Best love.

Jack

3. G.Y.K. = George Young Kinnaird (see Index to People).
4. Refers to 11th August 1892 vote of no confidence in the Conservative government moved by the Liberal Party:
   https://en.wikipedia.org/wiki/1892_vote_of_no_confidence_in_the_Salisbury_ministry

46. Letter from S.S. Trent while docked in Rio Janeiro, 4th August 1892

18920804 See an image of this letter, http://dx.doi.org/10.17613/j50q-j482

Per "Iberia"   Rio Janeiro   4th Aug. 1892

My dear Mother,

You see we have come so far all right – approaching the end of our voyage. I sent you a letter from Pernambuco. We reached Rio this morning & here we leave most of our passengers; – only 5 or 6 go on to the Plate.[1] I have just seen one friend & former fellow-passenger – young Youle, & I have accepted his invite to dine & spend the night with him as I did when going North.[2] Just now I am waiting in the agent's office to see a Dundee customer & as a mail leaves tonight I am turning the moments of enforced idleness (South American punctuality providing, as I well know, only too many of these) to good account in sending you "all's well" from the look-out. The "Trent" proceeds to-morrow & this day week I hope our somewhat tiresome voyage will have ended. I saw quite a number of old friends in Pernambuco & was very kindly welcomed. Young Gilroy, whom I met a few days before leaving Dundee, at dinner at Taylor's, came with the "Trent" from Pernam. to Bahia.[3] Some enthusiastic cricketers on board wanted to play a cricket-match against Bahia, & had wired a challenge from Pernam. to the English Club. My services were requisitioned, but the the match did not take place, the Club having received the telegram too late to make arrangements.

A final number or the "Trent Gazette" appeared y'day – the best of all. I contributed a skit on our whist party, entitled "Mr Prattle's" Opinions on Whist" (after Charles Lamb) which was much applauded & laughed at. The author preserved a strict incog. & made fun of himself as well as the rest, by way of blind; – as for instance "Mr Long-and-tall followed suit. He always followed suit, for he prided himself on playing whist according to Cavendish. But first he made himself comfortable by putting one leg out of the window of the smoking-room, & the other through the door on the opposite side". Mr Prattle I think I mentioned in a previous letter. He talked incessantly, from morning till night, & played the most extraordinary whist, so he was fair game, & he took all jokes good-naturedly. His real name is Williams & he drank a great deal of champagne & seltzer becoming rather lively at times in consequence, though he never forgot himself. Someone

---

1. The Río de la Plata, named River Plate in British English, is the estuary formed by the confluence of the Uruguay and the Paraná rivers at Punta Gorda. It empties into the Atlantic Ocean, forming a funnel-shaped indentation on the southeastern coastline of South America. Depending on the geographer, the Río de la Plata may be considered a river, an estuary, a gulf or a marginal sea. It is the widest river in the world, with a maximum width of 220 kilometres (140 mi). It is about 290 kilometres (180 mi) long and forms part of the border between Argentina and Uruguay, with the major ports and capital cities of Buenos Aires and Montevideo on its western and northern shores, respectively. The coasts of the river are the most densely populated areas of Uruguay and Argentina: https://en.wikipedia.org/wiki/R%C3%ADo_de_la_Plata

2. There were two Youle brothers, both "south American Merchants". Both of them died in Rio de Janeiro. (1) Frederick Louis Youle (b 1857, d Dec 1900), (2) Frank (Schwind) Youle (b 1866, d March 1900). I suspect the younger one was JMcC's greater friend. See Index to People for further details.

3. Not sure who Gilroy was but "Taylor of Dundee" is John Brown Taylor, of Affleck Castle, Monikie, Dundee (see Index to people). Linen and Jute Manufacturer& Merchant. Taylor was b 5th December 1853, m Julie Anne née Duff (b~1859), d 19th May 1932.

wrote some verses about him, – very funny, if perhaps of doubtful taste; – they began "You are boozed, Father Williams" – You know the original of the parody.[4]

Today & to-morrow I mean to look up the McKinnels, Allens, & other friends.[5] My next will be from B. Aires, to which place you can write. Best love

Jack

I send best birthday wishes to Addie.[6] I shall write to him soon – but too late for his fête.

4. The reference is to the poem by Lewis Carroll, published in 1865 in *Alice's Adventures in Wonderland*: https://en.wikipedia.org/wiki/You_Are_Old,_Father_William
5. McKinnels were mentioned before in JMcC's letter of 17 August 1890. He is English, she American. See Index to People.
6. Addie's (his younger brother – see index to people) upcoming birthday is on 23rd August – would have been his 27th (JMcC is 28 ½ when writing).

47. Letter from Buenos Aires, 13th August 1892

18920813 See an image of this letter, http://dx.doi.org/10.17613/kaj1-hg35

Headed notepaper: CASILLA DEL CORREO 226
Buenos Aires, 13th Aug.......de 189 2

N.º 1

My dear Mother,

Here I am at last in the old digs. Julian looks well, but is very neuralgic.[1] When the warm weather comes I expect he will feel better, & that will be very soon now; in fact it has almost begun, for the last two days have been perfect. We were off the Ensenada port by day-break of the 11th, but what with the health-visit, the delay of the special train, & the custom-house it was after three when we reached our lodgings. They look very nice now. Julian has made them brighter by draping the top of the piano with a piece of grey-blue cloth, & adding to the furniture a book-stand, & to the nicknacks some photographs, two lamps, ink-stands, & a china afternoon tea-set, – the last a present from a lady.

Julian got his presents on his 21st birthday, & was much pleased therewith.[2] I stood him – along with our companion in digs, Ferguson, the other 29th Feby.[3] man – a dinner in the Café de Paris, & we drank many happy returns to him in a bottle of fiz.

There is not much change in B. Aires in the last few months. The big boulevard, projected through the centre of the town, has advanced a block & one house in our street has been re-painted. Those are the only noticeable improvements.

At the same time there seems to be a little more stir in the streets & people tell me trade is improving. The revenue returns for the first half of this year are double what they were in the corresponding half of 1891, & the imports in the same time, excluding railway-materials have increased 50%. If they have only political quiet the country will come forward again. I only hope it will do so gradually & not too suddenly. We have had enough of booms here, & the Argentines easily lose their heads.

I want to write a line to the Pater, so this, my first from B. Aires, must be short. I hope you got my letter from Rio. I spent the night there with Youles & had a good game of whist.[4] McKinnels & Allens were out of town.[5]

Best love to all.

Jack

The p.o. box is now 226. But all letters hitherto addressed to 2260 will come right.

1. Julian Weinberg (see Index to People)
2. Julian Weinberg born 12th August 1871
3. Ferguson. Born on 29th February as JMcC – he appears in other letters too.
4. The Youle brothers – both merchants in Rio de Janeiro. See Index to People.
5. McKinnels, Allens: see Index to People.

48. Letter from Buenos Aires, 15th August 1892

18920815 See an image of this letter, http://dx.doi.org/10.17613/prk4-1e38

N⁰ 2   Casilla del Correo 226
"Trent"   *Headed notepaper:*   *Buenos Aires,..15th August.....de 189 2*

My dear Mother,

I wrote you by Pacific Mail two days ago. To-day is a holiday – lady-day is it not? – nevertheless I have been trotting round this morning & I have to see a man again at half past two. Till then I have three quarters of an hour & on the principle of "always doing something" I begin my rambling weekly for the "Trent", & so turn the spare minutes to some account. To be honest – this ceaseless activity is not perhaps my most remarkable characteristic, – but I am fresh on the field after a four-weeks' voyage, with a reserve fund of energy, & I must make it last for at least a day or two.

Last night we dined at Mortlocks'.[1] In a rash moment I volunteered to carve a turkey which our host was making rather a botch of. I prospected for the joint of the wing, & "fooled around" it for five minutes; – then I gave it up & helped the company to breast, of which there was luckily enough to go round. Meanwhile I joined in the conversation with a would-be-easy indifference. "The Opera, oh yes, very fine! (blow the tough old patriarch) – very pretty song indeed! (drat the flirty veteran). Yes, she gets up well, but she's not so young as she looks (May the old gentleman fly away with this turkey) – Inaudible asides in parentheses.

As we are dining out so often now, our "patron" gives us extra good breakfasts. Today, after fish & ragout, a plump martineta (a bird between a woodcock & a pheasant) roasted on toast with bacon, "a pretty dish to set before a king".[2] There is a Cinderella on Wed. evg. Julian is trying hard to beg, borrow, or steal a ticket for me, but I am afraid he is too late in the field.[3] The number of tickets is limited & all have been divided. I should like to go, for not a few people will be there whom I should like to meet again; besides I still enjoy an occasional hop.

This morning I had my hair cut. The artistic barber applied the curling-irons to the ends of my moustache & gave them a ferocious military {moustache – see illustration below}. I had to think of coffins & bones & other grave subjects to keep from laughing at myself & him.

Sketch by JMcC of his amusingly "military" moustache, as styled by a barber in Buenos Aires. Included in the letter from Buenos Aires of August 15th 1892.

1. Mortlock – unable to identify.
2. The elegant crested tinamou or martineta (*Eudromia elegans*) is a medium-sized game bird that can be found in southern Chile and Argentina in shrubland: https://en.wikipedia.org/wiki/Elegant_crested_tinamou
3. Julian Weinberg (see Index to People).

In this connection it is worth chronicling that Julian had a warm bath y'day. He renewed his youth like the eagle, & is now practising the pas-de-quatre behind me.

Time's up. "On! Stanley, on! were the last words of Higginbotham".

<u>16th Aug.</u>   Last night we dined with Roesli; – the first time on record.[4] He is not given to hospitality – though perhaps it is not fair to say so the day after being his guests. But he does not like spending the bawbees. His partner, Meili, told me once that when the firm did an extra good stroke of business, he, Meili, indulged in a pint of champagne with his lunch, while Roesli treated himself to a fried egg with his steak.[5] All the same we had a fine fat turkey, – of which a neighbour had made him a present. This evg. I dined with Darmstätter, our stock-broker-boating friend of the Tigre. We did <u>not</u> have turkey.

The general consensus of opinion seems to be that Argentina is round the corner. The value of land is up 25% – I am told – since this time last year. I wish I had a lot of land in or near Buenos Aires just now; – nevertheless I am not going to speculate, my reserve fund not being sufficient to warrant that little excitement.

The crops promise magnificently, but they are still very young, & much may happen before they are gathered in. There has been a plentiful rainfall & the weather now is perfect. The area under cultivation is larger than ever before.

Today I met a former fellow-passenger, Mr Angus, who invited me to visit him on his estancia early next month. – No time.

I hope you are all lively

Best love

Jack

Eudromia Elegans from W. H. Hudson (1893), Idle Days in Patagonia.

4. Eugen Roesli, b 15th February 1857 in Zurich (see Index to People). Of "Meili & Roesli" listed as "commission merchants" in Buenos Aires in the *International Bureau of the American Republics Argentina Handbook*, 1894
5. August(o) Meili, b 1853 in Zurich (see Index to People)

49. Letter from Buenos Aires, 22nd August 1892

18920822 See an image of this letter, http://dx.doi.org/10.17613/9pbf-x180

N.° 3

Headed notepaper: Buenos Aires, 22nd August....de 189 2

My dear Mother,

I wrote a long business letter to the firm y'day. & enclosed a few lines to Addie, but I had not time to write to you since my last by "Trent" – 15th Aug.[1] Three days ago I recvd. your welcome letters of 18th & 19th July, & to-day came that of 24th, as well as a long & newsful letter from Father, all in good spirits, so I was very glad to have them, & to learn that the result of the half-year was satisfactory, all things considered, & that expenditure was less. We must continue keeping latter down & working to improve the "biz", so as to put something to the good.

I hope to hear from Julie, after his return from Strone, how he got along, & whether he tried the fishing; – also how you liked the place.[2] In a letter to Julian[3] Mr W. says he has just been made J.P. for the county.[4] When the Conservatives come in again I suppose the next blushing honour will be "Sir" Isaac Julius.

Just now the Pater will be about starting for Russia. I hope he will secure bookfuls of orders & come home well & cheerful, & with whole shins.

No doubt the girls had a good time at Laurelvale.[5]

I hear Buckby is now in Rosario in a railway office.[6] I shall get his address & try to see him when I go there. Sorry not to have made Gideon's acquaintance, but shall perhaps have that pleasure some day in Berlin.

The first rush of dinner invitations is over now I am glad to say. Over-eating, if persevered in steadily is apt to upset the stomach.

23rd Aug. 11 p.m. I note the time so that you may observe that my industrious fit still lasts.

I have just come from the "office" (a back-room first floor, in the business centre) where I was doing my official correspondence. Massa Julian is out visiting. I think I shall send him up to the camp for a week, to let him have a little change, as his neuralgic headaches have returned.[7]

1. Addie: JMcC's brother (Ferdinand) Adolphus (see Index to People)
2. His brother Julius (see Index to People). Strone is a village on the Cowal peninsula in Argyll and Bute in the Scottish Highlands at the point where the north shore of the Holy Loch becomes the west shore of the Firth of Clyde. The village lies within the Loch Lomond and The Trossachs National Park. Julie may have gone there with the Weinbergs https://en.wikipedia.org/wiki/Strone,_Cowal
3. Julian Weinberg (see Index to People)
4. Mr W.: Isaac Julius Weinberg, founding partner of "Moore and Weinberg" in Dundee, father of Julian – see Index to People.
5. Laurelvale is a village in County Armagh, Northern Ireland. It was founded in the 1850s by Thomas Sinton JP (1826–1887) to house the workers in his linen mill of Thomas Sinton & Co. Ltd, which was in the village: https://en.wikipedia.org/wiki/Laurelvale and https://en.wikipedia.org/wiki/Thomas_Sinton (Sinton family: see Index to People
6. The Buenos Aires and Rosario Railway (BA&R) was the second largest British-owned railway company in Argentina by the 1890s and was effectively challenging the Central Argentine's monopoly of the north-west of the country: https://en.wikipedia.org/wiki/Buenos_Aires_and_Rosario_Railway
7. the camp = "el campo", the Argentine countryside

Two Whigs came out y'day.[8] I have only read one so far. I notice in it the death of William Campbell, Elmwood Avenue. Is that the old sexton?

A tennis-club has been started here since I left. There are four good earth courts, the lines marked by metal-tape, painted white. I had three sets with Julian the other day – very good exercise. I should like to have more of it, but I have not time to play more than once a week. The telegraphing to & from Dundee has already begun.[9] To-day they want to know what are the crop prospects, – not an easy question to answer when the wheat is just showing itself above ground & no more, with all the possibilities of bad weather, locusts, & so on. I am not going to begin another sheet so bye-bye. Best love

Jack

8. *The Northern Whig* newspaper. Its editorial line was liberal and unionist and it was seen as reflecting a Presbyterian slant on the news: https://en.wikipedia.org/wiki/Northern_Whig

9. "to and from Dundee" = i.e. the Moore and Weinberg office.

50. Letter from Buenos Aires, 28th August 1892

18920828 See an image of this letter, http://dx.doi.org/10.17613/km0w-hw02

N.º 4   "Thames"

Headed notepaper: *Buenos Aires,..28th Aug....de 189 2*

My dear Mother,

Another week's hard work, an afternoon's tennis, & cold weather. That is all I have to relate, compressed into one line, instead of being judiciously spun out to fill three pages. I shall pass lightly over the hard work, lest you should think it unusual by my dwelling on it, & I shall enlarge on the tennis to impress you with the conviction that the moments of relaxation are rare. There are four excellent courts at the club, laid with brick-dust sand. The lines are marked by thin slips of iron, such as are used for hooping bale, painted white.

> Writer: "It through my memory flashes
> I've said all this before;
> The thought me quite abashes
> Your pardon I implore."
> Polite Recipient:
> "Don't mention it! Your words are pearls, & greeted
> As like-sized gems in golden coil repeated."

Very civil of you to say so I'm sure, – but to proceed: – there is a swagger pavilion–grandstand–verandah– edifice on one side, &, on the other, excellent dressing-rooms, with luxurious shower-baths & so on. The founders of the Club came forward very generously & defrayed the cost, – one of the timber, another of the plumbing, another of the labour, so that the young institution was not burdened at the start. Balls sometimes go over the wall into the street & then someone must promptly run up the ladder to the "look-out", while the "fielder" goes round by-the door. If the first is not very quick the ball has disappeared into somebody's pocket long before the second has arrived on the scene. Today one was lost in this way & we strongly suspected the guardian of the public morals – the bobby at the corner – of having secreted it about his person in a moment of absent-mindedness.

There is to be a tournament on Tuesday next, for which Julian has entered. I was giving him some practice to-day.

And now to my third topic, the weather. For the last four or five days getting out of bed in the mornings has been an act requiring the courage, & indifference to physical discomfort, of a Spartan. At half past seven one awakes to a sense of the agreeable warmth of the blankets & the nippingness of the outer air. This pleasant consciousness is mingled with the melancholy realization that "it is time to get up", but the latter conviction is of slow growth & takes quite fifteen minutes to come to maturity.

> "And thus the native hue of resolution
> Is sicklied o'er with the pale cast of thought",

till a war-whoop from the next room announces that "the Mr Ferguson" is stirring. "How are **you**, Mr Loewenthal, &

how's the boy? – pretty well?", & with an answering "**Oh** yes!" I jump out to the middle of the floor, while "the boy" utters a deprecating grunt & turns over for another five minutes.

The late telegrams from Europe bring very bad news of the cholera epidemic.[1] In Hamburg the people seem to be in a state of panic & I see that one or two cases have occurred in London & in Aberdeen. I now take it for granted that the Pater will not have gone to Russia this year, perhaps not even to Berlin. Business must be at a stand-still in all the infected places.

The authorities here are adopting rigorous precautions to prevent the introduction of the disease. Quarantine has been declared for all vessels from Hamburg, Havre, Antwerp, & various other ports, & if the epidemic becomes worse it is quite possible they may refuse altogether to admit vessels coming from those places. But the summer is well advanced in Europe, & the colder weather will soon come, I trust, & gradually stamp out the plague.

A cholera disinfection team with their cart and buckets, Hamburg 1892

There has been a little flutter in Argentine politics this week. President Pelegrini was at loggerheads with the Chamber of Deputies & wanted to resign, but the president-elect, Dr Saenz Peña, would not take office before the appointed date; – everybody patted everybody else on the back – & everybody felt virtuous & happy. Which means, being translated, that Pelegrini withdrew his resignation & the cloud has rolled by for the time being, but the political atmosphere is still far from clear, & there are "rumors of wars".[2]

In Venezuela they are still cutting each other's throats, as last year they did in Chile. They are a pretty kettle of fish, these South American republics.[3] And now they are organizing balls & banquets in Valparaiso & Santiago to celebrate the anniversary of the decisive battle in the late civil war!

---

1. The cholera pandemic of 1881–1896 was the fifth major international outbreak of cholera in the 19th century. It spread throughout Asia and Africa, and reached parts of France, Germany, Russia, and South America. The 1892 outbreak in Hamburg, Germany, was the only major European outbreak; about 8,600 people died in that city.
2. The Argentine presidential election of 1892 was held on 10 April to choose the president of Argentina. Luis Sáenz Peña was elected president. He was inaugurated president on 12 October 1892. https://en.wikipedia.org/wiki/1892_Argentine_presidential_election; https://en.wikipedia.org/wiki/Luis_S%C3%A1enz_Pe%C3%B1a
3. The Chilean Civil War of 1891 (also known as the Revolution of 1891) was a civil war in Chile fought between forces supporting Congress and forces supporting the President, José Manuel Balmaceda. It lasted from 16th January 1891 to 18th September 1891. The war saw a confrontation between the Chilean Army and the Chilean Navy, which sided with the president and the congress, respectively. After the battle of Placilla, it was clear to President Balmaceda that he could no longer hope to find a sufficient strength amongst his adherents to maintain himself in power, and in view of the rapid approach of the rebel army he abandoned his official duties to seek asylum in the Argentine legation. On August 29th, he officially handed power to General Manuel Baquedano, who maintained order in Santiago until the arrival of the congressional leaders on the 30th: https://en.wikipedia.org/wiki/Chilean_Civil_War_of_1891

I just now recvd. your welcome letter of 2nd Aug. from Strone, & I am glad to have all your news.[4] I hope the change of air will have done you both good, also Julie from whom I suppose I shall have a letter soon. Miss Patullo is pleasant & chatty, is she not?[5] The primrose-league day must have been "great"[6] Wish I had been there to chaffy Mr W. – with all due respect – about the "intelligent cultivation of disinterested conservative principles by a generous distribution of tea & buns". Wouldn't I have got it hot!

Bye-bye. Love all round.

Jack

4. Probably with the Weinbergs.
5. Miss Patullo: See Index to People. Initially mentioned in the letter from Buenos Aires on 15th June 1890. She was friendly with the Weinbergs and at Fred Weinberg's coming of age dance at Fernbrae.
6. The Primrose League was an organisation for spreading Conservative principles in Great Britain. It was founded in 1883: https://en.wikipedia.org/wiki/Primrose_League

51. Letter from Buenos Aires, 4th September 1892

18920904 See an image of this letter, http://dx.doi.org/10.17613/kmd1-tx40

Nº 5

"Portugal"

Headed notepaper: *Buenos Aires,   4th Sept..........de 189 2*

My dear Mother,

My last went by "Thames". – Five letters in three weeks. – Really I am spoiling you! The worst of it is I am almost in as sorry a plight as Julian, who sits down opposite me each mail day, dutifully to write to his Father & Mother, brothers, sisters, & friends, who have sent him letters by the last hitherward mail, & asks me every five minutes with an air of hopeless vacancy on his face: – "What shall I say?" If I had not him to write about I don't know what I should do.

The other evening we had asked two friends to dinner. Julian always does the carving – Ferguson & I are too lazy – & we had a laugh at his expense. A roast fowl was brought in & Julian hacked away at it in several places for some time, until he discovered that it was upside down & that he had been trying to cut slices off the backbone! When a clean cloth is laid we always implore him to control his wrists & elbows & the gravy spoon, until sometimes he gets quite riled.

He goes to-morrow to Sērēs' estancia for a week or ten days. Now that I am here to look after the business he can take a holiday, & I think it will do him good. His headaches have been rather bad of late.

Last night we went to Lomas, a small town, almost half English about three-quarters of an hour by train from Buenos Aires, to hear a concert.[1] Mrs Gould sang, very well, "Goodnight" – a beautiful song, & as an encore, "Il Baccio". I spoke to her during the Interval, & she kindly asked me to dine with them on Thursday week – their "at home" night. After the concert there was a little farce, the most amusing part of which was the singing in well-sustained falsetto of the young fellow who was dressed as the heroine. He sang "Some Day" in clear soprano tones, making the shakes by moving his hand before his lips, & giving the last two notes of each verse in the deepest base. There were lots of topical hits & excruciating puns which caused plenty of laughter. The Miss Agars were there,[2] & the Hirschbergs,[3] with Miss Sanders, – not many others I knew. By the way you may perhaps remember my mentioning Miss Sanders's water-drinking capacity. Beer has christened her "Nada, the Water-Lily." Lovely! isn't it?   You ought to pass it on to Dundee, they would enjoy it.

I have another dinner to eat to-morrow chez Martinez. Young Mr has been three years at King's College, London, & came out by the "Trent". His people are, I understand, one of what the local papers call the "familias distinguidas de Buenos Aires".

Yet another invitation has been promised me: – to join a personage of a no smaller degree than the President-elect – Dr Saenz Peña[4] – & party in an excursion to visit a new national industry, the paper-mill at Zarate, some three hours by

---

1. Lomas is ca. 20 km south of the centre of Buenos Aires. Prior to 1910, when it was given city status, Lomas de Zamora was a residential town with a large British colony: https://www.britannica.com/place/Lomas-de-Zamora-county-seat-Argentina
2. Probably the twins, Catherine (later married Shearer), and Clementina Agar (later married Neild) b 23rd March 1872 in Blythswood, Glasgow. Their parents were John and Anne Maria Agar (nee Forrester), both listed in the Argentina National Census of 1895. Father, John Agar, was born in Ireland ~1829. He was a Cotton Goods Commission Merchant.
3. Edward Hirschberg (Merchant) was naturalized in Dundee in 1887. See Index to People.
4. Luis Sáenz Peña was elected president on 10 April 1892, and was inaugurated president on 12 October.

train distant from B. Aires.[5] There will be luncheon & dinner provided, with champagne ad. lib., good cigars & so on. If the invite comes I shall certainly accept it, & then I shall have something to write about.

The welcome warmth has come since I wrote last. We can leave the windows open during dinner, & a cold shower-bath is a pleasure, not as before – undergone from a sense of duty.

I am glad to see that the latest telegrams announce that cholera is decreasing in Europe & that so far it has not invaded England. Here they have quarantined vessels from almost everywhere, & Mr Meili[6] is just now (& will before the next 8 days) kicking his heels in the Lazaretto at Flores Island.[7] The authorities have become exceedingly energetic about drainage, whitewashing, & water supply, so that the scare is productive of some good. At present the public health is excellent in this town. No typhoid, small-pox, measles, nothing! About one third of the old town, & all the new, are drained according to the most modern system of sanitary science, & in about eighteen months this system will have been extended over the whole of Buenos Ayres, making it one of the healthiest towns in the world, as far as science can help; – & very different from what it was five years ago. So I am told by Ferguson who is one of the engineers under Government in connection with the water supply. The water furnished to the city is taken from the Riv. Plate & passed through an elaborate series of filters before going into the pipes.

Political parties are again at loggerheads chiefly owing to personal ambitions, & the way is not being made smooth for the incoming President.

I have spoken.

Best love to all

Jack.

For the Pater: – A small order will go by next mail from Petit y Piria through Paris.[8]

5. Zárate is a port city in the northeast of the province of Buenos Aires, Argentina. It lies on the western shore of the Paraná River, 90 km from Buenos Aires.
6. Mr Meili: August(o) Meili. He was on the passenger list (with wife Mathilde and child Adelite b~1887) returning from Hamburg on 11th August 1892. See Index to People.
7. The Lazaretto was the quarantine station of Montevideo, located on Isla de Flores - a small island in the Rio de la Plata, 34 km southeast of Punta Carretas, Montevideo, Uruguay: https://en.wikipedia.org/wiki/Isla_de_Flores
8. "Petit y Piria, Calle Rivadavia, 1423, Buenos Aires - a good concern making medium wool underwear and cotton stockings. The product is of a cheap to medium quality and is sold through the firm's own store in Calla Rivadavia, as well as to the wholesale trade. Employees number about 100, with 71 stitching machines. The firm is of French nationality." From US Bureau of Foreign and Domestic Commerce, 1917.

52. Letter from Buenos Aires, 12th-14th September 1892

Nº 6   Casilla 226
Headed notepaper: *Buenos Aires, 12/14th..Sept.....de 189 2*

My dear Mother,

Since writing you last – by my note, on the 4th – I received your welcome letter of 8th Aug., by which date you had returned from your visit to Scotland.

Your news of Sam Sinclair's engagement surprised me very considerably.[1] Sam is a very nice fellow but Miss Darbishire is a cut above him; a refined, nice girl, of high ideals, – perhaps with a longing to be a little more "blue" than her powers warranted –, whereas Sinclair never had an ideal in his life.[2] But if they are pleased with each other no one else need object.

Mrs McCallum tells me Sam's old flame in Brussels, a Miss Telford, was engaged about the same time.

You were fortunate in having dry weather at Strone. I hope the few days' change of air did you good.

Last Thursday I joined the distinguished guests invited to visit the paper-mill at Zarate, as mentioned in my last letter.[3] The special train left town shortly before 10 a.m. & carried us in less than two hours to Campana, where we had an excellent luncheon in the restaurant of the station. Mr Estrada, chairman of the board of directors had, on his right, Dr Gilbert, president of the Chamber of Deputies, &, on his left, Dr Cafferata, Governor of the Province of Santa Fé.[4] There were besides some 50 or 60 senators & deputies, & a few others. The only other Englishman present was Mr Waverly, sub-manager of the B. Aires & Rosario Railway, so he & I kept each other company. The luncheon was very elaborate & the wine-supply generous – sauterne, bordeaux, burgundy, champagne, & liqueurs – & decent Havana cigars. Some of the Fathers of the Country ate & drank as if they expected never again to have a square meal, until I became seriously alarmed for the collective healths of the legislature. After luncheon we proceeded by train to Zarate, the next station,

1. Samuel James Sinclair (b 1861 Belfast), son of yarn merchant Samuel Sinclair who died in 1905 at 22 University Square, Belfast, aged 75 years. He was the younger brother of Professor Thomas Sinclair (b 1857, d 1940) an eminent surgeon, war hero, and British Member of Parliament: https://artuk.org/discover/artworks/professor-thomas-sinclair-18571940-168970
2. Edith Mary Darbishire (b 6th October 1867, m 6th June 1893 in Belfast). They had six sons and one daughter
3. This was the first modern paper mill in Argentina, established in 1884 by entrepreneur José Mussini and the firm of Maupas, Escalada, Estrada & Cía. Zárate, a town close to the main consumer market in the city of Buenos Aires, on the Paraná river. This company, which was eventually to be named after Ángel Estrada (Mr Estrada referred to by JMcC below), quickly positioned itself in the market. The first production concentrated on packaging paper, but soon it covered all sizes and qualities providing everything from what was necessary for books to what was used by national newspapers. The mill is described further in Silvia Badoza and Emilio Ravignani (2013) "Origins, development and structural limits of the paper industry in Argentina, 1880-1940", *Revista de Historia Industrial* 22(53): 109-141: https://doi.org/10.1344/rhi.v22i53.21002
4. Juan Manuel Cafferata (b 1st January 1852, d 23rd September 1920) was an Argentine politician of the National Autonomist Party. He was the governor of the province of Santa Fé between 1890 and 1893: https://en.wikipedia.org/wiki/Juan_Manuel_Cafferata

where it was discovered that the President of the Chamber of Deputies had been left behind, & an engine & carriage had to be sent back for him.

After such hospitable entertainment everybody was prepared to be delighted with the factory, & really it did not require the stimulus to praise of a good lunch & a fragrant cigar. It was spotlessly clean, most orderly, & interesting to the last degree. I managed to secure as a guide Mr Dyke, English employé, & he explained & pointed out everything, from the cutting of the esparto,[5] the boiling of the rags, & the reduction of both to pulp, through the colouring, filtering, & drying processes, to the finished paper, in a very thorough manner. It was remarkable to see a broad shallow stream of apparently nothing but muddy water running quickly down a rippled board, which removes, in sediment, the heavier sand & dirt, over an endless sheet of fine wire sieve, which oscillates from side to side, allowing the water to fall through, & carrying on to the drying & pressing calender the thin resulting layer of evenly-spread pulp which is soon hardened into paper.

Another ingenious machine receives at one end a roll of paper & turns it out at the other end in bags, finished & gummed.

The factory employs some 500 people, among them about 70 women & girls. It works day & night, stopping only on Sundays. The operatives look strong & have a good colour, – very different from the pale consumptive-looking employees in factories at home. Most of them are paid by piece-work, & they can make such good wages that, I am told, it is very difficult to procure domestic servants in the neighbourhood; – they all prefer to work in the factory. One little girl of 10 was counting & separating into parcels of five the sheets of paper, & she did it so quickly that my eye could not follow the counting. She was earning about 6/- a week.

After seeing all that was to be seen, & when some of the ever-receptive law-makers had refreshed themselves with beer, we returned to Campana, where more champagne, beer, tea, & cold viands were served, & more cigars passed round.[6] The express train back to Buenos Aires arrived shortly after 7 & the directors stood hat in hand on the station to receive our thanks & good wishes. It was a pleasant & instructive excursion.

On Sunday evening I dined at Hirschbergs, & had rather a slow time, though they were, as always, very kind. Mrs Hirschberg & the children are well.[7]

Last night I was writing letters till 11. This – Tuesday evg. – I dined at Sērēs' house, left at 11 p.m. to send off a cable to Dundee, & thereafter sat me down to finish this. It now being 1 o'c. I shall go to bed.

On Thursday night I dined at Goulds'. To-morrow, by way of change, I dine at home at my own expense, or rather at Mr W.'s.[8] I should mention that on Saturday I dined at MacCallums' & had a pleasant little game of cards.

I want to be up early to-morrow: – "Tagus" mails close at noon.

Love to all.

Jack

---

5. Esparto grass is known for its use in papermaking: https://en.wikipedia.org/wiki/Esparto
6. Campana is located about 75 km from Buenos Aires, on the right-hand margin of the Paraná River. Campana and Zárate still make up an important industrial region: https://en.wikipedia.org/wiki/Campana,_Buenos_Aires
7. Edward and Selma Hirschberg, of Dundee – children Erika b 1887 and Frederick b 1890. See Index to People.
8. Mr W = Isaac J Weinberg, senior partner of Moore and Weinberg in Dundee. See Index to People.

53. Letter from Buenos Aires, 24th-28th September 1892

18920924 See an image of this letter, http://dx.doi.org/10.17613/990z-mw45

N$\underline{^o}$

Casilla 226,   Buenos Aires.

24th Sept. 1892

My dear Mother,

I have your two welcome letters of 15th & 23rd Aug. with interesting accounts of Lady Dixon's garden-party,[1] Mrs Carr's reception at Crawfordsburn,[2] & other entertainments, of your presents of grouse, & so on. I suppose the girls have too many occupations & amusements on hands to write to me, for during the six weeks since my arrival I have not been favoured with a letter from any of them.[3]

Julian came back from the camp two days ago, sunburnt & looking well, & with a healthy appetite.[4] He has been riding all day, helping to skin cattle, cure sheep of scab, & doing all kinds of regular "gaucho" work. He always maintains ranche life w$\underline{^d}$ suit him better than business.[5] By the way he showed me one of his letters from his mother, which began by stating that you had said to Mr Weinberg that Julian had no underflannels & that I had to buy them for him. I don't know what followed. But you must be <u>very</u> careful what you repeat. Things are so easily taken up wrong & I see every day mischief made by harmless remarks being repeated & misunderstood, so that I feel less inclined than ever to change my natural habit of eloquent silence, about which I am sometimes chaffed in Dundee.

On Monday night Ferguson was invited to a dance, & without consulting me he kindly asked his friends for permission to take me. I gladly availed myself of the invitation & spent a very pleasant evg., or rather night, for it was 4 o'c. in the morning when we returned to our digs. The dance was at Mr Seeber's,[6] ex Lord Mayor of Buenos Aires, & there were about fifty people there, of the "best families" (as those who are invited say) of Buenos Aires, among them Mrs Meyer,

1. Annie Dixon, née Shaw, was the wife of Sir Daniel Dixon, 1st Baronet, PC (Ire), DL (b 28 March 1844, d 10 March 1907). He was an Irish businessman and politician, educated at the Royal Belfast Academical Institution. He served as Mayor of Belfast in 1892 and as Lord Mayor of Belfast in three terms; 1893, 1901 to 1903, and 1905 to 1906. He was also a Member of Parliament for Belfast North as an Irish Unionist from 1905 to 1907: https://en.wikipedia.org/wiki/Sir_Daniel_Dixon,_1st_Baronet
2. Crawfordsburn is a small village in County Down, Northern Ireland. It lies between Holywood and Bangor.
3. "the girls" are JMcC's sisters, Annie, Emma, and Olga.
4. the camp = "el campo" = the countryside
5. Julian Weinberg, son of Isaac Julius Weinberg of Dundee (see Index to People), the gaucho – enjoying "ranche" life much more than business – a far cry from his German Jewish merchant parentage... Although Jewish gauchos were quite a thing in Argentina in the late 19th century – they did not usually originate from Germany – see https://en.wikipedia.org/wiki/Jewish_gauchos
6. Francisco Seeber (b November 15th 1841, d December 13th, 1913) was an Argentine military officer, businessman and Mayor of Buenos Aires. Son of German Argentine immigrants, he studied in Hamburg: https://en.wikipedia.org/wiki/Francisco_Seeber

sister of President Pellegrini, three sons, & a pretty niece, intimate friends of Ferguson.[7] At these native receptions people do not dance very much; most of the time is spent in lively conversation while walking round the room in couples. I was taken aback for a moment by the frankness of one sprightly young lady with whom I was promenading round the room in this fashion. She had informed that she was an "Oriental" (Uruguayan) & that her father had an estancia at Paysandú. I said it was only recently I had learned where that place was, though the name had long been familiar to me through the Paysandú tongues that were famous all over Europe. "Oh yes" she said with evident pride "those are ours!"[8] Young girls here do not wear low cut dresses – much to the credit of themselves & their mothers & of the prevailing modest good taste – but they have adopted the short trains.

There was a refreshment buffet open from about 11 o'clock on, with sandwiches & sweets, & a varied & copious supply of wines to which some of the young men did full justice. I am sorry to say that the interior decorations of various native houses I have seen here, belonging to the families in good position, are simply lamentable – the walls are hung with gaudy chromos & cheap German wooden carvings, & the other ornaments are in keeping. One rarely sees a passable oil or water-colour, or a decent engraving.

A week ago I was at a very pleasant dinner-party at the Goulds' – Mr Gould is traffic superintendent of the Great Southern Railway.[9] The guests were all English. I took in a Miss Barfield – a round-faced rather pretty young lady, who smiled frequently, doubtless oblivious of the fact that she had very nice teeth & that people saw them when she smiled. The pleasantest acquaintance I made there was Canon Pinchard, a young Church of England clergyman, to whom I "cottoned", – principally over the head of the "Barrack-Room Ballads".[10] He goes to Rio to meet his wife who is on her way out from England, & hopes I will gout to dine with them at Banfield on his return, if I am still here.[11] I dined once at the Hirschbergs, once with Mr & Mrs Enthoven, once with MacCallums, refused an invite to Mortlocks, paid my visit chez Martinez, & I think that is all; – no, I dined at young Sērēs' home one night & played that old exciting game of racing tin horses round a course marked with numbered lines on canvas, the steeds' progress or misfortune being decided by throwing dice.

I hope Jim is flourishing.[12] I have two letters from Julie to answer.[13] Glad to hear the old lady is hearty.[14] Any applicants for the house yet? How does Miss Buckly look? Has she changed since we were in Scotland? I have not heard anything of her brother, but before I go to Rosario I shall make enquiries. I am sorry to miss the Edenderry grapes & tomatoes.

<u>27th Sept.</u>   Last night we went to a performance of "Caste", given by the "Amateur Dramatic Society". The theatre was quite full, – not a vacant seat or box; – the whole English colony was there, & in grande toilette, so it looked rather

---

7. Carlos Enrique José Pellegrini (b October 11th 1846, d July 17th 1906) was Vice President of Argentina and became President of Argentina from 6th August 1890 to 12th October 1892.
8. Paysandu Ox Tongues were sold tinned in England
9. The Buenos Aires Great Southern Railway (BAGS) (Spanish: Ferrocarril del Sud) was one of the Big Four broad gauge, 5 ft 6 in (1,676 mm), British-owned companies that built and operated railway networks in Argentina. The company was founded by Edward Lumb in 1862 and the first general manager was Edward Banfield after whom the Buenos Aires suburban station of Banfield was named, when it opened in 1873. After president Juan Perón nationalised the Argentine railway network in 1948 it became part of the state-owned company Ferrocarril General Roca. The Goulds may be Diego and Elisa b 1850 and 1854 respectively.
10. Reverend Canon Edward Pinchard of the Anglican Church at Calle Almirante Brown is mentioned in *The Standard*, Buenos Ayres, on Sunday, September 18, 1892. The Barrack-Room Ballads are a series of songs and poems by Rudyard Kipling, dealing with the late-Victorian British Army and mostly written in a vernacular dialect.
11. Banfield is a city in the district of Lomas de Zamora in Buenos Aires Province, Argentina, 14 km (9 mi) south of the city center of Buenos Aires. Banfield railway station, named after the Englishman Edward Banfield, the first general manager of the British-owned Buenos Aires Great Southern Railway (Spanish: Ferrocarril del Sud), was opened in 1873. On August 19th, 1873, the first plots of land in the area were advertised for sale and extensive development took place from the 1880s onwards: https://en.wikipedia.org/wiki/Banfield,_Buenos_Aires
12. JMcC's brother James Moore (see Index to People).
13. JMcC's brother Julius.
14. Presumably Ann Isabella McCully (nee McCaldin), Jane's mother. She died 23rd November 1892, at Lennoxvale.

well. The acting was very creditable & there were no obvious hitches. I don't care much for the piece. We knew lots of people all round us, & everybody seemed to know everybody else; – so much so that the continuous exchange of bows & smiles, & of visits to the boxes, made the entertainment seem like a kind of private social reception rather than a public performance. There seems to be a considerable amount of dramatic talent & ambition among the English residents here. The Society is flourishing, & the immediate object of this performance was to increase the funds they have in hands for building a hall or theatre of their own for social meetings & entertainments.

28th Sept.   Last night there was a very nice dance given by people called Drabble. Julian went, but I was rather wild at having to refuse, because I had booked myself a week before, to go & play cards with old Darmstädter, & I could not get out of it without giving offence. I have not quite got over the disappointment yet, though D. hospitably entertained us with excellent Rhine wine, sandwiches, salad, & cigars, & we spent a very pleasant evg.

You have abt. enough now for this mail. I must soon think of putting an end to my stay here & moving northward.

Love to all,

Jack

54. Letter from Buenos Aires, 8th October 1892

18921008 See an image of this letter, http://dx.doi.org/10.17613/k210-1×47

N.° 8   Buenos Aires

8th Oct. 1892

My dear Mother,

I wrote you 28th Sep. by "Clyde" – I think that was the last, but I have got somewhat mixed in my numbers.

Many thanks for your long letter of 29th Aug. & the shorter one of 6th Sept.

I am surprised that the Pater went to Russia after all. He should not have done so I think. Business must surely have been very bad all over, & it was too serious a risk to run. When this reaches you I trust he will be back safe & sound & I shall be very glad indeed if he has done a fairly satisfactory business in spite of my expectations.

Best thanks to Annie & Olga for letters by last mail.[1] Glad to hear Jim is all right.[2]

I want to start for Montevideo & Brazil, if I can, in a fortnight or so. Business has been very good for Dundee, but it has become calmer this last week on account of locusts in the wheat-provinces. So far they have not done much damage; rain has fortunately come too, when it was badly needed, & the corn that was eaten to the roots will spring up again. The reports are contradictory, but I think we shall have a good harvest. For Belfast orders come in slowly. Politics are unsettled & will remain so until the new President is fairly started with some show of stable authority on his promised path of reformation. He takes office four days hence. The 12th too is the Columbus fête. Great preparations are being made here & in Montevideo to celebrate the anniversary of the discovery of America. South America has not much reason to be proud of the state of civilization & prosperity arrived at in 400 years. A civil war lately finished in Chile & one going on in Venezuela. Financial crises & continuous unrest of political factions in the Argentine, Uruguay, & Brazil. Paraguay almost dead, with a paper currency depreciated to one-sixth of its normal value. Peru in a bad way owing to the fall in silver. Altogether a cheerful picture. I wonder what it will be like in another 400 years. Still Mr Christopher would open his eyes could he come back on a steamer of 6000 tons, going 20 knots, telegraph his arrival to Cadiz, walk along the Calle Florida, & take the train almost up to the Andes. He would probably retire overcome to his room & amuse himself by balancing eggs on end for the rest of his days.

10th Oct.   We dined last week with people called Wallace. A sister of Mrs Wallace lives with them – a Miss Gilling-Lax – when not present usually called Miss Sealingwax.[3] She plays tennis & whist well & is a nice girl. I think I mentioned having been asked to a dance at Mr Drabble's but being obliged to refuse on account of another engagement. Julian & I went a week later & found the "party" reassembled, & we danced till 1 o'clock.

The tennis-club gives us the opportunity of taking some exercise which one needs, to keep one in good condition.

---

1. Annie and Olga, JMcC's sisters. Olga's 22nd birthday coming up on 6th November.
2. "Jim" is JMcC's brother James Moore.
3. Frederick L'Estrange Wallace (b 1853 Brooklyn, d 1925 Buenos Aires), wife Ellen Gwendoline Gilling-Lax (b 1860 Bedfordshire, d 1850 Buenos Aires). Miss Gilling-Lax ("Miss Sealingwax") is one of Ellen's sisters. Could be (1) Katherine Emma (b 1859 Bedfordshire, d 1943 Dorset) unmarried; (2) Agnes Maud Gilling-Lax (b 1862 Somerset, d 1924 Buckinghamshire) – unmarried; (3) Olive Mary Gilling-Lax (b 1866 Somerset, d 1942 Kent) – unmarried; (4) Ethel Gilling-Lax (b 1872 Somerset, m April 1893, d 1957 Surrey); or (5) Edith Margaret Gilling-Lax (b1873 Somerset, d 1945 Sussex).

We had some excellent games y'day afternoon. Lots of ladies go to Church on Sunday mornings & play tennis in the afternoons; everybody does it here & the English parsons do not object, & one could not spend the afternoon more profitably.

I see the MacCallums often.[4] They asked me up again last Sat. evg. but it was raining so hard that I remained indoors.

I wrote to Olga for her birthday by this mail. On the 12th inst two special "Columbus" stamps will be issued & I shall try to procure some copies for the collectors.

Love to all

Jack

---

4. See Index to People

55. Letter from Buenos Aires, 15th October 1892

18921015 See an image of this letter, http://dx.doi.org/10.17613/9z39-6b17

N⁰ 9   Buenos Aires   15th Oct.   1892

My dear Mother,

The Columbus centenary is over & the new President is in, for both of which consummations it behoves us to be devoutly thankful. For a month past the papers have been full of Columbus, & Caravels, & Cadiz, & Centennaries, & other big Cs, until America is sighing & groaning "What have I done that I should have been discovered?"

Also until the change of Presidents was effected everything was in suspense. If a man wanted to buy five thousand pounds worth of goods or to invest in a new hat the advice of the croakers was "Wait till after the 12th October" – "There will be a revolution" – "A military conspiracy in La Plata" – "A split in the ranks of the Acuerdistas" – "Saenz Peña refuses at the last moment to accept" – and so on.[1] Now that is all over & there is a sigh of relief all round.

Perhaps the most widely interesting feature in connection with the Columbus fêtes was the issue of two commemorative postage stamps. They were for inland postage only, – values two & five cents – a pretty design with the Caravel under full sail – & were sold only on the 12th October. The total issue of 400.000 was exhausted in a few hours.

On October 12, 1892, Argentina issued a two-stamp set depicting the caravels of Christopher Columbus – the Niña, Pinta, and Santa Maria. This is the five-cent one.

I enclose, for Julie's collection, an envelope with both these stamps, which he must preserve as a relic or a family heirloom.

Already at daylight of the eventful morning a large crowd had collected at the Post office. At 8 o'clock the sale began. A small door was opened, 30 or 40 people were allowed in, & the door was forcibly shut again by the officials aided by policemen. As soon as the first batch was served it was escorted out at another door, & another lot of 30 or 40 was admitted. The crush outside was something fearful. Several mounted policemen tried to keep the crowd back & the street clear. Scarcely a whole hat got through the narrow entrance. One man left half his coat behind & scarcely anyone escaped without some injury to his clothes.

Julian was in the crowd for two hours; twice he was pushed back just as he got to the steps; the third time he got in but a youth in front of him was lifted off his feet & went backwards over Julian's head – by the pressure of the crowd. This youth was so irritated at being thus forcibly ejected from his hard-gained position of advantage, that he gave the disappearing Julian a most vicious pinch – in the most pinchable part of his body. Julian could only get 10 two cent & 5 five cent stamps. He returned to the office his collar bent over, his

---

1. The Acuerdistas (= The Agreementists). In 1892, close to the end of the mandate as President of the Nation of Dr. Carlos Pellegrini, partisan disputes and the failure of an option presented by the National Civic Union, elections were held to succeed him and the victory went to the "agreementist" formula represented by the partnership of Luís Sáenz Peña and José Evaristo Uriburu, who assumed power on October 12, 1892: https://elarcondelahistoria.com/la-revolucion-radical-de-1893-30071893/

cuffs ruffled, his face black, & his hair down over his face, bathed in perspiration. He dropped into a chair & gasped for something to drink, & as soon as he had recovered a little he had to go home, & take a bath.

I hear these stamps are now being sold, used, at 6/- or 8/- each. In a short time they will be very valuable. Julie sh^{d} keep them on the envelope, which bears the postmark & the date.

I hope to have letters from you to-day. The Pacific mail is in. Just now recvd. yours of 12th Sept. I am glad you have good news from the Pater from Moscow. I hope soon to hear that he is safe at home again, with a good business done.

Mail closes early today.

Best love to all

Jack

Weather perfect.   Warm & bright – not too hot.   I have an invite to go yachting to-morrow, & there is no business "on" to prevent my accepting.

56. Letter from Buenos Aires, 19th October 1892

18921019 See an image of this letter, http://dx.doi.org/10.17613/0a1x-x056

N.º 10   Buenos Aires
19th Oct. 92

My dear Mother,

Two mails came y'day. & day before & brought me a number of letters, yours of 12th & 19th Sept., one from the Pater from St. Pertersbg., one each from Jim, Addie, & Emma, for all of which many thanks.[1]

I am sorry Olga has been unwell, & trust the visit to the country did her good. I send her a piece of music – a Spanish dance, rather pretty. What made you consult Dr Lindsay?[2] Is Dr Whitla not in town?[3]

The Pater expected to be home middle of October, so I hope by this time he is safe in the "bussom of his family". The Hamburgers seem to be justly indignant at the want of sympathy shown by the rest of Germany during the terrible epidemic.[4] I saw a printed manifesto to that effect which was sent out from the Hamburger Exchange.[5]

I am sorry about your neuralgia. This climate would do you good. My face has been like a ripe strawberry for the last two days & the skin is peeling now, so that I look as if I had powdered my cheeks & that badly. I had a magnificent day's yachting in the "Gladys", a neat little yacht belonging to Mr Kinch, vice-commodore of the Argentine Yacht Club.[6]

We were five – Young Kinch,[7] a fellow called Verschoyle,[8] Julian, myself, & one sailor, & we had all to assist in the navigation just at the start, for we had to get out of the very narrow entrance to the Basin against a strong wind & heavy sea, so that Kinch's orders had to be smartly executed. Once out on the river we had a glorious sail to the Tigre – some 21

1. Jim, Addie, and Emma are JMcC's siblings.
2. Dr Lindsay: James Alexander Lindsay FRCP (b 20th June 1856, Fintona, County Tyrone, d 14th December 1931, Belfast) was a British physician and professor of medicine: https://en.wikipedia.org/wiki/James_Alexander_Lindsay_(physician)
3. Sir William Whitla (b 15th September 1851, d 11th December 1933). At the time he was Professor of "Materia Medica" at Queens', and practiced at 8 College Square North, described as "the Harley Street of Belfast" at this period. https://www.ums.ac.uk/whitla_w.html. See also Index to People
4. The outbreak of cholera in Hamburg was reported in detail in the British Medical Journal of 1893, "The chief thing to be done in Hamburg now is a radical change in the water supply. But as long as there are sewers opening into the river, it will not be safe to take water for domestic use from the Elbe at any distance up the river." https://www.ncbi.nlm.nih.gov/pmc/articles/PMC2402644/pdf/brmedj08914-0037b.pdf
5. Referred to in the *Pall Mall Gazette* of 16th September 1892: "A meeting called by the Chamber of Commerce in the Hamburg Exchange for the purpose of forming a help committee for alleviating the distress due to the cholera epidemic": https://www.marxists.org/archive/aveling/1892/cholera.htm
6. The Argentine was the first yacht club to be founded in South America, and was granted legal standing on the 13th April 1892. Its first board of directors was composed of the "nine visionaries of the legend" - Aguirre, *Kinch*, Castro, Penard, Peña Salas, Wilding Kehlstedt, and Gainza. Robert H. Kinch, the founding first Vice President of the Argentine Yacht Club, was a British merchant (b Ardwick 8th June 1836, m Buenos Aires 1866). https://www.histarmar.com.ar/Veleros/ReseniaYachtingArgentino.htm
7. Most probably Robert Kinch's eldest son, Walter Halkett Hinch (b 1867). His other sons were Frank Somerville (b 1870), Harold Wright (b 1872), and Edgar Tudor Jordan (b 1874).
8. Robert Henry Verschoyle (b 11th October 1865 Sligo, d 1st December 1910 Waterford, Hants), listed as a "gentleman" on the passenger list sailing from Wales to Buenos Aires in 1898. He was the Chief Engineer on the Cordoba North Western Railway, Argentina, in 1902.

miles – the "Gladys" flying along at a fine rate & dancing over the waves. We stopped at San Isidro, on the way, rowed as near the shore as the shallow water permitted, in the dingy, waded the rest of the way, & cooked our own lunch. We had tender juicy steaks, preceded by sardines & tinned beef, & we walked into these good things. Then we paddled up the creek in the dingy, & walked inland through the trees – I with bare feet & my trousers rolled up to my knees, – a white flannel jacket of Kinch's coming down six inches below my own blue jacket. We then returned to the yacht & proceeded to the Tigre where the Kinches have a wooden house on one of the Islands.[9] At the Railway Station we had some tea, after which we returned to town by train in time for dinner, having spent a very jolly day.

Where did you read that extraordinary yarn abt. the steamer for B. Aires with Italian emigrants, 25 having died of cholera? So far there has not been a single case of cholera her or on any steamer hitherward bound.

Give my love to Aunt Martha when you write.[10]

20th Oct.

The skin is coming off my face in shreds & patches & I am a pretty object to look at. Am asked out to dinner to-night & to-morrow night & have no other complexion to put on. I have half a dozen troublesome small matters to look after – petty difficulties which are riling. Feel in a mood to light on somebody or to let off a little steam in a vinegar-pepper-& mustard letter to Dundee. Perhaps I shall feel better after breakfast.

Bye-bye.

Jack

9. Tigre is a city to the north of Buenos Aires. It sits on an island created by several small streams and rivers and was founded in 1820, after floods had destroyed other settlements in the area, then known as the Partido de las Conchas: https://en.wikipedia.org/wiki/Tigre,_Buenos_Aires

10. Martha McCaldin (b 1808, d 27 Dec 1897) was 86 when this letter was written. She was Jane's aunt (her mother's sister).

57. Letter from Buenos Aires, 30th October 1892

18921030 See an image of this letter, http://dx.doi.org/10.17613/6ebd-b806

<u>30th Oct. 92.</u>   Buenos Aires

My dear Mother,

I feel unsettled to-night, & not because we have had strawberries & cream twice to-day, but because I have decided to leave Buenos Aires this week & I have ever so many things to square up first, & they are chasing one another through my head. So much so that I cannot settle down to write even a common-place letter to you.

This is Sunday evg. I want to go to Rosario on Wednesday, return on Saturday & say good-bye to Buenos Aires & clear off to Montevideo.

I have been here longer than I anticipated, but business has been good for Dundee & I have been able to do something for Belfast. So long as there were orders to be got I felt unwilling to hurry away to some other place where the result might not be so satisfactory.

I must give it up. I can't write to-night. I shall turn in, rise early to-morrow, try to finish two ordinary days' business in one, & then perhaps I shall be clearer in my "mind". The worst of it is I have to think for Julian as well as for myself. With the best of dispositions he is not particularly smart at times, & he has no self-confidence whatever. His most fixed belief is that he good for nothing – not an encouraging point to start from, whereas he w$^{\underline{d}}$ do very well if he had a little more perseverance & faith in himself. He wants backbone.

<u>2nd Nov.</u>   Best thanks for your letters of 25th Sept & 3rd Oct. Glad that Olga is alright again. Also very pleased to have a letter from the Pater, Berlin, with good news.

What put it into your head that I sh$^{\underline{d}}$ have fever? I never had half an hour's illness of any kind since I began travelling. Many thanks for framing my water colour. This time I have not picked up any objets d'art.

Tigre Hotel with the Tigre river in the foreground, ca 1900.

I had a fearfully busy day on Monday & a ditto morning to-day. The day between was an "off" – a public holiday – & we spent it most delightfully with Mr & Mrs Wallace, Miss Gilling-Lax,[1] & young Goldsmid – brother of Colonel G.[2] – on the river at the Tigre.[3] We left town at 9.20 & returned at 7 – rowed to "El Toro", sandwiched & beered on the way, tongued & egged there, & picinic-tea'd half way back. In the evg. I went round to Wallaces' & had a very good game of whist. Altogether a record day. We had one of the club pleasure-boats, & the weather was perfect. A day's exercise like that in the open air does one a world of good.

I shall try to make my next letter more interesting. Meanwhile I must run out & look after abt. twenty different matters.

Best love all round

Jack.

1. For Mr & Mrs Wallace and Miss Gilling-Lax, see notes for letter of 8th October 1892, and Index to People.
2. Colonel Albert Edward Williamson Goldsmid MVO (b 6th October 1846 Poona, d 27th March 1904 Paris) was a British officer. He was the founder of the Jewish Lads' Brigade (in 1895) and the Maccabaeans. Colonel Goldsmid was an ardent Zionist, and head of the Hovevei Zion of Great Britain and Ireland. From 1896-1904 he was associated with Theodor Herzl as the head of the British Zionist movement and the key contact in the failed Zionist effort to establish a British Zionist protectorate in the Northern Sinai area of El Arish: https://en.wikipedia.org/wiki/Albert_Goldsmid
3. Tigre is an Argentinean town just north of the city of Buenos Aires. It's a gateway to the rivers and wetlands of the vast Paraná Delta. Also see footnote 9, letter of 19th October 1892.

58. Letter from Rosario de Santa Fé, 6th November 1892

18921106 See an image of this letter, http://dx.doi.org/10.17613/dm0b-9856

Rosario de Santa Fé[1]
– a very holy name but not a very holy place.
<u>6th Nov. 1892</u>   Sunday.

My dear Mother,

I came here on Friday, travelling previous night by "sleeper" from Buenos Aires, wither I intended to return to-morrow night. B. Aires is waking up again from its torpor (I'm not sure abt. that word torpor – but let it pass) but Rosario is still asleep. The streets are so quiet & neglected looking that it seems a city of the dead. Last night I went to the theatre to see "Caste" given by the same amateur Company that performed in B. Aires, for the benefit of local hospitals.[2] There every seat was taken & everyone was in full war-paint; – here the house was half empty & the general turn-out shabby. The weather may have had something to do with it. It had rained all day, & that makes the roads heavy & prevents people coming in from the Camp.[3]

The crops generally promise well now, but the harvest is three weeks later than last year. The wheat will have less straw & fuller ears than before. The harvest – "la cosecha" is the topic of absorbing interest at this time. All business depends on the result, & people have to make their calculations before-hand. It is difficult to form an idea of the vast areas under cultivation in the Argentine. When I was last here I was introduced to a man who had more than 50 square miles under wheat!

On Friday evg. I dined with a Mr Barge – managing director of the "Colonization & Land Company" which is in the hands of a few English people. They buy land in large tracts & sell it in small lots, or they rent it, or they go shares with the colonists they put on the land, taking a fixed proportion of their crops. They have various properties in the Province of Santa Fé. Whitehorn, who came out with me,[4] has been appointed manager of some of these Colonies, as they are called.[5]

1. Rosario de Santa Fé is 300 km northwest of Buenos Aires, on the west bank of the Paraná River. The city is a major railroad terminal and the shipping centre for north-eastern Argentina. Ships reach the city via the Paraná River.
2. *Caste* is a comedy-drama by Thomas William Robertson, first seen in 1867. The play was the third of several successes by Robertson produced in London's West End by Squire Bancroft and his wife Marie Wilton. As its name suggests, *Caste* concerns distinctions of class and rank. The son of a French nobleman marries a ballet dancer and then goes to war. When word arrives that he has been killed in action, his mother tries to wrest the child from his penniless widow: https://en.wikipedia.org/wiki/Caste_(play)
3. the Camp = el Campo = the countryside
4. ? Arthur Albert Whitehorn (b~1864), "rancher in Buenos Ayres" and registered "colonial Freemason".
5. The "Colonization & Land Company" was also known as the Santa Fé Land Company, Ltd, which was founded in 1881/1882 when a group of investors acquired a block of land from the Government of the Province of Santa Fé and formed the Santa Fé Land Company to sell lots. The prospectus appeared in July, 1883. The property was said to comprise about 650 Spanish leagues, or 4,336,150 English acres, and the price to be paid to the vendors was £1,050 per league: https://www.gutenberg.org/files/14366/14366-h/14366-h.htm#HISTORY_OF_THE_SANTA_FE_LAND_COMPANY_LIMITED

I got a coat & vest made in B.A. the other day – only a middling piece of work. That coat I set on fire before starting, which G.Y.K. helped to extinguish, was getting too shabby.[6]

Bye-bye. Love to all.

Jack

Albumen silver print of Rosario de Santa Fé in 1884 showing ships in the harbour. Unknown photographer, J. Paul Getty Museum.

6. George Young Kinnaird (see Index to People).

59. Letter from Montevideo, 13th November 1892

18921113 See an image of this letter, http://dx.doi.org/10.17613/ev9d-7d81

(Buenos) Montevideo   13th Nov. 1892

My dear Mother,

Having headed so many letters "Buenos Aires" during the last three months the force of habit made me begin this one with a capital B.

But I am glad at having at last said adios to the Argentine, – though I must return for a couple days at the end of the week to bid it a final farewell. Not that Buenos Aires is at all a bad kind of place to live in, – quite the contrary, particularly when one has a sufficiently large circle of acquaintants. But the restless spirit awakes again & makes me wish to "move on", – the effect of this wandering life. And I feel a kind of satisfaction in having "done" so much – finished a certain part of my journey – so that I can figuratively fold it up, write the name & date on the back, & put it away like an answered letter. I wonder does everyone experience that satisfaction of completion, the agreeableness of drawing a line through a reminder in one's note-book, – of reading the last page of a heavy book undertaken from a sort of sense of duty – of placing in definite & final order things that have lain in pending confusion in one's mind or in one's surroundings. This is, as Basil used to say, a line of thought that might be followed out, but I won't inflict on you any further reflections on the subject.

Last night I was reading a Spanish, or rather Argentine, historical novel, called "Amalia", but the irritation the opening chapters produced in me reached a climax when I came to the following description of a young woman, – "a waist twelve inches (!) in circumference, sustaining a delicate alabaster vase in which seemed to be placed, like a flower, that exquisite head"; – when I got so far I thought it was time to shut the book & blow out the candle.[1]

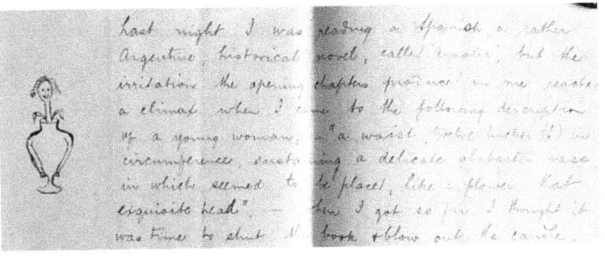

A sketch in the margin's of JMcC's letter, parodying the imagery of the Argentine novel Amalia

One of the characters, an old schoolmaster, makes the observation that it is the stupidest pupils who write the best hand, – the dunces, as some do, should add carelessness to their stupidity & scrawl, & imagine themselves geniuses in consequence.

---

1. Amalia is a 19th-century political novel written by the exiled Argentine author José Mármol. First published serially in the Montevideo weekly, Amalia (1851) is a semi-autobiographical account of the experience of living under a dictatorship. https://en.wikipedia.org/wiki/Amalia_(novel)

Something similar applies to a good many books. Because genius is sometimes eccentric not a few authors seem to think that is sufficient to be eccentric in order to be a genius. I am thinking just now of two shining lights but I am afraid to mention them lest I should be indignantly crushed by young ladies who have the advantage of attending lectures on literature. Ruskin is not one of them. I have a humble & enthusiastic admiration for him.

I have just read "Armorel of Lyonesse" by Besant, – a pretty story.[2] I like all Besant's books. They are very weak in places, but the man is "motived" by right principles, & his work is good, if not so good as it might be. A Ruskinian theory applies here, but as it rather savours of moralizing I will merely refer you to Ruskin for it. I like the humour in the book; – there is not too much of it this time (as there is in the "The Golden Butterfly").[3] There is a funny reference to a royal duke who used to murmur, during the weekly repetition of the commandments: "Never did that! Never did that!"

<u>16th Nov</u>.   Last Sunday afternoon I drove out to the very pretty country residence of Mr Alfred Thomsen (of Hamburg & Montevideo) father of our local agent. It is a drive of about an hour, in the course of which one has many a fine view over the broad bay & the scythe-like promontory on which the town is built, & up the slopes which culminate in the well-known "Cerro", a hill a few hundred feet high, referred to in the aforementioned historical novel as "that immense mountain!"[4]

An 1892 view of the old city of Montevideo with the Cerro hill (mountain) in the background.

Mr Thomsen's house stands in some 150 squares of land, say, at a rough guess, 200 acres, most of which is covered with trees 30 to 40 years old, – oaks, firs, cedars, magnolias, & eucalyptus, a very beautiful property in this almost treeless land. It is alive with birds, for Mr Thomsen allows no shooting in the place, & is very angry if anyone injures bird or animal. He has five sons & one daughter. The second son fell from his horse nearly two years ago & injured his spine & is now a helpless invalid. It is very sad. He was formerly the strongest & most active of the family & he now has to be wheeled about on a couch & cannot walk a step.[5]

The two younger boys, sturdy chaps of about 8 & 10 years, were galloping about all afternoon on horseback, without stirrups, saddle, or other bridle than a rope fastened to the bit – the horses quite barebacked! I believe the little girl, who must be about 9 years old, rides like her brothers, sitting crossways like them. They run about the place barefooted, as their father believes in making them hardy & strong. They all rise at half past five & have their cold bath, & at eight o'clock they are in town after their hour's drive – the father & eldest son at business, & the three young people at school. The youngest boy, aged 6, & the invalid, remain at the country-house.

2. Sir Walter Besant (b 14 August 1836, d 9 June 1901) was an English novelist and historian: https://en.wikipedia.org/wiki/Walter_Besant

3. *The Golden Butterfly* by Walter Besant and James Rice: https://www.gutenberg.org/files/43442/43442-h/43442-h.htm and https://www.bartleby.com/library/readersdigest/855.html

4. The Cerro de Montevideo is a hill located next to the city of Montevideo and the coast of the Montevideo Bay in Uruguay. With an altitude of 132 meters above sea level, it was the place chosen by the Spanish soldier Bruno Mauricio de Zabala for the installation of a surveillance post protecting the port of Montevideo against maritime invasions: https://es.wikipedia.org/wiki/Cerro_de_Montevideo

5. Alfred Thomsen (b 1843 Hamburg, d 1924 Buenos Aires). Sons: (1) Alfred Thomas Thomsen (b 1873) – would only have been 19 in 1892 – could he have been the agent?; (2) Emile (Emilio) Frederico Thomsen (b 1874, died 1893) - could he have been the "invalid"?; (3) Arturo Ricardo (b 1878); (4) Otto Hugh (b 1883) - he would have been around 10 in 1892; (5) Ervin Carlos (b 1887) - would have been 6.

This morning early I had a plunge in a fine saltwater swimming bath & another before dinner, – very refreshing now that the weather begins to get warm.

I shall have no letters from you now till I arrive at Rio. You can address there per return c/o Mr A. Spann, Caixa N$\underline{^o}$ 1.[6] In my next I shall likely give you another address.

Best love to all

Jack

6. Adolf Spann & Co was an "external" agent, a role described by Teresa da Silva Lopes *et al.* (2017) in their article "The 'disguised' foreign investor: Brands, trademarks and the British expatriate entrepreneur in Brazil," *Business History* 60(4):1-25: http://dx.doi.org/10.1080/00076791.2017.1287174

60. Letter en route to Rio de Janeiro, 27th November 1892

18921127 See an image of this letter, http://dx.doi.org/10.17613/vgcr-2w45

S.S. "Thames", Sunday 27th Nov 92

My dear Mother,

We are drawing near Rio & as the "Thames" will not stay very long in port I may as well have a few lines written to send on by her. We have had a pleasant run up. Most of the officers are old acquaintances of mine, particularly the chief officer, Mr Tyndall, in whose cabin we have had jovial sessions.[1] There are eleven young fellows from Rio on board who went down to the Plate to play cricket against Montevideo & Buenos Aires, suffering defeat in both places. They are all Englishmen & a merry crew. I knew two of them before. Youle, brother of the fellow who came out with me on this ship, & in whose house I have staid twice when passing through, & Keay who remembered having met me at McKinnels' dance, though I did not recognize him.[2]

I thorough enjoy this life on board. Glorious weather, bright sun, & sea breezes, nothing to worry me, salt tub in the morning, novels, whist, chess, & poker to amuse one. For four or five days it is splendid, & I can put up with even three weeks of it.

Julian came down to the Ensenada port to see me off. He is looking forward to his own going home in Feby./March.[3]

I am going to live out of town at Rio. Though there is not fever yet in town it will be cooler & pleasanter outside.[4]

I look forward to renewing acquaintance with old friends.

I hope to see Bertie Weinberg one of these days.[5] He is engineer, as you likely know, on the "Tagus", which is now in Rio or Santos.[6] She goes no further south, but returns to England via Rio after an eight days' stay at Santos. I don't much envy Bertie those eight days on the river at Santos. Fortunately the public health is now good there.

There must be several letters from you waiting for me at Rio. If we land this afternoon I trust Mr Spann will send a

---

1. Andrew Tyndall, engineer (b ~ 1853). See Index to People.

2. The Youle brothers – Frederick Louis (b 1857) and Frank (Schwind) (b 1866). "South American merchants." See Index to People.

3. Julian Weinberg. See Index to People.

4. "Between 1802 and 1849, cholera and influenza pandemics killed hundreds of thousands from Shanghai to Seville to New York, but these diseases did not dip below the South American portion of the equator. As a result, Brazil gained a reputation of good health, an opinion confirmed by European travellers and some provincial authorities. This rosy reputation wilted in 1849 when a yellow fever epidemic devastated several seaports, including the imperial capital of Rio de Janeiro. Following this outbreak, waves of epidemics swept the nation with unfamiliar and terrifying virulence. Brazilians were struck again and again by cholera, smallpox, yellow fever, and bubonic plague until the early 1900s." https://www.cambridge.org/core/journals/americas/article/abs/sickness-recovery-and-death-among-the-enslaved-and-free-people-of-santos-brazil-18601888/4E807636A7035B9C8014187CE0C4DA93

5. Herbert James Weinberg (b 1868 Belfast, d Perth, Scotland, 1896). Son of Isaac Julius Weinberg. See Index to People

6. RMS Tagus: Royal Mail Line – built 1871 – scrapped 1897. The Royal Mail line routes included: Southampton - Lisbon - Brazil - Uruguay - Argentina (1850-1980): http://www.roll-of-honour.com/Ships/RMSTagus.html

clerk to meet me with them.[7] On Sunday afternoons the offices are closed. To-night or early to-morrow morning I must write some other letters to go forward by this mail. I hope to have good news from you.

Best love

Jack

RMS *Tagus, built 1871. The ship on which Bertie Weinberg served as engineer.*

7. Adolf Spann. See Index to People.

61. Letter from Rio de Janeiro, 28th November–1st December 1892

18921128 See an image of this letter, http://dx.doi.org/10.17613/5xnd-7096

Rio Janeiro
28th Nov. '92

My dear Mother,

I wrote you a short letter on board the "Thames" & on landing I sent a few lines to the Pater to let you know I had come so far.

Resuming. – The steamer entered port at about five in the afternoon but as it was raining heavily I postponed going ashore till next day. This morning I rose at five, had my tub & started with my small bags in the first boat that came off. The "Tagus" was lying near, so I went on board & knocked Bertie out of his bunk, spoke to him for a few minutes, & then proceeded.[1] He seems to like his trip very well. He goes today to Santos & will be back here on Sunday next. No sooner did our boat pull off (Youle was with me) than the rain came down in torrents, driven by a stiff head wind that sent the choppy seas over the side & made our progress a kind of crawl.[2] In spite of umbrella & overcoat I was soon wet through & I felt as if I were sitting in a pail full of water & mops. The Royal Mail steamers anchor far out in the Bay, & it took our boatman more than an hour to row ashore, against the head wind.

Two "changadores" – porters – shouldered my bags (the heavy luggage is sent straight from the steamer to the Custom house) & off we started for Mr Spann's office near by. It was still closed, but luckily a few squares further on, just as I had decided to turn into a very shabby-looking hotel so as to get out of my wet clothes, I met Spann's clerk who advised me to

"Changadores" talking on a street. From Viaje por la América del Sur, 1892.

1. Herbert James Weinberg. See Index to People.
2. Frank (Schwind) Youle. See Index to People.

go on to Carson's English Hotel.[3] A tram, or "bond" as they call them, took me there in a quarter of an hour & my porters turned up immediately after.[4] My first care was to strip & rub myself with a rough towel & then swall a stiff brandy & tonic. In these countries one must be careful not to let wet clothes dry on one. Fortunately my small hand-bag had proved water-tight & I had put pyjamas, soap, brushes & baccy into it – the prime necessaries – so I was soon clothed in my favorite robes enjoying my coffee & bread & butter & thereafter a pipe. My under garments, about the seat, had dyed a rich mauve shade – the wedding-garment-tint which I have hitherto affected in unspeak-aboutables but shall eschew in future.

My hat-box instead of retaining its original shape had become so {see sketch of pulpy hat below} & was decidedly pulpy on the top, but the glory of the silk tile inside was untarnished. My black bag, containing books, correspondence, & writing materials had leaked "considerable", & these articles are now spread out to dry.

Sketch from the letter showing the "before" and "after" appearance of JMcC's soaked hatbox

Bye & bye the clerk arrived with my mail, twenty-eight envelopes, containing say thirty-five letters! The answering of them ought to keep me out of mischief for some time to come. I read the private ones, finished an "urgent" letter to Dundee & sent the clerk back to post it for the "Thames". By this time the waiter had brought back my clothes dried. He kindly offered to lend me a clean shirt of his own, which proposition I gratefully accepted. This is a republican country. I then had breakfast after which I felt sufficiently fortified to read the rest of my mail, & here we are!

Four "welcome weeklies" I found from you, 10th till 31st Oct. I am sorry for the old lady.[5] Her mind is so clear that she feels her helplessness the more.

Very glad to hear all the rest are well & lively. I hope you had an opportunity of dining Mr Murley Gotto for my acct.[6] I am very sorry they are not here just now. It is pleasant to read all your news about Belfast & Belfast people. The rain has cleared off now so I shall trot into town.

<u>1st Dec.</u>   The day after writing the foregoing I came up to the "Hotel Internacional" at the head of a valley above

3. From *Ninety Days in the Tropics – or Letters from Brazil* by W S Auchincloss (1874): "Thus far we have said nothing on the subject of hotels, and can only account for the omission by the fact that they furnish little for remark. There are very many in the city, but the preference must unquestionably be given to the two known as Hotel dos Estrangeiros and Carson's Hotel. We believe that few better investments can be made than the establishment of a first-class hotel in Rio de Janeiro. It is indeed strange that a city of 375,000 inhabitants, the capital of a vast empire, is no better provided with first-class hotels." https://digital.bbm.usp.br/bitstream/bbm/5096/4/002197_COMPLETO.pdf

4. In fact "bonde." https://en.wikipedia.org/wiki/Santa_Teresa_Tram

5. This refers to "granny", Jane's mother Ann Isabella McCully (b McCaldin). She died 23rd November 1892 (age 88) – so was probably dying when Jane wrote the most recent letter JMcC just received, written on 31st October 1892.

6. Percy Murly Gotto – civil engineer (b 18 April 1859 in London) and very much involved with Argentina / La Plata / Brazil in his dealings – landowner in Brazil. See Index to People.

the suburb of Santa Teresa, about 900 feet above the sea-level.[7] The surroundings are so exquisitely beautiful that they defy description. Behind us rises the precipitous peak of the Corcovado – "the hunchback".[8] To the right the deep valley divides us from the steep hills of Larangeiras, the sides of which are part sheer rock glistening with light reflected from the moisture that trickles refreshingly down its surface, part a dense growth of shrubs & trees festooned with trailing parasites.[9] In front & far below, the bay spreads out, the narrow entrance guarded by one or two rocky islands fringed with the white foam up by slow heaving swell. Inside the water is at perfect rest & the dark, piled-up hills in the distance are mirrored in the many winding bays & inlets.[10]

The Hotel Internacional in 1908 with Corcovado ("the hunchback") in the background.

7. The Hotel Internacional is referred to in the Almanak Laemmert of 1892. This publication was published in Rio de Janeiro between 1844 and 1889, by the brothers Eduard and Heinrich Laemmert.

8. Corcovado, which means "hunchback" in Portuguese, is a mountain in central Rio de Janeiro: https://en.wikipedia.org/wiki/Corcovado

9. Actually "Laranjeiras", an upper-middle-class neighbourhood located in the South Zone of Rio de Janeiro. Primarily residential, it is one of the city's oldest neighbourhoods, having been founded in the 17th century, with the construction of country houses in the valley located around the Carioca River, which bordered Corcovado Mountain. Because of this, the neighbourhood was previously called Vale do Carioca, or Carioca Valley: https://en.wikipedia.org/wiki/Laranjeiras

10. Such a poetic paragraph – reminiscent of the poem addressed to Jane McCaldin that starts this book.

I don't know at what hour of the day the scene is most charming. Whether in the early morning when the thin blue haze softens all the outlines & carries seemingly still further away the distant hills behind a half transparent curtain, or in the afternoon when the wreaths of cloud roll over the ridges, or later when all below is in darkness & the highest peaks catch the last glow of the settling sun. There is a peaceful intense silence, & yet the air is alive with the hum of insects, – so continuous & subdued that it does not break the calm.

When I think of you at home in mid-winter I am sorry for you that you cannot – presto-pass-magic-wand yourself over here & realize what I can only feebly tell you about.

The creature comforts of a fairly good hotel do not make it less easy to enjoy the beauty of nature. Here there are clean fresh rooms, broad beds with wire mattresses, & the best of shower-baths. The food is nothing to boast of, but that one does not mind so much if all the rest is right.

It takes one about an hour to come from the centre of town, by tram, cable rail-road, & tram once more. Two pages of description are sufficient infliction for one letter so I wont enter into detail about the delightfulness of the winding drive up the hill-side, through the trees.

Yesterday evg. I dined with the Youles & slept at their house.[11] I have been asked to do so again as often as I feel inclined. I have promised to pay visits to many other old acquaintances.

Christmas is near us once more. Good wishes all round for it, & a happy New Year to everybody. I don't know how many letters I shall get away by this mail; – not as many as I should like to I am afraid, but one or two I must manage.

I hear the Gottos are to be out again before Christmas.[12]

The weather is particularly cool & pleasant for this time of year. There is no yellow fever yet. It does not begin till about February, & the general health is now excellent. The particular health – that is to say _my_ health, is "como siempre". People tell me I look fatter & much stronger, – quite refreshing after a long course of sympathy for supposed delicacy. Adios. Best love.

Jack

<u>over</u>

....

By the garish light of day I am afraid I must admit that my enthusiasm about the cleanliness of this Hotel was a trifle "previous", & it is open to the suspicion of the faintest shade of over-colouring, seeing that during the process of disrobing last night I drowned seven fleas. I successfully stalked all I saw which proves me good sportsman considering the shyness of the game.

J.L.

---

11. Frederick Louis Youle and Frank Schwind Youle. See Index to people.
12. Percy Murly Gotto (b 1859), civil engineer, directed the Rio de Janeiro City Improvements Company, and his wife Jane Tulloch Fiddes Murly Gotto (b~ 1862). See Index to People.

62. Letter from Rio de Janeiro, 18th–20th December 1892

18921218 See an image of this letter, http://dx.doi.org/10.17613/jcre-v694

Rio Janeiro,   18th December 1892.

My dear Mother,

It is some time since I wrote to you – about a fortnight, I think, – 3rd Dec. was my last, but as I wrote meanwhile to Julie, Emma, & Annie, you will not have been without news from me.

And now I shall begin a letter so as to have it ready for the first steamer; though it probably won't get much beyond the beginning to-night, for I am somewhat tired, having spent ten hours to-day in train & boat; & further the gas will soon be put out. Still I find that once a letter is begun it somehow grows & ends itself, in spare moments, whereas the fixed resolution to begin & end a letter at one sitting is only born of a Sunday afternoon, or a holiday, when one can "laze" for a few consecutive hours.

Best thanks for your "Monday Pops." of 7th & 14th Nov., – the latter quite a long one with lots of news. You say there have been ever so many engagements in Belfast, but as you don't mention names I suppose they are people I don't know. I am not engaged myself so far, & though leap-year is almost over I have not had any proposals – at least no eligible one. It is thus that young women waste golden opportunities. Perhaps there is not enough gold about this here opportunity.

On Thursday I went to Campos, spent Friday & Saturday there, & returned to-day. Mr Kalkmann, partner of Mr Spann, went with me; – he will remain there for a couple of days still.[1]

It is a very fatiguing journey. It really began the night before, for I had to sleep in town, instead of out at my comfortable Hotel Internacional. We had to rise at 4 a.m. to catch the 5 o'clock steamer & there is no tram in from Santa Tereza at that early hour. The one hour's sail across the Bay in the fresh morning air, just about sunrise, is very pleasant. The near mountains, the wooded islands, & the winding channels, remind on of the Scotch lakes. From Nichteroy, on the north side of the Bay, the train starts at 6 a.m. & reaches Campos at 3 in the afternoon, a nine-hours' tiresome, dusty journey on hard cushion-less seats, in carriages that jolt so fearfully that one feels quite sore long before the ride is over.[2] The country is uninteresting; – covered mostly with virgin scrub, scarcely deserving the name of forest; – here & there scattered mud houses, & patches of land under maize or sugar-cane.

Campos itself is a flourishing little provincial town on the river Parahiba.[3]

[But the gas is out, & my candle is low, & it is 11.30, & I am dead tired, & –   Buenas Noches, or rather Boas Noites – for we must speak Portuguese here]

The rest in our next.

1. Campos dos Goytacazes is the largest municipality in the state of Rio de Janeiro and is 286 km from the capital city, Rio. Its name comes from the geographical characteristic of the region, very flat with fields (campos in Portuguese) and from the Goytacazes Indians, who were the original inhabitants of the region: https://en.wikipedia.org/wiki/Campos_dos_Goytacazes
2. The word "Niterói" comes from Tupi and means "water that hides". Often spelled Nictheroy or "Nitheroy", it was the indigenous name of the port of the city of Rio de Janeiro that was established around 1554: https://en.wikipedia.org/wiki/Niter%C3%B3i
3. Paraiba River: https://en.wikipedia.org/wiki/Para%C3%ADba_do_Sul

Campos is quite a small town, but it can boast of a large square with several palm trees & two electric lights. The Hotel is more like a family boarding house & the proprietor is so amiably pressing as he hovers round the dinner-table & so attentively solicitous for your comfort that you seem to be his guest, & you equal his politeness with assurances that you have nothing left to wish for.

The people are not yet spoiled by too much contact with European "civilization". They are still simple, confiding, & hospitable. Business begins in the stores at 6 in the morning & goes on without hurry till 9 at night. At half past nine the second breakfast is served in a room up-stairs for the principals & employees all to-gether, & dinner in the same way at four o'clock. If you are transacting business with the people when either hour arrives, as a matter of course you go up & take your seat at the table – if you are a stranger, at the head of the table. The food is good, plentiful & well cooked, & there is wine for everybody.

I was there for two days & did a good business.

20th Dec.   Have just recvd. your letter of 21st Nov. also a few lines from Father, written three days later, saying that the old lady had passed quietly away. Within a month of ninety years. It is a great age.[4] Poor old lady, at the end life was no pleasure to her. But that was only in the last few months. Till then her mind was clear & all her faculties strong. She enjoyed her books, her talks about old times, & the outlook from the window over the trees in which she watched the change of the seasons. What a good thing it was that her mind did remain clear as long as her bodily strength lasted. Old age with loss of reason is painful & pitiable.

It must have been a great strain on you looking after her when at last she became so helpless. You ought to go somewhere – Rostrevor[5] or Newcastle – for a few days' rest. I wrote to Julie to give you my Xmas present. I hope he got my letter all right & in good time.

I had a nice letter from Mrs Weinberg with a little pocket comb & glass & a very pretty card with a sprig of heather. Also a letter & a Christmas-card from Sissy. Very kind of them. I suppose I shall have a line from Mr W. & from Fred by next mail.[6] I don't think there will be any need for me to go back to Buenos Aires. I wired Dundee an order y'day. – also for a Campos firm, & I got besides two other small orders there for them, so I did not lose my two days.

Love to all
Jack

4. This is Jane's mother, JMcC's grandmother, Ann Isabella McCully (née McCaldin) (b 25th December 1803, d 23rd November 1892, Belfast). See Index of People.
5. Rostrevor is a village in County Down, Ireland.
6. Mrs Weinberg = Agnes Weinberg wife of Isaac Julius. Mr W = Isaac Julius Weinberg. Fred = their eldest son Frederick Simon Weinberg (b 1865). Sissy = nickname for their daughter Zerline Adele Weinberg born 1872 – there is a letter from her to JMcC written on 2nd September 1895 on the return from his final trip in this collection. See Index to People.

63. Letter from Rio de Janeiro, 27th December 1892

18921227 See an image of this letter, http://dx.doi.org/10.17613/xwqg-h666

Rio,   27th December 1892

My dear Mother,

Since writing you 18th/ Dec. by "Clyde" I recv^d your dear letter of 28th Nov. & the pretty Xmas-card sent two days later. I was also very glad to have letters from all the family. They arrived very timely on Christmas-eve.

You ask who the B. Aires Wallaces are. Mr W. is partner in the firm acting as agents for Lamport & Holt, the large shipowners.[1] Mrs Wallace was a Miss Gilling-Lax. Her sister lives with them. The Gilling-Laxes come from some place in Wales, where they had a nice country-house (according to photographs they showed me) & where they were apparently the "big" family of the district. Wallace himself is a decent little man; his wife & sister-in-law are exceedingly nice, & we were always glad to go to their house. They asked us often for dinner, whist, picnics, & so on. That reminds me I have to send them a New Year's card.[2]

Thanks for the "flour" suggestion. I'm afraid it won't do. I should look like a baker out for a holiday. Besides I don't give a cent what colour my complexion turns, so long as it isn't black or _too_ yellow, nor if it peels from time to time.

The card you sent me is a very pretty one indeed.

Well, I spent Christmas most pleasantly, – lighting on my feet as usual. I went up to Petropolis with Mr Allen on Saturday afternoon & returned on Monday morning.[3] On Xmas-eve we had a quiet family dinner – Mr & Mrs Allen, Captain & Mrs Williams (Mrs Allen's father & mother) & Allens brother, all of whom live in the house.[4] Afterwards we drove round to the Landsbergs – Mrs Landsberg is Mrs Allen's sister – who live near in a fine villa, though not such a

1. Lamport and Holt was a UK merchant shipping line. From its foundation in 1845 until 1975, the partnership was headquartered in Liverpool. It was in stiff competition with the Brazil Line in the coffee trade. Lamport and Holt would schedule its ships to leave Brazilian ports a few days before Brazil Line departures, and would even keep a ship stationed in Rio de Janeiro any time that a Brazil Line ship was in port. The company also waged a rate war against the Brazil Line with the result that it secured most of the Brazilian coffee cargoes to the US and left Brazil Line ships often sailing north only half-laden. In 1881 the Brazil Line again withdrew from the competition. Then in 1883 the Brazilian Chamber of Deputies awarded the Brazil Line a subsidy large enough to compete with Lamport and Holt. In 1890 the Brazil Line introduced two new ships. But UK-owned merchant houses, warehouses, insurers and banks supported Lamport and Holt, and the Brazil Line went bankrupt in 1893: https://en.wikipedia.org/wiki/Lamport_and_Holt
2. The Wallaces were Federick L'Estrange Wallace (b 1853 Brooklyn, d 1925 Buenos Aires), his wife Ellen Gwendoline Gilling-Lax (b 1860 Bedfordshire, d 1850 Buenos Aires), and Miss Gilling-Lax (referred to as "Miss Sealingwax" in earlier letters) one of the sisters of Ellen. See Index to People. The family actually seems to come from SOMERSET although Ellen and her sister's parents (George Robert Gilling-Lax and Ellen Mary Roberts) were married in Pentraeth, Anglesey in 1835.
3. Petrópolis, also known as The Imperial City, is a municipality in the Southeast Region of Brazil, inside the state of Rio de Janeiro state. It is located 68 km northeast of the city of Rio: https://en.wikipedia.org/wiki/Petr%C3%B3polis
4. See Index to People. John Roscoe Allen (b 14th January 1856 Lancashire, d 10th August 1946 in Rio De Janeiro - buried in Cimiterio do Ingleses Gamboa). He married Grace Elizabeth Williams (b 1867, d 1923) in 1888. Their daughter Grace Muriel Allen was born in 1890. Captain John Smith Williams (b~1835, New Orleans) and Laura Ursula Williams (b ~1844, nee Gilbert) were the parents of Mrs Allen and Mrs Landsberg. They married in Duxbury, Massachusetts, in 1864.

palatial residence as the Allens.[5] They had a children's party in the afternoon, & had re-decorated the Xmas tree from which we all got some little souvenir. There was a little dancing – cards – billiards – conversation & refreshments.

On Christmas day there was a grand dinner at Allens. We sat down, 16, to table at abt. half past 7 & rose at a quarter to 11. I took Mrs MacKinnell in to dinner & had Mrs Landsberg on my left & ours was the merriest corner of the table. Mrs MacKinnell I like very much.[6] Mrs Landsberg is young & handsome, & very lively. The table was beautifully decorated with ferns & flowers on amber silk I think, & lighted with candles in handsome silver "sticks", & there were lamps round the room. Each guest had his place marked by a card bearing some suitable quotation hand-painted on chamois. I enclose mine. It is a pretty idea & it started the conversation vigorously right away. Please keep this card for me.

Mrs MacKinnell was told to "Eat, drink, & be merry." (the sequel was left out), but there were other happier quotations. The only unmarried lady present was given "sweets to the sweet". The compliment was a little extravagant as "the sweet" was no longer in the first bloom of youth & she had a marked squint, but she seemed quite pleased. I can't give you the menu for I really don't remember what we had, – only that the succession of dishes seemed endless & all excellent (Mrs Allen pays her cook – an Englishwoman – £70 a year!).[7] At all events we wound up with the customary roastbeef, turkey & ham, plum-pudding, & mince-pies. After the soup there was a kind of liqueur-ice – a punch "romaine" is that ? – & the wines were all of the very best. Sherry, Hock, Bordeaux, Sparkling Burgundy, Champagne, & Port, – of brands & age to make a kernoozer's teeth water. Then coffee as they know how to make it in Rio & a good Havana, – & you will allow he must have been an odd mortal who w^{d} not have felt at peace with himself & the world.

In addition to being Xmas-day it was the anniversary of the Allens' wedding, – they were married in 1888. Everybody's health was drunk & there were supplementary toasts – "absent friends", – "sweethearts & wives" (with the usual small jokes). There was great fun over the crackers & the bran pie from which everyone drew a little present, the ring falling to young Allen who was feeding "the sweet" with American candies on the end of his fork.

Afterwards Mrs Allen sang "Love's old Song" & Mrs Landsberg "Connais-tu le pays?" from Mignon, & to-gether they sang two duets. It was a great treat, as they both have very much better voices & training than the average drawing-room singist.[8]

So ended a poor exile's Christmas.

Next morning we missed the train, but, thanks to Mr Allen's two good boys & a light victoria, we overtook it at the next station two miles further on, where the carriages are separated to be taken down the steep decline on the cog-wheel railway.[9]

The MacKinnells have asked me to visit them at Petropolis; the Youles where I dined & played whist last night (being Tuesday) have invited me to a dinner-party on New Year's eve & to stay over-night, & Murley Gotto, whom I saw y'day, asked me to stay over Sunday with him at Tijuca.[10] I hope I shall some day be able to make a return for so much kindness, & if not, a sort of sense of justice will oblige me, if ever I am in a position to do so, to show a corresponding friendliness to young fellows away from home.

Murley Gotto is an amusing fellow. I said to him: "So your brother has gone home to be married." "So I heard on my

5. Albert Landsberg (b 1851, d 21st November 1923) lived at Praca Liberdade, No 28, Petropolis. He was buried at the Cemitério do Cajú Município de Rio de Janeiro. Mrs Landsberg was Lucy Ethel Williams b 1869 (hence "young, handsome and lively"). She was married in Rio in 1886 (she was 17 – he twice her age). She outlived him quite a while and died in Rio de Janeiro in 1951. See Index to People

6. Mrs McKinnel is American. See Index to People.

7. In 1890 a British cook would make between £30 a year (in a modest house) and £300 a year (if a famous chef for a royal family). So £70 in Rio de Janeiro may be a reasonable salary.

8. "Mignon" is an 1866 comic opera in three acts by Ambroise Thomas, based on a novel by Goethe. "Love's Old Sweet Song" is a Victorian parlour song published in 1884 from a collaboration by composer James Lynam Molly and lyricist G. Clifton Bingham. 1913 recordings by the soprano Olive Fremstad are available for both songs from the Library of Congress: "Connais-tu le pays?" https://www.loc.gov/item/jukebox-649316/ and "Love's Old Sweet Song" https://www.loc.gov/item/jukebox-133342/.

9. The victoria is an elegant carriage style of French origin: https://en.wikipedia.org/wiki/Victoria_(carriage)

10. Tijuca is one of the most traditional districts of Rio de Janeiro and has the third-largest urban forest in the world: https://en.wikipedia.org/wiki/Tijuca

arrival" he replied. "There are two girls at home who believe themselves engaged to him. He has taken home a ring & some diamonds they tell me. If they don't do for one they'll do for the other."

Alfred Betzold comes to Rio on financial business by "Magdalena", due 11th Jany.[11] So Leppin tells me. Latter bewails high expenses in Brazil. Can't do much business here just now though he did pretty well in the North. Doesn't know where to go. Wanted to go to Rio Grande but affairs are son unsettled there. Has been here so long (I think nearly three months) that he must go somewhere. I feel sorry for the man. He doesn't seem to have many friends. He was "quite sad" when he left Belfast & not a soul came to say good-bye. Very sorry he ever left M. & W. – Mr L. was always so good to him. (Better not repeat any of this.)[12]

This is a long letter, I don't know how many other letters I have to answer nor when I shall do it. Paciencia! A great word but an unsatisfactory sentiment.

Papers say you are having great snow-storms. I hope your neuralgia is not troublesome. Here it still keeps cool (for Rio) & the public health wonderful. Death-rate 15 per thousand.

In Belfast it must be half as much more.

Mr Morley must feel his noblest feelings hurt at the want of gratitude on the part of the fenians![13]

Another revolution in the Argentine! – this time in the Province of Corrientes.[14] Sweet countries. Here they are issuing a few million more paper-money "to support local industry" & so raise the value (!) of the depreciated currency already existing, "so as to make a fresh loan in Europe on favorable terms." Enlightened financing!

Love to all.

Jack

11. Alfred Betzold, a linen merchant in Belfast originally came from Upper Saxony and was naturalized in 1871. *The Belfast News-Letter* of 8th September 1896 records that he later fell on hard times, "these bankrupts, Max Veitel & Alfred Betzold, carried on business at Fountain Street, Belfast, as linen merchants, and the case was listed for . . ."

12. Ernest Leppin was a disgruntled ex-employee of Moore and Weinberg in Belfast. Regrets he hadn't appreciated how good Julius had been to him. See Index to People.

13. John Morley, a Liberal politician, Chief Secretary for Ireland, and supporter of Home Rule: https://en.wikipedia.org/wiki/John_Morley

14. "The rebels in the province of Corrientes, Argentine Republic, have defeated the provincial troops in a number of skirmishes, and have seized the towns of Mercedes and Caseros and the railway lines of the district." *Indianapolis Journal*, 28th December 1892: https://newspapers.library.in.gov/

64. Letter from Rio de Janeiro, 6th January 1893

18930106 See an image of this letter, http://dx.doi.org/10.17613/v3n4-2015

Rio Janeiro,   6th Jany. 1893

My dear Mother,

I wrote you 16th & 27/8th December. The other day I recvd. to-gether your welcome letters of 5th & 12th.   You tell me you had a very bad cold. I trust you shook it off before Christmas. You ought to take more care of yourself. The winter seems to have begun with great severity. Here we had great heat all last week, but y'day it rained heavily & to-day is cool & delightful once more, as is always the case after rain. A telegram from Buenos Aires reports continued drought & great heat all over the South. Such a cool & healthy season in Rio is unknown "in the memory of the oldest inhabitant".

It is very clever of the girls to be able to earn pocket money through art-work. What kind of work is it?

What a shocking thing the sudden death of Mrs James Black. It seems no time since Addie & I went to the wedding reception.[1]

I had a newspaper, dated 14th from Dundee announcing the failure of Lipman & Co.[2] Did Mr W. lose anything?[3] I am sorry for Mrs Friedländer. The failure cannot really have been a great surprise in Dundee, as Lipmans were known to be short of funds considering their large business. I suppose the Wolffs lose everything.[4] It is hard lines on young Mrs Albert W. unless she has money of her own settled on her.[5]

I spent New-Year with the Youles, stopping with them from Saturday evg. till Monday morning.[6] Several guests disappointed them & there were no other ladies there, but some young fellows from the Bank came to dinner on Saturday, & we spent a pleasant & noisey (with or without e? without I think) evening, playing games, thought-reading, singing choruses & so on. Sunday was fearfully hot & we did not move about much, but we enjoyed our morning & afternoon cold baths. It must sound refreshing to you just now to hear of cold baths twice a day! Youles have a fine bath. One walks, in pyjamas & wooden slippers down the garden, under palms, bamboos, & bananas, to the clear tank, tiled

---

1. This is a reference to James Black's wedding in New York – described at length in letter of 29th January 1891. His wife was a Miss Russel. He was likely related to the Black "heiresses", neighbours in Lennoxvale.

2. Lipman and Co. were international linen and jute commission agents and merchants, providing both raw materials and made up cloth. Their first office was in Dundee in 1844 and then expanded to Hamburg, New York, Glasgow, Chicago, Gratz, Carelshaven and Belfast. Edward Friedlander had entered the firm of Lipman and Co. at some point during the 1870s. Born in Hamburg about 1848, he married in London and then entered business in Dundee. It was a spectacular bankruptcy. There seemed little warning of what was coming, but on the 12th of December 1892, Lipman sent out a letter to their creditors advising they could not pay their debts. It seems to have come as a surprise that the various rumours which had been circulating about the failure of an anonymous Dundee firm had been about Lipman and Co. It was said to be the "most serious to have occurred in Dundee for more than twenty years" and their liabilities were around £300, 000. Full account at: https://mcmanus168.org.uk/mcmanus168entry/lipman-co/

3. Mr Weinberg

4. There was a WULFF associate with Lipman & Co as a partner of the Hamburg firm of Lipman & Wulff – this was MALTA Wulff.

5. Albert Wulff, Jute and Linen Merchant of Dundee (b 27th January 1864 in Hamburg) married Olga Elias (b 21st October 1870) on 14th May 1892 in Hamburg. Albert lived in Dundee and was naturalized in January 1895. So, young Mrs Albert Wulff (age 22) had only been in Dundee for 6 months at the time JMcC wrote. (Albert died in Hamburg on 18th May 1938.)

6. Fred and Frank Youle. See Index to People.

with blue slabs, & rolls with luxurious laziness into the cool water. The tank is three feet deep & about ten feet square, so one can dive slowly from one end to the other, then float on ones back & kick, & afterwards turn on the copious shower overhead. Such a bath in itself makes life worth living.

To-day is another holiday – "Reyes" – the Magi or wise men of the East. There is a fearful band in the Garden of the Hotel, & their music reminds one of the flight of some birds that migrate in a long string, each one a little behind the other.

Interval for dinner.

Recipe for a nice fruit salad. Oranges, melon, & pineapple, cut in small pieces, grapes whole but separated, in a salad-bowl with ice. If all the fruit is sweet no sugar is needed.

Another culinary menu. A favorite breakfast dish of mine is eggs beaten-up with tomatoes.

In honour of the day several of the Brazilian families have seated themselves at the centre-table & are having a kind of banquet. It is pleasant to see them having a jovial time, but their table-manners might be a little more refined with advantage. If only the ladies would not put their elbows on the table, if the men would not cross their legs, nor throw one arm with careless grace over the back for their chair, if they would discriminate a little in their use of knife & fork, if the toothpicks were not so much in evidence all round!

It is funny to see how quickly they become bosom friends. Three or four families meet for the first time at the Hotel. On the second day they are inseparable. The women call one another by their Christian names & promenade arm in arm, four or five in a row.

I expect they will be up bye & bye to dance in the drawing-room & as it is next my room, with a thin door between, my writing will be interrupted. They danced vigorously the other evening, & politely pressed me to join them, but it was too hot & I did not feel in the humour so I politely declined.

The Readies have gone for a few days to Santos. I mentioned already that Mr Readie is manager of the Cable Company. They are very nice people. Mrs Readie kept me supplied in books. The last was the pathetic story of Little Nell. I wonder I never read "The Old Curiosity Shop" before. I recommend it to any emotional person who wants to "indulge in the luxury of a good cry." Dick Swiveller & the Marchioness playing cribbage make a very funny picture.[7]

In a very few days I am going for a flying visit to San Paolo & Santos & then I shall go to Bahia, where I shall likely be when this reaches you. Hence to Pernambuco.

There come the dancers & musicians, so I may shut up.

Glad to hear the Pater is looking well. I have a letter half-written to him, which I shall send by this mail. Best love to all
Jack

7. Novel by Charles Dickens, *The Old Curiosity Shop* was printed in book form in 1841: https://www.gutenberg.org/ebooks/700

65. Letter on board S.S. Magdalena travelling north from Rio, 24th January 1893

18930124 See an image of this letter, http://dx.doi.org/10.17613/0h0k-wc04

S.S. "Magdalena"   24 Jan. 1893

My dear Mother,

Here I am sailing North once more, having said good-bye to Rio y'day.

On my return from São Paulo I found a number of letters had come for me, including yours of 26th & 27th Dec., with an account of your Xmas doings. What a list of presents from everybody to everybody. I congratulate you on the acquisition of your spinning-wheel, your hand-glass, your toilet set, & all the little devils. Glad to hear Llyod was with you.[1] Thanks for her message & my love in return. I envy the skaters. During the last fortnight ice with us has been at a premium, – to put in the drinks –, for the heat has been very great.

On Saturday-week I left Rio for Santos by the Brazilian steamer. Young Kalkmann came with me.[2] The boat was so crowded we could not get berths & we had to sleep on the bench in the saloon, – very narrow & hard it was & we c$^{\underline{d}}$ not even raise a pillow or a cushion.

The passengers were almost all natives – some funny specimens among them. Opposite me at table was a fat good-natured woman who was going down to Montevideo to take the river steamer past Uruguay & Paraguay to Matto Grosso – a two months journey into the centre of S. America.[3] By way of making conversation I asked her how many inhabitants there were in Matto Grosso.[4] She could not tell me & the matter evidently weighed on her mind & she must have asked some of her compatriots, for next day as soon as we took our places she caught my eye, beamed upon me & before I c$^{\underline{d}}$ say good morning she began "Ya sei, Senhor, cuantos habitants tem Matto Grosso". – I know now, Senhor, how many inhabitants there are in Matto Grosso; – from seventy to ninety thousand!

I tried to look as if ignorance of this fact (more likely this fiction!) had deprived me of my night's rest & the knowledge she imparted w$^{\underline{d}}$ enable me to sleep calmly in future, & she seemed duly gratified.

At the corner of the next table sat a fidgety little man who thought himself ill-used because he had to wait till the stewards came round to him, instead of serving him first. His patience exhausted itself during dinner in shoulder-shruggings, piano-business on the table, & ejaculations of disgust. Towards the end of dinner he jumped up like a flash, made a stride towards us, & seized in his fingers a piece of cheese which lay on a plate on our table, flashed back to his place, & ate the cheese. The thing was done with the jerky rapidity of a Jack-in-the-box. We tried to look

---

1. Who was Llyod who spent Xmas with Jane & family (female, but no title ? servant). Perhaps Sarah Williams Llyod (b 1840 Liverpool, d 1912 Belfast), Housekeeper?
2. A. Kalkmann, German merchant (b ~1865), on passenger list from Rio de Janeiro to NY in Feb 1892
3. Probably along the Paraná river which today marks the border between Argentina and Paraguay and then Paraguay and Brazil.
4. Actually Mato Grosso. "The Bororo Indians live in the Mato Grosso area. As late as 1880, soldiers patrolled lands on the outskirts of Cuiabá, Mato Grosso's capital and largest city, to protect settlers from Bororo raids. Mato Grosso (lit. "Thick Bush") is one of the states of Brazil, the third-largest by area, located in the western part of the country. The state has 1.66% of the Brazilian population and is responsible for 1.9% of the Brazilian GDP. Current population ca 3.5 million!" https://en.wikipedia.org/wiki/Mato_Grosso

contemptuously disgusted, but the little man was too absurd, & we burst out laughing, which offended him, I think, much more.

Landing at Santos was not a pleasant matter. Our little steamer took a long time to get alongside the wharf, & the heat was very great. Then we had a long squabble with the porters who asked £3 ! to carry our luggage to the hotel; – they ultimately took abt 15/-.

If you want anyone to work for you today in Santos you must pay a very big price. There is a great demand for laborers & employees of all kinds, for the traffic of the port has increased enormously, & there are fewer people to do the work owing to the bad yellow fever season last year when so many died & so many others left the place. I was told by lots of people that the business firms cannot get ordinary clerks to go to their Santos branches even for £500 or £600 a year.

We spent one night there in a miserable hole of a hotel, & were glad to clear out next day to S. Paulo up in the hills. I once before described the cable railroad, the beautiful scenery, & the relief of passing from the damp stifling heat of Santos into the fresh air & cool breeze on the higher level.

Once more we had some curious fellow-passengers. We were much struck by the performance of one man who, leaning out of the window, called for a tin of water. He got about an ordinary tumbler full which he seemed to swallow, but he must have had the peculiar capacity of the camel for stowing away water in a kind of reserve cistern until required, for he proceeded to wash his hands with that water, spouting it out of his mouth again with lively satisfaction.

I remained six days in S. Paulo. The evening before I left there was a dance at the German Club, to which I went. I met there a Miss McCulla, aunt of your friend Dickie, a very jolly girl & a capital dancer. We danced the pas-de-quatre to the envy & admiration of the Germans & I expect it will be a feature of their dances in future.[5] Miss McCulla is governess with one of the leading German families there, the Nothmanns.[6] She said she knew my name because Dickie had mentioned the family in his letters. She had been in Newry & Dundalk – knew the Pattersons & McHinches – Nettie particularly.[7]

There was a Miss Park at the dance, also governess, & very lively. I enjoyed myself immensely.

I had only one hour's sleep that night for the waiter called me at half past three to catch the train for Rio – a tiresome, hot, dusty journey of nearly fifteen hours.[8]

Next day I said good-bye to my friends in Rio, got my letters, collected my baggage & came on board the "Magdalena". A friendly steward recognized me & took me off to a good cabin, & here I am.

I have now a lot of writing to do – a difficult business on board owing partly to the motion of the ship & partly to the many temptations to be lazy. But it's got to be done all the same.

I had letters from Father & Olga, for which best thanks. My last to you was a post-card on the 12th, & by the previous mail I wrote to Father, Addie, Emma & Olga.

Best love to all.

Jack

5. The "Pas de Quatre" was a version of the schottische couples dance popular in Europe in the late 19th century: https://www.libraryofdance.org/dances/military-schottische/
6. Victor Nothmann was a German entrepreneur in São Paulo who was responsible for several urban development initiatives in São Paulo, catering to wealth from the coffee trade. With Frederico Glette, Nothman launched Campos Eliseos (a literal translation of Champs Elysees) in 1872, transforming a former cottage farm into a modern, urban district: https://research-information.bris.ac.uk/ws/portalfiles/portal/56359897/Football_and_Urban_Expansion_Sport_in_History_revised_4_12_15_PURE.pdf
7. Nettie McHinch could be Matilda Antoinette McHinch (b 1859 Dundalk) who married Matthew Marshall Patteson (b 1850 also in Dundalk) in Belfast 1886.
8. No train apparently nowadays – but by coach it now takes about 6.5 hours

66. Letter from Pernambuco, 14th February 1893

18930214 See an image of this letter, http://dx.doi.org/10.17613/wwhy-ze77

Pernambuco   14th Feby. 1893[1]

My dear Mother,

Just come ashore from the "Trent". She leaves again at once so I have only time to scribble a few lines to let you know I have come safely so far.

Found here your welcome letter of Jany 23rd. You see I am nearer home now when we get each other's letters under 3 weeks instead of 4.

Mr & Mrs Hoyer & Mr Eggers came to see me off at Bahia & lunched with me on board.[2] Captain Milner, an old friend of mine, welcomed me heartily, said I was to get "the best cabin on the ship", & gave me a seat beside him at table. Next morning he knocked my out of my berth at 7.30. "What do you mean sir, by being in bed at this hour? Don't you know the regulations of the ship? Come up at once & have a cocktail." So up I went in pyjamas, paced the decks for a while & had the iced appetizer. After 8 o'clock one must appear respectably dressed.

I also found on board a fellow called Estil, who lives with Youles in Rio, a very nice chap.[3] Also the Englishman who showed me over the paper-mill at Zarate.   I am pretty well known on the Coast now, & wherever I go I meet acquaintances.

The "Tagus" passed the "Trent" between Bahia & Pernambuco so I did not see Bertie this time.

I shall write again by "Sorata" in four days.

Bye-bye meanwhile. I am glad to hear you are all well.

Best love.

Jack

---

1. Although JMcC refers to Bahia and Pernambuco as though they were towns, they are states in Brazil. The main city of Pernambuco is Recife, and of Bahia it is Salvador: https://en.wikipedia.org/wiki/Pernambuco and https://en.wikipedia.org/wiki/Bahia

2. For more information about the Hoyers and Mr Eggers, see Index to People.

3. Probably Harry George Estill (b 14th November 1866 Madras, India). He grew up in Lancashire, but lived most of his adult life in Brazil, working as a coffee exporter. In 1897 he married a woman 5 years older than him (Edith Jeavons) in Hounslow (he was then 30 and already listed as resident in Rio de Janeiro). They both died in Rio de Janeiro – she 20th August 1932, he 10th May 1955.

67. Letter from Pernambuco, 18th February 1893

18930218 See an image of this letter, http://dx.doi.org/10.17613/0147-3k78

Pernambuco.   18 Feb. 1893

My dear Mother,

Here beginneth the letter for "Sorata" promised in my last by "Trent".

To my disgust my baggage was sent to the Custom-house instead of being passed immediately on arrival. It was the last day of Carnival & a half-holiday.[1] At half past nine the Inspector had not put in an appearance so I said I w^d return later on. I asked the man if the Custom-house w^d be open in the afternoon. "Certainly it will", he said "We don't go out masquerading". At five minutes past twelve I returned & the whole place was shut up until next day. I had not a stich with me but what I was wearing, &, to rile me more, Tuckniss,[2] a friend of Keiller's[3], gave me a card for a ball at the Club that evening. I said I c^d not possibly go & told him of my fix. He said to leave the matter to him, – I sh^d go to the dance.

Through Mr Guimarães[4] I have been lucky enough to secure a room in an exceedingly nice English boarding-house owned by a Mrs Latham.[5] There are several English fellows living here & one of them said to me during dinner "That's all arranged". I asked him what was all arranged. "About this evening – I have had a telephone from Tuckniss". So after dinner this man, whose name is Shaw, introduced me to another fellow called Wilson, who again produced the keys of the private boxes of a third man, yclept Kanthack, to whose room, in the proprietor's absence but with his permission, we repaired, & there I was rigged out.[6] Shirt, collar, tie, gloves, underclothing, & dress-suit, were subscribed by one or other. Fortunately all the garments fitted pretty well. The only difficulty was pumps, – no one had a pair big enough, so I went to the ball & danced in my laced boots! At first I felt rather uncomfortable – the unwhisperables were tight in the legs & I had no place to put my thumbs for the pockets ran across, the tie was not clean, & I thought my boots must be remarkable. But afterwards I forgot about all these things & enjoyed myself thoroughly. I danced with Mrs Williams,[7] who asked about "my sister" – I suppose it was Annie she met – , also with her sister Miss Boxwell, a very pretty girl, just out from England for a short visit,[8] with a Miss Rawlinson, "the best dancer in Pernambuco", & a very lively young lady, etc.[9] We drove home about three in the morning after a jolly night.

---

1. The Carnival of Brazil (Portuguese: Carnaval do Brasil) is an annual Brazilian festival held the Friday afternoon before Ash Wednesday at noon, which marks the beginning of Lent, the forty-day period before Easter. During Lent, Roman Catholics and some other Christians traditionally abstained from the consumption of meat and poultry, hence the term "carnival", from carnelevare, "to remove (literally, "raise") meat." https://en.wikipedia.org/wiki/Brazilian_Carnival
2. (Benjamin) Howard Tuckniss (b 1863) lived in Pernambuco. See Index to People.
3. John Gibson Keiller. See Index to People.
4. Alfred Lopes Guimaraes (b ~1855). Merchant. See Index to People
5. Mrs Latham: see Index to People
6. "Kanthack" probably Ernest Kanthack (b 1867 Ceara). Merchant. Brazilian and naturalized English in Liverpool in 1885 along with father Emilio and sister Emilia and brother Francis. His sister Emilia Victoria Kanthack (b 1865) became a nurse at Barts hospital in London. See Index to People. "Yclept" = Old English gecleopod, past participle of cleopian 'call', of Germanic origin.)
7. Mrs Williams = Ada Boxwell's sister Edith Ann Boxwell (b~1862 married to Arthur Llewellyn Griffith-Williams). See Index to People.
8. Ada Boxwell. She features in later letters from Pernambuco. See Index to People.
9. Miss Rawlinson = possibly the daughter of William Rawlinson, Civil Engineer in Pernambuco, sister of Robert Purcell Rawlinson dentist (m to Carlote M Rawlinson).

Offices of the London and Brazilian Bank in Manaos, 1910.

Mrs Latham is a kind motherly woman, & a lady. Her husband had formerly considerable means but he came to grief. He is in Ceará on business just now. They have one daughter & three sons. Mrs Latham supplied me with comb & brush etc. & instructed the servant to leave pyjamas in my room – my things being still in the Custom-house. It was very thoughtful. And when I mentioned that my eyes were a little sore after the ball, she gave me some spirit of rum to bathe them with. The house is exceedingly comfortable. We have English breakfast in the morning, afternoon-tea for those who are home, & dinner at half past six. Mr Bilton, manager of the London & Brazilian Bank, is living here now, & there are in all eight boarders, – all gentlemen.[10] The tone of the house is excellent.

There is a grass tennis court in the garden. I have had one or two good games already.

I am glad to be so far north already. Rio is still healthy, according to the accounts, but here is now some fever in Santos & several vessels from there had cases on board & were quarantined at Bahia. It is surprising that the fever did not show itself sooner. The hot season will be over in another two months. But this hot season has been phenomenally healthy in Rio & Santos.

Keiller is very well & doing splendidly.[11] Two contracts he signed with Wilsons have been broken by the firm to sign others more favorable to him. He was a short time ago of some use to the new Cable Coy.[12] & the head office wrote to the directors of Wilsons asking permission to forward to Keiller a check for £200.[13] He has been appointed Danish Consul & altogether things have been going well with him. Miss Anderson made a mistake.

I have been getting your letters somewhat irregularly of late. 16th Jan. arrived after 23rd Jan. & several others in the same way.

---

10. W. H. Bilton Retired and returned to England in 1898. See Index to People. The London and Brazilian Bank was established in 1862 with the first branch opening in Rio de Janeiro in February 1863. Shortly afterwards branches were established in Bahia and Pernambuco and the Anglo-Portuguese Bank which had branches in Lisbon and Oporto was taken over. In 1864 a severe monetary crisis in Brazil, followed in 1866 by the repercussions of the Overend Gurney crisis in London, hit the fortunes of the new bank. A run on the bank in May 1866 resulted in the Rio branch being drained of over a million pounds within fifteen days. The bank only just survived. Head Office in London shipped gold to Rio as fast as possible. To obtain further funds the manager in Rio sold drafts to London to the value of £200,000. These events led eventually in 1871 to the bank being reorganised. The fortunes of the bank changed and by 1880 it was the leading foreign bank in Brazil with a wide network of branches from Manaus on the Amazon and Para and Maranhao on the northern coast to Porto Alegre, Pelotas and Rio Grande do Sul in the south. The bank and the London and River Plate Bank operated as friendly rivals for many years, sharing a similar tradition and outlook. In 1923 Lloyds brought about their amalgamation, the new name chosen was Bank of London & South America Limited (BOLSA). By this point, the London & Brazil Bank had offices in Buenos Aires, Rosario, Montevideo, Manchester, Paris, New York and several in Portugal: https://archiveshub.jisc.ac.uk/search/archives/49348d0b-a19f-3ecf-9d5b-c8bee0a1b948
11. John Gibson Keiller (b 9th July 1865 Dundee, d 24th February 1897 Pernambuco). His sister Grace Keiller (b 31st May 1870 Dundee, d 5th November 1935 London) married Frederick Simon Weinberg ("Fred") (Isaac's eldest son). See Index to People.
12. Probably the Western Telegraph Company: "In the mid-1880s the Brazilian Submarine Telegraph Company changed its name to the Western Telegraph Company. One of the first tasks undertaken by the new company was to lay cables from Para to Montevideo. CS Scotia undertook the laying. Para-Pernmabuco 1390 nm Pernambuco-Rio de Janeiro 1372 nm" https://atlantic-cable.com/CableCos/CandW/EATC/index.htm
13. In 1837, Edward Pellew Wilson and his brother Fleetwood Pellew Wilson founded Wilson Sons in Salvador, Bahia. One of the oldest companies operating in Brazil, it still prospers as in the areas of port, shipping, and land logistics services. Throughout the 19th century and the first half of the 20th century, the company supplied coal, the main fuel at the time, to Brazilian Navy arsenals throughout the country. After signing a contract with the Great Western of Brazil Railway Company Limited in 1879, Wilson Sons begins the construction of the Recife to Limoeiro Railway in Pernambuco. On October 24, 1881, the first two sections of the railway were inaugurated. https://www.wilsonsons.com.br/en/history/

The Rio Allens are nothing to the Allens you mention – so far as I know – I fancy they are a very different style of people.[14]

Am glad to hear the private news in your last letter, re finances. Hope next year will be better again.

Best love to all.

Jack

14. There are many English Allens in Rio de Janeiro – all buried in the Cemiterio dos Ingleses Gamboa: https://en.wikipedia.org/wiki/Cemit%C3%A9rio_dos_Ingleses,_Gamboa. It is also known as the English Cemetery or the British Cemetery Gamboa. For JMcC's friends John and Grace Allen, see Index to People

68. Letter from Pernambuco, 21st-25th February 1893

18930221 See an image of this letter, http://dx.doi.org/10.17613/sxxp-md37

Pernambuco   21st/25th Feby.   1893

My dear Mother,

I wrote you the other day by "Sorata". Since then the "Clyde" has come in with a large mail, which is not yet all sorted in the post-office though it is now twenty-four hours since the steamer landed the letter bags – a fair sample of Brazilian official despatch. But I have received two letters from you, 30th Jan. & 6th Feby., two from the Pater, & one each from Julie & Annie, the last from London.

Many thanks for all birthday wishes. Last night we were speaking of birthdays & abt. mine being 29th Feby & not coming for eight years after 1896 – a fact very few people are aware of. Mrs Latham expressed her astonishment & then said thoughtfully "So you'll celebrate your real birthday again in 2004". I said I should if I lived so long but I did not expect to, at which she looked as startled & distressed as if I had told her that I had only a few days to live. Curiously I made the same mistake myself not long ago quite overlooking the fact that the next century is 1900 & not 2000. I like Mrs Latham very much. She is such a sympathetic motherly woman, & gives me little bits of kind advice; – not to walk in the sun without keeping my umbrella up, not to get wet, not to smoke too much, & so on.

Everybody is much concerned now about the English parson, Mr Ding, who is dangerously ill. His wife & two children came out by "Clyde" y'day, & they knew nothing of it till their arrival. It must have been a great shock for the poor woman.[1]

In my last I told you about my going to the ball in borrowed plumes & meeting Mrs Williams & her sister Miss Boxwell.[2] I forgot to mention that Miss Boxwell was at school with Miss Violet Dunlop[3] & was over on a visit to the Dunlops last year. – It must have been the week before Sissy Weinberg's visit[4] for Miss Boxwell left the week before Dixons' dance.

Mrs Williams is living with her uncle Mr John Boxwell[5] & she asked me to call, so I went up on Monday evg. Mr B. asked me for dinner the following evg. – they were having some people. I accepted but early next morning I remembered I had already made an engagement for that evg. so I at once sent a note of apology. I was very sorry for the Boxwells are nice people, as well as being in a way the magnates of the English Colony here, so I should have had a good dinner & likely met some other nice people.

The other engagement was to the Tucknisses. Keiller lives there & both he & young Tuckniss had asked me some days before for that evg. Tuesday being their at-home night.

---

1. Rev William Ding, the British Consular Chaplain (b 20th November 1854 in Papworth St Everard, Cambridgeshire). His wife Elizabeth was on board ship with their children en route to Brazil when he became ill. Their children William Rowland (b 1885) and Doris Mary (b 1890) were age 8 and 3. See Index to People
2. Mrs Williams: Edith Ann née Boxwell, b~1862l. Miss Boxwell: Ada Boxwell, b 1870. Both daughters of William James Boxwell, "Cotton Broker", b~1833 in Co Wexford. See Index to People.
3. Violet Madoline Dunlop b 1872 in Belfast. See Index to People.
4. Sissy: Zerlina Adele Weinberg, Isaac and Agnes' daughter, b 2nd November 1872 in Dundee. See Index to People
5. John Havey Boxwell, "Brazilian Merchant", b~1845 Co Wexford, brother of William James Boxwell. See Index to People.

Mrs Tuckniss is a pleasant, dignified, middle-aged lady, whose heart I won by listening with interest to her account of the different ages at which her children had had measles. Miss Tuckniss is really a nice girl, rather pretty, pleasant, graceful & musical. Confound that adjective "nice"! But there are no other words to convey the same meaning, so I may as well plunge at it "right away" & say that Harold Tuckniss, the son, is one of the <u>nicest</u> fellows here, & the whole family among the <u>nicest</u> in Pernambuco.[6]

I dined one evg. at Mr Guimarães.[7] Both Mr & Mrs G. are English. Mrs G. is young, pretty, & lively. She was very amusing about her own name. In England she is called Mrs Jimmyrags or Mrs Jimmyrash. Here when she goes shopping the people ask "What name please?" – "Mrs Guimarães." – "I beg pardon?" – "Mrs Guimmer-rangs" (very distinctly) – "Excuse me, would you mind writing it" – "Certainly, so!" – "Ah! – you mean Gueemaraingsch!"   And then she feels so small at being told how to pronounce her own name.

I was at a pleasant little tennis-party given by Mr Guimarães, & we had afternoon tea &cake, rather a treat out here. I was asked to call on some people called Rawlinson, whose at-home is this evg. but the parson lives near, & his illness has upset the arrangement.

To-morrow is a half-holiday & I have been asked to go out by four o'c. train & visit & dine with the Gatises, – former fellow-passengers.[8]

Glad to hear all your chatty news about people. Lots of engagements & marriages, but I don't hear of any of the numerous heiresses "going off". Perhaps they are all too difficult to please.

Mr Jim Ferguson is a promising youth. What's he going to do in New York.

Annie is in luck, "doing" London; – very kind of Derenbergs.[9]

I congratulate you on the new carpet. It was certainly about time to replace the dining-room one. When you took it up to clean it you must lately have had some difficulty in knowing which side to turn up.

By the "Clyde" Mrs Adamson & her little daughter also came out from England. Mrs A. is a daughter of Mrs Tuckniss & is married to the Commander of the cable-ship "Viking". We were fellow-passengers on the "Clyde" last year. The little girl is a dear little child, with blue eyes, & always laughing.

<u>25th Feb.</u>

The parson, Mr Ding, died y'day morning at 10 o'c. & was buried same afternoon at five.[10] It is fearfully sad. His wife only arrived three days ago, & she returns to England to-morrow by "Thames". The occurrence has cast a gloom over the whole English community. Mr Ding was very popular. Only a week ago I was present while he conducted a glee practice at Mrs Latham's house. He had been seedy for some time & was not strong, & instead of taking care of himself he worked too much, imprudently exposed himself & got a chill which became serious & he had not strength to rally.

I went to Olinda y'day afternoon to the Gatises.[11] Olinda is a bathing-resort about half an hour from here, an old town with lots of old Dutch houses built before those early colonists were driven out by the Portuguese. Mr & Mrs Gatis, the

6. "Harold Tuckniss" = (Benjamin) Howard Tuckniss (b 1863, d 1927 Pernambuco), railway manager. He was the son of Benjamin Tuckniss (b 1826 Yorkshire, d 25th June 1896 Pernambuco) and Leonora Eliza Tuckniss (b Taylor 1842 in Camberwell, d 13th January 1931). They are Keiller's best friends. See Index to People.

7. Alfred Lopes Guimarães (b 1855) . See Index to People

8. Mr and Mrs G Gatis. See Index to People.

9. Presumably Edward Derenberg and his wife Anna Henriette (née Karpeles) whom he married in Hamburg in 1885. They lived in London at 67 Evelyn Gardens, SW. Edward was Elsa Iklé's uncle (his sister Clara Derenberg was Elsa's mother) and his mother Louise Derenberg was born Samson in Hanover in ~1810. Julius' mother Minna was born Samson in Hanover in 1803. They are presumed to have been sisters, making JMcC and Elsa second cousins and Edward and JMcC and his sister first cousins once removed.

10. He was 38. His death was due to "Yellow fever contracted while taking Holy Communion with a sick parishioner". His wife Elizabeth was 36.

11. Mr G C Gatis and Mrs Mary Fredina Gatis (b 1854) had seven children. See Index to People.

governess, Miss Browning, & another guest, Mr Fletcher, all came out with me last year on the "Thames".[12] We had a pleasant quiet dinner & a walk on the beach afterwards.

I was rather busy y'day forenoon – took three orders – small ones – for Belfast, & now I must write them out. I think I shall go on board the old "Thames" tomorrow, Sunday, morning. Keiller has offered to take me in his launch. A boat costs £1, – big surf-boats with six men to row & one to steer, so that luxury is better avoided.

Best love. I hope there will be another mail in a few days to send you "many happy returns" of the 17th March.[13]

Jack.

12. Clara Annette Browning (b 1st August 1864 New Brompton, Kent). She immigrated to the USA in 1904 and married William Wright Wesley in New York in April 1927. She became a naturalized US citizen in 1940. See Index to People.
13. Jane's 57th birthday.

69. Letter from Pernambuco, 28th February and 6th March 1893

18930228 See an image of this letter, http://dx.doi.org/10.17613/2kjq-f715

Pernambuco   28th Feby. 1893

My dear Mother,

It occurs to me just now that this is my birthday. Many happy return of it to all of us. 29. Oh Jupiter! Well I don't <u>feel</u> any older than when I was 21, that's surely a good sign.[1]

The other day I sent you a long letter by "Thames". After posting it I took the train out to Jaquera[2] where the Boxwells & Williams live, & joined their picnic-party to Jabotão.[3] There were twelve of us; – Mr & Mrs Williams & their little daughter, Miss Boxwell, a Miss Conolly, old Mr Harvey Boxwell & two nephews, a brother of Williams, myself & two others.[4] We had a jolly drive of over two hours in a kind of char-a-banco drawn by four mules.[5] The road was bad & several times we were nearly upset, which rather added to the fun. At Jabatão we lunched by the river where the water forms a pretty little fall of foaming rapids & the trees on the bank give a pleasant shade. We were all very hungry & thirsty after our drive, & the iced claret-cup & cold chicken, turkey, & tongue were worth a king's ransom, & the good Havana which followed simply priceless.

I wanted to return by rail as I was engaged to dine with the Tucknisses, but there was no train between 3 & 7 p.m. so

1. JMcC birthday on 29th February, born 1864.
2. Likely "Jaqueira" – a neighbourhood of Recife (capital of Pernambuco).
3. Jaboatão, city, eastern Pernambuco state. It is located on the Jaboatão River, just west of Recife, the capital of the state. The site of two battles in the 17th-century war of the Portuguese against the Dutch, Jaboatão was elevated to city status in 1884. It is an increasingly industrial sector of the greater Recife metropolitan area.
4. From the passenger list of the "Clyde" coming from South America, we see the Boxwell clan arriving in Southampton on 28th April 1893 (2 months after this letter from Pernambuco). Mr W J Boxwell age 60 (b ~1833) embarking in Rio was William, the father. His daughters "Miss Boxwell" (Ada) and Mrs Williams (Edith) both embarked in Pernambuco. Edith was accompanied by her four children: Henry aged 6 (b~ 1887), Alice aged 4 (b ~1889), John aged 3 (b ~1890), and Annie age 1 ½ (b ~1891). Also embarking at Pernambuco were Mr John Harvey Boxwell age 48 (b~ 1845) – this is William's brother and uncle to both Edith and Ada who must have been staying with him. So on the picnic we may have: Mr and Mrs Williams and their little daughter -Arthur Llewellyn Griffith-Williams and Edith Williams with possibly Alice Williams (Annie may have been too young); Mr William's brother with Miss Connolly; Mr (John) Harvey Boxwell Sr and his two nephews: his brother William's sons, John Harvey Boxwell (b ~1868) and William E. G. Boxwell (b~ 1870), both of whom are listed as "Cotton & Sugar Agent Broker" and "Cotton & Sugar Merchant in Brazil" in the 1901 Birkenhead Census. Also in the 1901 Census, Ada aged 30 and still single is living at home with her parents William and Mary – as are her sisters Frances aged 36, Eleanor aged 27 and Sarah aged 38.
5. A charabanc or "char-à-banc" is a type of horse-drawn vehicle, usually open-topped. It has "benched seats arranged in rows, looking forward, commonly used for large parties, whether as public conveyances or for excursions". The name derives from the French char à bancs ("carriage with wooden benches"), the vehicle having originated in France in the early 19th century. https://en.wikipedia.org/wiki/Charabanc

there was nothing for it but to make what apology I might to Mrs Tuckniss.[6] Boxwells had told me they w^d be home at 5, but instead it was ½ past 7.

On the drive home we were very merry – played up-Jenkins & spelling games & told storied. Soon after 6 the sun set & the moon came out. A drive in the tropics by moon-light, with the tall palms standing clear against the red glow in the west, & the polished leaves of the tropical trees glistening in the moonbeams & gently fanning themselves in the cool evening breeze, – and – and – a pretty girl to talk to; – well a fellow might be worse off. I am merely stating a case – generally.

By the time I had changed my clothes & gone round to Tucknisses it was half past 8 & I had been asked to come in the afternoon & stay for dinner! I was awfully sorry, & I w^d not intentionally have been so rude for anything. But I explained how it was & they were very nice about it, – did not take offence at all, – but on the contrary asked me for another day & also to come to their usual weekly musical evening. In the course of the evening Mrs Tuckniss told me the family history – how they were connected with the Wentworth family – Lord Strafford[7] – & that Mrs Tuckniss' grandfather had the same coat of arms which she produced, – all gorgeous in gold & blue on parchment) as the present Lord Fitzwilliam[8], whose arms she pointed out in a late number of the Graphic.[9]

People tell me all kinds of funny things: – I suppose because I am a good listener. Mrs Tuckniss imparted all this information to me not at all in a spirit of brag, but in a chatty fashion. The conversation turned upon it because I mentioned that Mrs Latham was connected with the family of Lockhart[10] – Scott's biographer & son-in-law, & she had a Lockhart family heirloom in the shape of a gold chatelaine.[11]

By the way Julie might buy, for my account getting McClury to charge me the cost, this Biography of Scott. I bought it before leaving but gave it to Julian. It was published last year in two vols., cheap edition, plain blue cover with white label I think, costing abt. 3/6 or 4/- for the two vols. I want it sent by book post, registered, to Mrs Latham, address as noted at end of this letter.

I send you a photo taken by my friend Hoyer in Bahia.[12] For amateur work, & that amateur a beginner, & the photo not retouched, it is not bad.

Y'day a man stopped me in the street & shook hands with me – I did not recognize him, but I have a bad memory for faces & I see so many new faces every day, that I thought he might be a customer & have given me an order for handkerchiefs or hessians. So I smiled & hoped he was very well. After the usual interchange of compliments he began:

"About that business, you know, it's all right, but are your parents alive & do they live here or on the other side?"

I thought the question rather strange, but perhaps he wanted to know if my father was in the firm. Still I could not see what that had to do with handkerchiefs or bags. However I told him they were alive & lived on the other side.

"And your future wife?" But this "floored" me, & I stared at him with my mouth open, & as soon as I had recovered sufficiently from the shock, I said to him. "I think the Senhor must be making a mistake. I haven't found out yet myself

6. Mr Benjamin Tuckniss (b 1826, d 1896) and Mrs Tuckniss, parents of Benjamin Howard Tuckniss (b 1863, d 1924). Keiller lodged with them in Pernambuco. See Index to People.

7. Thomas Wentworth, 1st Earl of Strafford, 1593-1641: Royalist politician; President of the Council of the North (1628), and Lord-Deputy of Ireland (1632); Lord Lieutenant of Ireland (January 1640); 12th January 1640, created Earl of Strafford; supported Charles I, 1639-41; executed.

8. William Thomas Spencer Wentworth-FitzWilliam, 6th Earl FitzWilliam, KG (b 12th October 1815, d 20th February 1902), styled Hon. William Wentworth-Fitzwilliam 1815–1835, and Viscount Milton 1835–1857, was a British peer, nobleman, and Liberal Party politician: https://en.wikipedia.org/wiki/William_Wentworth-Fitzwilliam,_6th_Earl_Fitzwilliam.

9. The Graphic was a British weekly illustrated newspaper, first published on 4th December 1869: https://en.wikipedia.org/wiki/The_Graphic

10. John Gibson Lockhart (b 12th June 1794, d 25th November 1854) was a Scottish writer and editor. He is best known as the author of a biography of his father-in-law Sir Walter Scott (https://www.gutenberg.org/ebooks/24497), which has been called the second most admirable biography in the English language, after Boswell's Life of Johnson: https://en.wikipedia.org/wiki/John_Gibson_Lockhart

11. https://en.wikipedia.org/wiki/Chatelaine_(chain) and https://www.langantiques.com/university/chatelaine/

12. Georg Hoyer (b 1860, m to Mararethe) from Germany. See Index to People.

where my "futura" lives." "Are you not the Senhor Kanthack?" he asked, pulling out a legal looking document. "No, I only live in the same house with him", & – I might have added – "I wore his clothes the other night & they fitted me to T, so your mistake is excusable".

It seems Mr Kanthack is about to be married, so I suppose it was the license or something of that sort.[13] He was the man who lent me the dress suit to go to the ball in, when mine was in the Custom-house.

6th Mar

There has been no mail in or out since I began this letter, so I have had no news from you nor have I had any further opportunity since my last of sending you my birthday wishes.[14] I shall drink your health & prosperity to Ireland on the 17th.

I have not much to add. On Thursday evg. I dined again with Mr & Mrs Guimarães, & last night at the Tucknisses'. Business has been going pretty fairly, though, as usual, better for Dundee than for Belfast.

Best love to all.

Jack

13. Ernest Kanthak, merchant (b 26 May 1866 Ceara, Brazil, naturalized with father and siblings in Liverpool in 1885) married Josephine Maria (née Dowsley, b 19 March 1869 in Pernambuco) approximately 1893/4. Both died in Bournemouth; he in 1953, she in 1946. See Index to People.

14. It would be Jane's 57th birthday. She was born 17th March 1836.

A list of passengers arriving from Brazil to Southampton on the SS Clyde, showing many of the picnickers described in this letter.

NAMES, &c., OF CABIN PASSENGERS.

Ports of Embarkation.	Names of Passengers.	Age of each Adult of 12 years and upwards. Married. M.	F.	Single. M.	F.	Children between 1 and 12 years. M.	F.	Infants. M.	F.	Profession, Occupation, or Calling of Passengers.	English.	Scotch.	Irish.	Foreigners.	Ports at which Passengers have been landed.
		28	19	41	15	8	7	1	1		74	5	5	36	
Rio de Janeiro	Mr W. J. Boxwell	60								Merchant	1				Southampton
	Miss Ada Boxwell				22						1				
	Mr Chas A Carlisle	38								Merchant				1	
	Mr Carlisle			22						—				1	
	~~Mr~~														
	~~Mr Luca~~														
	Mr H Livock	32								C. Engineer	1				
	. Leo Hess				41					Merchant				1	
Bahia	. Henrique Costa	35								"				1	
	Mrs Costa		32											1	
	Mr Francisco Andrade				43					Merchant				1	
	Mrs Pott		36							—		1			
	Mrs Morrison		57							—		1			
	James Pott (child)					8				—		1			
	Dorothy — (child)						6			—		1			
	Ruth — (child)						4			—		1			
	John — (child)					2				—		1			
	Mr H J Dutton	50								Merchant	1				
Maceio	. Chas Goble	42								Merchant	1				
Pernambuco	Mrs Williams		32							—	1				
	Henry — (child)					6				—	1				
	Alice — (child)						4			—	1				
	John — (child)					3				—	1				
	Anne — (child)						1½			—	1				
	B Mansfield (nurse)				50					Nurse				1	
	Cecilia Jackson (nurse)				30					—		1			
	Mr D Bury	32								Civil Engineer	1				
	Mrs Bury		31							—	1				
	Sybel Maud Haigh (child)						4½			—	1				
	Cecil Oliver Haigh (child)					3				—	1				
	Agnes Ramsey (nurse)			39						Nurse	1				
	Mr Chevallier				24					Telegraph Clerk	1				
	. Alfonso Maia	42								Merchant				1	
	. Geo J Boxwell	48								—	1				
	G. Pycroft				22					Telegraph Clerk	1				
	Mrs Dunsmure		26							—	1				
	Miss Ralston				21					—	1				
	Wm Wood (manservant)				21					Servant	1				
	Mr Sze Ferreira Valle	46								Naval Officer				1	
Rio de Janeiro	Mr Domingos Braga	38								Merchant				1	
	Mrs J. F. Braga		29							—				1	
Buenos Aires	Mr Salvador Izguerdo	35								Merchant				1	
	Mrs J Izguerdo		28							—				1	
	Raul					5				—				1	
	Salvador					4				—				1	
	Delia						3		3	—				1	
	Roguel					1				—				1	
	Maria (nurse)				30					Nurse				1	
	TOTAL CABIN ...	40	30	46	19	15	14	1	1		101	5	5	55	

70. Letter from Pernambuco on board S.S. "Seguranca", 13th March 1893

18930313 See an image of this letter, http://dx.doi.org/10.17613/ybsk-y128

S.S. "Seguranca"   Pernambuco
13th Mar. 1893

My dear Mother,

Owing to an off-shore wind & consequent low water on the bar this steamer which was to have sailed last night, has had to remain inside the reef till to-day & now we expect to get out abt. 10 o'clock a.m. This gives me time to write a few lines to you & leave the letter here for the "Tagus" which is due here the day after to-morrow.

I had at first intended going to Maranhão by this ship, but somewhere near Bahia she stuck in the mud & was detained for a couple of days, & then she altered her route omitting Maranhão & going direct to Pará.[1] Then I thought of taking the Brazilian steamer "Pernambuco" y'day for Maranhão, but I was so strongly advised not to do so by everyone that I gave up the idea. Brazilian boats are small & very dirty & the food is not eatable, & this particular one, the "Pernambuco", is the oldest & worst of the lot, & will take 6 or 7 days to get to Maranhão as she touches at all the small ports on the way. The "Seguranca" goes in 4 days to Pará & from there I shall have no difficulty in getting a steamer back to Maranhão.

There has been a lot of talk about an expected row in Pernambuco. The Governor & the Legislature can't agree.[2] On one side is the military & on the other side the police.

They were to have fought it out on the 6th & then again last night but I expect it will all end, as it has begun, in talk. Unfortunately it interferes considerably with business.

The French packet "Equateur" is lying outside.[3] I expect she brings letters for me but I shan't get them. Mr Guimarães does not come into town on Sundays & anyway the mails will scarcely be sorted by 10 o'clock.[4]

Keiller[5] came on board last night to see me off; – also Shaw, Harburger,[6] & Harrington, all friends I have made here; – the two latter having also other acquaintances on board to say good-bye to.

---

1. Pernambuco, Maranhão, Bahia, Pará: These are all STATES of Brazil, but names used interchangeably with their respective capitals at the time, i.e. Recife, São Luis, Salvador, Belém.
2. Barbosa Lima was Governor of Pernambuco at the time. A supporter of the proclamation of the Republic, Lima was elected deputy to the Constituent Congress for Ceará. From 1892 to 1896, he was governor of Pernambuco. From 1896 to 1899 he was a deputy for Pernambuco, starting to represent Rio Grande do Sul in the lower house from 1900 to 1905 and the Federal Capital from 1906 to 1911 and from 1915 to 1917. He was elected senator from Amazonas in 1923. In 1919, he was appointed director of Lloyd Brasileiro. Defender of abolitionist ideas, during the Republican period he stood out during the government of Floriano Peixoto, of whom he became a trusted person during the Armada Revolt and the Federalist Revolution: https://pt.wikipedia.org/wiki/Barbosa_Lima
3. Rather than "packet" being an "anglicisation" of paquebot, it is in fact the other way round. Paquebot comes from the English "packet-boat" and is used here to mean a mail boat.
4. Alfred Lopes Guimarães. See Index to People.
5. John Gibson Keiller. See Index to People.
6. Julius Harburger (b 18th March 1863 Frankfurt) became naturalized as a US citizen, 16th July 1891. He was a merchant in Pernambuco.

On Friday night I was at a small dinner-party at Boxwell-Williamses', – took Miss Boxwell in to dinner & had the only other young lady present, Miss Connolly, on the other side.[7]

A pleasant party, good dinner, ditto wines & cigars, & some music.

I must tell you a rather funny piece of absent-mindedness on my part. I was dressing for dinner & had just begun to brush my hair when a fellow called Wilson passed my window. I called him in to speak about another man, Baillie, who was unwell, upstairs, suffering from nervous prostration & sleeplessness through worry & over-work (he was a little off his head & I sat up with him part of one night). When Wilson left I finished dressing but quite forgot I had not parted my hair but only brushed it down over my forehead. I only remembered when I got to the station. At first I thought of waiting till I got to Boxwells' & finishing my toilette in Williams' room, but luckily (for the ladies were sitting in the hall when I arrived) I changed my mind & turned into a bachelors' "chacra" on the way, where there were four men I knew already sitting at dinner, & there I borrowed a brush & comb. I think this proves conclusively that I am not in the habit of looking at myself in the glass very much.

Half past eight.   Breakfast gong.   Adios.

I have enjoyed my stay in Pernambuco very much. Left two photographs of myself ! & several awfully nice friends there.

Best love
Jack

---

7. Probably Lucy Connolly (b ~1870 Pernambuco). She was the daughter of Richard Hamilton Conolly (b 1844 Dublin, d 1905 Recife) and Emma Raymond Gatis (b 1844 Lancashire, d 1923 Lewisham). She never married. She was also on the Boxwell picnic described in the previous letter

71. Letter from Pará, 30th March 1893

18930330 See an image of this letter, http://dx.doi.org/10.17613/tc01-p286

Pará,   30th March 1893

My dear Mother,

It is just a fortnight since I sent you my last postcard by the "Anselm", & I have had no news from you meanwhile.

I have been waiting for three days for the steamer to take me to Maranhão. It is not there yet but it will surely be in today. I mean to make only a very short stay in Maranhão & then to return here & sail for Barbados about the 10th April. These boats that go to Barbados are uncertain in their dates but I expect positively to arrive there between the 15th & 20th April & I am very pleased at the prospect. I think I shall very soon turn homewards now, say inside three months.

There are not many Englishmen here. I have made the acquaintance of two very nice fellows – Power & Duff, & dined once or twice at their house.[1]

Power was former manager of the London & Brazilian Bank here, but had some difference of opinion with the home board & resigned. He & Duff are now in partnership as brokers. They keep house together & their place is a kind of gathering point for the Englishmen here. Duff is from Aberdeen, where his people have a nice house, judging from photos he showed me. Here their house is arranged with all bachelor comforts, – straw lounging-chairs with rugs thrown over them, plentiful pipes & ash trays, & a good supply of English magazines, – a pleasant place to spend a Sunday afternoon.

To-morrow will be Good Friday. To-day – Holy Thursday – I see people are trooping to Mass all dressed in black. But this day is evidently not so strictly observed as in many other Catholic countries. For instance I see carts going about the streets & the trams are running. You do not find that in Colombia nor in Spain. Here, since the declaration of the Republic, the people profess to be "emancipated".

Business begins early in Pará. I have several times had appointments with customers between half past six – seven in the morning.

In Pernambuco I had two suits of pyjamas made. I told the man to make them loose as they would likely shrink, & he has done so with a vengeance. They would do for a man six times my size. The collar measures 22 ½ inches, whereas 16 to 17 would have been ample, & the other measurements are in proportion. I can sleep in them but I cannot go to my bath in them; they look too absurd.

There are two married couples stopping in the same hotel. Mr & Mrs Vaz, Brazilians, & Mr & Mrs Parodi, Venezuelan. Mr V. speaks a little of several languages. The Parodis speak Spanish only. Mrs V. speaks French. Then there is an Englishman who speaks some German. In the evening we sometimes have a game of farthing nap,[2] & then we jabber in Portuguese, Spanish, English, French, & German, – a funny mixture.

When I was sitting in Power's office the other day a gentleman came in & said to me in Spanish: – "Oh, how do you do, Señhor? I hope you are very well." I did not recognize him at first but he reminded me we had met in Barbados. His name is Cabral – a doctor in laws. He is a prominent monarchist & a man of some influence here. When the Republic

---

1. Other mentions in the letters from Pará of 19th-26th April 1893 and 4th March 1894. See Index to People
2. Napoleon or Nap is a straightforward trick-taking game: https://en.wikipedia.org/wiki/Napoleon_(card_game)

was declared he thought it well to go to Barbados for a time. He gave me his card with a great coat of arms on it – lions rampant with goats friskant or something of that kind.

As a souvenir of Pará I have bought a small box of leaves, – gold & silver & slate, some with a metallic polish, others with a mossy surface. They are brought from the interior by Indians & negroes & are sold as curiosities.

<u>Good-Friday</u>.　　The English mail is in & no letters from Belfast – only one from Dundee. I am disappointed. I suppose I shall have none now till I reach Barbados.

I leave this afternoon for Maranhão.

Best love to all.

Jack

72. Letter from Maranhão, 3rd-5th April 1893

18930403 See an image of this letter, http://dx.doi.org/10.17613/zy12-d263

Maranhão
<u>3rd April 1893</u>

My dear Mother,

I wrote you on the 16th March by the "Anselm", & on the 30th by the "Sobralense", both from Pará.[1]

On Good Friday I left that place by the "Pernambuco", a dirty old Brazilian boat & arrived here on Sunday morning. Pará is some 80 miles from the mouth of the river of the same name, one of the mouths of the mighty Amazons that spreads its huge arms north, south, & west, for so many thousands of miles, through the heart of Brazil, up into Bolivia, Peru, Ecuador, Columbia, Venezuela & the frontier of British Guiana.[2]

The smaller river Guamá flows into the Pará just above the town, & in the spring tides I am told a tidal wave some five feet high rushes up it.[3] But in one of the twisting channels on the north side of the large island of Marajó,[4] in the delta of the Amazons, one of the most remarkable tidal waves in the world is to be seen. It is said to be about fifteen feet high. Its limits are marked on the navigating charts of the place.[5]

The Amazons, & its immense tributaries the Rio Negro, the Purus, the Madeira, & many others, are navegable for immense distances. The "Brazilian Lloyd" have a fleet of steamers that ply up & down the coast, leaving Rio de Janeiro at weekly intervals. Some go south as far as Rio Grande. Others come north & these all go up the Amazons to Manáos which is some 800 or 900 miles from Pará – 3 or 4 days' voyage. Mr Brocklehurst (of the firm Singlehurst Brocklehurst & Co)[6] told me that one of their largest steamers from Liverpool, drawing 22 ½ feet, went up to Manáos & back without difficulty.

From Manáos smaller steamers ply far into the interior. One goes every month to a place called Yquitos away up in Peru. It is worth while opening the map to form some idea of this. On the Purus & Madeira there are rapids which steamers cannot pass, but steam launches have been taken up in pieces & put together to ply above these rapids; beyond this again canoes penetrate still for hundreds of miles.

Not infrequently people living up in Bolivia or Peru & wishing to go to some place on the other side of the impassable Cordillera, perhaps not more than one or two hundred miles away as the crow flies, perform a journey of 60 days in canoe & steamer to Pará, & thence go round north by Panama, or south by the Straits of Magellan, to some port on the West Coast.

---

1. Name of the state, but used instead of the name of the capital Belém.
2. British Guiana was a British colony, part of the British West Indies, which resided on the northern coast of South America, now known as the independent nation of Guyana since 1966.
3. https://en.wikipedia.org/wiki/Guam%C3%A1_River. The Guamá River is located in northeast Pará state in north-central Brazil. Its mouth forms the southern border of the state capital, Belém.
4. The largest delta island of the islands in the Marajó Archipelago. https://en.wikipedia.org/wiki/Maraj%C3%B3
5. The "Pororoca": a tidal bore, with waves up to 4 m high that travel as much as 800 km inland upstream on the Amazon River and adjacent rivers.
6. See Index to People.

These waterways are of incalculable value in developing the resources of the country, & all along the rives there is a lively trade. But between the rivers there are still immense regions in the interior of Brazil that have never been explored.

It would be very interesting to go up one or two of these rivers as far as possible, with a proper outfit. Lots of sport one might have, from alligators to South American tigers, besides doing valuable original work in the way of botany, natural history, geographical research, & learned "ologies".

<u>5th April</u>.　　It is just as well I felt in a humour to write the other day, else my letter might have been a very short one. The post closes this afternoon for the direct mail steamer. We all counted on having another two days.

This morning I visited a jute mill recently started here & did some "biz" for Dundee, about which I have still to make out my report. The two Scotch foremen were pleased to have a chat with a countryman.

Letters please to Curaçao <u>via New York</u> c/o Rivas Fensohn & Co[7]

Best love to all

Jack

---

7. Rivas Fensohn & Co was a trading company in Curaçao that issued private paper money in 1893. See Index to People.

73. Letter from Pará, 17th April 1893

18930417 See an image of this letter, http://dx.doi.org/10.17613/0snh-eq10

Pará   17th Apl. 1893

My dear Mother,

Just finished writing to Dundee & to Pater & it is now 2 a.m. I must make this a very short letter, merely to let you know I am flourishing, as usual. I arrived to-day from Maranhão where I spent just a fortnight, – not unpleasantly. There is a very nice clean hotel there with good French cooking, at which I was agreeably surprised. I made the acquaintance of some pleasant people, & usually spent the evenings playing chess or dominoes. I was taken to one ball given by a club. All present had a title for the occasion, & I was honoured with the dignity of "Baron de Gingerale", that being considered "quite English". It was very good fun. I shall give some account of it in my next which I promise to make longer.

After a long interval without news I was glad to find here to-day your letter of 6th Mar. & to hear about all.

I am disappointed to find I shall likely be stuck here for 3 weeks for want of a steamer to Barbados. It is riling as it delays my home-coming by so much. The two that were expected sailed on the same day while I was in Maranhão whereas I thought there w^{d} be fully a week between them. I <u>may</u> get one on the 26th but more likely it will not call at Barbados & I shall have to wait till the 6th May.

Paciencia! It can't be helped, but when I was so informed I felt like the Bishop who asked some layman to say something suitable to the occasion.

Now, good-night. My letters have to be at the Post by 7 to-morrow morning, or rather this morning.

Best love.

Jack

74. Letter from Pará, 19th–26th April 1893

18930419 See an image of this letter, http://dx.doi.org/10.17613/921j-9g28

Pará[1]
19th April 1893

My dear Mother,

In my short letter posted y'day I mentioned having just rcv[d] your letter of 6th March. Today I was glad to get two more – 12th & 20th March, bringing the home news more up to date. Jim 6ft 0 ¾![2] Jupiter! The Baby of the family. Why it's no time since he was a kid in a blue jersey & corduroys. No more cutting down of discarded garments for the small boy. I was thinking of taking home a pair of trousers worn through in that part that suffers most from the friction of cane chairs, saying to myself that twelve inches or so cut from the legs would serve to repair the other place. But I look at them now with a tender regret that a deficiency of six square inches in their structure should prevent their further usefulness to our family.

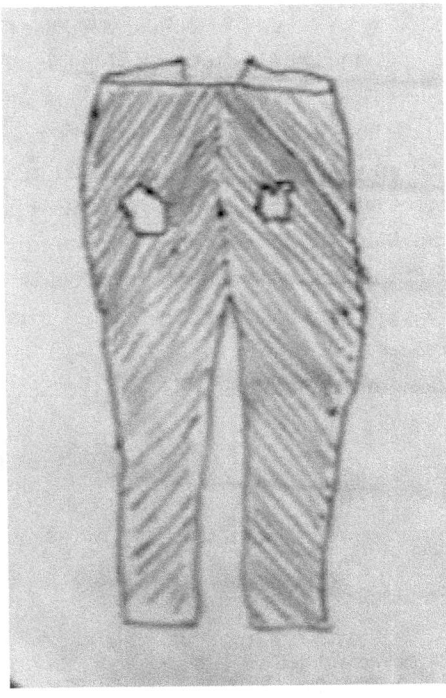

A sketch by JMcC of the location of the holes in his trousers (over the buttocks) that constant sitting in cane chairs has caused

1. The last letter from this packet, ending one day before being able to set sail to travel home via Barbados.
2. This is JMcC's baby brother James Moore, the youngest child in the family, born on 19th November 1874. He is 18 ½.

Well! Well! G.Y.K. reduced to rocking a cradle & wheeling a perambulator![3]

It is well it is a girl, for if it had been a boy he w$^{\underline{d}}$ have had to wait for me to come home to stand god-father to it at the christening.

You must be glad to have your house-cleaning over. People don't bother much about that kind of thing out here, as you would say if you saw the cobwebs on the ceiling & the thousands of ants running over the floor.

An English Commission of Astronomers came to Ceará to observe the total eclipse of the sun last Sunday.[4] On that day I was at sea, between Maranhão & Pará. The sky was perfectly clear & we had a good opportunity of watching the eclipse, which was only partial, about three-fourths of the surface of the sun being covered. I had some amusement in discussing the eclipse with the natives on board. Having made a hole in a card & allowing the sun to pass through it, the eclipse was reproduced on a paper held some little distance behind the card. Then every eyelet in the awning caused the sun to be reproduced on the deck in the shape of a crescent. They maintained this was owing to the cord passing through the eyelets to lace the awning. But when the cord was removed & the crescent remained they could not understand it at all. I should much have liked to have seen the total eclipse. There was nothing very remarkable in the partial eclipse as we saw it. It became a little darker but not very much, & even when the sun was most covered one could not look at it without shading one's eyes or using coloured glass.

I promised to tell you something about that ball at Maranhão. It was given at the house of one of the members of a club formed among the Marahense families for mutual entertainment. I went in a cab with three other gentlemen & one lady, all five inside, & we congratulated ourselves that the resurrected crinoline had not yet come into fashion in Brazil. After fifteen minutes jolt over the deplorable streets, in the course of which we were nearly upset, we came to the house standing in a garden illuminated with Chinese lanterns. As soon as we were inside the gate I was startled by the band striking up a few bars of a march fortissimo as a kind of salvo of welcome. This performance was repeated on the arrival of each batch of guests. The stewards at once rushed forward to receive us & to escort the lady up the steps.

Between 9 & 10 the President, a Prince for the occasion, took the chair, surrounded by his council of Dukes, Marquises, & Counts, & another band inside struck up the Club March, composed for the occasion. Then there were a couple of speeches without which no Brazilian gathering of any kind would be complete. After this dancing began & was kept up till about 3 o'clock. The two strangers, Mr Millet (Frenchman) & I, were summoned to the presence of the Prince, dubbed Barons de Poulet-Canet & de Gingerale respectively, presented with button-decorations & the freedom the guild in a dish of very unsavory "Cariru" which politeness obliged us to swallow.[5] As they were all very kind & attentive to us it is perhaps not fair to make fun of them but really the scene at times was very comical. Many of the guests were coloured – not black – but with a touch of tar. The ladies' dresses were mostly cotton prints with all possible combination of colour. The dancing was bad. The quadrilles are danced pretty much according to the fancy of the master of ceremonies who calls out his instructions in Portuguese French. En avant! En arrière! Balancez vos dames! A vos places!

I saw one young man twice leave his partner to expectorate out of the window! And remember this was the best society of Maranhão.

3. G.Y.K. = George Young Kinnaird. See Index to People. The baby girl referred to was Margaret, his eldest child. George Kinnaird (b ~ 1854) was married in 1892. His wife Letitia was 16 years younger. George's eldest daughter Margaret Kinnaird was born in early 1893 (he was the ripe old age of 39) soon to be followed by her sister Elizabeth H. Kinnaird (a close friend of JMcC's 4 daughters) born 2nd June 1894. George ended up having eight children; including son John Loewenthal Kinnaird (b 19th April 1896).
4. The Brazilian expedition was led by Mr A. Taylor, assisted by Mr. W. Shackleton. "The members of the expedition to Brazil will leave Southampton by the Royal Mail steamer on February 23 for Pernambuco, arriving at the latter place on March 12. They will take passage by the local mail steamers to Ceara, at which place they will arrive about March 20." More from this account from *Nature* of February 2, 1893, is reproduced below.
5. Cariru (*Talinum triangulare*) is a herbaceous plant very common in Tropical America; it reaches up to 60 cm in height. In the Brazilian Amazon region, it is a traditional plant used in different ways in local gastronomy, and it plays an important part in the culture of Amazonian people. Both leaves and stalks of this green can be consumed: https://www.fondazioneslowfood.com/en/ark-of-taste-slow-food/cariru/

There was supper during the evening. In fact on entering I was presented with a card which I took to be the dance-programme but which, on examination proved to be the menu.

Supper was served on little tables in the garden. Altogether it was very good fun.

You would smile sometimes if you saw me saying good-bye to my Brazilian customers.

Perhaps a fat little man in shirt-sleeves: he puts his arm round me & pats me on the back; I do the same to him & look over his shoulder, feeling a strong inclination to "put my thumb up to my nose & spread my fingers out."

The Brazilian coasting-steamers are not very pleasant for an Englishman to travel on. They are fearfully dirty & there is no discipline or decency. The pillows & bed-clothes are taken out of the cabins & dragged all over the place. The first-class passengers sprawl on the deck on the benches, in the music-saloon, & the steerage passengers hang their hammocks forward & amid-ships & along the passages. There they swing & eat bananas & oranges & smoked codfish, & litter the deck with bones & peel. The smell is abominable. The cabins are filthy. On the last trip, at dinner one day I had to give back three forks to the waiter, which he brought me one after the other as clean. The food is mostly uneatable. Fortunately I had brought a bottle of wine & a tin of sardines.

I should like to have taken some photos of the "deckers". One family had brought their flat-bottomed canoe with them & they were camped in it on deck. I saw one young woman with a long comb sticking out of her "chignon", balanced in front by a briar pipe which she smoked with evident enjoyment.[6] It is quite a common thing to see these emigrants carrying about with them the most intimate articles of domestic furniture with entire unconcern.

I received y'day a letter from Bahia, written 7 weeks ago. Of course it was one to which the writer wanted an immediate reply. It went first to Dakar on the coast of Africa, then down to Rio, then to Pernambuco, from which place it was sent here.

<u>21st April.</u> Hurrah! I shall not have to wait here 2 weeks after all. The "Lisbonese" leaves in four days & calls at Barbados. I shall soon be able to wire what steamer I am coming home by.

This afternoon I drove out in the tram to see Mr Rand's garden.[7] He is an American who has spent 14 years in Brazil & devotes himself to botany, particularly to orchids of which he has a very fine collection, one of the finest, I believe, in the world. He is a member of many Botanical Societies in Europe & contributes to their various magazines. I had a very interesting conversation with him. He told me a lot about orchids & showed me round his garden. Unfortunately it was a wet afternoon, & he has not very many orchids in bloom just now, so his collection did not look so imposing as I dare say it would at another time. He has a bright & a rolling eye; – only one, for the other is of glass, which gives his face a somewhat wild expression. He is an animated talker, but not easy to talk to for he is very deaf. Mr Rand has done a good deal of original work & has discovered various new species of orchids. I sh^d like to have bought some Amazonian orchids for Fernbrae[8] but I am told you can't get much from him for less than £20 & that is beyond my means.

6. The majority of pipes sold today, whether handmade or machine-made, are fashioned from briar (French: bruyère). Briar is a particularly well-suited wood for pipe making for a number of reasons. The first and most important characteristic is its natural resistance to fire. The second is its inherent ability to absorb moisture. The burl absorbs water in nature to supply the tree in the dry times and likewise will absorb the moisture that is a byproduct of combustion. Briar is cut from the root burl of the tree heath (*Erica arborea*), which is native to the rocky and sandy soils of the Mediterranean region. Briar burls are cut into two types of blocks; ebauchon and plateaux. Ebauchon is taken from the heart of the burl while plateaux is taken from the outer part of the burl. While both types of blocks can produce pipes of the highest quality, most artisan pipemakers prefer to use plateaux because of their superior graining: https://en.wikipedia.org/wiki/Tobacco_pipe#Briar

7. Edward Sprague Rand (b 1834 Boston, d 1897 Para): "American horticulturist. Born into a wealthy family in Boston, Edward Rand graduated from Harvard in 1855. He thereafter devoted his life to the study and cultivation of tropical plants at his home in Glen Ridge near Boston, especially collecting orchids and rhododendrons. Rand made several trips to Brazil to collect plants and wrote a number of books on the orchids of South America and on cultivating plants in greenhouses. He died while in Brazil." https://plants.jstor.org/stable/10.5555/al.ap.person.bm000006844

8. The Weinberg family home. See "Weinberg" in Index to People.

Just now our afternoon thunderstorm is going on, & the rain is coming down in torrents. How would you like to live in a country where there is a thunderstorm almost every afternoon?

<u>26th April.</u>   Still here. Steamer detained two days waiting for a Bill of Health from Ceará. They need it for Barbados & as they had not at first intended going there they did not get it when in Ceará & now they have to wait for it. But we are to sail positively to-morrow morning.

Last night I gave a little dinner to five fellows who have shown me much hospitality. Mr Power (who describes himself as "once a bank-manager & a gentleman, now a broker", – but makes as broker twice as much as he made when manager of the London & Brazilian Bank), Mr Duff, his partner,[9] Singlehurst, partner in Singlehurst, Brocklehurst & Co owners of the direct line of English Steamers,[10] Jordan, manager of Sub-marine cable station, & Mr Brown "of New York", who wants to electric-light Pará. All very good fellows. We were a merry party. After dinner we adjourned to Jordan's & sang songs till mid-night. Jordan has a good voice & Singlehurst is an excellent musician. The others have voices pretty much like mine.

I shall post this here, & begin a fresh letter at Barbados. Love to all

Jack

Nature February 2, 1893, p. 317

The Approaching Solar Eclipse, April 15-16, 1893

The total solar eclipse of April 15-16, 1893, is not only one of the longest of the century, but is the last of the century from which we are likely to get any addition to our knowledge of Solar Physics. The longest duration of totality of this eclipse is 4 minutes 46 seconds, and as the path of the moon's shadow is to a great extent on land, there is a considerable choice of possible stations with long durations of totality. Commencing in the Southern Pacific the line of totality passes in a north-easterly direction and enters Chili at Charañah in 29° southern latitude, crosses the South American continent, and issues at Para Cura, a village near Ceara, at the north-east corner of Brazil, in latitude 3° 40′ south . . . The eclipse will be observed by several parties of astronomers in Chili, Brazil, and Africa, there being almost absolute certainty of fine weather in Chili and Africa, and a reasonable probability in Brazil. The English arrangements to observe the eclipse have been made a joint committee of the Royal Society, the Royal Astronomical Society, and the Solar Physics Committee of the Science and Art Department, South Kensington; Dr. A. A. Commons, LL.D., F.R.S., undertaking the duties of Secretary. Two expeditions will be sent from England, one to Africa and the other to Brazil, the expenses being defrayed by a grant of £600 from the Royal Society.

---

9. For Mr Power and Mr Duff, see Index to People.
10. Singlehurst, Brocklehurst & Co: Merchants and Shipowners at Liverpool, and merchants at Pará, Brazil. See Letter from Maranhão 3rd April 1893

PART V

THE LETTERS: VOYAGE TO SOUTH AMERICA, 1893-1894

Map of the 1893-1894 voyage by John McCaldin Loewenthal. Note that JMcC refers to Brazilian cities by the names of the states that they are part of. These are shown in parentheses on the map. A high-res version is available online: https://doi.org/10.17613/1cwx-7880 (Original map by Thomas Bachrach)

75. Letter from S.S. Magdalena, 28th August 1893

18930828 See an image of this letter, http://dx.doi.org/10.17613/km0w-hw02

S.S. "Magdalena"
to be posted from Lisbon <u>28th Aug. 93</u>

My dear Mother,

You will have seen from my wires that I reached successively London & Southampton without mishap. In London it rained in the morning but was fine in the afternoon, & I got my shopping done. I hope the Pater got the Picquet box I forwarded as forfeit from the Stores, & you the cap.[1] If latter does not please or is too similar to the last one they will be pleased to change it.

I could not find anything suitable for presents to my lady-friends but I bought a couple of pipes & two pencil-cases – not dear ones – for the males.[2]

I put up at Charing + Hotel but did not like it.[3] The food & accommodation were not in keeping with prices charged. In the evening I spent an hour at Simpson's Divan – saw Bird & Blackburn & other masters.[4] Afterwards I dropped in at the Empire expecting to run across some of the people who w<u>d</u> be going out to S. America next day but did not see any one I knew. But at Waterloo I met a crowd of old acquaintances next morning. Mr Boxwell, Willson, & another from Pernambuco, old McLalennan, a Mr & Mrs Jackson, Mr Abraham Q.C., Mr O'Meara from Rio, & several others with whom I have travelled before.[5] My cabin is not bad, but it might be better & I shall try to have it changed after Lisbon. Until the purser knows how many he has to provide for there nothing can be done.

We have made up a jolly little table of eight & we certainly have more fun than any of the other tables. The other passengers look round with envious enquiry as to the joke when they hear our almost continuous laughter at dinner.

In the carriage with Julian[6] & me going down to Southampton there was a young & pretty American lady with whom

---

1. Picquet (alt spelling of piquet) can be "a trick-taking card game for two players, using a 32-card pack consisting of the seven to the ace only".
2. Presumed to be his sisters and brothers.
3. Till now he always stayed at 205 Adelaide Road when passing through London with Uncle Addie and family – why this change?
4. Simpson's-in-the-Strand is one of London's oldest traditional English restaurants. After a modest start in 1828 as a smoking room and soon afterwards as a coffee house, it gained a reputation as a place to play games. Chess matches were played against other coffee houses in the town, with top-hatted runners carrying the news of each move. The Grand Cigar Divan soon became recognised as the home of chess in England: https://en.wikipedia.org/wiki/Simpson%27s-in-the-Strand. Joseph Henry Blackburne and Henry Edward Bird were noted players of the day, https://en.wikipedia.org/wiki/Joseph_Henry_Blackburne and https://en.wikipedia.org/wiki/Henry_Bird_(chess_player)
5. Mr Boxwell = Mr John Harvey Boxwell (b ~1845) of Pernambuco (confirmed on passenger list); Mr Willson not identified; McLalennan /McLolennan / McClalennan / MacLennan ?; Mr Abraham Q.C. = Mr P. B. Abrahams on passenger list (b ~1849); Mr O'Meara = Patrick O'Meara, Civil Engineer (b 1834 Negagh, co Tipperary, d 1st of April 1898 Harrismith South Africa). Mr O'Meara's obituary in the Minutes of the Proceedings of the Institute of Civil Engineers notes that "in September, 1883, he went to Brazil as Chief Resident Engineer of the Brazil Great Southern Railway, on the completion of which he undertook the duties of general manager as well as engineer. In 1889, he was appointed by Messrs. Punchard McTaggart and Company to take charge of the construction of the Ceará Harbour Works in the North of Brazil. He resigned that post in 1893."
6. Julian Weinberg. See Index to People.

we soon made friends, & by the time we got to Southampton were quite chummy. She goes out to join her husband, an officer on the U.S. cruiser "Yantic", stationed at Montevideo. Julian has made great friends with her little boy, a rather naughty youngster of two summers. This American lady, Mrs Jewett, is the life of our table.[7] Someone was being chaffed about having been seen at the bar early in the day. He explained that he went there merely to have a pencil pointed. "I guess you write considerable" said Mrs J. in inimitable Yankee manner. It was very rich.

She came from N.York by the old "City of Paris" – now the "Paris" – arriving at Southampton on Wednesday afternoon.[8] She did not want to leave England next morning without having "done" London, so she went up with some fellow-passengers, arriving at 10 p.m. ! & coming back perfectly satisfied by 10 a.m. train next morning.

We have about 150 "firsts" on board & I think the voyage will be pleasant. As far as the weather goes it has begun well except for a fog off Finisterre that lost us a day. We should have been in Vigo y'day instead of this morning, & in Lisbon to-day – Sunday – but it will be early to-morrow when we enter the Tagus.

The Bay of Biscay was like a mill-pond & scarcely a passenger has failed so far to turn up at the call of the dinner-bell. The fog was rather a nuisance. When not completely stopped we were going dead slow with the fog-horn blowing constantly.

I have not had any whist so far. It becomes more & more difficult every voyage to arrange a rubber. Poker has almost annihilated its more sober rival. I have played several games of chess, read a novel & a half, & written several letters.

Julian, who just now nearly sat down on my ink-bottle, desires me to note his kind regards.

I sh^{d} have mentioned in due order that I saw the two younger Miss Blacks at Larne & had a five minutes chat with them. They wished me a pleasant voyage in a most friendly manner. Mrs Black has benefited much by the change of air.[9]

On the Stranraer steamer I made friends with the chief engineer who invited me in to look at the engines, & we had a long chat. He pointed out to me an appliance which indicates in the chart-room the number of revolutions of the paddle-wheels, so that in foggy weather the Captain knows by this alone when he is about "there".

I had no letter or wire from you at Southampton, but I hope to hear from you at Lisbon. Julie will give you my address which is c/o O. Letzgus[10], box N° 1 ? 1, B. Aires.

You need not expect news from me for fully a month – a fortnight out to P'bco. & a fortnight back. Best love.

Jack

Monday 28th Aug. 93

Just anchored in the "Tagus".

Last night had a long chat with a charming little woman, Mrs Jackson, who goes out with her husband to Rio.[11] She knows McKissacks very well, especially Mrs McK., has visited them several time in Belfast, & several other Belfast people.[12] She has been in Rio before & knows the Gottos & others there & will be a pleasant addition to my circle of friends.[13]

Bye bye. Hope you are all flourishing & that I shall have news to that effect this afternoon.

Love to all

Jack

7. Lida Eliza P Jewett (b 4th September 1869 New Jersey [née Polhemus]). She is nearly 24 with a two-year old son, Harry Jewett (b 1891). Her husband, Harry Erradt Jewett (b 1868) is indeed an officer on the US cruiser "Yantic": http://www.navsource.org/archives/12/09904.htm. The whole family is on the passenger list returning from Montevideo to Southampton on 8th November 1895. Little Harry dies in 1900 aged 9, by 1910 she will be divorced. She remarries in 1914: https://www.ancestrylibrary.com.au/family-tree/person/tree/87237708/person/422090608466/

8. The "City of Paris", renowned as being the 1889 Trans-Atlantic record-breaker, was renamed "Paris" in 1893.

9. Miss Blacks (the heiresses) from across the way of Lennoxvale and their mother Mrs Black.

10. Ottmar Letgus. See Index to People.

11. On passenger list – going to Rio – traveling with 1 Servant (unnamed!)

12. McKissacks of Belfast – unidentified friends of the Jacksons.

13. For the Gottos, see Index to People.

76. Letter from S.S. Magdalena, 5th September 1893

18930905 See an image of this letter, http://dx.doi.org/10.17613/5ava-fn29

S.S. "Magdalena"   5th Sept. 1893

My dear Mother,

I suppose you got both letter & p.c. from Lisbon. Thanks to Julie for his notes which were delivered to me after the ship sailed.[1] We are now eight days out from Lisbon.[2] We sighted Grand Canary on the third day & since then we have not seen land but to-night we shall view Fernando Noronha & to-morrow reach Pernambuco.[3] These big ships have ceased calling at St Vincent (Cape de Verde), a comfortable omission: – the place is so barren & parched that I never was tempted to land there & the ship, when coaling is going on, is horribly dirty.

The weather has been perfect all along. Not a single rough day, & the heat has not been oppressive.

I mentioned that my cabin was not a good one & that two Brazilians were booked to enter it at Lisbon. Well they came, & the purser held out small hopes of being able to do better for me as the ship was so full. I wondered if my luck was going to desert me, but it didn't! On the second day I was moved into one of the best cabins on the ship, – better than Julian's who paid £7-10-/ more for his ticket.[4] My room-mate is a very nice old gentle-man called Fraser, who does not mind at what hour I come to bed & who turns out before six in the morning leaving me room to dress leisurely. He further gives me an occasional cigar & we get along famously.

We are having a very jolly voyage. I have not played cards much – in fact the smoking-room has not known me, except two nights when I joined a table of small poker which the old Pernambucanos run. There are no whist-players – though half a dozen are willing to play, but they don't know the elements so I seldom cut in: – it's no fun & it's apt to ruffle one's equanimity.

I have a very tough & come-up-again-smiling opponent at chess in the 2nd officer, Mr Joliffe.[5] Y'day we had a hard battle lasting two hours almost. I go to his cabin usually twice a day, before lunch & after dinner; we light our pipes & fall to.

Y'day we had a game of euchre[6] in the Captain's cabin, where we took afternoon tea: – Mr & Mrs Broad, Mrs Jewett & myself.[7]

I the morning y'day Neptune came on board & delivered some amusing letters to various ladies, causing much amusement. In the afternoon he came back & held a court. About a dozen of the young fellows who had not yet crossed

---

1. Julie = JMcC's brother Julius.
2. The duration of the journey from Southampton to Pernambuco was 13 days. Southampton to Lisbon took four days (delayed by one day by fog). As per the previous letter, the journey from Lisbon to Pernambuco was nine days.
3. Fernando de Noronha is an archipelago in the Atlantic Ocean, part of the State of Pernambuco, Brazil, and located 354 km offshore from the Brazilian coast: https://en.wikipedia.org/wiki/Fernando_de_Noronha
4. For Julian Weinberg see Index to People.
5. Probably Austin Joliffe (b 1859 Lincoln), registered as First Mate by Merchant Service in 1887 and Master Seaman in 1891.
6. *Euchre* or *eucre* is a trick-taking card game commonly played in Australia, Canada, New Zealand, Great Britain, and the United States: https://en.wikipedia.org/wiki/Euchre
7. Mr and Mrs Broad are on the passenger list as travelling with 3 children – nil else. Lida Eliza P Jewett, an American lady travelling with her 2-year old son Harry, is described in the notes to the last letter.

the line were shaved with a wooden razor after having been lathered all over the face with a white paste liberally laid on by a white-wash brush, & then chucked head over heels into a sail containing about three feet of water, where four of Neptune's sea-police ducked them about unmercifully.

In the evening there was a very good concert in the 2nd class,[8] which we all attended, the poop being prettily decorated with flags & electric light.[9] We had lots of songs, comic & serious recitations, step-dancing, banjo-playing, & nigger business.

The "nigger" told a funny story about his "gal" having met with an accident. She climbed a peach-tree, got out on a branch, tried to get a peach on the top of the tree, the branch broke & she fell down "peach-less"!

It has been so calm that several nights there has been dancing on deck, to the rapturous delight of two sweet gushing young ladies & the more moderate pleasure of those of more sober age.

The passengers are all pleasant companions, some of them very nice indeed. An engineer who superintends various bridges & water-works under construction in Brazil, Mr O'Meara (Irish of course), whom I knew before at Rio, gave us the other night an interesting lecture on the eclipse of the sun at Cerarã, illustrated by magic lantern slides.[10] He had much to do with the Commission that was sent out from England to observe the eclipse, & lately, when at home, he had an opportunity of examining papers & photographs & learning results which have not yet been published. I have had many conversations with Mr O'Meara & he has lent me a delightful book on Astronomy.

Many thanks to the girls for my plum-cake (I think it was Annie who baked it this time).[11] Several ladies said it was the best cake they had ever tasted, & I was able to have several little afternoon tea-parties, invitations to which were much coveted. And the chocolate creams which were used as padding for the tin made me very popular.

Just now there are two little girls, Silvia & Lucy, who want to be sweethearts to me so I cannot write any more.

Bye-bye. Love to all.

Jack

8. HE was travelling in 1st class (see previous letter, "We have about 150 "firsts" on board . . .")
9. The poop is the aftermost and highest deck of a ship, especially in a sailing ship where it typically forms the roof of a cabin in the stern. Word origin: 15th century from Old French *pupe*, from Latin *puppis*.
10. Patrick O'Meara, Irish civil engineer – see notes to previous letter.
11. "The girls" are his sisters. His sister Anne Isabella Loewenthal (b 1867) baked the cake. See Index to People.

77. Letter from S.S. Magdalena, 15th September 1893

18930915 See an image of this letter, http://dx.doi.org/10.17613/vh8w-dr59

S.S. "Magdalena"   15th Sep. '93

My dear Mother,

By this time you will know more about the Revolution in Brazil than we do. When we arrived in Pernambuco, from which place I posted my last letter to you, there were rumors of trouble somewhere. Cable communication was interrupted & it was said that the Province of Rio Grande, always in hot water, had revolted once more. At Maceió, the new next port of call we learned that the fleet had sided with the Rebels & that we might have difficulty in entering Rio.[1] So we were all up early on Monday morning & there was much excited speculation among the passengers as to what might happen.[2] We steamed up to the fort near the entrance & awaited the usual visit, but no visit came, & the English gun-boat "Sirius" at once signalled to us that no communication was allowed with the shore, but that we might go up to our anchorage & they w^d send an armed escort on board, & that they were prepared to take German subjects, as well as English, under their protection.[3] The English gun-boats "Racer" & "Beagle" were also lying near,[4] & soon the pinnace[5] from the "Sirius" was alongside with a lieutenant & some blue-jackets, & we proceeded to the usual anchorage in the inner harbour rather more than a mile from the shore. There were likewise three Italian men-of-war, & one French, signalling by flags & semaphore to one another. The customary vast amount of shipping was anchored round, but we noticed that none of the steamers were discharging or taking in cargo. On the north side of the Bay the Brazilian fleet was in line, to-gether with all the National coasting steamers, which they had taken possession of, requisitioning their coals & stores. We learned from the officers of the "Sirius" that there had not been much fighting in Rio itself but a hot struggle had been going on for several days on the north side, at Nitheroy, where there is a Government arsenal which had been taken & re-taken more than once by the opposing factions.[6] Later in the day & after much interchange of communications between the fleet & the "Magdalena", we sent some of our Rio passengers & the mails ashore, escorted by the pinnace flying their white ensign, our own boats proudly showing their Union Jack, & they were not molested. That night the Brazilian fleet kept up a vigorous canonade on the forts at Nitheroy, & in the morning between 8 & 9 o'c. there was quite a bombardment, answered sharply by the guns on shore.[7] We were anchored a couple of miles away & we watched it all through glasses without being able to discover whether the fleet had succeeded in landing troops & retaking the arsenal, which was evidently their object. During the night the electric search lights flashed frequently over the Bay & we heard a desultory firing.

1. The journey south to the River Plate and Buenos Aires continues – first port is Maceió: https://en.wikipedia.org/wiki/Macei%C3%B3
2. Presumably outside Rio de Janeiro (Monday 11th September).
3. HMS Sirius was an Apollo-class cruiser of the British Royal Navy which served from 1892 to 1918 in various colonial posts such as the South and West African coastlines, as well as off the British Isles: https://en.wikipedia.org/wiki/HMS_Sirius_(1890)
4. HMS Racer was a Royal Navy Mariner-class composite screw gunvessel of 8 guns (https://en.wikipedia.org/wiki/HMS_Racer_(1884)) and HMS Beagle, launched 1889, was a Beagle-class 8-gun screw steel sloop (https://en.wikipedia.org/wiki/Beagle-class_sloop).
5. a small boat, typically with sails and/or several oars, forming part of the equipment of a warship or other large vessel.
6. Actually Niterói, across the bay northeast of Rio de Janeiro.
7. The monarchist navy revolt in 1893 damaged productive activities and forced the transfer of the capital's headquarters to Petrópolis.

HMS Sirius, the Royal Navy ship protecting English shipping, in 1890.

By the Admiral's orders no one was to be away from the ship after dark. Boats flying a foreign flag were unmolested during the day-time, but two nights before some men from the Italian Legation were returning in a boat from the man-of-war after dinner & they were fired on & one killed. Next day the Italian Admiral sent a boat ashore to demand £5000 indemnity, which was promptly paid.

The Agent managed to come off from the shore & to secure a couple of lighters[8], but we only got about half of our cargo out & we left the lighters anchored there in the Bay. There was no coal to be had either but fortunately we had enough to take us on.

On Tuesday morning, the 2nd officer was going ashore in the steam-launch & just as he went down the ladder he asked me w^{d} I care to go with him. I did not wait for a second invitation but slipped into the launch. The Captain was not pleased about it, I heard afterwards, but there really was no risk. We came ashore & everything seemed to be going on almost as usual. Most of the shops were open & the trams were running, but the Banks had only half a door open, ready to close in case of a row. I saw some of my friends. Youle pressed me to stay overnight, but luckily I preferred returning to the ship.[9] Luckily – because though we expected to be detained several days, we were informed that the Brazilian Admiral had given formal notice of his intention to bombard the town & the United Foreign Ministers had only been able to obtain a postponement of the bombardment till 8 o'c. next morning, so our Admiral advised the Captn of the "Magdalena" to clear out at day-break, which we did.[10] Had I remained ashore, I sh^{d} have been left behind.

As it was the passengers for Santos – some twenty, including several ladies & children – were very much in a fix. They were making enquiries about some steamer to take them to Santos & some had gone ashore & left their baggage on board, while some had remained on board & sent their baggage ashore. Those who had staid with us were transferred at 4 o'c in the morning to a cargo boat belonging to one of our passengers, a Mr Holland, who ordered it to clear

8. flat-bottomed barge or other unpowered boat used to transfer goods to and from ships in harbour
9. Probably Frank (Schwind) Youle (b 1867, d 1900 Rio de Janeiro). See Index to People.
10. This would have been Wednesday 13th September (see below) – when bombardment of the fortress held by the Army began.

out at once, & we left immediately afterwards. As we sailed we saw the foreign men-of-war changing their position, presumably to be out of the line of fire.

Of what has happened since we are of course in entire ignorance. The general opinion seems to be that the Navy, under Mello, backed by Rio Grande, will speedily gain the upper hand, & the President Floriano Peixoto will be deposed.[11]

We have one refugee with us – a little shrimp of a man who has done more harm to Brazil in recent years than any other – Ruy Barboza, finance minister, some say of the last cabinet, some say (& I think) of the present one.[12] But in any case it looks like the rats leaving the sinking ship.

Last time I went north he was passenger from Rio to Bahia, his native town, where he was received with a steam tender decked with bunting, bands of music, rockets, huge bouquets with satin streamers & vivas to the "ilustre Bahiano".

I did not see Murly Gotto at Rio but I left Miss Gotto's parcel, with a note, at the Roy. Mail Agency & they were to deliver it.[13] Neither did I see Spann, Allens, or McKinnels, none of whom were in town that day.[14]

You see we have had some little excitement. As likely the ship has not been wired from any Brazilian port I purpose sending a telegram to the office on arrival at B. Aires.

We are now speculating as to the possibility of quarantine at the River Plate. Recent Roy. Mail ships have had to undergo it – why I don't know unless on acct. of cholera in Europe. Moreover we had to leave Rio without a bill of health or other customary papers.

At Pernambuco I saw Keiller, who had quite recovered from a severe attack of yellow fever, & many other friends.[15] At Bahia I saw no one because it was a strict church holiday & I had not been able to wire from Pernambuco for anyone to meet me.

Since leaving Rio we have had rather rough weather & the fiddles have been on the tables for the first time.[16]

The voyage altogether has been very pleasant. Julian has not suffered much this time from head-aches though he had one or two bad ones.[17]

Now I hope soon to have settled down to work. I trust the Pater has done well & will soon be home in good health & spirits.

Best love to all

Jack

11. Rebels joined forces with the naval rebellion of Admiral Custódio de Melo to oppose the republican regime of Floriano Vieira Peixoto. It was a very bloody revolt – harshly suppressed in the end (not as predicted by JMcC). https://www.encyclopedia.com/humanities/encyclopedias-almanacs-transcripts-and-maps/federalist-revolt-1893. More broadly, this was the second Brazilian Naval Revolt which had started in March 1892, when thirteen generals sent a letter and manifesto to President Floriano. This document demanded new elections be called to fulfil the constitutional provision and ensure internal tranquillity in the nation. Floriano harshly suppressed the movement, ordering the arrest of their leaders. Thus, not legally solved, the political tensions increased. On September 13 (a Wednesday), the fortresses in Rio de Janeiro, held by the Army, began to be bombarded. The rebel forces' fleet consisted of navy vessels and civilian vessels of Brazilian and foreign companies. In the Navy, the rebels were the majority but faced strong opposition in the Army, where thousands of young people joined the battalions that supported President Floriano. State elites, especially Sao Paulo, were also in favor of Floriano: https://en.wikipedia.org/wiki/Revolta_da_Armada

12. Ruy Barbosa de Oliveira (b 5th November 1849, d 1st March 1923), also known as Rui Barbosa, was a Brazilian polymath, diplomat, writer, jurist, and politician: https://en.wikipedia.org/wiki/Ruy_Barbosa

13. This is Percy Murly Gotto, civil engineer and director of the Rio de Janeiro City Improvements company (see Index to People). Percy Murly Gotto's brother, Arthur Charles Gotto (b 1853), lived in Belfast on the Malone Road and had given JMcC the introduction to Percy. I cannot find a record of a daughter but there could have been a Miss Gotto, niece of Percy, or else it was from Mrs Margaret Mary Gotto – Percy's sister-in-law.

14. Adolf Spann was an external commercial agent- his company Adolf Spann & Co. facilitated the development of the Brazilian textiles industry and export. McKinnels JMcC had met on the steamer going to Pernambuco in 1890.

15. This is John Gibson Keiller (b 9 July 1865 Dundee, d 1897 Pernambuco), Fred Weinberg's future brother-in-law. See Index to People.

16. A *fiddle* in nautical settings is a guardrail used on a table during rough weather to prevent things from slipping off.

17. Julian Weinberg (see Index to People).

78. Letter from Buenos Aires, 22nd September 1893

18930922 See an image of this letter, http://dx.doi.org/10.17613/rvwk-8m78

Headed notepaper:　　　　　　　　LENNOXVALE, BELFAST

Friday
<u>22nd Sep. 1893</u>

My dear Mother,

I posted a long letter with an acct of affairs at Rio on arrival of the steamer at Montevideo. We were at once put into quarantine in the Plate, so I did not land at Montevideo, & only y'day came ashore here, as we were allowed to spend the four days on board the "Magdalena" instead of having to go to the lazaretto at Martin Garcia.[1]

There are rumours of revolution too, with actual trouble in the provinces, & the local Radical leaders have been arrested.[2] Consequently business is said to be at a stand-still, – not a pleasant look out. I saw MacCallum[3] y'day, & a number of other old friends.

Julian has gone back to his old digs at Belgrano.[4] I prefer staying in town. I have put up at a Hotel, but I am going out now to look for a room.

I felt quite sorry to leave the ship, having become so accustomed to it during the four weeks we were on board, and it is not pleasant to say good-bye to fellow passengers one has come to know so well on the voyage.

It is still very cold here, at night particularly. I had to put my rug on the bed.

The English paper announces among arrivals by the "Magdalena" the name of Mr J McClournthal.

In the present state of affairs I scarcely know what address to give you, but you had better continue writing here c/o Mr O Letzgus, Casilla 1296, subject to change of instructions by wire.[5]

Best love,

Jack

---

1. Marin Garcia island is an island in the Rio de la Plata – where they had a quarantine station: https://en.wikipedia.org/wiki/Mart%C3%ADn_Garc%C3%ADa_Island
2. The Argentine Revolution of 1893, or the Radical Revolution of 1893, was a failed insurrection by members of the Radical Civic Union (UCR) against the government of Argentina: https://en.wikipedia.org/wiki/Argentine_Revolution_of_1893
3. James MacCallum. See Index to People
4. Belgrano is a northern and leafy barrio or neighborhood of Buenos Aires.
5. This is Ottmar Letzgus, merchant, (b 1861 Germany) resident in Buenos Aires.

79. Letter from Buenos Aires, 28th September 1893

18930928 See an image of this letter, http://dx.doi.org/10.17613/6vsd-t179

"Magdalena"
On headed notepaper:
O. Letzgus   *Buenos Aires, ...28th Sept.................de 189 3*
Casilla de Correo 1296
TELEGRAMAS :   LETZGUS

My dear Mother,

Your first letter, 28th Aug., has just come; – very welcome. Very glad to hear your cap came safely & that you liked it. You write that the Pater has just left.[1] When you get this he will be back again. Telegrams about cholera in various parts of Europe are not reassuring. Nevertheless I trust the Pater did a good business. It seems that several Italian steamers have arrived at Brazil with cholera on board. They are invariably given provisions & sent straight back to Europe. In former years cholera has caused such ravage in South America that the natives have a wholesome dread of it, & the precautions now taken to prevent its re-introduction are so rigorous that it is almost impossible it will ever obtain a footing. We had to spend four days in the River, – that is the ship was in the River, & we were too one afternoon when the skipper allowed us to have a swim. Fortunately we were allowed to remain on board instead of having to go to the dirty quarantine station at Martin Garcia.[2]

The papers will have told you something about the state of affairs here. A foreigner coming to South America for the first time, say by the "Magdalena", must have formed a curious idea of these Republics. At Rio the Navy in revolt & bombarding the town. In the Argentine the whole country in turmoil.

In the streets of Buenos Aires nothing unusual is to be noticed. Shops are open, trams run, & people go about as usual. But business is at a stand-still.

It is not very easy to understand what all the trouble is about. You must know that the Argentine Republic consists of fourteen provinces. There is one Central or Federal Government at Buenos Aires with two Houses of Parliament – Senators & Deputies, but besides that each Province has its Governor & two chambers with Home Rule all round ("Unionists" are welcome to their "there you see"s). The Provinces elect their own Governor & Members, but as the elections are always manipulated, these Governors are practically at the outset nominees of the Party that happens to be in power in the Central Government, though afterwards they frequently, through motives of jealousy & such, strike out in an independent line.

The party now in power comprises several sections of moderate Republicans. Against them are arrayed the Radicals, – now in active protest. There are revolts in the Provinces of Buenos Aires, Tucuman, Santa-Fé, & Catamarca;[3] – revolts in the first place against the Provincial Authorities. Besides that there are various reports, very contradictory that all or part of the Navy is disaffected, & part of the Army. The Government has intervened in the Provinces, sometimes by arms, sometimes but rarely, siding against the Provincial Authorities, & has just now succeeded in restoring Tucuman

---

1. in the letter of 11th October we read that he has safely arrived in St Petersburg, via Berlin
2. Martín García is an island in the Río de la Plata.
3. All provinces in Northern Argentina

to order. According to latest news it w$^{\underline{d}}$ seem that the Government will obtain the upper hand in the other Provinces too, though at first it looked as if the Radicals w$^{\underline{d}}$ triumph. The latter have considerable support but they are scattered & disjointed, whereas the Government has acted energetically & concertedly.

Two days ago a decree was published calling out the National Guard. This is a very extreme step which has not been taken since 1880. It means that all able-bodied men between 18 & 35, born in the country, even of foreign parents, have to go to the barracks. It is not expected that arms will be given them. People say the Government wants to have them under control, knowing that the Radicals count many adherents among the young men.

This leaves many places of business almost without employees, – often without chiefs too. At Sérés' for instance the three sons & the partner Lacaud have been called & there is no one left.[4] Three Kinch boys, – English, but born here, have had to present themselves.[5]

The Consulates are besieged with foreigners taking out their protective "papeleta", a document stating where they were born & giving descriptive particulars of their persons.[6]

I do not think there will be any serious row now. One officer induced two torpedo-boats to escape from the dock-yard at the Tigre & try to win over the rest of the fleet. But they were pursued by another torpedo-boat & one captured after getting a shot into her boiler killing three men. The Government seems to be winning along the line.

Though I cannot do any business for the moment I shall wait here meanwhile in hopes of a speedy settlement. If Brazil is quiet first I shall go there, but I rather think Argentina will soon be quiet & things will resume their normal course.

I have seen many friends already. MacCallums are very well – the Baby all right again.[7]

No time for more. You can write to the address noted on this paper unless you get contrary news from the office. Best love to all.

Jack.

There is no occasion in the world to be uneasy. I shall keep clear of all rows.

4. Unable to find any information on them

5. Sons of Robert Hall Kinch (English), of the Yacht Club, and Flora (Argentinian). From the Buenos Aires 1895 Census, their ages in 1893 were: Walter Halkett aged 26 (died in Kent in 1935, buried in Folkestone), Frank Somerville aged 22, Harold Wright aged 20, and Edgar Tudor Jordan aged 19.

6. Noted that passports requirements were not introduced until WWI.

7. Likely James MacCallum (merchant) and baby Doris born 1892. From Buenos Aires 1895 Census: Doris MacCallum aged 3 ½ (i.e., born around 1892 – no doubt the baby in question); parents "Diego" (probaby James) MacCallum (b ~1849 Scotland) and Emily (b ~1865, England); and baby brother Hector. On passenger manifesto sailing to Southampton from Buenos Aires in July 1895: James and FLORENCE MacCallum with daughter Doris and son Hector. See Index to People.

80. Letter from Buenos Aires, 5th October 1893

18931005 See an image of this letter, http://dx.doi.org/10.17613/gg18-xn85

c/o O. Letzgus, Casilla 1296[1]

B. Aires 5th Oct. 1893

My dear Mother,

A few days ago I sent you a long letter per "Magdalena", giving some account of the recent state of affairs here. Since then the Government has rapidly gained the upper hand, & the Revolution seems to be at an end for the time being. The Radicals made their last stand at Rosario. There was a naval combat between two men of war. One nearly sank the other, & during the fight some of the shells lit in the town, – one passing through two walls & coming to rest on the top of the elevator in the office of Mr Goodwin whom I know. The Government finally retook the town & arrested the principal Radical leaders. We have had only very meagre news all the time, for the Press was under a strict censorship & many papers have been "suspended" for a term of weeks for publishing or commenting on political news. The National Guard has been practically disbanded, & the gold-premium, the real public barometer has fallen from 250 to 240.

Business is still paralized, & there have been several failures in town during the last few days.

Meanwhile I have met many old friends. I was at a little dinner-party at Goodwins, who are at present living in town. I was asked to oblige them at the last moment by filling a gap. As they had asked me to dinner only the week before when I was unable to go, & as I know them very well, I willingly accepted an invitation which from anyone else I sh[d] have declined. It was a very pleasant evg. indeed. We were eight in all. I took in a Miss Troutbeck, a very nice lively girl, & Mrs Goodwin was on my left.[2] She made me sit at the end of the table as otherwise there would have been two ladies to-gether & two gentlemen ditto, & I did a little carving. Two of the other guests I knew already. The conversation was animated & we had lots of fun, not separating till nearly 12 o'clock. We often go to the tennis-club abt. ½ past 4 or 5 & never fail to get a game. Tea is provided there almost every day by some lady member.

My old fellow traveller & twin, Ferguson, (we were born same day & year) told me an amusing story abt. the little Irish doctor on the "Coleridge". He went home again on that old tub, of which I have a lively recollection. On some particular occasion the doctor's table arranged to have a special festivity at dinner. The bell rang & the other passengers took their seats & were astonished to see this particular table gaily decorated with paper flowers & napkins in gala fold but no diners. Finally, when all the rest were seated, in walked the little doctor with a lady on his arm, followed by the other "guests" two & two, all in full evening dress, the gentlemen wearing paper flowers that had been made by the ladies. They had a lively evening, champagne flowed freely, speeches were made, & the festivities were kept up till a late hour. Next morning the little doctor did not turn up at breakfast & a deputation went to his cabin to see what was the matter. They found him in his berth, a towel round his head, & in the rack his paper rose carefully placed in a glass of water!

---

1. Ottmar Letzgus (b 1861 Germany), Merchant, resident in Buenos Aires.
2. Possibly Victoria Troutbeck (b 27th March 1874 Buenos Aires, d 11th December 1937 Sussex). She would have been 19. She married Robert Lawrence Scott-Moncrieff in Buenos Aires on 1st June 1897. Daughter of John Brown Troutbeck from Lancashire and Mary Ann Linay, married in Buenos Aires in 1856. Victoria had several sisters, so it could also have been one of them, but I would have thought all too old except for Charlotte Anne Manuela - who would have been 21. The sisters were: Annette (b 1857), Agnes (b 1858), Mary Jane (b 1860, d 1863 aged 3), Margaret Watson (b 1862), and Charlotte Anne Manuela (b 1872).

I have read since my arrival Hudson's "Naturalist in La Plata", – a most delightful book.[3] You sh^d certainly get it from the Library. I don't know when I read a book with so much pleasure. It is not at all heavy, – quite the opposite, full of curious & interesting accounts of the habits of birds & beasts on the Pampas. Some of the things he tells, such as the dances of birds & the huanacos going to a certain spot to die, are like a fairy-tale.[4]

I paid a hurried visit to La Plata Museum one day but there is no time to tell you abt. it now. It must wait till my next for post closes in a few minutes.

Best love,

Jack

"The Dying Huanaco" from W. H. Hudson's The Naturalist in La Plata (1892).

3. William Henry Hudson, *The Naturalist in La Plata*, with illustrations by J. Smit. Published London: Chapman and Hall, 1892. The first edition appeared in February 1892 in an edition of 1,000 copies, the second edition in June 1892 in an edition of 750 copies. Text available online: https://www.gutenberg.org/ebooks/7446

4. The guanaco (*Lama guanicoe*) is a camelid native to South America, closely related to the llama. Its name comes from the Quechua word *huanaco* (modern spelling *wanaku*).

81. Letter from Buenos Aires, 11th October 1893

18931011 See an image of this letter, http://dx.doi.org/10.17613/j2d2-4746

Buenos Aires   11th October   1893

My dear Mother,

I sent you a letter Oct. 5th by Italian steamer "Orione". Since my arrival I have recvd. three letters from you Aug 28th, Sept. 4th & 11th, – the last came this morning.

Your mention of Somerville reminds me that I looked up his cousin here, Mr Warden, who seems a decent sort of fellow. About a week ago he became a happy father; – a daughter & mother doing well.[1] As soon as things resume their normal course at his house I am to visit him. His wife is American & said to be very pretty. They live at Adrogué[2] & are friends of the Goulds with whom Julian & I dined last night. Mr & Mrs Gould & family are very well & they have not suffered through the Revolution, though for a week they were cut off from communication with Buenos Aires. They gave us a hearty welcome & we spent a pleasant evg. with music & so on. Mrs Gould's cousin, Miss MacKern, from Limerick, is staying with them, a jolly Irish girl whom one might describe as "plump".[3]

So the wonderful summer weather still continues with you. Here it is fine but cold. The morning shower-bath is not yet a complete delight, & an overcoat is needful in the evenings & occasionally during the day.

Very glad to hear of the Pater's safe arrival at St. P. & of orders taken in Berlin.[4] I hope business is better with him than it is here. It is depressing to visit firm after firm & hear them all lamenting the bad trade. My hope is that now tranquillity is restored business may take a speedy turn for the better as it has done before.

Lucky Mr John Ward with his copy books.[5] That is our neighbour, is it not.   More heiresses! Julie & Jim really must take advantage of the <u>golden</u> opportunities that Addie & I have lost.[6]

---

1. The Warden's baby girl is probably Eleanor Margaret (b October 1893).
2. Adrogué is a city in Greater Buenos Aires, Argentina, located 23 km south of Buenos Aires.
3. Elileen MacKern b 1871 (so aged 22 at the time of this letter) sailed from Newport in Wales to Buenos Aires in March 1893 on the Australian and New Zealand Line of Packets ship the "Hawkhurst". In the 1901 Census she was a nurse (single) at the London Hospital in Whitechapel. The MacKerns were (and remain) an important Argentine family. William MacKern with his brother Hector had arrived in the River Plate on 17th November 1843 on the "Talintyre" after a voyage of 77 days. They were among the earliest Irish settlers in Argentina, moving from Limerick where their family had a printing business. Their older brother, George MacKern arrived in 1847 and in 1860 opened a separate business in Montevideo, though returned to Buenos Aires two years later to be made a partner in Mackern Bros. The MacKern brothers' stationery and printing shop, LIBRERIAS MACKERN HERMANOS, was originally located at San Martín 20 in the centre of Buenos Aires (today the site of a cathedral). The company expanded over the years, opening new branches in Buenos Aires and Rosario, but became over-extended and went bankrupt in 1886. The branches in Constitución and Mar del Plata stations, and Rosario survived the bankruptcy but in 1892 Robert MacKern closed Rosario and the other two branches passed into the name of Charles MacKern, son of John (grandfather George de Limerick's first son). http://garycolquhoun.com.au/judaft/genealogy/bridger_daft/aqwn370.htm. LIBRERIA MACKERN continued as an English-language bookseller well into the 20th century and was a favoured haunt of Argentinian intellectuals like Jorges Luis Borges: https://norabenedict.github.io/borges/about.html
4. I presume St Petersburg – did he travel there by train?
5. Probably John Ward, Bookbinder (b ?1856) who lived 15 mins walk from Lennoxvale (Ulsterville Gardens) in 1911 and in Napier Street in 1901 (18 mins walk).
6. More heiresses (not just the Blacks) in Lennoxvale? Or more Black girls?

You are all right in pit at Carl Rosa if you can get in without crush.[7] Quite right about saving money. I am going to be economical. As a matter of fact my board & lodging here cost me very little, – about half of what Julian pays.[8] I have a very nice room, with balcony to the street & view of the river, in a clean & respectable lodging house where several fellows whom I know live: 70 paper dollars per month including coffee in the morning – about £ 4. Then I have "pension", lunch & dinner, at an English Restaurant, clean, good service, & excellent table, for 60 dollars, – in all, board & lodging under £ 8 a month. Of course there are a good many extra expenses, but I never lived here so cheaply & so well before. "The Brunswick" Restaurant is patronized by almost the whole English Colony. All the Bank Clerks go there & it is really, with the exception of the two "swagger" Restaurants, "Paris" & "Mercer", the best place in town. Lunching & dining there without "pension" costs quite three times as much. If often take a friend there to dine & pay $ 3.50 for him, for the same dinner that costs me $ 1.

I suppose the deafness you complain of is the result of that wetting. You should be more careful. I hope it is all right again now. Julian still suffers from head-aches but is otherwise all right. He lives at Belgrano[9] – 20 minutes by rail from town, then 10 minutes walk, with people called Getty. Getty's father was, he told me, mayor & later member for Belfast,[10] & he, the son, is a cousin of the Crossleys.[11] He married a widow with two or three daughters, Foster by name. He is a clerk in the British Bank, with not too large a salary, & Weinberg & another lodger help to pay the household expenses, without which I fancy Getty would have some difficulty in making ends meet. I have not been to the house, but I have spoken to him here in town. He seems a very good-natured fellow, & they certainly looked after Julian well when he was ill.

The Revolution is over now in the Argentine though the state of siege is still in force, by which military supersedes civil law. Part of the National Guard will remain under arms for some time.[12] In Brazil the state of things is still worse than before. During the bombardment a clerk of the London & Brazilian Bank was killed, – a young fellow who had only been in the country a few months. It was his own fault for being in town when all foreigners had been advised to leave.

"Trent" leaves to-day, but I send this by French S.S. "La Plata", which is probably quicker.

Best love

Jack

7. The Royal Carl Rosa Opera Company performed at the Theatre Royal in Belfast 11th–16th September 1893 One can leaf through the programme and read the admission prices here: http://www.digitaltheatrearchive.com/archives/2330 . Performances among others: *Carmen* (11th September), *Rustic Chivalry* (12th September Matinee), *Orpheus and Eurydice* (12th September evening), *Pagliacci* (13th September), *Postillion of Lonjumeau* (14th September), *The Daughter of the Regiment* (15th September Matinee), *Othello* (15th September). Prices of admission: Dress Circle 7/6; Orchestra Stalls 5/-; Upper Circle 3/-; Pit 2/- (*very thrifty of Jane!*); Gallery 1/-
8. Julian Weinberg (see Index to People).
9. Belgrano is a northern and leafy *barrio* or neighbourhood of Buenos Aires, Argentina.
10. Samuel Gibson Getty (b 30th November 1817 Belfast, d 15th Dec 1877 Kensington) was Mayor of Belfast 1856–1859. He was married to Emily Crossley (b 23rd December 1830 Ireland, d 1884 Kensington) and had 3 sons: William (b 1853), Arthur Radcliffe (b 1861), and Walter Baron (b 1862) . . . none of whom I can trace to Argentina.
11. His mother was née Crossley, daughter of William Crossley (b 1797 Londonderry) who had three brothers and three sons. The Crossleys were a well known Belfast family.
12. Argentine Revolution of 1893. 28th July–25th August and 7th September–1st October 1893. Locations: Buenos Aires, Santa Fe, San Luis, Tucumán and Corrientes, Argentina. Action: Attempt to depose the fraudulent government of the National Autonomist Party and to call national elections. Result: Revolution crushed by the government after revolutionaries temporarily took power of the provinces of Buenos Aires, Santa Fe, San Luis, Tucumán and Corrientes and Alem was proclaimed president in Rosario.

82. Letter from Buenos Aires, 25th October 1893

18931025 See an image of this letter, http://dx.doi.org/10.17613/yew0-pp39

Buenos Aires   25th Oct.   1893.

My dear Mother,

I have not had any letters from you since I wrote last some twelve days ago.

I hope you liked the photos of your daughters & were as entirely surprised at seeing them as was intended.[1] Yes, I <u>did</u> have a letter from you, – Sept 18th, – which I have not acknowledged yet, – the "Opera" letter. I am treated to an opera here every morning. There is a man in the next room whom I should like to strangle. As soon as he rises he breaks forth in song, or rather in inarticulate hum – ah – eh – oh – hummings with trills & operatic flourishes which he keeps up till he has finished dressing. I don't think he even stops while he brushes his teeth. I have tried to whistle him down, I have tried jumping the coffee-tray up & down, hammering on the table, banging the chairs about; – it is all of no use. I understand the man on the other side has made a compact with him that he may gurgle & chortle all the week if he will only be quiet on Sundays. And so on Sundays he starts suddenly on the high C, remembers, chokes, & is silent for three minutes. Then comes another burst & another choking. I fear this weekly effort to suppress himself is slowly undermining his constitution.

You have <u>still</u> strawberries & we have strawberries <u>already</u>, but those here have not much flavour yet. They will be better bye & bye. I wish the warm weather would come. Those woollen socks are very comfortable & I usually wear my top-coat. It is a <u>very</u> late season. As a rule October is quite warm.

I have just exhausted myself in a letter to Olga & have told her about a big auction, where I might have picked up some nice trifles for Mrs John D. had she given me a commission to spend a few hundred pounds for her. Auctions are a characteristic feature in Buenos Aires. All the large importing firms have regular auctions of goods, – not of odds & ends that they want to clear out, but of current merchandise. The great bulk of the live stock, both imported & bred in the country, is disposed of by auction, & in half a dozen marts in the centre of town there are almost nightly auctions of furniture, books, wines, & every conceivable thing.

The occupation of auctioneer is considered quite a distinguished career. Ex-president Pellegrini is partner in a firm of auctioneers of live-stock. The former Lord-Mayor of Buenos Aires, Mr Bollini, was & is an auctioneer. The Bullriches, auctioneers, are well-known & wealthy people, & so on.[2] To be a "rematador" is to be "somebody" in Argentina.

I was hungry for breakfast this morning & I had some very good porridge & cream, an omelet, an excellent chop & a glass of beer, all for one & three-pence. That is no exorbitant, is it?

The fighting still goes on at Rio. The Pacific steamer in to-day brings the latest news, as per paper I send to Julie. A piece of a shell lit on her decks as she was steaming out.

Here we are quiet & the gold premium has fallen, but business is still as bad as it can be.

This Pacific mail brings me your letter of 25th Sept., also one from Pater from Berlin.

---

1. His sisters (Annie aged 26, Emma aged 24, and Olga not quite 23). I wonder when and where he arranged this for Jane.
2. "On April 8, 1867, a key character in the history of our city, Mr. Adolfo J. Bullrich –Mayor of Buenos Aires under the presidency of Gral. Roca- set up the Firm under the name of Adolfo Bullrich y Cía: https://bullrichcampos.com/en/historia/

Mrs MacCallum will be glad to have her mother here.[3] I was at MacCallums' on Saturday evg. They are most likely going to Quilmes, a few miles out of B.A., to live.[4]

I wish there was some business doing. I am in hopes of an improvement from day to day. If only the summer would begin, the buyers would come in from the country for the new season's goods & things would begin to move all round.

Mr Hischberg is back here again.[5] There is something the matter with his eyes, but he hopes they will be all right again soon.

I must trot out again now & see if I can find a customer who will cheer me with a prospect of business. Most of them will do nothing but bewail the sad times & talk of failures happened or impending. It will all come right – bye & bye.

Best love

Jack

3. James (b 1849 Scotland), Merchant, with his wife Emily (or Florence? - see previous letters -, b ~1865) and daughter Doris (b 1892). See index to people. No indication as to Mrs MacCallum's mother was.

4. Quilmes is a city 17km south of Buenos Aires. During the first British invasion, lasting 46 days in 1806, the British arrived from Montevideo through Quilmes and went to Buenos Aires from there. Quilmes was also inhabited by British immigrants: Juan Clark, born in Yorkshire, England, was president of the municipality in 1855. The Clarks were owners of land in Quilmes, and were linked to the Irish and Scottish community, established in the area since 1830s: https://en.wikipedia.org/wiki/Quilmes

5. Edward Hirschberg (b Pomerania 1851, naturalized Dundee 1887), Merchant. See Index to People.

83. Letter from Montevideo, 9th November 1893

18931109 See an image of this letter, http://dx.doi.org/10.17613/vvpd-rh90

Montevideo   9th Nov.   1893

My dear Mother,

For the last few days I have been here, on the "other" side of the "River". Business is not brilliant here either, but at all events it is a little better than in Buenos Aires, & it is a relief to be able to send even a few small orders. I wrote you by "Thames" 26th ult. Before leaving B. Aires I got your letter of 2nd Oct. Julian went to the Camp for a week.[1] His neuralgia was bad again. I do not see so much of him now that he lives in Belgrano but we usually meet once or twice a day. Josephy will be there for a few weeks more.[2]

Very sorry to hear of James Black's serious accident.[3] How is he now?

This place is full of Argentine political refugees; – Radicals who sided with the Revolution & who now deem it prudent to take a little change of air. One of the leaders is Dr Ayerza, a lawyer, whom I have the honour of knowing.[4] Y'day he raised his hat to me, bestowed on me the sweetest of smiles, & made kind enquiries as to my health. I forthwith became a convert to Radical (want of) Principles.

But this is not my only acquaintance of standing. To-day I was greeted politely by a real live Belgian Count, a former travelling companion. To be sure his standing is only about four feet six, but he makes up in distinction what he lacks in height.

The "Tagus" passes homeward to-morrow. I shall try to find time to go on board to pass the time of day to Bertie.[5] It was only y'day I heard he was still on the old ship. I thought he was to be transferred to one of the new ones.

The weather all last week has been perfect. Spring & Autumn are the two delightful seasons in the Plate.[6] Clear skies & summer warmth tempered by light breezes. I do no care much for Montevideo for I know scarcely anyone here, & life is very quiet, but the town, though smaller than B. Aires, is brighter, cleaner, & more imposing. The broad well-paved streets & the many stone houses give an air of solidity & respectability to the place, beside which B. Aires seems shoddy.

On Sunday young Thomsen drove me to his Father's country-house – the "Chacra", & I stayed overnight.[7] For this part of the world it is a beautiful property, – not the house, but the grounds which are wooded with firs, oaks, eucalyptus, palms & many other trees.

1. Julian Weinberg (see Index to People). The "Camp" = "the countryside" = the "bush" in Australia.
2. Albert Josephy (b 18th January 1859 Mecklenburg-Schwerin). Connected to Moore & Weinberg. See Index to People.
3. James Black who got married in NY in Jan 1891 – probably related to the Black "heiresses" across the way.
4. Francisco Ayerza (b 1860 Buenos Aires, d 1901 Argentina) was a photographer and founding member of the Argentine Photographic Society. He studied jurisprudence without this preventing him from participating in politics, since he not only intervened in the Revolution of 1890 but also held, although for a short time, a seat in the Chamber of Deputies. https://second.wiki/wiki/francisco_ayerza#Enlaces_externos
5. Herbert Weinberg – working as ship's engineer. See Index to People.
6. The River Plate ("Rio de la Plata" Spanish for "river of silver") is formed by the confluence of the Paraná and Uruguay rivers near Buenos Aires. It lies both in Argentina (to the South) and Uruguay (to the North).
7. Likely Alfred Thomas Thomsen (b 1873 Montevideo), the son of Alfred Thomsen (b 1843 Germany) and Helena Tomkinson (daughter of Thomas Tomkinson 1804-1879). Thomas Tomkinson was involved in many aspects of trade and finance development in the River Plate area.

In Rio the revolution continues. It will cost the country a mint of money. In spite of the sanguinary reports the bloodshed will, I fancy, not be found to be in proportion to the expenditure of powder & shot. There is a reluctance on both sides to kill, partly owing to an appreciation of the fratricidal nature of the struggle, I suppose, & partly to the fear of consequences to each should the other side ultimately triumph.

I have a good deal to do for tomorrow's mail, which means writing for some hours this evg. after dinner. I do not at all fancy it, but once I settle down to it & get over my first feeling of sleepiness it usually goes all right. This morning I was up at six. Now the warm mornings have come it is much easier to rise.

Best love,

Jack

84. Letter from Buenos Aires, 15th November 1893

18931115 See an image of this letter, http://dx.doi.org/10.17613/7wk2-k357

Buenos Aires,   15th Nov. 1893.

My dear Mother,

My last letter was from Montevideo, 9th inst. I came back y'day. to B. Aires & recvd. your letter of 17th Oct. & the photos which I like very much indeed. I think they are all good. I shall get them framed & covered with glass in portable fashion. Many thanks to Julie for sending his too.

So the Pater got quarantine for 48 hours. I hope he had someone to play piquet with, or was he reduced to "patience"? Give my love to Aunt Martha. Is she so very deaf now that she requires an ear-trumpet?[1]

I saw Bertie at Montevideo, on his way home, not altogether pleased at being still on the old "Tagus" instead of on one of the new ships, but still satisfied with the life & with his independence.[2] Your last letter came by the "Nile": – her first voyage.[3] She is considerably bigger than any of the other steamers of the Roy. Mail Co. When she has completed her four days quarantine I shall go on board. I know all the officers, & "chummily" the 1st, Mr Tyndale.[4] There is some talk about a ball to be given on board, – by the Agents I suppose. It is just possible I may go up to Bahia by the "Nile", to-morrow week.

Since the warm weather began I rise regularly between six & half past. It is not yet 7 a.m. How's that for energy?

Julian is back from the Camp & considerably better. A German doctor here, whom he consulted, said his neuralgia is nothing but the contraction of a little nerve in the forehead, which he proposed to cut out – an operation, if it can be dignified with the name, which he says he performs frequently, & with success. But I don't think Julian will allow any cutting to be done without consultation at home. The doctor thinks it a very simple matter. Meanwhile he has given him some ointment which has done him good.

I have written this letter with copying-ink, not because it is even more uninteresting than usual, but because two steamers leave to-day, the "Galicia", Pacific S.S., & the Italian "Perseo",[5] & I do not know which is quicker so I send a copy by each, which is as good as two letters. I wrote to Pater last mail & to Jim by this.

Love to all

Jack

1. Martha McCaldin: Jane's unmarried maternal aunt, now 85 (born 1808).
2. Herbert Weinberg (see Index to People). He is engineer on the "Tagus" – built in 1871 (so 22 years old at the time, only removed from fleet in 1897).
3. S.S. Nile. Royal Mail vessel. Built by J&G Tomson Ltd, 1893 in Glasgow.
4. Most likely Andrew Tyndall, engineer, (b ~1853) on passenger list sailing on the S.S. Nile from Buenos Aires to Southampton, arriving 17th December 1893. (See Index to People).
5. The "Galicia" operated by the Pacific Steam Navigation Co. Built by Robert Napier & Sons, Ltd., 1873 in Glasgow. Decommissioned 1898. The "Perseo" operated by Navigazione Generale Italiana. Built by Robert Napier & Sons, Ltd., 1883 in Glasgow.

85. Letter from S.S. "Nile" near Bahia, 1st December 1893

18931201 See an image of this letter, http://dx.doi.org/10.17613/shse-j012

S.S. "Nile", near Bahia   1st Dec. '93.

My dear Mother,

You will have heard of my telegram to the office giving Bahia as my address. To-morrow I expect to arrive there, so I am writing this to send on with the steamer. Before leaving B. Aires I recvd. your welcome letter of 9th Oct which was a long time on the way. Perhaps I acknowledged it in my last of Nov. 15th though.

As things are still so bad in the Argentine I have come up here to try Bahia & Pernambuco with the intention of returning to the "Plate" if business improves there.

I scarcely expect it to be very good in Brazil either with the fighting still going on in Rio, but it can't be worse than in B. Aires & I must go somewhere. We spent a day in Rio Harbour & had an excellent view of the proceedings as we lay not much more than half a mile away from Admiral Mello's flagship the "Aquidaban", which was engaged with three shore batteries, and about a mile from Fort Villegaignon which was being pounded by Santa Cruz & Lage Forts & a heavy battery on the hills.[1] The expenditure of powder & shot, & the consequent noise & smoke, were most impressive, but the only damage done, as far as we could see, was to the Rebel Fort Villegaignon, where about one shot in five or six took effect, sending the masonry flying & raining clouds of dust, while the rest fell into the water, sending up columns of spray.[2]

---

1. The Brazilian Naval Revolts, or the Revoltas da Armada (in Portuguese), were armed mutinies promoted mainly by Admirals Custódio José de Mello and Saldanha Da Gama and their fleet of Brazilian Navy ships against the claimed unconstitutional staying in power of the central government in Rio de Janeiro. The revolt included the powerful battleship "Aquidaban" and a collection of small ironclads, modern cruisers, and older wood 'cruiser' or steam frigate type ships. https://en.wikipedia.org/wiki/Revolta_da_Armada. The "Aquidaban" was a Brazilian ironclad battleship built in the mid-1880s. https://en.wikipedia.org/wiki/Brazilian_battleship_Aquidab%C3%A3

2. Fort Coligny was a fortress founded by Nicolas Durand de Villegaignon in Rio de Janeiro, Brazil in 1555, in what constituted the so-called France Antarctique historical episode. For protection against attacks by hostile Indians and the Portuguese, Villegaignon built the fortress with the help of the 500 colonists who travelled with him in two ships armed by the king of France, on a small island called Serigipe by the Indians of the region, near the mouth of the large Guanabara Bay. The island was rocky and almost barren, but served Villegaignon's purpose of being near the shore, at the same time achieving a good defensive position against attacks from sea and land. The fortress fell and was destroyed on March 17, 1560 under the siege of Portugal's navy and troops under the command of Mem de Sá, third Governor-General of Brazil. Villegaignon had already returned to France, in 1558. The fortress was named as such in honor of Villegaignon's supporter and friend, the French Admiral and leader of the Huguenots, Gaspard de Coligny. After the foundation of Rio de Janeiro in 1565 by Estácio de Sá and the expulsion of the French in 1567 a new fortress was built there by the Portuguese, in order to defend the mouth of the Guanabara Bay, by crossing fire with two other fortresses, Guajará and Santa Cruz. This fortress was almost totally destroyed by bombardment in a revolt of the Navy, in 1893. Today, the island, which was renamed Island of Villegaignon, is home to the Naval School (since 1938) and is permanently connected to the mainland, near the Santos Dumont Airport. https://en.wikipedia.org/wiki/Fort_Coligny

This map will give you an idea of the position. All forts are on the Government (Peixoto's) side except Vellegaignon which after two months neutrality, declared for the revolted fleet.

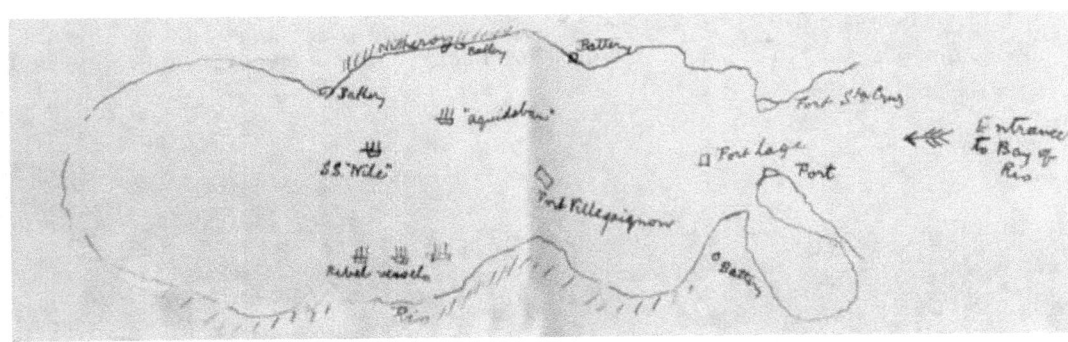

Map of the Rio harbor showing positions of the various ships on December 1, 1893, and the three forts that guard the mouth of the Guanabara Bay. Sketch by JMcC.

We were stopped outside the Bay by the Govnmt. forts to land Rio passengers, others not being allowed to leave the ship. This measure is to prevent Mello's emissaries from coming & going freely. We steamed up to our anchorage before 9 o'c. a.m. & the firing began very soon after.

From Sta Cruz to Villegaignon is about a mile & a half.[3] The Rebel vessels anchored close to Rio did not take an active part that day. The United foreign war vessels of which there are some 15 or 18 in the Bay will not allow them to fire on the town itself.

I have written a long description of it all to Mrs Weinberg, by way of a Christmas letter & I don't like writing about the same thing all over again. Besides the above is really all there is to tell, in fewer words.

A friend of mine who joined us at Rio knows all the leading men personally, & he says that there will be a restoration of the Empire within six months & the grand-son of the late Emperor will be called to the throne. It is all arranged. Mello is to leave Rio, & Admiral de Gama[4] is to unite various elements that have declared their readiness to support him, get rid of Peixoto, & give the country the opportunity of recalling the Imperial family. My friend declares the Country will acclaim the restoration, having had quite enough of Republican Government. He speaks very positively about it & he has special opportunities of obtaining inside information.

The "Nile", this new steamer of the Roy. Mail Co, is a very fine ship. She has a magnificent promenade-deck & there are notable improvements on the last built vessels in the smoking-room, the ventilation, & the general arrangement.

I know almost all the officers & I have had a cabin to myself for the 9 days' run from B. Aires to Bahia.

The voyage has been very quiet; I have written a lot of letters & played a good deal of chess, but I would much rather be working with some result if I could manage it.

There is an American lady on board whom I met once in B. Aires. She is unmarried, not very young, & not very pretty, but bright, amusing, & well-informed. Well, at Rio six or eight middies from an American man-of-war came on board, and after dinner one of them turned to me on deck, – begged pardon – was I a passenger – his friends had come to see him off – would I introduce them to some of the young ladies!!! For calm glorious sublimity of cheek give me the stars & stripes! I smilingly acquiesced, begged to be presented to his comrades & having obtained the American lady's

3. Apart from Fort Villegaigon, there were two other forts - both guarding the mouth of Guanabara Bay. Fort Santa Cruz (https://en.wikipedia.org/wiki/Fortaleza_de_Santa_Cruz_da_Barra) and Fort Lage (https://pt.wikipedia.org/wiki/Forte_Tamandar%C3%A9_da_Laje).
4. Luís Filipe de Saldanha da Gama (b 7th April 1846 Campos dos Goytacazes, d 24th June 1895 Campo Osório, Rio Grande do Sul) was an admiral of the Brazilian Navy. He led the Revolta da Armada against the Brazilian Republican government with Custodio Jose de Melo and was killed by Brazilian government forces in the Federalist Riograndense Revolution. https://en.wikipedia.org/wiki/Saldanha_da_Gama and https://history.state.gov/historicaldocuments/frus1893/d86

permission I led them up to her & introduced them in a batch, & then left her holding a court. I had to go away & have a quiet chuckle to myself.

Please send your letters to Pernambuco c/o Mr Theo Just.[5] I am somewhat uncertain where I shall go next. It depends on circumstances, but the letters will be forwarded wherever I may be.

I hope to have another opportunity of writing in time for Christmas, but if not, a merry one to everybody, with good cheers & a pleasant outlook for the coming year.

Best love,

Jack

The Aquidaban bombarding the forts of Rio de Janeiro, print by M. Fouqueray, copied from a photograph. Reproduced in the Le Monde Illustré of 16th December 1893.

5. Theodor Just. Moore & Weinberg agaent in Pernambuco. See Index to People.

86. Letter from Bahia, 12th December 1893

18931212 See an image of this letter, http://dx.doi.org/10.17613/y85q-4756

Bahia   12th Dec.   1893

My dear Mother,

I wrote you by the "Nile" on my arrival. There has been no time for letters to come here yet except a couple that were forwarded to me from Buenos Aires, with three Whigs that will take me as many weeks to read. Last time I was in Bahia I had a room in a private German boarding-house, which this time is full unfortunately. I went to a hotel the first night, got a small dirty room & was nearly eaten up by mosquitoes so next morning I removed to another hotel where I am slightly better fixed, but it is an uncomfortable change from the clean lodgings & decent food of the South to the dirt & uneatable provender of Bahia. I was allowed to bring only my small things – a hand-bag or two – with me from the steamer; my trunks were sent to the custom-house, &, Sunday intervening, I could not get them till Monday. A disagreeable surprise was in store for me. My smoking-jacket, dress-trousers, & black tailed coat, all as good as new, were missing, but whether stolen from my cabin, or from the lighter that brought the trunks to the custom-house, I cannot say. I think the former, for the lock of my big leather trunk is good & not easily picked. It is the first time that I have anything stolen while travelling. I purpose wiring to the Chief Officer on the "Nile" to Lisbon to have a search for them. It will cost another £2 or so, but the things are worth £10.

Business for the moment is not bad in Bahia, but there are several holidays this month, & towards the end of the year people are difficult to persuade to do business, as they have stock-taking before them.

It was your letter of Oct 23rd I sh^{d} have acknowledged in my last. I sh^{d} have much later news from you now by next mail.

A good friend of mine, Mr Hoyer, who took that photo with the straw hat, asked me to stop with him for a few days at the "Barra", so I was there from Thursday till Monday. His wife is English & he has three nice little children.[1] The "barra" is about an hour by tram from the centre of town, on the sea, round the lighthouse which stands on the point at the entrance to the bay.[2] I had a swim every morning at six o'clock, walking down from the house in pyjamas, even thus much clothing being considered "dressy" by the inhabitants. Then a cup of coffee & some eggs at seven, & into town by ½ past eight.

On Thursday night I was at a very pleasant dance at the English Club; – got a pair of "bags" made that day by an obliging ebony tailor. There were a few Brazilians at the ball, as well as English. I was introduced to one young lady. She wrote her name on my programme – "Elisinha" – nothing more. Imagine a young lady in England, introduced to a man at a dance, writing "Mary-Ann" on his programme. I had to leave early with Hoyer & there was not time to explain to the ladies "booked", so I gave my list to another man, asked him to apologize for me & claim the dances. I have an idea from what I heard since, that he did so with the good-looking girls & the good dancers, & forgot the rest. It was only later that I remembered the descriptive notes on my programme – corals, pink & flowers, blue stripes, & so on.

---

1. George Hoyer, merchant (b 1860 - ? Germany), wife Margaret (b ~1869), Vera (b ~1888), Alice (b ~1890) and Olga (b ~1892) See Index to People.
2. South of the city of Salvador, Barra is a vibrant seaside district home to the bayside Porto da Barra beach, with its calm waters and 17th-century fort, and ocean-facing Farol da Barra which has surf-friendly swells. Dating to 1698 and famed for its sunset views, black-and-white-striped Barra Lighthouse also houses a museum displaying nautical artifacts.

To-night I am invited to play whist with a Mr Oakes, – married to a German lady, but as he does not believe in playing "according to rules & books" it will scarcely be satisfactory, but there will be some families there whom I know.

We have no news here at all about affairs in Rio, & the people don't seem to trouble themselves much about the revolution, so long as they are left in peace. The merchants wisely say "We don't care if we have an Empire or a Republic or no Government at all, if they will only leave us alone."

13th Dec.   Admiral de Gama has issued his manifesto as predicted.[3]
Very hot here & much rain. I had a good swim this morning. Hope to have news from you soon.
Best love, & a happy new Year to all.
Jack

3. Luiz Felipe Saldanha da Gama was the rebel leader resisting the military coup of 1889 and calling for a national plebiscite to determine the nature of government most appropriate for the future of Brazil. Here is a nice pen portrait of the man, "The personality of the Admiral alone kept the revolt alive. Luiz Felipe Saldanha da Gama was a man of exceptional ability, who had become Rear-Admiral in the Brazilian navy after long service. A descendant of Vasco da Gama, he had the pride of family tradition deep-rooted in his heart. The subservience of political principles to personal motives had no place in his life. He had traveled extensively, and his knowledge of English, French, Italian, Spanish and German enabled him to profit from his journeys. Whilst holding aloof from political affairs in Brazil, he frequently expressed to his more intimate friends his contempt for the politicians who had dragged his country down since the abolition of the imperial regime. He condemned the dictatorial methods of Peixoto, and at heart was a devoted servant of the exiled royal family. His personal inclination was for its restoration, but he never proposed to re-establish monarchy by force." https://www.globalsecurity.org/military/world/war/brazil-1893-2.htm

87. Letter from Bahia, 20th December 1893

18931220 See an image of this letter, http://dx.doi.org/10.17613/1yvp-k387

Bahia,   20th Dec.   1893

My dear Mother,

I wrote you some 7 or 8 days ago, when I also sent a scrawl to Emma, – by German steamer. Y'day I recvd. some letters from B. Aires – among them yours of Oct 30th & Nov 6th – a little old, but welcome all the same. Your chat about people & things is very interesting. So Miss Dunlop was at Fernbrae & they gave a dance![1] I wonder has Miss Boxwell been in Holywood since visiting the Dunlops.[2] Bob Fuhr has passed at last, has he?[3] Do you ever hear anything of Harry Fuhr.[4]

I hope Annie is better. Many thanks to her for her letter, which Julie enclosed.[5]

Answering your questions, – I left MacCallums very well indeed.[6] A few days before sailing from B. Aires I dined with them in their new home at Quilmes, about 40 minutes by train from B. Aires.[7] It is a comfortable, roomy, one-storied house with a small garden which Mrs MacC. hopes to have in nice order shortly. The little girl Doris is a fine fat child, about two years old now. She is beginning to talk – in French, for they brought a French nurse with them. Mr MacCallum consulted me privately about some new business he thought of entering, & I gave him, I think, some good advice, if he will only follow it. I expect Josephy left B. Aires y'day by the "Clyde".[8] He intended doing so.

Glad that all your news, except abt. Annie, is good. You will now be busy with Xmas' preparations. Jim will have at least three days with you. I suppose the girls were at Mrs Carr's dance. I trust their cash held out for the dresses. They would not let me have the satisfaction of putting something to their bank acct. They might very well do it now & let Julie get it

1. Fernbrae was the Weinbergs' residence near Dundee. Miss Dunlop was last mentioned in a letter dated 21 February 1893, "In my last I told you about my going to the ball in borrowed plumes & meeting Mrs Williams & her sister Miss Boxwell. I forgot to mention that Miss Boxwell was at school with Miss Violet Dunlop & was over on a visit to the Dunlops last year. – It must have been the week before Sissy Weinberg's visit for Miss Boxwell left the week before Dixons' dance." This is Violet Madoline Dunlop (b 22nd June 1872 Castlereagh, Belfast). She was the daughter of Dr Archibald Dunlop and Elizabeth and was resident in Holywood, Co Down in the 1901 Census. Violet married Elliot Hill in 1898.
2. The Dunlop family lived at 64 High street, Holywood, Co Down. Ada Boxwell was the daughter of William J and Mary Boxwell (b 18th August 1870 Childwall, Lancashire). Her father was a Cotton Broker from County Wexford, Ireland. JMcC had met her in Pernambuco in early 1893. See Index to People.
3. Dr Robert Strickland Hannay Fuhr, LRCP, LRCS, Edin (b 27th August 1871). The reference is probably to Robert, Harry Fuhr's brother, passing his medical exams. Robert Married 1st January 1896 (having first been baptised on 9th December 1895). He was a Lieutenant Colonel in the Royal Army Medical Corps during WW I
4. Henry Agustus Fuhr (b 1868 Belfast) was a Civil engineer and the son of Ernest Agustus Fuhr and Dorothea Hanney Fuhr. See Index to People.
5. Annie and Julie were JMcC's siblings.
6. James MacCallum, Merchant, (b ~1849 Scotland), his wife Emily (b ~1865 England) and baby Doris (b 1892 Buenos Aires). See Index to People.)
7. Quilmes is a city in the province of Buenos Aires, Argentina, on the coast of the Rio de la Plata, south-east of Greater Buenos Aires.
8. Albert Josephy (b 18th January 1859 Schwerin) was connected to the management of Moore and Weinberg. He was a "commercial traveller" frequently moving between England and Argentina. Albert was the son of Simon and Franziska (née Jaffé) Josephy who were registered in Mecklenburg-Schwerin during the census of 1867. By 1899 they were resident in Broughty Ferry, having naturalized in January 1899, and Simon Josephy was listed as a linen and yarn merchant. See Index to People.

for them. I shall be exceedingly pleased if they will. I shan't want any money till I get married & that won't be for a few months yet.

Y'day I went on board the Roy Mail Steamer "Tamar". Mr Guimarães was passing through to Pernambuco.[9] He came from England by the Clyde which was not given pratique at Pernambuco but was sent to be disinfected at the Quarantine Station, Ilha Grande, near Rio, because she touched at Vigo on the way out.[10] It is a great shame – they make passengers go a thousand miles beyond their destination & back, entailing great expense & loss of time, to go through the farce of having a few drops of carbolic acid sprinkled in their cabins, a matter of half an hour, instead of having a quarantine station at Pernambuco. The cargo too for these northern ports is taken right down to Buenos Aires & back, & delivered about a month late, with 25% extra freight to pay.

The revolution in Rio is in a worse stage than ever. Passengers who came up by the "Tamar" report that the town is completely blockaded now & the bullets of the machine guns are flying about in-discriminately. The ordinary landing-place at the Custom-house is continuously peppered with shot, & it was only with the greatest difficulty & danger that the passengers were able to embark at another quay. The British minister has issued a proclamation informing British subjects that he can no longer protect them if they wish to come ashore or embark, & that if they do so it is at their own risk.

The gold deposits guaranteeing the note issue are said to have been all used up, & unauthorized emissions of paper money have been made, & the country is virtually bankrupt in the opinion of most foreigners. It is a sorry state of affairs.

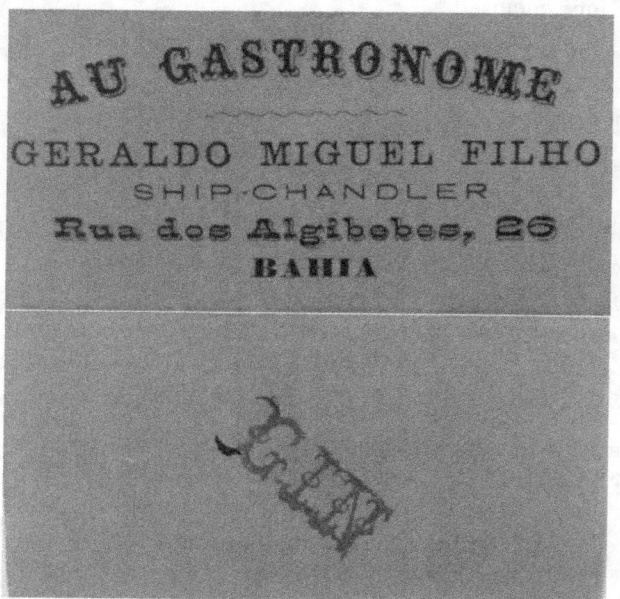

Front and back of a cardboard "cheque to bearer" used by individual businesses in the absence of a functioning currency during the political upheaval in Brazil in 1893.

Here, as I wrote before, people so far don't trouble themselves much about it. They have unauthorized currency, but of another kind. There is such a dearth of small change that every shopkeeper, restaurateur, & hotel-proprietor issues money of his own in the shape of "vales", or "cheques to bearer", on slips of cardboard like tram-tickets. In order to keep within the law these vales are not for 100, 200, or 500 reis (1d, 2d, 5d) but for "1 soup 200 rs" "1 gin, 100 rs" "1 cocktail (spelt "coqdeal") 500 rs. & so on; & they are accepted as current coin. I enclose a couple to show you what they are like. Eggers[11] has a collection of some 17 different kinds. One must see such a thing to believe it.

I purpose going by the "Clyde" this day week to Pernambuco. I might have gone by the "Tamar" but in the week between Xmas & New Year it is next to impossible to do any business & so I have remained here to pick up one or two small orders.

Please tell the Pater I am not writing to the firm by this steamer. The "Clyde"'s mail will be in a day or two later.

Best love to all,

Jack

---

9. Alfred L Guimarães. See Index to People.

10. Ilha Grande ("Big Island") is an island located off the coast of Rio de Janeiro state: https://en.wikipedia.org/wiki/Ilha_Grande

11. John C Eggers, commission agent. See Index to People.

88. Letter from Pernambuco, 31st December 1893

18931231 See an image of this letter, http://dx.doi.org/10.17613/qkns-e969

Pernambuco   31st Dec.   1893

My dear Mother,

Just come ashore from the "Clyde". Before going out to my old lodgings at Mrs Latham's I will scribble a few lines to go forward by the steamer.[1]   In Bahia I recvd. your welcome letters of 20th & 29th Nov. Hope the great dance was successful. I had nice Xmas letter from Mrs Weinberg & Sissie, & a few lines from Mr W. From Fred a Xmas card – "The Lord's Prayer Almanack"![2]

I spend Xmas quietly at the Hoyers' & had my usual morning swim.[3] There was another dance at the English Club, after a concert. It was very pleasant and lively.

I saw Keiller, who looks well, & a number of old acquaintances on landing this morning.[4] Also on board ship there were a good many old pals, as usual.

The last day of the old year. I hope 1894 will be good to us all. I have my coat & vest off & am streaming at every pore, while you are trying to keep close to the fire. To-morrow, New Year's day, is a holiday. I shall take advantage of it to put my clothes & papers in order, & perhaps to begin a longer letter to you. No time for more now.

Best love,

Jack

1. Mrs Latham runs an English boarding house in Pernambuco. See Index to People.
2. "Mrs Weinberg" is Agnes Weinberg, the wife of Isaac Julius, "Mr W", founding partner of Moore & Weinberg. Sissie (which has also been written as "Sissy") is their daughter Zerline Adele (b 2nd November 1872) and "Fred" is Frederick Simon Weinberg (b 5th August 1865). See Index to People.
3. George and Margaret Hoyer, and their family. See Index to People.
4. John Gibson Keiller (b 9th July 1865 Dundee, d Pernambuco 1897) was Fred Weinberg's future brother in law (Fred married his sister Grace Keiller in August 1894). See Index to People.

89. Letter from Pernambuco, 1st January 1894

18940101 See an image of this letter, http://dx.doi.org/10.17613/zr1r-3095

Pernambuco   1st Jan.   1894

My dear Mother,

My yesterday's letter was so short that I will forthwith begin another.

I am back in my old digs chez Mrs Latham.[1] She refused another lodger, the house being full, but could not say <u>no</u> to <u>me</u>, so she turned out one of her sons to make room for me. It is a little box of a room, but the house is English & clean, & there are several pleasant boarders living in it among them the new English parson, Mr Macrae. I went to Church last night! Later, towards midnight several of us went to the Cable Quarters to see the New Year in & drink a glass of punch, evidently having begun early in the evening to celebrate the occasion, we did not stay long. This morning I have been putting my clothes in order & writing to Julian.[2] The heat is very great but the general health of the town is excellent & there is no fever.

Alfred Guimarães, who lives some miles out of town with three other men, had a narrow escape three nights ago.[3] Hearing the dog bark loudly he got up & fired his revolver to frighten anyone who might be there, whereupon four fellows who had come to steal the horses sprang out & attacked the house firing through the doors & windows. One bullet passed through Guimarães' clothes & grazed his shoulder. Finally the men went away leaving a trail of blood for some distance. There were fifteen shots fired.

A torpedo-boat & two of the armed cruisers bought by President Peixoto in the United States have arrived here & people are now curiously speculating what is going to happen, whether these vessels are going to join the rebels, or fight them, or simply avoid them.

This place has been in a state of siege for some time as the Govnmt. anticipated trouble here. No code telegrams can be sent. To oblige a German acquaintance on the steamer I sent a cable to his family in Düsseldorf – "Prosit Neujahr".[4] The telegraph clerk looked at it suspiciously & asked what it meant.

I went to see the Tucknisses this afternoon, – the people with whom Keiller lives.[5] I meant to stay half an hour but Mrs T. has such a plentiful gift of language that I could not get away under an hour & a half.

There has been a romance in the family meanwhile. Howard, the son, was very attentive to a Miss Braga who came out as governess with Mrs Ding, the wife of the Parson who died.[6] Miss Braga returned to England some months ago &

---

1. Mrs Latham was previously mentioned in the letter of 18th February 1893: "Through Mr Guimarães I have been lucky enough to secure a room in an exceedingly nice English boarding-house owned by a Mrs Latham .. a kind motherly woman, & a lady. Her husband had formerly considerable means but he came to grief. He is in Ceará on business just now. They have one daughter & three sons." See Index to People.

2. Julian Weinberg. See Index to People.

3. Alfred Lopes Guimarães (as in back of envelope in last letter "A.L. Guimarães"). Merchant b ~1855. See Index to People.

4. "Prosit Neujahr" (German) = Happy New Year

5. Mr Benjamin Tuckniss (b 1826, d 1896), Mrs Leonora Eliza (née Taylor, b 1842, d 1931). Keiller: John Gibson Keiller. See Index to People.

6. Benjamin Howard Tuckniss ("accountant"), b 1863 and lived on in Pernambuco. He married Constance Mary Braga in Liverpool on the 15th November 1893. "A friend of Keiller's" in letter of 18th February 1893. Daughter: Mary Tuckniss (1903-1983). Howard died 24th Dec 1924 in Pernambuco. See Index to People.

Howard followed & married her.[7] Mrs Keiller went to the wedding which took place in Liverpool.[8] I don't think old Mrs Tuckniss was very pleased with the match, as she expected her son to look higher, but she has wisely decided to make the best of it, & anyway the ci-devout Miss Braga is a very nice girl.

Keiller looks well, but he tells me he is nervous & unstrung through worry & overwork & he requires a change. He will probably go home in abt. a month.

We had English-made plum-pudding for dinner to-day. I hope I shall not suffer in consequence.

Love to all.

Jack

---

7. Constance Mary Braga came out to Pernambuco as a governess to the children of Mrs Elizabeth Ding and the Rev William Ding who died of yellow fever on 24th February 1893, days after his wife arrived to join him in Brazil. Miss Braga looked after their children William Rowland and Doris Mary who were 8 and 3 respectively when their father died. She was born in Pernambuco ~1871, the daughter of José Fernandes Marquis Braga (Brazilian merchant, owned his own business, b 1839 Pernambuco, later naturalized) and Barbara Braga (b 1840 in Lancashire and recorded in the 1881 Census as living in Formby, Lancashire). See Index to People.

8. Presumably the mother of John Gibson Keiller, Mrs Grace Ann Keiller of Dundee.

90. Letter from Pernambuco, 14th January 1894

18940114 See an image of this letter, http://dx.doi.org/10.17613/qcvx-bv08

Pernambuco   14th Jany   1894

My dear Mother,

Since I wrote to you by last mail, abt a fortnight ago, I have recv$^{d.}$ several letters from you, – the last one dated Xmas day.   There sh^d be one of the 18th Dec. but it seems to have gone to Bahia & I shall have to wait a few days for it. No doubt it contains an account of your dance. Sorry to hear Jim was unwell but I hope he soon got alright again.

In the way of letter-writing I have done rather well this last week. A few days ago I wrote to Annie & to Olga by a small German steamer, not a regular mail but an outsider that ought to reach Lisbon before this by the "Trent", & I have a letter ready to post to Emma, besides my usual business correspondence.

Mr Guimarães had an auction of his furniture two days ago, & he has gone to live at a boarding-house opposite.[1] He was rather upset by that night attack on his house when he was nearly shot, & a few days afterwards Mr Felton, an old gentleman, one of those sharing the house with him, fell ill & died, so Guimarães decided to give up the house & to live in digs till he goes home in April next.[2]

Y'day the occurrence that most interested Pernambuco society was the arrival by the "Tagus" from England of Mr & Mrs Howard Tuckniss. Mrs H.T. was the governess who came out with the family of that unfortunate parson who died of yellow fever. She remained here for some months at Mrs Latham's & a marked flirtation sprang up between her & Tuckniss, which was not approved of by old Mrs Tuckniss, nor by Mrs Latham, who had given the young lady a home here meanwhile, so Miss Braga was sent back to England. Tuckniss followed soon after & married her.[3]

All this has taken place since I was here last March. This is such a small place that a tiny romance gives food for copious gossip, & it is whispered that there were one or two disappointed young ladies, Mr H.T. having been something of a butterfly. No doubt they will soon find consolation.

We had a game of whist last night, Mr & Mrs Latham, the parson, a man called Anstruther & myself, cutting in, but we were all rather sleepy.[4] You see here we are all astir soon after six o'c. in the morning.

Anstruther has been telling me so much about Iceland that I have resolved to go there to fish, some day. Cost of living 1/3 ½ per day including washing, trout & salmon just waiting to be caught. Will you come? You can sit & paddle your feet in a geyser while I fish.

I have never before felt it so hot in Pernambuco. I have had to change my clothes two & three times a day. When I come out of town in the afternoon I am always wet through with perspiration, though I move about slowly & always have an umbrella up in the sun.

1. Alfred Guimarães. See Index to People.
2. Richard Felton (Pernambuco Brazil railway manager) died on the 7th January 1894. Here is the announcement: "FELTON Richard of Jaqueira Pernambuco Brazil railway manager died 7 January 1894 Probate London 31 March to Herbert Forbes Felton engineer Effects £5886 6s. 1d.
3. Already discussed in more detail in the letter of 1st January 1894. Howard Tuckniss Benjamin Howard Tuckniss married Constance Mary Braga in Liverpool on 15th November 1893.
4. The Lathams were mentioned previously in a letter of 18th February 1893: "Mrs Latham is a kind motherly woman, & a lady. Her husband had formerly considerable means but he came to grief. They have one daughter & three sons."

While the others were out at church this morning I have kept comparatively cool in tennis flannels, & have written this letter. I hear them coming in just now & luncheon-bell will go in a minute.

To-morrow afternoon I got to a place out of town where a man I know has a sugar-estate & refinery. He is to put me up over-night. On Wednesday I am to dine at Gatis's, very nice people. Tuesday night there is whist at the cable-quarters. Mr Bilton, Manager of the Lond. & Braz. Bank is to fix an evg. for dinner & whist, so there is altogether no reason to be dull at nights.[5]

There goes the bell.

Best love.

Jack

5. As well as being Manager of the London and Brazilian Bank in Pernambuco, Mr. Bilton lived at Mrs Latham's when JMcC was there in February 1893: "Mr Bilton, manager of the London & Brazilian Bank, is living here now, & there are in all eight boarders, - all gentlemen. The tone of the house is excellent" he wrote on 18th February 1893. Bilton retired from his position and returned to England in 1898. From *The Brazilian Review* 23rd August 1898:

> "We regret to hear that Mr. Bilton so long and favourably known in Pernambuco is leaving the London & Brazilian Bank to retire to England. He will be much missed in that community. The brokers presented him with a handsome farewell gift in token of their friendly appreciation and good will. Mr. N. J. Harding the accountant has been named to take Mr. Bilton's place pro tem, and Mr. R. King to substitute Mr. Harding as accountant. It is thought that Mr. Harding who has shown great ability will probably be definitely confirmed in the post."

91. Letter from Pernambuco, 29th January 1894

18940129 See an image of this letter, http://dx.doi.org/10.17613/z4c4-bk69

Pernambuco,   29th Jany.   1894

My dear Mother,

This morning I am making and early start; –   6.30 a.m. & I have already had my tub & a cup of tea, but the "Magdalena" comes up today & I did not get all my writing done y'day.

In my last letter – I think abt. 14th Jan. – I acknowledged your Xmas-day letter. Since then no less than three have come, one so far back as 18th Dec., the others 1st & 8th Jan.

I was surprised & shocked to hear of young Clarke's death. I did not think he was so ill. York St. will not easily find another man as good a traveller. They treated him very well & he must have saved money.[1]

A photograph of ca. 1900 showing the York Street Spinning Mill in Belfast.

Very sorry my letters to Jim & Julie cost 7 ½ each. I wonder how that was. Were there not stamps on the envelopes? As a rule I post my letters myself & am very careful to see that they are rightly franked.

---

1. JMcC mentioned Clark(e), see Index to People, in previous letters, for example, his letter from Barranquilla of the 21st February 1891. "York St. will not easily find another man as good a traveller." York St. may refer to the "York Street Flax Spinning Company", which appears to have been quite a serious concern.

<u>Much</u> interested by your account of the dance, which seems to have been a complete success as was to be expected. I hope lots of nice girls asked for me & deplored my absence, but you don't say anything about that. Belfast seems to have been very gay just about New Year.

Here we have had a lively time too. Last week I was at a pleasant little dance at Mr Mackintosh's, one of the nicest houses here. To-night Mr Bilton, the jovial & popular manager of the Lon. & Braz. Bank, gives a dance.[2] He has also sent me a card for the carnival fancy-dress ball at the International Club on Saturday. Mr Gatis, an old whist friend & fellow traveller, gave me an <u>excellent</u> dinner & a good rubber.[3] Mrs Gatis is a clever pleasant woman, & Miss Browning, the governess, is very popular in P'buco society.[4] Williams gave me a little dinner-party to discuss a piece of corned beef just arrived from England. I sat on Mrs W's right & enjoyed myself, though the corned beef was rather tough.[5]

On Sat'day I dine at a Mr Levy's, also a former travelling acquaintance.[6] The roast guinea-fowl was good & we had a game of chess after it.

I think that is nearly all, but here may have been one or two dinners besides that I have forgotten to chronicle.

Josephy leaves by this steamer.[7] I am sending a barrel of pines by him. I hope they will reach you in good condition, though it is a little late in the season, & if they go bad you must be satisfied with the good-will. I send a barrel & a little jelly (you don't appreciate jelly) to Taylor in Dundee.[8] As Josephy is probably bearing gifts to Fernbrae I am not sending any there.

I have done a fair business here. Shall very soon leave for the north. I don't relish that part of it much, but must take it as it comes.

Best love to all.

Jack

2. Mr. W. H. Bilton. See Index to People.
3. Mr. G. C. Gatis and Mrs. Mary Fredina Gatis (b 1854) with seven children.
4. Clara Annette Browning (b 1st August 1864 New Brompton, Kent). She emigrated to the USA in 1904, married William Wright Wesley in New York in April 1927, and became a naturalized US citizen in 1940.
5. Mrs Williams (Edith Ann née Boxwell, sister of "pretty" Miss Ada Boxwell) and family. See Index to People.
6. Likely Enrico Salvator (Harry S) Levy (b ~1861), native of the US, and citizen of Malta, "merchant".
7. Albert Josephy, a "subscriber" to Moore and Weinberg and connected to the management of the firm. See Index to People.
8. John Brown Taylor, of Affleck Castle, Monikie, Dundee. See Index to People.

92. Letter from Pernambuco, 1st February 1894

18940201 See an image of this letter, http://dx.doi.org/10.17613/6bkm-5v71

Pernambuco,   1st Feby.   1894

My dear Mother,

I wrote you the other day by "Magdalena". After this French mail there will not be another for some time, so I think it best to send you a few lines now, to make the interval shorter. I went on board the "Magdalena" on Monday & was cordially received by the Skipper & Officers & by various acquaintances from the Plate, Rio, & Bahia, homewards bound; – took one or two drinks & refused a great many more. Josephy left entrusted with my pineapples.[1]

That same evg. I was at the Biltons' dance. Mr B. is manager of Lond. & Braz. Bank.[2] They live some two miles out along the railway & all the guests – 60 or 70 came trouping up by the 8 o'c. train. It was very funny to see the invasion. Mrs Bilton's arm was quite sore shaking hands with so many. I danced right through the programme & my collar was like the side of a concertina. The "12.30" special train home left some time after 2 o'clock; you see after the dancing ceased it took about an hour to emphasize the fact that Mr Bilton was a jolly good fellow, that Mrs Bilton was a jolly good fellow, & that we were all jolly good fellows. We had lots of fun at the dance, lively lancers, a pas de quatre, spirited polkas, & so on.[3]

The Lancers' Quadrilles, from A Complete Guide to the Art of Dancing, 1863, by Thomas Hillgrove.

There was nearly an accident which might have been very serious. Between two dances, the oil in the globe of a lamp took fire, & the lamp fell in a blaze on the floor. Several fellows kicked it out through the door to the verandah where it lit between two ladies with flimsy skirts. One of the ladies jumped right over it. I expected to see her in a blaze next instant. Fortunately she escaped with a fright, & after a little hesitation decided not to go into hysterics but to dance through the rest of the programme.

There is another dance to-morrow night but I do not know the people. Mrs Latham was asked to bring any young men she liked & she invited me to go, but I don't care to on that kind of invitation.[4] In confidence between you & me, I may boast that I shall be missed a little, for men that can waltz decently are not too plentiful, though the ladies almost all dance well, & I know three or four nice girls who would be pleased to honour me with two waltzes each instead of having some partner who will tread on their toes.

However the next night there is a carnival fancy ball for which I have a card. It is under Brazilian management, but several English families I know are going – Mr & Mrs Bilton, Mrs & Mrs Williams & some others.

---

1. Albert Josephy. See Index to People.
2. Mr W. H. Bilton. See Index to People.
3. The Lively Lancers and Pas de Quatre are both dances for formations of four, in the case of The Lancers a group of four couples. The Lancers became popular in the late 19th century as a variant of the Quadrille. There is a video of it at https://youtu.be/fcCfQZlNqLA
4. Mrs Latham. See Index to People.

I shall leave in a few days now for the north. My clothes are not in very good condition , as the robbery at Bahia left me with a small wardrobe which must in consequence do extra duty. Mrs Latham kindly had the cuffs of some shirts mended for me. She is a very motherly woman, – most kind & thoughtful. When I had a cold she made me drink hot milk & so on; – gives me good advice about not being too much in the sun.

There is no fresh development, so far as we are aware, in the revolution.[5] The Governor here issued a decree the other day threatening with dire punishment to originators & spreaders of false reports as to the state of affairs in Rio.

A story is told of two Englishmen in a tram at Rio. 1st E. "The rebel man-of-war "Aquidaban" came into the Bay this morning". 2nd E. "Is that true?". 1st E. "Yes, I heard it as a fact this morning". Police officer sitting just behind, touching 1st E. on shoulder "The Governor has not heard this fact & will no doubt be interested to learn the news. Kindly come with me & tell him!" –   showing that it is safer not to talk politics in open places.

3rd Feb   Just this moment got your letter of 15th Jan. I hope Mrs Black, next door to you, recovered.[6] The girls are young to be alone in the world.

I don't think I shall write to anyone else by this mail, but by next Roy. Mail I hope to get some letters written.

Best love to all

Jack

5. The Brazilian Naval Revolts were armed mutinies promoted mainly by Admirals Custódio José de Melo and Saldanha Da Gama and their fleet of Brazilian Navy ships against the claimed unconstitutional staying in power of the central government in Rio de Janeiro. The second revolt started in March 1892, when thirteen generals sent a letter and manifesto to then-President Marshal Floriano Peixoto. This document demanded new elections be called to fulfil the constitutional provision and ensure internal tranquillity in the nation. Floriano harshly suppressed the movement, ordering the arrest of their leaders. Thus, not legally solved, the political tensions increased. The revolt broke out in September 1893 at Rio de Janeiro, and was suppressed only in March 1894 after a long blockade of the city. With many of the Brazilian Navy's most powerful ships either in the hands of the rebels or under repair, the Brazilian government had to improvise a new fleet to battle the rebel fleet. The revolt included the powerful battleship Aquidaban, build in the mid-1880s, and a collection of small ironclads, modern cruisers and older wood 'cruiser' or steam frigate type ships.

6. The mother of the heiresses next door in Belfast. It sounds like she was a widow. Possibly also the mother of James Black who had the posh society wedding in New York in 1891, attended by JMcC.

93. Letter from Pernambuco, 8th February 1894

18940208 See an image of this letter, http://dx.doi.org/10.17613/g5w3-7×80

Headed notepaper

Coquille **II**. 9 Kos.	en 4 Nr. 645
vélin, réglé bâtonné.	en 8 Nr. 690

Pernambuco   8th Feby.   1894

My dear Mother,

Mr Just[1] owes me thanks for the obliging readiness with which I use up his old samples. The other day I appropriated an ingenious & elegant machine for making cocktails, which formed part of a sample collection of glass-ware thoughtfully sent out by a French firm. To-day, having noticed a block-book with various qualities of writing-paper it struck me that I might spend a leisure half-hour usefully & inexpensively in beginning a letter to you.

Last night I dined with the Tucknisses, a quiet family dinner. They have a small dinner-party to-night & had invited me, but my steamer was posted for to-day so I refused & they asked me to go last night instead. I am sorry now, for the sailing has been postponed a day. I declined another dinner invitation for to-night as well.

I am very sorry to leave this place. Business has been fairly good with me, though others complain very much, & I have had a good time. I have lived in a civilized English house, where my washing was properly looked after, where there was a decent bath, meals served in order & cleanliness, & educated people to talk to. Pará will be different. Dirty hotel, impossible food, insects, no ice, no English ladies & scarcely half a dozen respectable Englishmen. However, as I said before, one must take it as it comes.

As the state of siege still prevails here I must have a permit from the Chief of Police to leave the town. Without that they would not let me go out of the harbour. While I am getting the permit I shall also get some tinned food to eat on the six days' voyage to Maranhão.

Mrs Tuckniss is a very estimable lady & nothing could exceed her affability to me personally, but "Mr Tuckniss's family" is the one engrossing subject of conversation. I have a commission from her to look up connexions & find out relationships in Barbados. Her children try to change the conversation or gently to make fun of her but you might as well try to stop Niagara.[2]

"And so, Mr Loewenthal, as I was saying, Mr Tuckniss is second cousin; – no third, – let me see, yes, third cousin to Lord Aberdare. Mr Tuckniss's grandfather, Hugh Austin, & so on ————- A daughter of Paul Wentworth must have been married in Barbados; if you w^d find out for me I sh^d be <u>so much</u> obliged. Wentworth is the family name, – the Straffords you know, – Jane Seymour was of the family, – it makes it so interesting, you know, Mr Loewenthal, to read English history, – don't you think certain features & expressions are hereditary in families – the overhanging brow so marked in Mr Tuckniss's face – the same as Earl Strafford they say – the great Earl, he was called – Richard Austin, first bishop of

---

1. Theo Just, M&W agent in Pernambuco. See Index to People.
2. "Mrs Tuckniss" was Leonora Eliza Tuckniss née Taylor (b 1842, d 1931), aged 52 at the time of this letter.

Demerara, was first cousin, the Austins of Barbados, whom you know, must have been the elder branch, Mr Tuckniss's family came from Barbados" _____there is no end to it.[3]

Keiller leaves abt. the 18th inst. so he will be in England about the time this arrives or soon after.[4]

This morning an English lady Miss Peyton, was married to a Mr Hood, at the British Consulate.[5] The Vice-consul, who performed the ceremony, is about my age. Three days hence the couple will be married again at the Intendencia, where the civil contract, obligatory under Brazilian law, will be signed. After that they will be married in the English Church. When this is all over the knot will surely be so tightly tied that there will be no undoing it.

3. Unravelling Mrs Tuckniss's tales about Mr. Tuckniss's family:

- "Lord Aberdare" = Baron Aberdare of Duffryn, a title created on 23rd August 1873 for the Liberal politician Henry Bruce. He served as Home Secretary from 1868 to 1873. Bruce was born at Duffryn, Aberdare, Glamorganshire, the son of John Bruce, a Glamorganshire landowner, and his first wife Sarah, daughter of Reverend Hugh Williams Austin: https://en.wikipedia.org/wiki/Henry_Bruce,_1st_Baron_Aberdare
- "Wentworth is the family name, - the Straffords you know" = Paul Wentworth (b ca. 1736, d 1793) was a British intelligence agent and politician who sat in the House of Commons briefly in 1780. Wentworth may have been born in Barbados. https://en.wikipedia.org/wiki/Paul_Wentworth_(spy). Although Thomas Wentworth was the name of the first Earl of Strafford, he seems to be totally unrelated to Paul Wentworth! https://en.wikipedia.org/wiki/Earl_of_Strafford
- "Jane Seymour was of the family" = The weakest link in Jane Seymour's royal descent was Mary Clifford, Dame Wentworth: https://royaldescent.blogspot.com/2010/02/weakest-link-in-jane-seymours-royal.html
- "Richard Austin, first bishop of Demerara" = Richard Austin, a clergyman and slave-owner in Surinam. From a Barbados family, brother of William Austin and Thomas Austin (both British Guiana slave-owners) but by 1832 the owner of 250 enslaved people in Surinam. Father of Wiltshire Stanton Austin, Charles Adye Austin and William Paul Austin. Reported to have died in Surinam in 1851. More information from the Centre for the Study of the Legacies of British Slavery mentions a connection to Benjamin Fuller Tuckniss, father of Benjamin Tuckniss (b 1826, d 1896) JMcC's friend: https://www.ucl.ac.uk/lbs/person/view/2146647831

> The will of Richard Austin was made 14th April 1824 when he was 'about to make a voyage to Europe to arrange various family concerns.' He appointed his two beloved sons, William Paul Austin and Charles Adye Austin, and the husband of his daughter Mary Jane named **Benjamin Fuller Tuckniss** as his executors to take possession of his rights etc which are now claims on Plantations Kleinhoop, L'Assistance and a third estate which appears to be Appecappe, of which he was in possession not only by virtue of his marriage to Joanna Wentworth niece and co-heir of Paul Wentworth, but also by virtue of a contract between him as attorney to the guardians of the late [i.e. the former] Jane Elizabeth Smith now married to the Rev. Bruce of Belfast in Ireland. He left the estates to his three children, subject to a legacy of £1000 to the Rev. Wilshire Stanton Austin, his son by a former marriage and the transfer of specified enslaved people who had belonged to Sarah Stanton his first wife ('men - Sam. Walker Jos.Tom and a woman named Rose').

4. John Gibson Keiller. See Index to People.

5. Ellen Paton (b 1st November 1871 Brazil, d Jan 1920 in Hendon, England) married Thomas Macdonald Hood (b 1865, d 1939) on 10th February 1894 in the British Consulate Chapel in Pernambuco.

A postcard image of the Intendencia (town hall) of Recife, Pernambuco, at the turn of the century. Published by Ramiro M. Costa.

It is still very warm here. While writing this letter I sit mopping myself. Now I must go & have a lemon-squash & continue my preparations for to-morrow.

Best love.

Jack

94. Letter from Maranhão, 12th–14th February 1894

18940214 See an image of this letter, http://dx.doi.org/10.17613/f5ws-6p22

<u>Feby 12th 94</u>

My dear Mother,

I left a letter in Pernambuco to be forwarded to you by first mail. It took me several afternoons & evgs. to say goodbye to my friends there. Among the last to speed me was Keiller who stood champagne, partly, I suppose, to drown his grief at my departure & partly to celebrate his own approaching home-going. Two days before I left, a lady, young & charming, gave me her album in which to write some poetry. Being busy I put it off to the last moment – literally to the last half-hour – when I scrawled the following where she could tear it out without injury to the book.

> My hair is grey, but not with age,
> No – it grew white
> In a single night
> Through thinking what on earth to write
> On this devoted page.
>   Byron.

& sent it to her with my apologies on a card. I am afraid it smacks of rudeness & shows poverty of imagination, but to write something "real pretty" requires favorable conditions & a calm mind.

This is the third day out from Pernambuco & there are fortunately only two days more to be endured. And no slight amount of endurance is required. The steamer is filthy. The habits of the passengers are too disgusting to be described in detail. I took a corner seat at a table so that I could look away from the feeders who plunge their forks, just used, into all the dishes & the pickle-bottles, & their knives, also just used, & that not legitimately, into the salt & mustard. The table-cloth looks as if it had not been washed for years & the waiter evidently looks upon me as a crank because I prefer my own napkin to someone else's, since they don't give me a clean one. The stench below one might cut with a knife. I sleep in my deck-chair till I feel stiff, & towards 1 o'c in the morning I go unwillingly to my cabin to leave it again at 6.

Last night before falling asleep I killed a cockroach & frightened away a rat; – happily perhaps, the light was too dim to see anything else that might be there. From some of my letters you might think it was all beer & skittles for me, but you see it is not <u>all</u> unmixed enjoyment.

We sailed from Pernambuco on Friday evg. On Sat'day morning we arrived at Cabedello, a village at the mouth of the river Parahyba & some 40 minutes by train from the town of that name.[1] I went up by the 8 o'c train (which started at 9.30), & spent a couple of hours in having some breakfast & walking over the little town, which contains nothing remarkable except an extraordinary number of churches. At the station I met, very unexpectedly a Mr Sumner, who sat at the same table on the "Magdalena" coming out. He is manager & engineer of the little railway. He w^{d} have taken me to his house for breakfast had it not been mailday. When I took my ticket on the railway, the station master, ticket-clerk, &

---

1. In the late 19th-century, Parahyba was a rapidly-growing port city with 18,645 residents (1890). It was the starting point of a railway to Independencia and the interior of Brazil as well as entrance to the Parahyba do Norte River.

factotum, volunteered the information that I must give one half of said ticket to the collector & keep the other half for the return journey. He saw I was a foreigner & evidently thought that in foreign parts they had not advanced so far as return tickets.

Next day we touched at Natal or Rio Grande do Norte, but as the steamer lay outside the bar & only remained a couple of hours I did not go ashore.

To-day we are at Ceará. The steamer is anchored in the small open bay, not more than 200 yards from the broad sandy beach on which the ground-swell breaks into heavy surf. Passengers land in strong boats, two or more men rowing, & one steering with an oar over the stern. About 20 yards from the edge the men jump out, up to their waists in water while the waves frequently pass over their heads; they push the boat as far up the sand as they can while a crowd of jabbering niggers rush into the water & fight for the privilege of carrying the passengers to dry land at 2^d a head. I felt rather funny as I was lifted like a long baby in the arms of a muscular mulatto. He did not seem very secure. I think he was tormented by doubts as to whether he had <u>all of me</u> out of the water or not.

<u>Maranhão 14th Feby</u>. Arrived. Glory be! Safely fixed in the comfortable little hotel. I wrote the above on Monday. Tuesday morning[2] we were off Amaraçao[3]; – nothing to be seen but a bank of sand & some tree-tops behind. Half a mile from the shore a bar over which the big waves broke threateningly. Two boats came off, shipped a lot of water, took two passengers & some mail-bags, & away we went. Glad I was not going there. Not long ago two boats capsized on the bar, everyone drowned.

The next mail leaves here abt. 22nd S.S. Brandenburg for L'pool. So you may expect a letter abt. middle of March.

Best love,

Jack

Letters Barbados Mess. Da Costa & Co[4]

2. the day before

3. amarraçao: portuguese for "mooring"; no place found of that name

4. Large trading house in Barbados owned by an influential family. See Da Costa in Index to People.

95. Letter from Maranhão, 20th February 1894

18940220 See an image of this letter, http://dx.doi.org/10.17613/fbpc-xr64

Maranhão,   20th/   Feby. 1894

My dear Mother,

One letter I left in Pernambuco to be posted by Roy. Mail Stmr. to you; another written in pencil, went on with the "Olinda" to Pará, meant to catch the mail there for Lisbon. I hope you got them both. It is now almost time to send you my best wishes for many happy returns of your birthday, as there will scarcely be another opportunity after this of sending a letter in time for the 17th March[1]. I hope this birthday will find you strong & well & jolly, & every succeeding one more so.

Praça Benedito Leite square in the historic center of São Luís, Maranhão. 1908 photograph by Gaudêncio Rodrigues da Cunha.

I did not give any address here so I do not expect letters before arriving at Pará. There is not much to write about from this place. It is as dull as Pernambuco is lively. There are no English people except a few factory managers, head-weavers, & the like, who have come out to superintend the fitting-up of various mills & factories & to teach the natives the practical work. For last year a craze took possession of the inhabitants of Maranhão for organizing limited companies to build factories for making everything under the sun; – among those that are completed are the concerns for producing jute bags, brown cottons, bleached cottons, shot, boots & shoes, clothes & shirts, stockings, & several other things I have forgotten. One & all these companies spent about three times as much money in their buildings & machinery as they had calculated beforehand, & now they have had to go borrowing money on mortgage & by various other means so as not to let their pet schemes fall to the ground.

The consequence is that there is very little money left in the town. The merchants owe in Europe & are being dunned by their creditors who must just have "paciencia". Half of the circulation consists of debentures issued by the various companies, a most extraordinary condition of things. Of course the custom-house & government offices do not accept such currency, but the merchants are obliged to for there is so little cash to be had. I have seen these so-called "debentures" for various values down to 10 mil.reis, say 8/-, each, bearing interest at 10% & amortization of 20% yearly.

I don't know if these "debentures" were subscribed for in the usual way. I expect they were merely launched into circulation, with the 10% interest as a bribe; but the financing going on at present in Brazil, national & commercial, beats cockfighting.

It is very doubtful whether many of these concerns will ultimately pay, in spite of the very high duties, monopolies,

1. Her 58th birthday.

etc., by which they are protected. They are limited companies, – promoted by people who knew nothing whatever about what they were undertaking, – they have had to buy their experience, they have made lots of mistakes, & the factories have cost three times what they ought to have cost. Then there is the difficulty of training native operatives, &, in fact, of inducing them to work at all. If it is a wet morning half of them do not turn up, & the machinery is idle. But these difficulties might all be conquered if there were only one good businessman, as we understand the word, at the head of each concern, but these people have no more idea of business out of their own little grooves, than the man in the moon.

The wet season has begun here & it has rained heavily for the greater part of the last week. But the town is hilly & the streets mostly well paved so it soon dries under foot, but one's clothes feel damp & everything of leather becomes blue-moulded. Fortunately this little hotel if very clean & comfortable. It is run by two Frenchmen who themselves superintend the cooking so we have decent food. The shower-bath is excellent, my room is large & fresh, & there is a hammock to swing in if I don't feel inclined to go to bed. Here when the houses are built, hooks are fixed in the walls of all the rooms for slinging hammocks. In the country everyone uses them. In town the lower classes have hammocks only & the well-to-do people always have them in addition to beds in the rooms.

The other evening I dined on the English cable-ship "Norseman" which was in the port. I made the acquaintance of Mr Cummins, electrical expert & he took me on board & showed me the ship, with the appliances for laying cables, testing them, finding out when they are broken, where the break is, & so on, – all very interesting.[2]

Cable Ship Norseman, built 1893.

This ship does duty between B. Aires & Pará & mends the cable on an average a dozen times a year. The most frequent cause of the cable breaking is friction on a sharp rock, but sometimes in or near ports vessels dragging their anchors foul the cable.

The "Norseman" has now gone to pick up the two ends of the cable where it is broken between this place & Ceará, about sixty miles from this end, as they have calculated by means of their "resistance" instruments, & having picked them up, to splice them & drop them again.

Cane-chairs are very destructive on certain garments. I have had to go to the tailor here to get a new "garment", & to have armour plating put inside the old one, the effect of which latter, showing sky-blue through grey, like a rift in rain-clouds, is iligant intoirely.

In further encouragement of native industry I took my "trees" to the boot-factory & ordered a pair of boots. I had to explain what I wanted to six men & one girl, successively, who seemed never to have seen anything in their lives so fine

2. This was probably the second Cable Ship to have the name Norseman. It was built in 1893 by Ramage and Ferguson, Leith, for the Western and Brazilian Telegraph Company. If it was indeed this new ship, Mr Cummins would have been excited to show it off. https://atlantic-cable.com/Cableships/Norseman(2)/index.htm

& large as my foot. I am in fear & trembling that they will make the boots pointed & turned up at the toes, as the natives like them

thus! {a small sketch of the turned-up boot shape is inserted into the letter here. See image below.}

I go to Pará next week I hope, & then to the West Indies. Ho!

Best love to all.

Jack

96. Letter from Pará, 4th–12th March 1894

18940304 See an image of this letter, http://dx.doi.org/10.17613/jnvq-d580

Pará   4th   March   1894

My dear Mother,

My last was dated 22nd Feby., from Maranhão. Here I am, one step further on, & at the last place I have to visit in Brazil. I have your letters of 29th Jan. & 5th Feby. – that of 22nd Feby. seems to be still short.

I am very sorry to hear of the death of Mrs Kamcke.[1] I don't know what they will do without her. It is well the young people are all independent, & Meta, I think is a good housekeeper. How is Victor?[2] I think he was very devoted to his mother. She was a good woman, if ever there was one. The Miss Blacks will feel lonely – three young girls all by themselves.[3] They have no near relatives, have they? What is the matter with Mrs James Carr? I did not know she was ill.

I wish old Campbell had left some of his money to his former neighbours instead of to his wealthy relatives.

Many thanks for your good birthday wishes. Into the thirties, high-ho![4] Seems no time since I was half that age. I really must come home & marry some girl who will support me in comfort & affluence during my old age. What do you think? You might put an advertisement in the paper. Best thanks to Emma, Julie & Jim, for their letters. I also had kind birthday wishes from Dundee.

Thanks to an old acquaintance, the manager of the Cable Station here, to whom I spoke along the wire from Maranhão carrying on a conversation with him free of charge, I got a fair room he reserved for me in the best of the hotels here (but bad is the best of them!). The rainy season is in full swing here & to-day, they say, is the first day with dry intervals they have had for a fortnight.

Most of my acquaintances of a year ago are here still. Two fellows who were kind & hospitable during my last stay – Power & Duff[5] – partners as exchange brokers – have had rather a tough time. They lost about £ 3000 through people speculating for a rise in exchange, who omitted to pay up differences when exchange dropped instead of rising. They have let the pleasant house where they used to give nice dinners, & have gone into lodgings. Otherwise things seem to have gone on pretty much as usual in Pará.

I have spent the greater part of to-day writing letters, & have now several briefs ready for the mail which will carry this. When it reaches you I hope to be in Barbados, if there is a convenient steamer, a matter for investigation to-morrow.

Mosquitoes & the late hour remind me that it is time for me to retire to the restful shelter of my curtained couch. I must be astir at 6 a.m. to-morrow for our agent, Mr Kolb, goes up river to Manáos & I have several matters to settle with

---

1. Mrs Helene Emilie Kamcke (b ~1837 née Rung in Danzig) who died "suddenly" in Belfast at 73 University Road, on 26th January 1894 age 57, buried Belfast City Cemetery 29th January. She was the wife of William Roderick Kamcke (b ~1825 in Danzig, d 27th November 1896 Belfast). He arrived to Belfast in 1848 as "apprentice to a merchant" and later established "Kamcke WR, & Co., flax , yarn & linen merchants". They were married on 28th July 1861 in Danzig. See Index to People.
2. Victor Kamcke, born William Victor Rung Kamcke in 1863 (contemporary of JMcC), became a missionary in Bengal; married Mabel Eliza Llyod, the daughter of a missionary, in Bengal, in 1902.
3. These are the "heiresses" next door. No clues as to their identity.
4. JMcC b 29th February 1864 – 30th birthday just been! – no mention of any celebrations . . .
5. See Index to People.

him before he leaves. Manáos is 900 miles up the Amazon – four days by steamer.[6] I sh$\underline{^d}$ rather like to make the journey too, & if Mr Kolb w$\underline{^d}$ wait 10 days or so I might go with him, but having just arrived here I want to see what's to be done here first.

7th   Still waiting for the mail steamer for England to come down from Manáos. She ought to have left five days ago & she is not even here yet. Perhaps stuck in the mud somewhere. There was a steamer <u>from</u> England this morning. Left Lisbon abt. 22nd Feby. Brings letters up to 17th or 18th but none for me. Expect mine have gone via Pernambuco. Last I got from Belfast 7th Feb. Dundee 9th Feb. This was one of Singlehurst's regularly advertised steamers, the "Sobralense", but all my writing & preaching to watch the sailing-bills of direct steamers to Pará via Lisbon seems to be of no use.[7] The English Bank got their mail & all the firms, but not even a newspaper came for me.

Pará 12th   "the office" –   Kolb's that is, not the police

Waiting for a fly who promised to walk into my parlor at 9.30. He is only 10 minutes overdue & as he won't turn up for another half hour I may as well go on writing to you & so keep my idle hands out of worse mischief. One "client" was here already by appointment at 8 o'c. but merely to say he couldn't stay, on account of the "mail". So meanwhile I went out & "got a line" – i.e. took an order – for the old man in Dundee[8]. That is friend Power's little joke; – when we meet each one asks the other "Got a line to-day?"

He describes himself as "Once a bank-manager & a gentleman, now a broker", & me as "Once a gentleman, now a drummer". He is an awfully good fellow. He was telling me y'day abt. his family skeleton. He sends home every year two or three hundred pounds toward the sinking fund, a matter of twelve thousand pounds which his sister's husband misappropriated in a Bank, & which he & his brother made good to save a prosecution. The fellow w^d have got 15 years penal servitude, & for their sister's sake the Powers paid the money & shipped the man off to New Zealand.

Power is in partnership with another very nice fellow – Duff, who comes from Inverness, where his people have a nice place, to judge by photographs.[9] Last year Power was offered the sub-managership of the Lond & Riv. Plate Bank at Rio with a salary of £ 1200 & a free house, but he refused, for there was a speculative boom in exchange at the time, at the rate of six or eight thousand a year. When the Revolution came exchanges dropped & several of their clients failed to pay up their differences & Power & Duff were responsible & lost some £ 3000. Then of course the speculation stopped & Power is now sorry he did not accept the Rio offer, which was a certainty. But having been full manager in Pará, he did not like to accept a sub-managership.

Blow this mail. It has been "leaving to-morrow" ever since the 2nd & this is the 12th & it is still there. It upsets things horribly. When one approaches the merchants about business they all say – "Awfully busy, steamer to-morrow for

6. Manáos is an old name for Manaus, a city in Amazonas, Brazil. Manaus, on the banks of the Negro River in northwestern Brazil, is the capital of the vast state of Amazonas. It's a major departure point for the surrounding Amazon Rainforest. Just east of the city, the dark Negro River converges with the brown, muddy Solimões River resulting in a striking visual phenomenon called the "Meeting of the Waters." The combined tributaries form the Amazon River.

7. Robert Singlehurst & Co was founded in 1869 to operate a cargo and passenger steamship line from Liverpool to Northern Brazil. In 1882 a joint Red Cross-Booth Line service started from Manaos and Para to New York and an Amazon feeder service to Para commenced in 1887. In 1897 the Red Cross Iquitos Steamship Co was founded to operate services 2,000 miles up the River Amazon to Iquitos, Peru. Robert Singlehurst retired in 1901 and the company amalgamated with Booth Line. S.S. Sobralense was built 1884 and owned by Robert Singlehurst & Co. till 1901. It was then owned by Li Lai Chuen, Hong Kong, and mined off Port Arthur on the 12th May 1905 when en route from Newchang for Kobe with a cargo of beans & bean cake.

8. Mr Weinberg

9. JMcC talked about them very effusively when he last wrote home from Para nearly a year prior (letter of 30th March 1893): "Power was former manager of the London & Brazilian Bank here.. Duff is from <u>Aberdeen</u>, where his people have a nice house, judging from photos he showed me." In the current letter he writes: "Duff, comes from <u>Inverness</u>, where his people have a nice place, to judge by photographs" See index to People.

Europe, kindly call again after it goes." Of course such delay is unusual. It is bungling in the steamer agency. – Putting in one cargo first, then taking it out to make room for a more valuable one. "Cosas de España"!

There is an Italian opera company here now & the tenor is practising Aida next door. When I have done this letter I shall put my head round the balcony & tell him that if he wants to get rid of a throaty tone he must sing koo-koo-koo-koo-koo-oh-a.

The other day a Brazilian gun-boat blew up in the river. The explosion shook the town. Four or five men were killed, & all you can see now is a bit of a mast above the water. The cause is unknown, but it must have been accidental. No one w^{d} do such a thing with the men on board, asleep. Probably carelessness – smoking cigarette in the powder magazine; – they do that kind of thing here.

Seldom if ever, felt so dry of material for a letter. Obliged to look for moisture & matter in a bottle of Apollinaris, – positively without anything else in it, in view of your warning, except a piece of ice.[10]

Meant to pay a visit to-night, but sat in deck-chair after dinner & read through a novel, one of seven I borrowed just before dinner from the Bank quarters. Mostly rubbish, but short & big print. Wouldn't attack a novel in 3 vols or one printed in small type, – not for Joseph.

In the house opposite there lives a comical bird. He struts up & down along the little ledge that connects the window-balconies. He has a peculiar note, or rather two notes, {see sketch below} something like the tuneful song of the common or garden donkey. I have found out that by whistling those two notes – like the domestic donkey ^{m} / $_{e}$ – I can set that bird going. You have no idea the amount of entertainment I derive from that bird. I come to my window & whistle a challenge. He forwith cocks up one eye, jerks his head out, straightens his long neck, & finally with beak wide open to the sky he answers ten times more shrilly. If I am in a bad temper I can set that bird going just about the siesta time of the surrounding neighbourhood, it soothes me & makes me feel quite cheerful again.

JMcC notation of what the friendly bird sings, inserted in the letter.

10. Apollinaris is a German naturally sparkling mineral water (now owned by Coca Cola). The spring was discovered by chance in 1852 in Georg Kreuzberg's vineyard, in Bad Neuenahr, Germany. He named it after St Apollinaris of Ravenna, a patron saint of wine: https://en.wikipedia.org/wiki/Apollinaris_(water)

<u>Same, 11.30 p.m</u>.

Got two spiders after all & did a fair day's work, – from 8 pretty steadily through till 11 – for, glory be, the mail is really going out to-morrow morning & after my customers left me at 4 I had to set to & write. Then the English steamer came in this afternoon, & brought letters, – from you one of 12th Feb. – that of 22nd Jan. came two days ago from Pernambuco. I am very sorry your neuralgia is so troublesome this winter; but March is half over now & the summer always agrees with you better.

When you get this I shall likely be in Barbados, but I shall not stay there long. I want to get along quickly to Curaçao, after which I shall probably soon turn home (unless I get other instructions) as I don't know many more places where there is money to be made.

Write to Curaçao,   c/o Mess. Rivas Fensohn & Co & put on envelope[11]

                    via New York

                    thence per Red D Line.

Best love.

Jack

11. Mess. Rivas Fensohn & Co was a trading company in Curaçao. Their business in Curaçao was principally as an agent for the American Red D Line. See Index to People.

97. Letter from Pará, 18-20th March 1894

18940318 See an image of this letter, http://dx.doi.org/10.17613/x0t2-hb75

Pará
18th Mar. 1894

My dear Mother,

I posted a rambling letter to you about a week ago. Since then I have not heard from you. Yesterday I proudly wore in my buttonhole the sprig of shamrock that came on your Christmas card, in your honour & St. Patrick's, & the fellows all exclaimed, with envy & admiration: "Shamrock, bedad! Where on earth did you get it?"

There is not much to record for the past week. I have been working at full pressure, with the intention of finishing business in time to catch a steamer for Barbados posted to sail y'day, but fortunately delayed for another two days.

There has been a flutter of excitement in town on the recpt. of news that the rebels had abandoned their ships, the officers taking refuge on the foreign men of war, & exchange has improved for the moment owing to the idea that the civil war is at an end. But I scarcely think it is finished yet. Admiral Mello is still in the south with a couple of the strongest vessels & the Province of Rio Grande do Sul is in a state of independence with considerable armed resources.

A few days ago I recv^{d} the accompanying nice note from Taylor.[1] He does not say "Oh, those things are very cheap out there. What did you pay for them?" I am very glad the pines arrived in good condition & I hope yours did too. I scarcely expected they would.

I had a letter from Julian W.[2] the other day. He does not say how his head is, but complains that his memory is very bad, – an old failing. He says business in general in B. Aires is still very bad indeed, & that two old English firms, Bates Stokes & Hill Bellamy, have called meetings of their creditors.

To acknowledge some old scores I was so extravagant as to take a box at the Opera the other night.[3] I invited some fellows who have shown me much kindness, & we heard Verdi's "Mask Ball" very well given.

Last night I dined with Power & Duff & to-day I lunch at Brocklehurst's.[4] In the latter I have a willing chess adversary, whom I just manage to beat, but who comes up smiling again after each defeat.

When I arrive at Barbados I am going to hang myself in the sun with all my goods & chattels for a whole day. Every-thing I have is blue-mouldy; – trunks, clothes, boots, brushes, tobacco. If you saw it & smelt it you might find it unpleasant not being used to it. In Pará it is always so in the rainy season. I sleep on my back to keep my nose as far away as possible from the mouldy smell of the pillow. But these are trifles.

---

1. The sending of the pineapples was mentioned in JMcC's letter from Pernambuco of 29th January 1894. The recipient was John Brown Taylor (b 5th December 1853, m Julie Anne née Duff, d 19th May 1932) who lived in Affleck Castle, Monikie, Dundee, and was a "Linen & Jute Manufacturer and Merchant". See Index to People.
2. Julian Weinberg
3. Most likely at the Theatro da Paz, build 1869-1874: https://en.wikipedia.org/wiki/Theatro_da_Paz and https://theatrodapaz.com.br/
4. For Power and Duff, see Index to People. Brocklehurst was a ship owner whose partnership was mentioned a year earlier in JMcC's letter from Pará 19th-26th April 1893: "Last night I gave a little dinner to five fellows who have shown me much hospitality. Mr Power (who describes himself as "once a bank-manager & a gentleman, now a broker", - but makes as broker twice as much as he made when manager of the London & Brazilian Bank), Mr Duff, his partner, Singlehurst, partner in Singlehurst, Brocklehurst & Co owners of the direct line of English Steamers."

The food in the hotel has been much better this time than it was in the other hotel I put up at last year. There is a Frenchman here who goes to market & always secures something special for me.

I am using up some stamped envelopes for my letters to you, for the Pater protests against my putting business letters in them & sends me the dilapidated remains of one in justification. But my autographs to you are neither so bulky nor so valuable, so I run the risk in the interest of collectors.[5]

19th Mar.

My steamer sails to-morrow for Barbados. I hear from a friend in the cable-service that a telegram has arrived for me from Dundee. I shall see it to-morrow, but from what he says I gather that the purport of the message is that I should return to Maranhão. Not for Joseph! more especially as I do not believe my going back there could possibly advance the business in hand. It w^d go very much against the grain to turn back now that I am just on the point of saying good-bye to Brazil. But perhaps I had better not say much until I see the telegram.

In quiet towns like Pará I find my chess-board a great source of entertainment in spare moments. With a few English newspapers containing problems or games I can always enjoy myself till bed-time if I have nothing else to do. I am out of books now but I can always fall back on old William S. with fresh delight. He never gets stale.

20th   I find the telegram is not such a serious business after all. Steamer postponed another day. I have just posted my business letters, which is rather a weight off my mind. But I have about fifty things to do to-morrow so that there is still sufficient weight left on it to prevent my indulging in flippant nothings, so I had better shut up as I have no serious matter to indite.

Best love,
Jack

18940218 Letter of thanks for "pines" from Taylor of Dundee, image: https://doi.org/10.17613/0a7n-cd68

AFFLECK,
MONIKIE
NR DUNDEE

18th February 1894.

My dear Loewenthal,

It was indeed very good of you to send us such a handsome present and my wife joins me in thanking you sincerely for your kind remembrance.

The Pines arrived in splendid condition, and have been much appreciated by ourselves & our friends; and the "dose" too is splendid, but as it will keep it has not been so freely sampled. I don't remember ever to have seen preserved Cajus before, they are very good indeed, & the flavour reminds me of many a "Cajuada" in the old Bahia days.[6]

I hope it may not be long before we have the pleasure of seeing you here again, and my wife asks me to say that she

---

5. His stamp-collecting siblings.
6. Caju is the Portuguese name for the fruit of the cashew tree: https://en.wikipedia.org/wiki/Cashew. Cajuada is a sweet (jam or ice cream) or drink made from pulp of caju.

hopes you will give us a little more of your time & a little more warning than usual so that she may be able to arrange a rubber for you.

Heartily reciprocating your good wishes, & with renewed thanks and kindest regards from both of us,

I am,

Yours most sincerely

J.B. Taylor

My wife has had a very sharp attack of Influenza from which she is now slowly recovering, and as the pines arrived just when her appetite wanted humouring they were doubly appreciated & most welcome.

98. Letter from S.S. Gregory sailing to Barbados, 25th-28th March 1894

18940325 See an image of this letter, http://dx.doi.org/10.17613/qz01-qg73

On headed notepaper: LENNOXVALE, BELFAST.
S.S. "Gregory"
Easter Sunday, 25th Mar. 1894

My dear Mother,

It would do you good if you could be here this Sunday afternoon instead of shivering at home, with neuralgic March winds blowing & the rain probably beating down with steady perseverance from a grey sky.

I am sitting in my deck chair, gently rocked as the steamer lazily rises & falls over the long low waves. The sun is almost overhead, & my feet, resting on the rail, are nursed by its comfortable warmth, while the awning keeps the glare from my head. Over my shoulder comes the soft cool breeze of the north-east "trades", filling out the sails & raising white crests on the little waves that dance in joy over the more grave & serious ocean-swell.

The sea is deep blue – nothing can rival that glorious depth of colour – each plunge of the ship takes down millions of tiny air-bubbles which come seething up in great swirls of grey-blue & snow-white veined marble. The flying-fish, frightened by the ship & taking her for one of their natural enemies, start from under the bows, & sail with outspread fins, low up & down like a sea-gull skimming over the waves, & take a fresh spurt with a quick wriggle of their tails, if they happen to touch the top of a wave, until they fall with a splash two or three hundred yards away.

Now & then a nautilus floats by, with inflated sail, transparent blue edged with pale pink, like a delicate shell of iridescent crystal.[1] No other living thing to be seen, & not a ship, nothing but the ocean all round to the horizon.

Anyone with a turn for it can moralize or be inspired to write poetry, according to his bent. As for me I merely feel that it is good to sit here & do nothing, think of nothing; – just to breathe in the pure air & let it sweep the dust & cobwebs from one's lungs & brain.

<u>28th March</u>   Just come ashore at Barbados. The steamer goes on at once so I shall send this on without postage. It ought to arrive some four days before the next packet, & so you may pay fivepence on it for the satisfaction of knowing as soon as possible that I have left behind the delectable Brazils & have arrived at this happy island.

Your letters of 5th & 12th March were waiting for me. Very glad to have news only 16 days old & to know you are all well. Best love, Jack

---

1. Thank you to Richard Boyd, grand-son of JMcC, for his explanation. The "Nautilus" (not a Nautilus as we now know them – these are confined to the Indo-Pacific apparently, and are marine molluscs of the cephalopod family; not surface living) is *Velella velella* (the By-the-Wind-Sailor) "a monospecific genus of Hydrozoa in the Porpitidae family; a cosmopolitan free-floating Hydrozoa that lives on the surface of the open ocean." A very eccentric sort of jellyfish. Deep blue, with a little sail. Found all over the tropical oceans: https://en.wikipedia.org/wiki/Velella

99. Letter from Barbados, 6th-7th April 1894

18940406 See an image of this letter, http://dx.doi.org/10.17613/pthm-sg36

Barbados,   6th April 1894

My dear Mother,

You must have had fivepence to pay on my last letter, which I sent on by New York, but you can set that against the sixpence you would have given me on my birthday if I had been at home, & can forward one penny to my credit.

Thanks to Miss Dora Sinton for her affectionate greeting which I reciprocate.[1] If she wants a courier for a tour round South America I am ready. She has about <u>done</u> Europe & must be sighing for fresh worlds to conquer.

I have had a pleasant stay here in a quiet way, but not such a gay time as previously, owing chiefly to the absence of the Da Costas who were very kind to me on former occasions.[2] They return from Europe by next mail.

Last night I was at a chess-gathering at Mr Alex Laurie's house & was fitted against a champion who metaphorically wiped the floor with me.[3]

There is not much change in the place or people since I was here last. The old black "nurse" beamed on me when I arrived "How <u>is</u> you Mr Lowentall? I'se <u>very</u> glad to see you, sah! How's your health, sah!"

She had not the proper kind of cotton to darn my socks, but she remembered that I used to carry some in my housewife, & asked for it.[4] She comes in the morning to settle the room & puts her head in at the door "Good morning, sah! Is you dressed yet sah? Did you sleep good, sah?" And Thomas, the black boss-waiter, who orders the under waiters about with an authority that admits of no dispute, comes to the breakfast table, salutes respectfully with his forefinger, "Good morning, sah! You eats very little, sah. Your appetite is very delicate, sah. Try a little fried flying fish & sweet potato, sah." No doubt he thinks I am flattered to hear that my appetite is very "delicate", & so I shall tip him the more generously for his observing thoughtfulness. But he unblushingly makes this assertion daily after I have eaten a large plateful of porridge, some bacon & three boiled eggs, & he looks sympathetically sorry when I say "No thank you. I am not very hungry this morning, I will have some marmalade & bread & butter now, nothing more." I must say that the eggs are not very large here, & that, further, it would be difficult for Thomas to blush under that dusky skin of his.

1. Dora Sinton is related to the Quaker linen and flax family. https://www.genealogy.com/forum/surnames/topics/sinton/14/ She is likely to have been Dorothy Hesilridge Sinton (b 29th June 1863), daughter of Thomas Sinton who married Elizabeth Hesilridge Buckby in 1859: https://en.wikipedia.org/wiki/Thomas_Sinton? If so, Dora never married and died on 5th October 1949 at Laurelvale. See Index to People.

2. JMcC mentions them in his letter to Jane in December 1889. He probably visited Darley and Ellen who were both born around 1844 and were part of the Da Costa Family of Barbados: http://freepages.rootsweb.com/~wheelwright/genealogy/dacosta.htm. See Index to People

3. Possibly Archibald Laurie (b 1854 Barbados, m 21st August 1877 in Barbados to Frances Ann Lawrance).

4. A "housewife" (and its derivatives) is a sewing kit. While women certainly carried and used them, housewifes are most associated with sailors and soldiers. Soldiers on both sides of the conflict brought their own kits in the American Civil War. An 1855 investigation into the poor performance of the British army in the Crimean war pointed out that the Russian soldiers all carried hussifs, and that if the English army had done the same, English soldiers would not have been in rags at Sevastapol. In WW I and WW II they were popular items for women's sewing groups to make to include in care packages: https://thedreamstress.com/2015/11/a-lucky-sixpence-hussuf-and-what-are-hussuf-or-housewives/

<u>7th April.</u>   Last night a musical & tea-sical evg. at Mr Rickford's.[5] He made me stay over-night & this morning we had a swim, walking down into the water from the house – very delightful it was.

This morning I went off to the Roy. Mail S.S. "Dee" to congratulate my old friend Tyndall who has lately been promoted from "Chief" to Captain.[6] He was very glad to see me & when I would not stay to breakfast made me promise to go back to-morrow. He dines with me to-night. To-morrow night I dine with some people called Challenor.[7] Mr Austin also asked me for dinner to-morrow but I had to refuse.[8]

I am just finishing my mail. The steamer just in from Pará brought one Dundee letter, but nothing from Belfast. The direct mail from England comes the day after to-morrow. I am still short two letters of yours before the last two. I don't understand it. They ought to have come up by this last boat from Brazil.

Two days hence I leave for Trinidad. A week later, or by first opportunity, I shall go on to Curaçao.

Best love.

Jack

5. The name pops up in Barbados records – likely to be an established family of English settlers.
6. Andrew Tyndall (b ~1853). See Index to People.
7. Like Rickford, the name Challenor pops up in Barbados records – likely to be another family of English settlers.
8. The Austins are mentioned at length in JMcC's letter of 14th December 1889: "And now I will tell you who these Austins are. Mrs A. is a sister of Mrs John Taylor of Drum, & I don't know what relation to Dr Jack Brown – the Fergusson's Dr Brown. Mr Braithwaite is also related to the Austins & Taylors by marriage I think. I am not very clear about the whole connection, but possibly you may know more about it. Mrs Austin & also her son & daughter have been in Belfast at different times staying with the Taylors at Windsor." The only other mention of Austin in Barbados relates to the Tucknisses of Pernambuco – where Richard Austin (clergyman and slave owner) of a Barbados family was the maternal grandfather of Howard Tuckniss (who married the governess) Richard Austin's brothers were William and Thomas Austin – both British Guiana slave-owners. His sons were William Paul and Charles Adye.

100. Letter from Trinidad, 13th April 1894

18940413 See an image of this letter, http://dx.doi.org/10.17613/83ry-f908

Trinidad   13th April 1894

My dear Mother,

I arrived y'day at Trinidad, having left Barbados two days before on the "Trent". That morning the English mail brought your welcome letters of 19th & 23rd March, written in good spirits when the whole "fambly" was going off on holiday making. Well I hope you all enjoyed yourselves at Ballycastle, & returned much the better for the outing.

I found a lot of friends among the officers on the various Roy. Mail stmers at Barbados. The three Intercolonial boats meet the fortnightly packet there.

I breakfasted with Capt. Tindall on the "Dee"[1] – an awfully nice fellow – & had a little refreshment with Capt. Milner on the Pará. – Was invited to go off & visit Chief Offic. (acting captain) Doughtie on the "Solent", but c^d no manage it. With Bolland, 4th on the "Trent", I have now made four voyages inside eleven months. It is comical the way we dodge each other round on different ships. I did not know him at first when I caught a glimpse of him down in the hold, for he had cut his moustache short & it now reminded me, as I told him, of a worn-out tooth-brush, but he came running up with his hand outstretched & his face beaming; – very good fellows they are, almost all of these officers.

This is not a regular mail – merely an outside steamer to N.York, but I thought I w^d send you a line to say "all's well".

Best love,

Jack

Curaçao
Rivas Fensohn & Co

---

1. Andrew Tyndall (b ~1853) had been promoted from Chief Engineer and JMcC has made frequent references to him. See Index to People.

101. Letter from Trinidad, 19th April 1894

18940419 See an image of this letter, http://dx.doi.org/10.17613/sfjg-8597

Trinidad 19th Apl 1894

My dear Mother,

To-morrow I go on to Curaçao. Just sent off six letters by this mail & now I come to yours, which must be short.

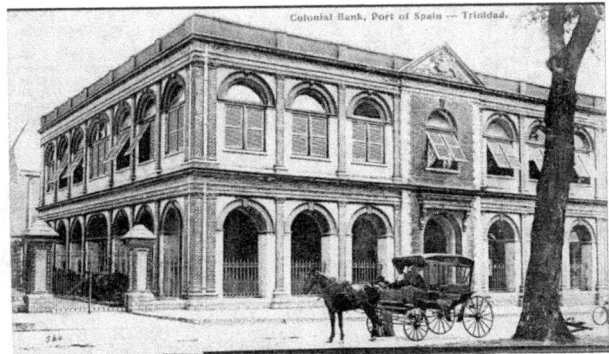

The Colonial Bank in Port of Spain, around 1898.

Business has been dull here & so have I. Last night I had a very good game of whist, & the night before some chess – not so good. To-night I dine out, – with a man called Twose, in the Colonial Bank, a nice fellow with whom I have spent most of my leisure hours here. He has asked Henry Tate to meet me, one of the long family that used to live at Queen's Elms.[1] He is now Govmt. Analyst in Trinidad. I have not met him yet, but I think he was a "small boy" at the Inst. when I was there.[2]

These West India Islands are very beautiful. At the back of Port of Spain there is an amphitheatre of low hills, covered with palms, & mangos, bread-fruit trees, acacias, banyans, cocoa-trees, – the usual tropical vegetation. Right at the foot of them is Government House, a fine residence, with the Botanical Gardens. In front of them the magnificent Savannah stretches out, two & a quarter miles round, & between it & the sea is the town.[3]

The Savannah is the public park & play-ground. In the afternoons you may see cricket, golf, polo, kite-flying without end, & other sports going on, & several pretty girls with their attendant swains having a fine canter on horseback over the green turf.[4]

---

1. Henry Tate (born 2nd February 1867 [youngest of 13 children], d 18th August 1894). He died aged 27 just 4 months after JMcC met him in Trinidad. From *Belfast Newsletter* of the 8th September 1894 – Death notices: "TATE – August 18, at Trinidad, of malignant fever. Henry, Assistant Government Analyst, youngest son of Alexander Tate, Longwood, Belfast." Henry's father Alexander Tate (b 1st July 1823 in Barnes, Surrey, d 29th July 1904 Rantalard, Whitehouse) had married his Belfast mother Margaretta Creery (b 9th September 1826 Ireland, d 21st June 1911 in Whitehouse, Antrim) on 16th July 1846 in Kilcoo Co Down. At the time of his death, was noted as being the 'father" of the Institution of Civil Engineers of Ireland (which he had joined in 1844): https://www.dia.ie/architects/view/5265/tate-alexander

2. "the Inst": The Royal Belfast Academical Institution is an independent grammar school in Belfast, Northern Ireland. With the support of Belfast's leading reformers, it opened its doors in 1814. Locally referred to as Inst, the modern school educates boys from ages 11 to 18: https://en.wikipedia.org/wiki/Royal_Belfast_Academical_Institution. JMcC attended this school and was associated with it all his life.

3. Queen's Park Savannah. Known locally as simply "the Savannah," it is Port of Spain's largest open space: https://en.wikipedia.org/wiki/Queen%27s_Park_Savannah

4. A "swain" is a male admirer or suitor.

Government House in Port of Spain, Trinidad, in 1895

Coming from Barbados our steamer called at the pretty little islands of St. Vincent & Grenada.[5] At the latter place I went ashore & took a walk round the hills at the back of the town. A three-feet-of-ebony offered his services as guide for a penny. I asked him if he knew of a school master called Chitty, a man I used to know in Barbados. He thought the gentleman was at the Grammar School. I asked my guide if he went there. "Oh no, Sah, only white people's childrens goes there". He told me that the Governor's Lady was pretty, & she had a daughter as big as herself, & "when they drives out to-gether you'll think its sisters". No courtier could have paid the Governor's Lady a prettier compliment. We found our way to the Botanical Gardens where there were a dozen convicts trimming the flower beds, – a pleasanter occupation than breaking stones. On the top of the hill was the dismal prison. I asked my guide if people ever did anything wrong in such a lovely little island, so as to get locked up. "Oh yes, Sah." & after a time, as if proud of Grenada being up to date "they sometimes kills people."

In the town I was amused at the frank directness of the public-house signboards, "Licensed to sell intoxicating liquors."

The greatest drawback to one's appreciation of the surroundings in all these places is the omnipresent "corbo", or big, repulsive carrion crow, the town scavenger, which it is forbidden to molest under a heavy penalty.[6]

Now, Misses, time's up & I must trot off to post with this.

Best love

Jack

5. Grenada may be pretty but is has a dismal colonial history: https://en.wikipedia.org/wiki/History_of_Grenada
6. A Grenadian Black Crow: https://www.pinterest.com.au/pin/65935582017939564/

102. Letter from Curaçao, 29th April 1894

18940429 See an image of this letter, http://dx.doi.org/10.17613/tt8d-se35

Curaçao,   29th April 1894.

My dear Mother,

On my arrival here y'day I recv$^{\underline{d}}$ a whole batch of letters, among them yours of 31st March, by way of New York, & an old one of 26th Feby. which had followed me from Brazil. There is still one short – 19th Feb – which will perhaps follow me round to Belfast. Though the one letter is two months old it is quite interesting reading as it contains quite a lot of chat about festivities & people. Glad to hear the pines were so good. Do you remember the previous ones I brought home, which had been packed in a salt-fish barrel & had little bits of dried cod sticking all over them?

I say, if you <u>will</u> open letters that come to me in ladies' handwriting, to save postage when forwarding, some day you will get a shock perhaps, & be sorry you did not leave them closed!

It is good news to hear that the "Craigside" is earning good dividends again. On the other hand "Ensenadas", I see, are quoted at abt. £ 35.[1] By the way, did you see Mr Pearce Edgcumbe in "Punch"?[2] You seem to have enjoyed the visit to Ballycastle. I did not know there was fishing in the neighbourhood.

Business reports from Venezuela & Colombia are so very bad that I am seriously thinking of returning home from here in about a fortnight. A good many travellers have turned back & all agree in the most dismal accounts.

The steamer "Yucatan" by which I came here from Trinidad was two days in La Guaira,[3] so I had time to go up to Caracas, & see what people had to say. Business is at an absolute standstill. Pardo tells me he has decided, if this state of things continues for two months more, to give up his agencies & take to travelling again, for he is not paying expenses & has about gone through what money he had put to the good.[4]

I saw all his family & many other old acquaintances. I am so well known round here now that almost daily someone says to me "Oh, I met somebody in Colombia – or Brazil – or on board such a steamer – who was asking for you." And when I arrive at a place after an absence of three years or so, it is not easy to remember just at once who everybody is who comes up, shakes me cordially by the hand, & welcomes me with gratifying smiles. It is exceedingly pleasant to be kindly remembered by people. At Puerto Cabello, where our steamer also called, I went to see a Mrs Rodriguez with her son & daughter, who were very kind to me before[5]. When I went away last time they gave me a basket of their own grapes & that tin of preserved bananas which, by the way, no one appreciated at home. This time they gave me the only

---

1. "Craigside" and "Ensenadas" likely to represent investment shares. No information found on "Craigside". Ensenadas could refer to investments in the English Mexican Land and Colonization Company which attempted to develop the area of Ensenada, one of the first settlements founded in the Californias, when it was designated the capital of Baja California in 1882. It is now a coastal city in Mexico.
2. Sir (Edward) Robert Pearce Edgcumbe (b 1851, d 1929) was a pioneer of the smallholdings movement and author. His portrait is in the National Portrait Gallery: https://www.npg.org.uk/collections/search/portrait/mw166472/Sir-Edward-Robert-Pearce-Edgcumbe
3. La Guaira is the capital city of the Venezuelan state of Vargas and the country's main port. It was founded in 1577 as an outlet for Caracas, 30 kilometres to the southeast.
4. Not clear who Pardo was.
5. She was previoulsy mentioned in letter of 17th May 1891.

bunch of grapes that had ripened, & said they had often spoken of me – only a short time before this bunch of grapes had brought my previous visit to their minds so that it seemed quite a proper coincidence my turning up to eat it.

I had written to Mr van Kleunen here to say I was coming though I did not say by what steamer.[6] But I was recognized by somebody as the "Yucatan" came into port & before I had put foot ashore my name was down in the Strangers' Book of the Club.

Changes take place in three years though. I found that my old boatman was dead. Two men I used to know pretty well in Puerto Cabello had also died meanwhile. I am always afraid to ask people about their friends & relatives I used to know for someone is certain to have dropped out. I spent y'day evg. with the van Kleunens at whose house I have had many a jolly time, but now they are in mourning for Mrs van K's mother. They tell me there are some people here "anxious" to make my acquaintance – Dr & Mrs Cole (?). Mrs Cole – née Greer – is from Belfast & "knows my family", so I am to be taken there to be presented.

This little place would be a paradise for the water-colour sketcher. The little harbour is like a long narrow split in the reef, leading to the lagoon which opens out behind the town. The town is built on the two sides of this "split", the houses are of Dutch style with unexpected gables, built of limestone & stucco painted yellow with red tiles, & steps leading from left & right up to the odd little porches. It always reminds me a box of German toys.

The harbour – or "split" – is about 220/300 yards across, of deep blue water, – at the entrance are the two old-fashioned forts; – a little further in is the pontoon bridge, opened, with important puffs, by the tiny engine in the end pontoon on the approach of a steamer.[7]

The pontoon bridge that connects Punda and Otrobanda in Curaçao was opened on May 8, 1888, and named after Queen Emma. It has operated ever since.

All is clean, even glaring. There is no mud, & no room or spare rain to make it, only a good deal of dust when the wind is strong from the white coral or limestone roads. My "hotel" (save the mark) is on the wharf, & I can lean out of the

---

6. Probably Jacob van Kleunen, "Merchant", a Dutch citizen who lived his whole life in Curaçao (b 27th November 1859, m Margaretha Louisa Moors 31st August 1881, d 25th October 1912).

7. The Queen Emma Bridge (Koningin Emmbrug) is called the "Swinging Old Lady" and was built in 1888 as a pontoon pedestrian bridge which opens laterally for passing ships.

window & distinguish the people on the decks of the steamers as they come slowly past, turn round cautiously & warp alongside.

To pass over the pontoon bridge I put down a Venezuelan "real" – about 4 ¾ – & received in change twenty three copper coins, – cents of a "florin" – the toll being two cents. Had I taken off my boots & carried them across I should have had to pay one cent.

The inhabitants of this side of the town are mostly Jews, – of the other side Christians.[8] Yesterday being Saturday most of the shops & stores were closed, & to-day, Sunday, all of them are.

If I return from here it may be by New York, or it may be by Royal Mail, the cost is about the same. In any case if you hear positively I am coming you might write on spec to New York. I don't know if Walter Portheim[9] is there now, so better address c/o Boulton, Bliss & Dallet.[10] Mr J.L. passenger from Curaçao.

Best love,

Jack

8. The Mikvé Israel-Emanuel Synagogue, in Willemstad, Curaçao, is the oldest surviving synagogue in the Americas.

9. Walter Portheim was previously mentioned in a letter from New York in Jan. 1891, when JMcC and Addie paid him a visit. Possibly an American merchant b~1862.

10. This refers to the Red D Line, which was the main transportation link between the United States and Venezuela from 1820 to 1936. The line took its trade name from the red D on its white flag, which stood for the line's founder, John Dallett, a Philadelphia merchant. Dallett travelled to Venezuela in 1823, where he went into business with the influential Venezuelan merchant, John Boulton. The first Bliss to be involved in the Red D Line was William Bliss who was born in Chipping Norton, England on July 4th, 1833. Many generations of Bliss, Boulton and Dallett family members were involved in the Red D Line and the long-standing history and their ties were of great importance in the strength and longevity of the company. The Red D Line is considered to be the oldest and longest-running merchant shipping line in American maritime history.

103. Letter from Curaçao, 9th May 1894

Curacao   9th May 1894

My dear Mother,

Since I wrote you last I have recv^{d} several letters from you, the long lost 19th Feby. Did they get back the 15/1 or part of it, paid on barrel of pines? Anyway I want that charged to me – please tell Julie. Perhaps Josephy thought it best to forward them by passenger train for fear they sh^{d} go bad, which w^{d} have been reasonable enough.

9th April 16th " 21st ") {these dates are shown listed with a single parenthesis to the right in the original letter} all very welcome, – last two came just ten minutes ago. N. York steamer came in this noon & the other is just making ready to leave so I must be quick with my answer.

I am sorry Rose & Bella are leaving. They were good servants & having been in the house so long knew the ways. New servants are a nuisance & it will give you trouble to drill them.

I wonder will English travel for J. Stewart & partner. In Barbados I saw sples. they had sent to a customer of ours, but I think those sples. went into the waste paper basket. People tell me when English was here he was never sober. This is a big smash of the Belfast Warehouse Co. £ 4 per share is not pleasant.[1]

Business is bad all round here. There was a big earthquake in Venezuela & Colombia the other day, several villages destroyed, this on top of bad trade is rough on the countries. Some people say they felt the earthquake here.[2]

I can't write very much in view of the fact that I may be starting for home before you get this. If so, – by steamer "Caracas" to N. York (Red D line) arrive there abt. 27th May.[3] Belfast say abt 10th June.

I have had a quiet time here, Van Kleunens are in mourning. So usually in the evgs. to Dr Cole's, – told me last night an early sweetheart of his was Jenny Wright, the fat girl, niece of Rev. Andrew.[4] He comes from Clones. Mrs Cole (née Greer) is a pleasant jolly sort of person, not particularly refined, but kindly. They have three small children with whom I have become great friends.

No more this time. I hope to have a telegram in a few days.

Best love.

Jack

---

1. The Belfast Warehouse Company company "failed" in May 1894 with the owner, J. S. Boyd, having "overextended" himself with the bank.
2. Likely the earthquake in Meridá on 28th April 1894. "1894 Mérida earthquake – On 28 April, a Richter scale 7.0 magnitude suffer the Venezuelan Andes called "Great Earthquake De los Andes" at 22.15 local time, shattered Santa Cruz de Mora, Zea, Mérida, Tovar, Mesa Bolivar, Lagunillas, Chiguará and other areas. There were a total of 319 victims and many injured." https://zimsen.kiwix.campusafrica.gos.orange.com/wikipedia_en_all_nopic/A/List_of_earthquakes_in_Venezuela
3. JMcC arrived in New York on 26th May – his name is on transit passenger list arriving from Curaçao.
4. The Reverend Andrew McCaldin, a relative of Jane's. See Index to People.

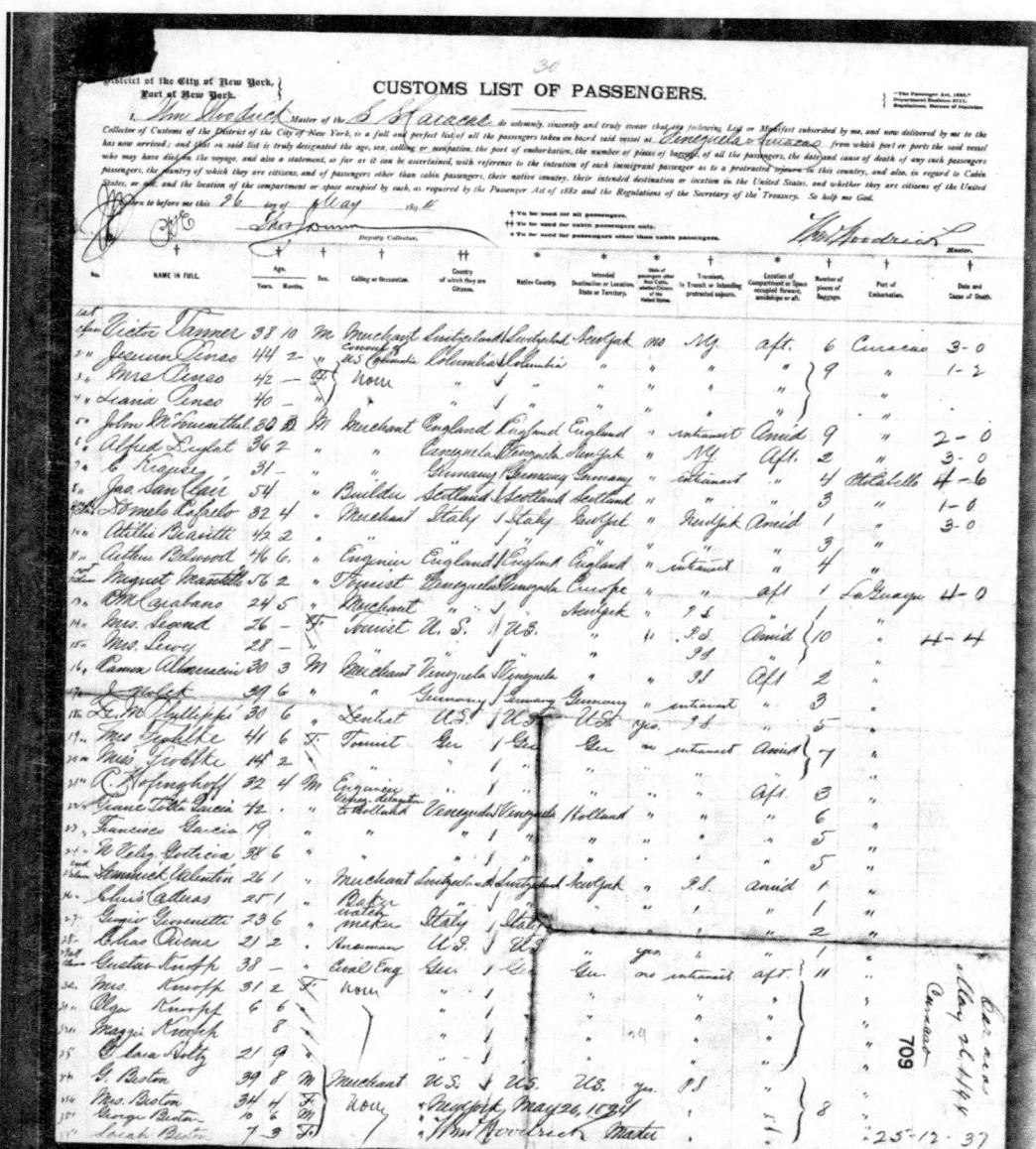

Customs List of Passengers arriving in New York on SS Caracas on 26th May 1894. JMcC is the fifth down on the list.

PART VI
THE LETTERS: BRAZIL AND ARGENTINA
1894-1895

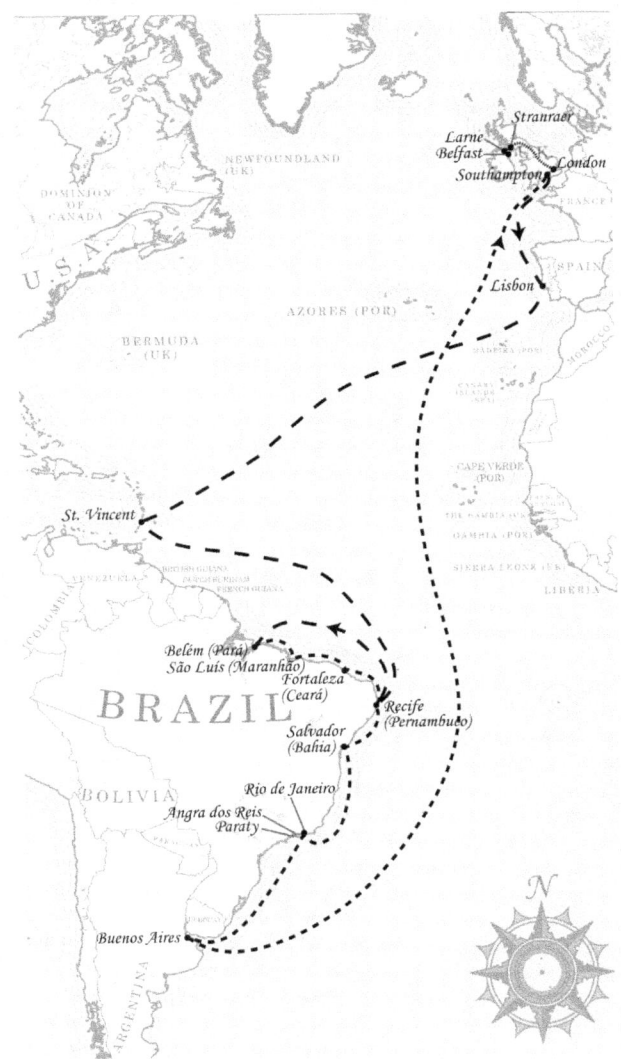

Map of the 1894-1895 voyage by John McCaldin Loewenthal. Note that JMcC refers to Brazilian cities by the names of the states that they are part of. These are shown in parentheses on the map. A high-res version is available online, https://doi.org/10.17613/8h4p-0p15 (Original map by Thomas Bachrach)

104. Letter on S.S. Nile about to sail from Southampton (sailing to Brazil via Lisbon), 7th September 1894

18940709 See an image of this letter, http://dx.doi.org/10.17613/zyfr-dw87

The letter is undated but possibly Friday 7th September 1894[1]

R.M. S.S. "Nile"
Southampton
Friday 2 pm

My dear Mother,
Just rcvd. your welcome wire. Many thanks. I have a good cabin & a pleasant mate. Everything has gone well so far. I shall write you from Lisbon. You may expect a letter about Thursday, then no more for about 5 weeks.
There are several nice old acquaintances on board, besides officers I know, & I shall be all right.
It is a lovely day. Our voyage begins well.
c/o John Eggers[2]
Caixa 114
Bahia
I purpose writing to Julie & the Pater from Lisbon.
Bye-bye
Best love
Jack

1. I wonder if this is the start of his trip to Brazil of September 1894 to August 1895. That trip started with a letter dated 8th September 1894 from the Bay of Biscay and written from S.S. Nile. The 8th September 1894 was a Saturday and this note was written at 2 pm on a Friday (no date). How long would a steamer have taken from Southampton to the Bay of Biscay in those days? 24 hours is long enough I think . . . so I believe this letter was written on 7th September 1894
2. Their agent in Bahia. See Index to People.

105. Letter from the Bay of Biscay on S.S. Nile, 8th September 1894

18940908 See an image of this letter, http://dx.doi.org/10.17613/txtj-bb41

S.S. "Nile"   Bay of Biscay
<u>8th Sept. 94</u>

My dear Mother,

I sent you a wire from London, another from Southampton & a few lines in pencil from the steamer, the first a little late in the day perhaps, but I hope you were not uneasy.

I paced the decks of the Stranraer steamer most of the time talking to Mr Pirrie. He was going to London first & then to Scarborough to join Mrs P. He asked me if I had ordered my "sleeper"! He says he is now extravagant in travelling, but economizes in other things. When he was a clerk in Harland & Wolff's[1] at a salary of £80 a year he crossed frequently to & from Liverpool, & used to take a steerage ticket, paying the first mate 4/- for the use of his cabin, thus saving about 6/-.

Stranraer ferry from an early 1900s postcard of the piers.

THE PIERS, STRANRAER

---

1. Harland & Wolff = the famous Belfast shipyard.

However a modest shilling to the guard at Stranraer secured me a comfortably cushioned 3rd class carriage to myself as far as Carlisle & subsequently every ticket-checker that appeared locked the door, so I had the whole compartment to myself from Stranraer to Euston without any further tips to pay. I pulled down the blinds, stretched myself on the seat with my rug & pillow & slept the sleep of the just. I dined and slept at Adelaide Road & was treated with the usual kindness.[2]

I am comfortably fixed on board. My room mate is a young fellow called Nicholson. He hails from Edinburgh & knows Miss Robertson, the charming young lady who was visiting the Barretts, very well.

The Captain, Chief Off., 2nd Off., D^{r}, Chief Engineer, & Purser, are all old acquaintances of mine & I know several of the passengers; – Mr Boxwell of Pernambuco, Messrs Gildermeister & Wilson, of the same place, Mr Hampshire, of Santos, & a few others.[3]

The Chief Engineer asked me to join his table, but unfortunately my neighbour on the right is very deaf & if I want to converse with him I have to shout. The ship is nearly full – about 120 1st saloon passengers I think.

I had letters from Bertie, Sissy, & Mr W., at Southampton, & I shall answer them meanwhile collectively.[4] Besides I want to write from Lisbon to the Pater. I have finished a letter to Julie.[5] So having so much correspondence I cannot make this letter any longer.

The photo sent to Southampton was a group of "the bridesmaids" for myself – very nice indeed.

The pillow was very useful in the train, & Mrs Wilson, a nice little Irishwoman from Cork, was very grateful for the use of it today. The cake is to be produced tomorrow at afternoon tea, & there are several people looking forward to tasting it.

Bye-bye,

Best love to all

Jack

2. 205 Adelaide Road (Hampstead) was the address of JMcC's uncle Ferdinand Adolph Loewenthal (senior) and his family. He was known as Adolf (or uncle Addie), was Julius' brother and the one who registered their mother Minna's death in Hamburg along with Abraham Lewandowsky, Minna's sister's son in law

3. John Harvey Boxwell (b ~1845 Wexford), "Brazilian Merchant". In references to "The English Pernambuco" one reads that Boxwell & Co. were the largest cotton baling establishment locally. See Index to People. W. Gildermeister was a frequent traveller between Southampton and Pernambuco, noted as "single and foreigner" on ships' manifestos.

4. Bertie = Bertie Weinberg (Herbert James Weinberg), son of Isaac Julius Weinberg. Sissy = Sissy Weinberg (Zerlina Adele Weinberg), daughter of Isaac Julius Weinberg, Mr W = Julius Isaac Weinberg, co-founder and senior partner of Moore and Weinberg. See Index to People.

5. Julie = JMcC's younger brother Julius.

A train at Paddington station in 1892.

106. Letter on board SS Nile and St Vincent, 14th September 1894

18940914 See an image of this letter, https://doi.org/10.17613/hfk1-9c88

S.S. "Nile",   near St Vincent
<u>14th Sept '94</u>

My dear Mother,

I was very glad indeed to have your letter at Lisbon.

I had also a long & interesting letter from Julie, one from Emma & a few lines from Addie along with some notes about business.[1]

Nothing reached me from the Pater.

We have had fine weather & a pleasant voyage so far. A chess tournament is going on, in which I am one of eight competitors. The life on board has been as usual, a daily sweep on the prow, some whist & poker, reading, sleeping, flirting, & pacing the decks. To-night there is to be a dance. I have not yet produced my cake, partly because one lady who provides afternoon tea for us had another cake, & partly because the mate of the hold will not be able to get at my box till to-morrow.

We have a very pleasant & lively set of passengers, – lots of girls & consequently entertainment "galore", as Mrs Wilson, a jolly little woman from Cork, would say. There is a Miss McClymont, whom I have seen at the Tennis Club in B.Aires; – a tall & rather pretty girl. She was lately staying a Banbridge with the Dicksons, to one of whom Norman Ferguson is engaged & she knows the Fergusons well.[2] She was at a garden party at the Fergusons' but does not remember having met any of the Sintons.[3] I wonder if Dora was there & if she remembers this young lady.

There are several newly-married couples on board. One does not notice them very much during the day, they are at their best by moonlight.

<u>Friday</u>.   The dance is over & the cake is found, so we shall have some of the latter for supper to-night. The "ball" was very good. Our band was composed of two nigger musicians, – one played the flute & the other the violin. We danced till about half past eleven, wound up with Sir Roger & then had supper.[4]

Cricket is played with a ball tied to a string, so that a "boundary hit" (overboard) may not result in a "lost ball". Miss Bridges, the belle of the ship, has just been batting vigorously while her numerous admirers bowled & fielded & chorused

---

1. Julie = JMcC's brother Julius. Emma = his sister. Addie = his younger brother Ferdinand Adolphus.
2. Norman Dickson Ferguson of Clonaslee (b 24th November 1866 Banbridge) married Jessie Mary Dickson (b 29th August 1865 Edinburgh) on the 23rd July 1895. Her parents were Andrew John Dickson (Supreme Court Solicitor in Edinburgh) and Isobella Culbert Dickson.
3. Dora Sinton and her family. See Index to People.
4. Sir Roger: One of the most popular dances in the history of social dance, Sir Roger De Coverley (later known as the Virginia Reel), is a fun, easy group dance with long-lasting appeal. Many 19th century sources propose that it was (and should be) danced as the final dance of the evening.

approval. You remember the name of Mrs Gotto's[5] friends, the Schwinds.[6] One of them is on board, a young fellow of 22 or 23, a very good sort & a good-looking youngster. I think the lady who was at Newcastle is his aunt. There is a Mrs Hockin, a very nice woman, with two children, a bright little girl & a boy of 15 or so. She wears a peculiar dress for dinner, a sort of tea-gown I suppose it is, cream-coloured, with long floating sleeves. This has earned for her the name of Cleopatra – I don't really see why – but she is rather stately.

St. Vincent, Sat'day 15th

Just about half the voyage over now. We stay here a day to coal, a very dirty, disagreeable proceeding. The black dust penetrates every-where & there is no getting away from it. The island is so hot & uninviting with its bare jagged rocks that I have never been tempted to land.[7]

I must close this now to send it off with the agent.

Love to all.

Jack.

5. Mrs Gotto = likely to be Margaret Gotto (b 1853) wife of Arthur Charles Gotto. They lived on the Malone Road. See Index to People.

6. The Schwinds = Probably Charles (South American merchant) and Eliza Schwind of Lancashire. Their son Harold Schwind, "Merchant", (b ~1874 Brazil), was a frequent traveller between the UK and Buenos Aires. Would have been 21 at the time JMcC wrote.

7. Saint Vincent is an island is in the Lesser Antilles chain; it is 29 kilometres, long and 18 kilometres wide and it is located 160 kilometres west of Barbados. It is very mountainous and heavily forested.

107. Letter from Bahia, 22nd September 1894

18940922 See an image of this letter, https://doi.org/10.17613/rbqf-2z26

Letterhead:

JOHN EGGERS

CAIXA 114

Telegrammas:

ATLANTIC-BAHIA

Pelo vapor ....

Bahia.........22$\underline{^{nd}}$ *de* September.......... *de* 189 4

My dear Mother,

Here I am once more on the old hunting-ground. The "Nile" arrived y'day. – just a fortnight since we left Southampton. Eggers & Hoyer came on board to meet me & the latter took me straight out to his house, where he had a room ready for me, so I shall not have to go to one of these filthy hotels.[1] It is very kind of him & I am only too glad to accept his hospitality. There at least I have a clean bed, nice food, a header & a swim in the sea every morning at six o'clock, & altogether the comfort that one can never have in a hotel, – no objectionable neighbours, no noise of billiard balls nor reek of smoke & eternal smell of cooking. His wife is very nice & I am a favourite with the children to whom I gave some little presents last Christmas.[2] To Mr & Mrs Hoyer I sent some nice hankerchiefs not long ago, with which they were much pleased.

The voyage was a very pleasant one. There were lots of nice people on board. In the evenings we had dancing or played games on deck – dumb crambo, up Jenkins, clumps & so on, & as I had a good deal of experience & knew the ropes pretty well on board they always looked to me to help to organize entertainments. There was also a chess tournament, in which very much to my own surprise, I divided the honours of first place with a Mr Mackenzie, who goes to Rio as manager of the Lond. & Braz. Bank.

At Pernambuco, on the way through, I saw many old friends & I have no doubt of a kind reception when I go back there. Keiller looks very well.[3] The date of his marriage will not be fixed until his business arrangements are settled. All the boarding houses in Pernam. are full but I know Mrs Latham will make room for me somehow.[4]

Here too I have greeted a lot of old acquaintances. Before leaving the steamer I was told that I was to be taken to an entertainment that evg. At the British Club, & as the customs officer would only let me have a hand-bag with me (the rest had to remain in the custom-house till next day) I opened my trunk on deck, took out a more sober pair of unwhisperables to replace my tennis bags, & the boatman carried them down the ladder under his arm. The English gunboats "Sirius", "Beagle", & "Barracouta", are at present in the Bay, & the entertainment was a very fair Christy Minstrel Concert by some of the officers & men. Afterwards there was some dancing, & we did not go home till after one o'clock.

---

1. John C Eggers and Georg Frederick Hoyer. See Index to People.
2. Mrs Margaret Hoyer, and Vera age 6, Alice age 4 and Olga age 2. See Index to People.
3. John Gibson Keiller. See Index to People
4. Mrs Latham who runs a "nice English boarding house" in Pernambuco. See Index to People.

<u>28th Sept.</u>

Leppin is here – has been here for some weeks.[5] He is rather "down" about business & says his trip has not been nearly so good as last.

I was lucky in having no trouble at all in the custom-house this time. There was so much luggage that the man did not look at a single thing – in two minutes all was ready, – nor did I come away minus a part of my wardrobe as on the last occasion.

Eggers has just moved into a new office – much more comfortable than the old one, which was up two flights of rickety stairs. On the first floor there was a tailor who had always a fire on the lobby outside in one of those iron stands the street-plumbers use. He used the fire to heat his smoothing irons & he burnt all his old rags in it until the smoke & stench filled the whole house. I often tried to persuade Eggers to pour a jug of water into it from above.

The new office is large & airy, with one flight of stairs & no tailor, though the former occupant was of that trade, & made me, in my need, a pair of dress trousers in eight hours. At the door sits Eggers his faithful body-guard, an old nigger with white hair, who sweeps the floor & employs his leisure moments in plaiting straw-hats. I have given him a commission to make me one.

This goes by the "Thames". I want to go on board if the ship comes in on time.

The Pater will now be on his way home. When this arrives I suppose he will be back. I hope he has had a good trip. I shall write to the girls soon in answer to their letters which I was glad to get at Southampton & Lisbon.

I have got quite fat this week with the good living at the Barra & the sea-bathing.[6]

Best love to all.

Jack.

5. Ernest Leppin (b ~1861? in Germany), commercial agent and a disgruntled ex-employee of Moore and Weinberg in Belfast. See letter from Rio de Janeiro of 27th December 1892 and Index to People.
6. Barra is a vibrant seaside district of Salvador, Bahia, and home to the bayside Porto da Barra beach, with its calm waters and 17th-century fort, and ocean-facing Farol da Barra which has surf-friendly swells.

108. Letter from Bahia, 8th October 1894

18941008 See an image of this letter, https://doi.org/10.17613/bkyt-3m83

Bahia   8th Oct. 1894

My dear Mother,

I was beginning to think myself rather ill-used when the Royal Mail came, a fortnight after the "Nile" and brought no letter from you. However y'day the French steamer which left earlier and arrived later brought me several letters, yours of 10th & 17th Sept. among the number, so I have calmed down again.

I hope the Pater has done well in spite of Mr Wallace and the cholera.[1]

Here I cannot say that things are very brilliant and Leppin has been here for a long time.[2] Still I am doing something. The orders are not very big, and one must run after the people time after time to bring them up to the scratch at all. But a few years ago we were doing nothing at all in South America, and now our connection is gradually growing.

I am glad to hear good news of Julie. Olga sent me half a letter, and you the other half.[3] I return it as I dare say you will like to keep it. Do so anyway, for Julie will like to read later the account of his first experiences abroad.[4]

I hope Lloyd is better.[5] I am glad Aunt has safely arrived at Warrenpoint.[6] Perhaps the change will do her good. So Andrew McC did not profit much by the lesson at Bangor.[7] He is evidently bent on killing himself, and that soon.

I have written a letter to Annie[8] and told her what I am doing here and how we live at the "Barra", so there is not much left to write to you about.[9] Your mention having tea in the porch on an odd day when it is still warm enough to sit out. Here we stay indoors because it is too hot to sit out. I have just bought a very thin brown calico coat to wear in town and I only wear my ordinary jacket coming down to the office and going home.

English servants are perhaps not always all that might be desired but I wonder how you would like Brazilian domestics. They are of course all negroes. They wear no stockings – only wooden clogs, and cleanliness is not their most striking characteristic. Hoyers have three servants.[10] The cook comes in the morning and leaves after dinner. There is a toothless old nurse to look after the children, and there is Fortunata. Fortunata is about the blackest blackie I ever saw. As a rule

1. The fifth cholera pandemic lasted from 1881 to 1886. It spread throughout Asia and Africa, and reached parts of France, Germany, Russia, and South America. The Pater (Julius) may well have been on a business trip in Russia – where the pandemic claimed 200,000 lives between 1893 and 1894.
2. Ernest Leppin (b~1861 ?in Germany), commercial agent. Ex-employee of Moore and Weinberg in Belfast. He appeared often in earlier correspondence from Brazil. See Index to People.
3. Olga Loewenthal, JMcC's sister.
4. Julius Loewenthal Jr, JMcC's brother – on first business trip in Spain. Tragically died on his trip to Brazil in 1896. See Index to People.
5. Probably a servant in the family household. She appeared in a letter regarding the 1892 Christmas at Lennoxvale.
6. Warrenpoint is a small port town and civil parish in County Down, Northern Ireland. It sits at the head of Carlingford Lough, south of Newry. "Aunt" is likely to be Jane's aunt Martha McCaldin (b 1808), unmarried, who died in Newry on 23rd December 1897.
7. Could be the Rev Andrew McCaldin who died on 29 Nov 1894 (see Index to People), or possibly Jane's first cousin (son of her uncle James McCaldin, brother of her mother Ann Isabella McCully née McCaldin) Andrew McCaldin (b 1852). Bangor is a town in County Down, Northern Ireland. It is a seaside resort on the southern side of Belfast Lough.
8. Anne Isabella Loewenthal, JMcC's sister.
9. Barra is a neighbourhood located in the south zone of the city of Salvador, Bahia, Brazil.
10. Georg Hoyer and his family. See Index to People.

these darkies have a sort of shiny appearance, as if they oiled themselves, but Fortunata is of a dull lustreless black and when she opens her head to smile the effect by contrast of her ivory teeth is positively dazzling.

The other day when Mrs Hoyer was out two lady visitors called. "And what did you say to them Fortunata?" asked Mrs Hoyer. – "I said you were out and told them to come back to-morrow," ! she replied with a smile of satisfaction which implied "Oh you don't need to tell me. – I know what's the proper thing to do."

Mrs Hoyer has a comfortable arm chair in her room, in which the other day after dinner she found Fortunata fast asleep her head comfortably propped up on the best cushion.

Not to be behind one or two other men I have a mind not to go to Rio from here now but to go north to Pernambuco and on up the coast. I have not quite decided but anyway please address letters to <u>Pernambuco</u> c/o Mr <u>Theo Just</u>.[11] (no further address is needed). If I am not there he will forward the letters and there will be no time lost.

On Saturday I was at a tea-fight and musical evening chez Mrs Hill, a lady who came out on the same steamer with me last year. The principal performer was a Mrs Mackay, a rather gook looking young married woman, inclined to be modern but not very good form. She delights in shocking the properer section of Bahia society by singing the latest burlesque and music-hall songs, – and she sings them well for she has a really good voice. But Miss Jones, Mrs Hoyer's maiden-aunt, a prim elderly lady of the old school and a great friend of mine, does not approve of Mrs Mackay at all.

It is very funny when I happen to meet Miss Jones going to or coming from the sea-bath – I in pyjamas, she trying to hide her Bloomer-costume under a large bath-sheet, with a deprecating smile and her eyes modestly fixed on the ground.

Miss Jones has kindly procured me an invitation to a dance tonight to which the Hoyers are also going. I think it will be very nice. That will be something for my next letter.

Best love,

Jack

11. Theo Just was a Commercial agent in Pernambuco.

109. Letter From Bahia, 23rd and 27th October 1894

18941023 See an image of this letter, https://doi.org/10.17613/e0bw-vx60

Bahia, 23rd Oct. 1894

My dear Mother,

My last letter went by the "Nile" a fortnight ago. Since then I have recv^d your welcome letters of 24th Sept. and 1st Oct. I am exceedingly sorry to hear of the death of my friend Ferguson. How did the Weinbergs know of it? Was it through Julian?[1]

I am finishing up here. My steamer, which will take this, comes in in three days. I have done a fair business, all things considered, and have considerably extended the list of our customers here. I have never done so much in Bahia before.

The Hoyers have been awfully good to put me up all this time and they have not shown any impatience to get rid of me.[2] On the contrary they ask me to stay longer. I must think of some present to send them, and as I have no hotel bill here (except at the restaurant where I lunch) I think the firm must pay for it or for the greater part of it.

S.S. "Clyde" 27th Oct.

I did not get any further with my letter on shore, so now I must finish it on board, so as to send it on by this steamer.

Mr & Mrs Hoyer came off to the steamer with me to say good-bye. Eggers came too & a number of the English fellows were on board so there was the usual thirsty leave-taking.[3]

We are due in Pernambuco to-morrow, Sunday, morning. It is rather an uncomfortable day for landing as the customhouse is closed and the luggage must remain there till Monday. It is difficult to find porters too, but I expect there will be someone on the look-out for me as I wired I was coming.

The officers on the Clyde have all been changed lately. I know the purser Dyer, – a friend of Taylor's of Dundee, – and Capt. Bell slightly, none of the others.[4]

The passengers mostly belong to an Italian Opera Company, – fat women and stagey men, not particularly clean. They are going to Lisbon I suppose.

It is always an effort to write on board, so I will cut this letter short, and make the next one longer. There will be a French steamer in a week or ten days.

Best love to all,

Jack

---

1. Julian Weinberg, son of Dundee Weinbergs, had been travelling with JMcC. See Index to People.
2. The Hoyers have been accommodating JMcC at their home. See Index to People.
3. John C Eggers, the commercial agent. See Index to People.
4. John Brown Taylor, Linen & Jute manufacturer & merchant. See Index to People.

110. Letter from Pernambuco, 4th November 1894

18941104 See an image of this letter, https://doi.org/10.17613/4vc5-dg21

Pernambuco,
4th Nov. '94

My dear Mother,

I have not heard from you since I wrote to you last, by the "Clyde". My letters have gone on to Bahia, but they will be sent back in a day or two.

They have given me a comfortable room at Lathams', though the house was pretty full[1]. Some fellows fortunately left just at the right moment. Mrs Latham has been in England for some months, putting the youngest boy to school. She is now on her way out and will arrive in about a fortnight. There are still several men living here who were in the house when I was last in Pernambuco, and altogether it is very social and pleasant. Frank Youle whom I knew so well in Rio is living here.[2] He is in the London and River Plate Bank – Accountant – and has come to this Branch for some six months. He has done very well. He came out with me in '91, and to become full accountant in three years is quick promotion.

The Parson, Mr Macrae, is still here, – a capital fellow, fond of chess, whist and tennis. Mr & Mrs Alfred Guimarães arrived from England by last steamer.[3] I have almost quarrelled with him. He told me they were in Belfast when I was there and never came to see me. He said I had not written to him this time though I knew he was in England. I said I was only a home for a short time, that I was running about a great deal – in Scotland – in London – and so on. I reminded him that the year before I had written to him asking him to stay with us and that I had enclosed a note from you to Mrs Guimarães, and that after that I took it very much amiss that he had not even looked me up in the office. As a matter of fact I consider it very rude. If it were anyone else I should say that he did not want to see me. But I know it is not so with him. He thought I might have written again and not having done so he would not come and seem to fish for an invitation. He is an extraordinary fellow, – always ready to imagine a slight. He said he even put a dress-suit in his bag and told his wife to take a couple of dresses in case they might hear from me at the last moment. I believe they went on to Killarney, but I was so much annoyed that I did not ask him any questions. I went, two nights after their arrival, to pay them a short formal visit out of politeness, for they were very kind to me when I was here before, but I don't think they will ask me to dinner this time for I think he understands that I should certainly decline any invitation.

I have already received many invitations from other sides and others are threatened. Keiller is not back yet from the South, but I called on the Tucknisses.[4] I also dined with Mr & Mrs Howard Tuckniss who are the happy parents of a four-weeks-old daughter.[5] Mr and Mrs Santos gave us an excellent dinner the other evening, fiz and all the rest of it. Mr Santos is the leading exchange-broker. His wife was a Miss Thom. The Thoms are an old Pernambuco-English family. We

---

1. Mrs Latham's English guest house in Pernambuco. See Index to People.
2. Frank (Schwind) Youle (b 1867) was 27 when JMcC wrote and died 9th March 1900 (only aged 33) in Rio de Janeiro. He was buried in the Cemiterio dos Ingleses there. See Index to People.
3. Alfred Lopes Guimarães. See Index to People.
4. Benjamin and Leonora Tuckniss. Keiller lodged with them in Pernambuco. See Index to People.
5. Benjamin Howard Tuckniss and Constance Mary Tuckniss née Braga from Pernambuco, who were married in West Derby on the 15th November 1893. The daughter was Irene Mary Barbara Tuckniss. She returned to the UK and became a teacher. Her married name was Penrose Pilgim and she died in Devon in 1968. See Index to People.

were three guests: – Youle, myself, and a Mr Fletcher, manager of the railway. After dinner we had a good game of whist. Altogether I have had a lot of whist this week. Two nights here, one at Santos', and one at a Mr Comber's; – the last was a meet of the local whist-club.

I have been to call on the Williams family,[6] and last night I went to visit Mr & Mrs Wilson, who came out on the steamer with me. In the afternoon if I have finished my business early enough I usually have a game of tennis and the exercise does me no end of good.

There will be another homeward mail five days hence. I will write by it if I can, but I don't promise.

Love to all.

Jack

6. Arthur Llewellyn Griffith-Williams and Edith Ann Williams (Mrs Williams was born Boxwell, sister of "Miss Boxwell"). See Index to People.

III. Letter from Pernambuco, 8th November 1894

18941108 See an image of this letter, https://doi.org/10.17613/r97q-w931

Written on notepaper printed with the letterhead below:

MOORE & WEINBERG

DUNDEE,

AND

BELFAST.

Spanish V Consulate

Address Telegrams:

WEINBERG

Pernambuco ~~Dundee~~..............................189 4

<u>8th Nov.</u>   My dear Mother,

As I am writing in the office and have no private letter-paper. I may as well use some of the Dundee stationery of which I have still a remnant left of my old supply. I don't get very much from the Dundee firm for nothing so it is at least a gratification to have some sheets of paper gratis.

Your two welcome letters of 8th & 15th Oct. came two days ago via Bahia. The pater must have been home a day or two after the latter left, so I expect to hear from him by next mail. I hope Julie is getting along well. I should like to have more news from him. Now that the winter gaieties have commenced with dances at Sinclairs' and Gottos', the girls will miss the society young man who has trotted them out since I was put on the shelf.[1]

Last night I dined at the Biltons' and spent a very pleasant evening.[2] Mr Bilton is the Manager of the London & Brazilian Bank, a most popular man. His house is a nice one to go to, – there is always lots of fun. After dinner at least twenty people came trooping in, all of whom I knew, and we had songs and lively conversation till our train came along at half past ten. And coming down the line we had a long carriage to ourselves and we entertained the other passengers with more music and very vigorous choruses.

I am out dining or visiting almost every evening. I have a very large circle of friends and acquaintances here, and they are all very hospitable. Yesterday the Pacific steamer passed south. I am sorry I did not go on board as I heard afterwards that Mrs Watson and Miss Moores whom I knew very well in Buenos Aires were passengers.

The Tucknisses were all charmed with Mrs Fred.[3] I believe they mean to stay here on their way north, – I mean Fred and his wife. I have not heard from them at all.

I don't know very well how I am going to get this posted. This is Sunday, the steamer comes up this afternoon, & the mail closed this morning. Don't scold me if you have to pay 5^{d}.

Best love,

Jack

c/o Mr Theo Just   Caixa 68   Pernambuco

1. The Gottos: These would be the Belfast Gottos. See Index to People.
2. The Biltons. See Index to People.
3. Most likely the wife of Fred (Frederick) Weinberg, he married Grace Keiller in London on 14th August 1894. She was the sister of John Gibson Keiller, the "Keiller" who often was in Pernambuco with JMcC, and used to lodge with the Tucknisses. It sounds like they have just returned as newly weds.

112. Letter from Pernambuco, 24th November 1894

18941124 See an image of this letter, https://doi.org/10.17613/vvjm-4p63

Pernambuco
24th Nov. 1894

My dear Mother,

My excuse for not writing longer letters from Pernambuco you will perhaps not admit to be a very good one. It is that I have so many invitations for dinners, whist, music, dancing, & friendly visits that I am out every evening, while during the day business and business-writing keep me fairly well employed.

For the next mail I must get some Christmas letters written and I shall have to put on the break and remain indoors a little more. Last night I dined with the Williamses, who were at Dundee once upon a time.

On Tuesday there was a ball at the International Club, to which I had an invite. It was very gay. All the Pernambuco-English belles were there and I had several charming partners. But in this climate I don't attempt to dance right through the programme and the extras – it is much too hot work and one becomes very limp quite early in the proceedings unless one carefully sandwiches intervals with hops.

On Thursday I dined again with Howard Tuckniss. His sister, Mrs Adamson, arrived from England by last steamer. She has a dear little four-year-old girl – a pretty child, very old-fashioned and out-spoken. I happened to go on board the steamer the day they arrived and as I was walking along the deck this little mite looked up and asked me "Are you Uncle Howard?".

I have just been writing to wish the Pater many happy returns.[1] My letter ought to arrive within a day of the 7th.

Mr Leppin has been laid up for some days – inflamed mosquito bites on his feet. I took him round some papers to read, for which he was duly grateful.[2] He has instructions to go to Pará and does not like the prospect a bit.

Keiller was to have come back yesterday from Rio.[3] I suppose he has done so.

1. Julius Loewenthal Sr (b 7th December 1834). His 60th birthday.
2. Mr Leppin. See Index to People.
3. John Gibson Keiller. See Index to People.

Floriano Vieira Peixoto, the second President of Brazil (b 1839, d 1895).

The old President has at last resigned the reins and the new one has come in, and the change has been effected quietly. Many people expected that Mr Floriano Peixoto, having bossed the show for so long, would decline to retire at the last moment.[4]

I must go to breakfast now, and then run into town. It is Sunday, but the mail does not wait. There is always general disgust among the young fellows when the mail comes up on Sunday, for most of the offices, even the English ones, open then.

So far I cannot complain of business here, though every one tells me things are very dull. It requires patience and imperturbability and if one has not lots of both one can do nothing at all out here.

Bye-bye.

Best love

Jack.

4. Floriano Vieira Peixoto (b 30th April 1839, d 29th July 1895) was the second president of Brazil. His government was marked by several revolutions. Ruling in an authoritarian fashion, Peixoto defeated a naval officers' rebellion against him in 1893–1894 and the Federalist Riograndense Revolution in the States of Rio Grande do Sul and Santa Catarina. He is often referred to as "the Consolidator of the Republic" or "The Iron Marshal." He left the presidency on 15th November 1894. In spite of his unpopularity, he was responsible for the consolidation of the First Brazilian Republic. He was succeeded by Prudente José de Morais e Barros who was nominated by the Republican Federal Party, founded by Paulo Glicerio Francisco in 1893. He won the presidential election on 1st March 1894 and took office on 15th November that year, becoming the first president of Brazil to be elected by direct vote and the first civilian president of Brazil. https://en.wikipedia.org/wiki/Floriano_Peixoto and https://en.wikipedia.org/wiki/Prudente_de_Morais

113. Letter from Pernambuco, 30th November 1894

> 18941130 See an image of this letter, https://doi.org/10.17613/sprc-p584

Pernambuco
30th Nov. '94

My dear Mother,

Since I wrote to you by last Royal Mail, about a week ago, I have had two letters from you, – one via Rio, dated 22nd Oct. & one of 12th Nov. The two between will no doubt come back from Rio one of these days.

I am glad to hear that Mr W. has got back £10.000.[1] So Bertie is giving up engineering for business. I dare say it is a very good arrangement, but there will be moments when he will regret his former happy independence.[2]

Jack Keiller tells me his father has been appointed treasurer to the Dundee hospital, at 100 guineas a year, which is, I am sure, a very welcome addition to his some-what precarious income.[3]

On Tuesday last I dined at Howard Tuckniss's, to meet Captain Adamson.[4] After dinner we had billiards and a little music. Before dinner little Nellie Adamson (aged 3), whom I have mentioned in a former letter, made me play hide and seek with her. She pronounces my name quite correctly, with a proper German accent, and she amuses me very much by saying "Now you must keep your eyes shut Mr Loewenthal dear!". She is old-fashioned and uses very big words for such a little mite. "Mother, if I say a thing and you say it isn't, isn't that contradicting?" she asked. Another favourite expression of hers is "That's bidiculous".

I shall very soon be moving further north now. There is not very much business to be done for the moment, which I regret, for privately, I like the life here very much. It makes such a difference living in a decent English boarding-house, and this of Mrs Latham's is an exceptionally nice one – it is more a family life than an ordinary boarding-house existence.[5] The people in the house are a very pleasant set, and all the surroundings – the little things that are so important – are civilized.

I hope the Pater's sciatica is long since gone; it is a painful thing. I travelled with a man from Pará to Barbados who had a bad attack of it and he seemed to suffer a good deal of pain.

It will be very nearly Christmas when this letter reaches you. I think there will be another mail arriving home just about the 25th and by it I must try to send several letters, but it is not a very easy matter to get them written.

---

1. Isaac Julius Weinberg, founding partner of Moore & Weinberg. See Index to People.
2. Bertie: Herbert Weinberg, the ship engineer and son of Isaac Julius Weinberg. He was sent to Buenos Aires by his father to replace his brother Julian with the firm Weinberg and Crank. Tragically he took his own life in June 1896, aged of 28, prior to arriving back in Dundee. For more see Index to People, and refer to I. J. Weinberg's memoir: *Reminiscences of My Life: Written from Memory for My Wife and Children*, pp. 128-129: http://dx.doi.org/10.17613/ch97-0r17
3. John Gibson Keiller (b 9th July 1865 Dundee, d 24th February 1897 Pernambuco. See Index to People. His father mentioned in this letter was George Clark Keiller (b 1833, d 1919) who was a Dundee merchant and commission agent (in New York) with many local connections. He was the grandfather of Grace Weinberg. He had a long and successful career and acted as secretary of the Dundee Chamber of Commerce for 27 years, rendering valuable services to the commercial community of Dundee: https://mcmanus168.org.uk/mcmanus168entry/george-c-keiller/
4. Captain Adamson was the husband of Howard Tuckniss' sister (mentioned in the last letter dated 24th November 1894). Their daughter Nellie was born ~ 1891.
5. For more about Mrs Latham, see Index to People.

In other places where the social life is not so pleasant and where I have to spend my leisure hours in my bedroom in the hotel I am a much better correspondent. Here I have no leisure hours.

The other day Mr Williams made me a present of a box of 25 of his extra-specially good Havana cigars.[6] When we were in Dundee together I remarked one day that the best cigars I had ever smoked were "Hoyo de Monterey N$\underline{o}$ 6", whereupon he produced two from his pocket and said they were the brand he always smoked.[7] So in town two days ago he stopped me to say that he had just received a fresh consignment and would like me to try them, and he insisted on my taking a box, which at first I was very unwilling to do.

<u>3rd Dec</u>.   Yesterday I dined with our agent here, Mr Theo Just.[8] He is German, his wife is Brazilian, and of course the whole family is very Brazilian, – three grown-up daughters, one son, a daughter-in-law, and a grandchild. There were four other guests, young Germans, and we sat the men all on one side, the ladies on the other side of the table. It was rather funny. The conversation was carried on in Portuguese, German, and English. The dinner was very good, except that there was too much of it, and I was devoutly thankful when the last of the dishes was taken away.

I must go now.

Best love to all

Jack

---

6. Probably Arthur Llewellyn Griffith-Williams, husband of Edith Williams née Boxwell. See Index to people.
7. Hoyo de Monterrey is a cigar brand established in 1865. The range historically comprises light strength cigars, using tobacco from the premium Vuelta Abajo region. There is a non-Cuban brand with the same name.
8. Theodor Just (b 23rd May 1839 Zittau, Saxony, Germany). See Index to People.

114. Letter from Pernambuco, 7th December 1894

18941207 See an image of this letter, https://doi.org/10.17613/abcj-2216

Pernambuco,   7th Dec. 1894

My dear Mother,

I wrote to you only a couple of days ago by Pacific steamer, so this goes as a short supplement to carry my best wishes to all of you for Christmas and the New Year.

This is the Pater's birthday: – Hoch soll er leben![1] I hope he has neither gout nor sciatica to prevent his dancing a jig today should he feel so inclined, and may he have every reason to be merry, even if he may not be disposed to give vent to his rejoicing in such playful gambols. I expect a playful gamble at threepence a point will be more to his taste.

I expect to leave next week for Pará. At the end of the year business is always dull. Stocktaking is approaching and people are not willing to give orders till their yearly balance is over and they see how they stand. I might almost as well stay here over Christmas and have a good time, but I have only a few more little orders to get from reluctant customers, and in another week I shall have no further pretext to remain. Pará is a very sorry place after Pernambuco and I go there the more regretfully at this time as business is reported very dull there.

The London and River Plate Bank building in Recife, Pernambuco, ca. 1909.

Last night I dined with the Ellises. Mr Ellis is the Manager of the London & Riv. Plate Bank here. Mrs Ellis was a Miss Mawson of Bahia – I know her people very well. She has some pretty sisters and she herself is very pretty and bright – quite a young woman.[2] They have asked me to dine again there on Saturday, – Youle is going and two Miss Needhams – belles of Pernambuco.[3] On Wednesday I dined at the Biltons', with a Mr Webster.[4] Mr B. is Manager of the rival English Bank, and Mr W. of a local Bank, so as I said in my letter to Addie I am moving just now in lofty financial circle. Mrs Ellis very kindly asked me to dine on Christmas-day with them, but I shook my head mournfully.

I hope you will all have a jolly Christmas. Is Julie home again, or is he still in Spain?[5] I presume he is to be home for Christmas, but I mean to write to him in Madrid (if I don't change my mind & send it to Belfast). You don't say anything about expecting him home.

It is fearfully hot. I don't feel the heat so much as most of the other Englishmen but even I sit here "mopping". I am the

---

1. "Hoch soll er leben" is a German song often sung on birthdays, loosely translated as "long may he prosper". Example here: https://youtu.be/hC8gBHdMoDc. It was Julius' 60th birthday.
2. The Mawson girls – daughters of Joseph Mawson – were all born in Bahia (Blanche Gabb b ~1867, Winifride Mary b 1876, Geraldine Teresa b 1880)
3. This is Frank (Schwind) Youle. See Index to People.
4. Mr W H Bilton. Manager of the London and Brazilian Bank in Pernambuco. See Index to People.
5. His brother Julius Loewenthal Jr, on his first business trip in Spain.

only one who comes home in the afternoon with an uncrumpled collar. Those of the rest are all in moist uncomfortable creases, and at a dance they envy me my immaculate shirt-front.

    Bye-bye.   Best love and all good wishes.

    Jack.

    This ought to arrive about Xmas-eve. I don't know if there will be another mail arriving before 2nd Jary. If not, many happy returns to Emma & my letter will follow.[6]

6. JMcC's sister Emma Loewenthal, her birthday 2nd January 1869, she will be 26.

115. Letter on way to Pará 22nd December 1894 and from Pará, 1st January 1895

18941222 See an image of this letter, https://doi.org/10.17613/madg-5c57

Pernambuco
<u>22nd Dec. 1894</u>

My dear Mother,

I wrote to you by the last Royal Mail about a fortnight ago, and to Emma and Julie by Pacific steamer leaving yesterday. I have your letter of 26th Nov. but I don't seem to have received one of the 19th – whatever has become of it. Otherwise the series is complete Monday by Monday. I am very sorry to hear the Pater was still poorly when you wrote. It is a very tedious and troublesome thing and must try his patience.

I hope Gideon enjoyed his plum-pudding. Why did you not send me one? Well anyway I am to have a piece of an English-made plum-pudding. Youle had one sent out to him, together with a plum-cake, and he gave them both to Mrs Ellis who has invited us to dinner on Christmas-day.

S.S. "Kaffir Prince",   <u>31st Dec. 1894</u>

I did not proceed with above because I did not want to post another letter from Pernambuco; – I wished to be fairly on my way to Pará before putting pen to paper again.

This steamer was so long coming and, when it did come, remained so long – a whole week – in P'buco harbour that I really lost patience. However that's the way they manage things out here, and finally we embarked on the 26th, the steamer sailing early next morning.

The one compensating consideration was that I was able to spend Christmas-day among friends. The Ellises gave us a nice dinner, and afterwards the Thom connection came around,[1] – three ladies and three men and we spent a right merry evening, dancing and singing about every song that has a chorus. It was two o'clock when we separated. We had plum-pudding (the ring falling to my share), mince pies, and champagne.

I may mention that I went to church on Christmas-day. There was a choral service, the church was nicely decorated, and the parson gave us a very good discourse. The English colony turned out in force: I think the congregation numbered over 130 not counting children and there was a highly satisfactory collection for the Church of England Society for Waifs and Strays.

I have not yet received my Christmas letters. It was very aggravating that the "Kaffir Prince", having waited so long, did not stay a few hours longer, for we saw the English mail steaming in as we went out, and I shall now not get them for another ten days at least.

Mr Leppin has come up with me from Pernambuco and has been a most pitiable object, – abjectly seasick the whole time, and unable to eat or drink anything.[2] For five days and nights he did not take his clothes off and he moaned constantly as if he were just about to die. Luckily I am a good sailor and I can adapt myself to circumstances. I like a comfortable bed with a spring mattress but if there is not one to be had, why I can sleep soundly in a bunk like a

---

1. In letter of 4th November1894: "The Thoms are an old Pernambuco-English family"
2. The pitiable Leppin is an ex-Moore & Weinberg employee. See Index to People.

scooped-out board with a few dozen cockroaches crawling around. I enjoy a good dinner and a bottle of iced Heidsieck dry Monopole, but I can satisfy the pangs of hunger and thirst with leathery beef and lukewarm water.[3] This adaptability is not entirely desirable, I am quite aware, but it makes life much more pleasant.

This 1901 advertisement for Heidsieck & Co's Monopole champagne features art by the Czech Art Nouveau artist Alfons Mucha.

I had an exceedingly pleasant stay at Pernambuco this time. Everybody was as kind and hospitable as I could possibly wish. The only returns I made were, – a box of French sweets to Mrs Howard Tuckniss on Christmas-day, a share in a little present of a silver-topped scent bottle to Mrs Latham, and a merry little farewell dinner-party to five fellows in a small inn at Capongá, one of the suburbs. The dinner was a great success, I bore with me, I really think, a great deal of good will, on leaving kindly Pernambuco.

I had an invitation to the "Bachelors' Ball" which will have taken place on the 31st. I was rather sorry to miss it. The previous one, on the 6th Janry. last, was one of the jolliest dances I have ever been at. The supper alone on these yearly occasions costs about £150, and everything is done as well as it can be done.

As I mentioned, I had to go on board on the evening of the 26th. Three of the fellows with whom I have been most chummy, Youle, Shaw, and Phillips, actually left in the middle of dinner, and that is a severe test of friendship, to come down and see me off.[4]

Pará 1st Janry. 1895.

A happy New Year to you all. Here I am safely ashore. I send this off to-day via Pernambuco. I am afraid it will be rather long on the way, but there is no direct mail from Pará till the 10th Janry. I cal'clate you will have this about the 26th. You had better address c/o Theo Just who will forward letters from Pernambuco to wherever I may be along this northern coast.[5]

Best love to all

Jack

3. Heidsieck & Co "Monopole" is a champagne house located in the Champagne region of France. It was founded in 1785 by Florens-Louis Heidsieck: https://en.wikipedia.org/wiki/Heidsieck_%26_Co

4. Frank Youle is the only one he has really mentioned before. See Index to People.

5. Theo Just was the Moore & Weinberg agent in Pernambuco. See Index to People.

116. Letter from Pará, 4th January 1895

18950104 See an image of this letter, https://doi.org/10.17613/4ce2-ww88

Pará , 4th Janry. 1895

My dear Mother,

Taking advantage of a steamer leaving today for New York I send these few lines that way on the chance that they may reach you sooner than a letter will by the next direct mail on the 10th.

Two days ago I posted a letter to you, written while on the steamer coming north, via Pernambuco. There are so many different routes for homeward mails from Pará, but most are very uncertain in the time required for letters to reach their destinations.

Once more I have fallen on my feet in the matter of lodgings. I had only to spend one day in the dirty hotel when I was offered a room in a house shared by two old acquaintances. Power and Duff, – about the best men here.[1] Power is now manager of the London & River Plate Bank in Pará, and Duff is an exchange-broker. They have a most comfortable house, arranged according to English ideas, and a good cook. We breakfast and dine there, and we lunch in town. They allow me to pay something, – but it is much less than what the beastly hotel would cost one.

Another acquaintance, Mr Oakes, is manager of the other English Bank (London & Brazilian). He is married to a German lady who is very nice – speaks English fluently. They were formerly in Bahia where I knew them and used to play whist with them. I dined at their house the day I landed here and I go there again to-night.

Our Agent, Mr Kolb, is at Ceará, but he returns in a few days. I have been round seeing our "customers"; they are all busy with their stock-taking and I shall not be able to do much before next week.

Am waiting impatiently for my Christmas letters by next boat from P'buco. You had better still address there c/o Mr Theo Just.

Best love to all

Jack

---

1. Power and Duff. Old friends in Pará. See Index to People.

117. Letter from Pará, 10th January 1895

18950110 See an image of this letter, https://doi.org/10.17613/nfkj-7c72

Pará   10th Janry   1895

My dear Mother,

I don't understand it at all. I have waited till the last moment allowed for this mail so as to be able to acknowledge the letters that I counted on for certain by a steamer just in from Pernambuco, but nothing whatever has come. Unless Mr Just has regt^{d} them – which would cause some delay – I shall be much disappointed. I have not yet had any Christmas letters from home.

Here I am all right, – very comfortable out at Power's house – dined three times this last week with Mr & Mrs Oakes, at whose house we had some mild whist.[1]

The rainy season is beginning. Torrents of rain every afternoon. One's clothes always feel damp & everything becomes mildewed. Mosquitoes vigorously on the warpath.

I expect to turn south again in a week or so. Maranham – Ceará – & P'buco.

I wrote you two letters since arrival here, one via N. York, on via P'buco, and now I shall wait till I get some news. Have had none for ever so long.

Best love to all,

Jack

---

1. Mr Oakes is the manager of the London & Brazilian bank. He is married to a German lady who is very nice and speaks English fluently (all from JMcC's last letter of 4th January 1895. Not otherwise identified.)

118. Letter from Pará, 16th January 1895

18950116 See an image of this letter, https://doi.org/10.17613/qgy6-c802

Pará 16th Janry. 1895

My dear Mother,

Since my last, posted 10th inst. I cannot complain that I have been neglected by the Post Office. In the course of three days I received some twenty letters and now I have a task before me to answer them all. Three of yours came together, 3rd, 10th, & 17th Dec., and two very pretty cards, for all of which many thanks. I am very glad to hear the Pater is better. In the last few lines received from him, dated Christmas-eve, he tells me Julie returned looking very fit.[1] I can imagine his feelings at coming home for Christmas after his first journey.

I am sorry to hear of Mills death, he was a very decent fellow. I saw a paragraph in the Whig about the Rev. Andrew.[2] There are not many McCaldins left now.

Pleased to know the pines were good. Those I sent to Mrs Barret seem to have arrived in even better conditions. She wrote me a very nice letter piling on the thanks and saying that not even one pine was bruised. I am very glad I sent them a barrel, they were so pleased to be remembered. Did you enjoy the entertainment at Fergusons'? I am sure they gave you a good supper – they always do the thing well and I was quite sorry to have to slip away last time from their garden party without a share in the banquet or a skip at the dance.

Among my letters were one each from the girls, Addie, and Jim; two from Pater, one each from Mr & Mrs Weinberg, one from Victor Kamcke.[3] From Mrs Latham I had also a letter and a pretty card, as well as two introductions for Ceará. Both Shaw and Youle, – the two fellows I was most chummy with in Pernambuco – wrote giving an account of the Bachelors' Ball, the great social event of the year, and of other doings since I left.

I am getting along here quietly. Business is not very lively and several small orders were sent direct before my arrival. We have the painters out at Powers's house and the place reeks of paint and varnish. My room is finished but the floors are still dirty and in consequence I found one of those little insects called "jiggers" in my toe the other day – a new and interesting experience.[4] I extracted him and examined him under the microscope with great curiosity. He is built rather like a tiny flea.

There is a ball given here at the "Assamblea" once a month. Having received an invitation I went to the last "meet".

1. His brother Julius Jr, just home from his first business trip in Spain. Tragically he died of yellow fever in Brazil on his business trip there barely one year later (28th March 1896). See Family Tree.
2. Jane's mother Ann Isabella McCully was née McCaldin. Jane had both an Uncle and a cousin called Andrew McCaldin. However, neither were Andrew McCaldin, a retired Presbyterian minister who died on 29th November 1894 aged 75 (b ~1819) at his residence, The Manse, Richhill. He was likely a more distant relative. https://apps.proni.gov.uk/WillsCalendar_IE/willsSearchResultsDetails.aspx
3. "The girls" = his sisters Emma, Annie and Olga. "Addie" = his brother Ferdinand Adolphus. "Jim" = his brother James Moore. "Pater" = his father Julius Sr. "Mr & Mrs Weinberg" = Isaac Julius Weinberg and his wife Agnes. "Victor Kamke" = the son of William Roderick Kamcke, "Flax, Linen Yarn, and Linen merchants" who became a missionary in Bengal. See Index to People.
4. *Tunga penetrans* (commonly known as a jigger or jigger flea, but also known as chigoe flea, nigua, or sand flea) is a parasitic insect found in most tropical and sub-tropical climates. It is the smallest known flea, at only 1 mm, but when embedded under the stratum corneum layer of the skin, it may reach up to 1 cm across. In Brazilian Portuguese known as Bicho de pé ("foot bug"): https://en.wikipedia.org/wiki/Tunga_penetrans

There were about 80 or 100 people there, including about a dozen young Englishmen but only two English and one German ladies. The ball-room was a fine large hall with a good floor and the band discoursed excellent music. I danced about half a dozen times in all, with the three "European" ladies. The native Senhoras were not remarkable for beauty, – in fact I did not see a really pretty girl among them all, and so I was not tempted to neglect the refreshments. After two cups of chicken-broth I had some chocolate and a few meat puffs with sugar on the top. It seemed sort of mixed but I required something to sustain me till three o'clock in the morning. With regard to dancing in Pará, the game is scarcely worth the candle; – one is in a bath of perspiration all the time, even when sitting still or moving slowly, and after waltzing three times round a ball-room ones appearance is positively disreputable.

Out of the house our costume is free and unconventional. We never wear collars or ties, and it is only at dinner that a coat is "de rigueur". As soon as coffee is served off go the coats.

The real boss of the house is Power and Duff's old servant and factotum, Manoel. If we play any mild practical jokes on each other or indulge in any pranks he smiles indulgently. At dinner if he grasps what we are talking about, – and he understands the drift of most things, – he joins in with a remark in Portuguese or even ventures on a word in English. Then there is the fat smiling old mulatto cookie Joanna, who has a son called Procopio. These people do choose the most extraordinary names for their children. I don't know how they invent them but nothing under three or four syllables is entirely satisfactory.

I dined with the employees of the London and Brazilian Bank – with the staff I should rather say – very nice fellows they are, and the other day I lunched with Jordan, – manager of the Submarine Cable Coy. Here. There are three or four houses where I might turn up when I liked and simply say I have come for lunch or dinner. It is quite usual here. Sometimes four or five men turn up unexpectedly at Power's and if there is not enough to go round, the cook can always make something quickly with eggs, ham, caviare, or sardines.

Young Brocklehurst, my old chess opponent, has asked me several times to lunch and dinner, but I have always declined. He is the local boss of Singlehurst, Brocklehurst & Co of Pará and Liverpool, one of the leading firms here.[5] I like him very much, but he lives in town over his office, and in the afternoons I like to go out to Power's place as soon as I have finished work, and change my clothes. Then after dinner it is rather an undertaking to dress again and go out. But Brocklehurst is not to be done out of a game of chess, and some nights ago he came along and brought his board with him and we had a two hours' tussle.

Though Pará is not a bad sort of place for a short visit I am glad I do not have to live here. The mosquitoes are too voracious and the damp heat saps all the energy out of one. When you get this I shall likely be in Maranham and I shall likely move along the coast with very short delays to Rio.[6] Letters c/o Theo Just Pernambuco.

Just now I am reading a rather interesting book, by an American called Hill, on Brazil, and particularly the river and valley of the Amazons. This river carries down to the sea more water than any two others in the world. Now there is a steamer once a month from Pará right up into Perù, so that there is nothing wonderful in such a journey. But it was different when the old Spanish conquerors and explorers crossed the cordillera from the Pacific by way of Quito, and came down the Amazons, across the continent in canoes; – a much more remarkable performance, I think, taking their limited knowledge and resources into account, than any of Stanley's achievements in Central Africa.

You upbraid me with my last "note" from Pernambuco, so this time, though I have not said much, I have spread the ink of over three sheets of paper and I guess you have about enough.

Bye-bye. Love to all.

Jack

5. The company at that time consisted of "R. Singlehurst & Co". - Merchants and Shipowners in Liverpool – "Singlehurst, Brocklehurst & Co." - Merchants in Pará – "Brocklehurst & Co" - Merchants in Manaos. As of 1st January 1892, the company was run by Henry and Septimus Brocklehurst (I have been unable to find which one is the chess player). Septimus was born in Liverpool in 1840 (in census "retired shipbuilder") and died 1914 -extremely wealthy!
6. Maranham = Maranhão , a state in Brazil located in the country's Northeast Region.

119. Letter from Pará, 25th January 1895

18950125 See an image of this letter, https://doi.org/10.17613/q66g-gc71

Pará,
25th Janry. 1895

My dear Mother,

My last letter went about ten days ago, by the last mail, S.S. "Lanfranc". To-morrow I leave for Maranhão. Beyond this I have very little to report. No letters from you since and nothing out of the usual routine, except that last night I dined once more with the Oakeses – had a pleasant little dinner and a mild game of whist.

26th   Just receiv$^{\underline{d}}$ your welcome letters of 24th & 25th Dec$^{\underline{r}}$.

Have had a very busy day to-day. Packed last night from 10-12 o'c. & this morning from 6 till 7. Then into town. Did my last "biz" between 8 & 9 o'c. Since then have been writing, running about, paying bills, & changing money. Now I am just about to go on board my steamer for Maranhão.

I have really no time for more. After all I am fairly satisfied with the result of my visit to Pará.

Best love to all

Jack

120. Letter from Maranhão, 29th January and 1st February 1895

18950129 See an image of this letter, https://doi.org/10.17613/0ve8-tg20

Maranham
<u>29th Janry.</u> 1895

My dear Mother,

Here I am – one step further on my journey. Just before leaving Pará I sent you a hasty line to say I had received your two welcome letters of 24th and 25th Dec. and very pleased I was to have them, and to hear you were all spending a merry Christmas to-gether. I am duly gratified to know that Mrs Moore enjoyed her pineapple.[1]

I left Pará in great style on Saturday evg. The S.S. "Clement" was lying out in the river, and Mr Marrack, assistant-manager of the Amazons Steamship Company placed a steam-launch at my disposal to take me on board. He himself came with me and I was further accompanied by two **B**ank **M**anagers and a leading **E**xchange **B**roker! – Messrs. Power, Oakes, and Duff, who kindly wished to have the melancholy pleasure of speeding me on my way.[2] Very good fellows they are, all of them, and I am much indebted to them for making my stay in Pará as pleasant as possible. It is a pleasant boast that I think my special friends are among the nicest people all round of the English colony in the various places I visit in Brazil.

The "Clement" is a small steamer – took from Saturday night till Tuesday morning to come here. But they made me comfortable on board. The Chief-steward even giving his sofa-bunk to a "Brazzy" so as to let me have a cabin to myself. The food was excellent and I had a fine breakfast of haddock omelette and bacon before coming ashore this morning – "Gather ye roses while ye may", which being interpreted means – "On the coast of Brazil take a good English feed when you can get one."

My chief regret on leaving the steamer was that I was not able to finish the pretty story of "Judith Shakespeare" by Black.[3] I borrowed it on board but had only time to read half of it.

Perhaps you do no remember my telling you last year that at Maranhão there is a good little hotel, clean, French cooking, an A^1 bath, not many mosquitoes, and the rain it raineth not every day but only about five days out of seven, so there is much for which to cultivate a grateful spirit.

There are no English people here except some mechanics, and a Mr Airlie – and he's a Scotchman and married into the country – . Therefore I shall not have many visits to pay in the evenings, and I look forward to getting a good many letters written. This is an earnest of my good intentions, and following as it does close on the heels of my last, and having come to the foot of the page, and contarning to boot, awl I have to say – all I mean, 'twas a slipper the pen – this leather must now come to an end. Love to all.

Jack

---

1. Eliza Moore (1813-1895) – widow of James Moore, founding partner of Moore & Weinberg. See Index to People.
2. No information about Mr Marrack, but Messrs Power and Duff are longstanding friends (see Index to People) and Mr Oakes was previously mentioned as a manager at the London & Brazilian bank.
3. *Judith Shakespeare: Her Love Affairs and Other Adventures* by William Black, novelist (b 1841, d 1898). Originally published 1884: https://www.gutenberg.org/files/37788/37788-h/37788-h.htm

<u>1st Feby. '95</u>

To-day I had quite a cheerful packet of letters via Pernambuco, – two from you, 31st Dec. and 7th Janry., besides letters from the Pater, Annie, Olga, Addie, and Julie, and a couple of others enclosed. A card from Dresden puzzles me; – "from a doubtless long-forgotten acquaintance" – in a lady's handwriting; – haven't the faintest idea who the (of course) fair one is. I wish people would not give one enigmas of this sort to solve. As the Pater sent it without envelope or remark I suppose it came addressed "J. Loewenthal". Perhaps it was meant for <u>him</u>!

I must find out somehow.

I am glad to read all your praises for the pines. Since they were so acceptable I am sorry I did not send you two barrels so that you might have been able to distribute some more liberally among your friends.

You seem to have had some lively storms about Christmas-time. I hope the ill winds blew somebody good, but the collateral blessing does not seem to have come Belfast way.

I had a letter from Mr W. y'day regretting I was not able to go to Rio to settle some serious troubles there about which I wrote you already.[4] As it is the matter will probably have to wait till I go there.

Quite interesting to read about all your "porties" – frivolous folks that you are.

I must trot out now and try not to let the day pass without making some money.

Best love.   Jack

---

4. Mr Isaac Weinberg, the boss in Dundee.

121. Letter from Ceará, 16th February 1895

Ceará, 16th Feby. 1895

My dear Mother,

Just before leaving Maranhão, three days ago, I received your welcome letter of 14th Jan. which, by the way, was posted with 1^{d} stamp, so the lynxeyed P.Office clerk pounced on Mr Just at Pernambuco for 3^{d}.[1] But as I got two gorgeous unpaid letter-stamps and as Mr Just paid the 3^{d} we will say no more about it.

The weather seems to have been terrific at home. I hope it has become milder since and that your neuralgia has gone away with the frost. About a fortnight ago I had a slight twinge of neuralgia or rheumatism in my arm. It was very slight and it lasted only a couple of days, but I can imagine what it must be to have that dull constant pain badly.

From the accounts of all the balls and other entertainments it w^{d} seem that the winter has been a gay one in Belfast, and Julie has come in for a fine fling. I had a letter from him along with yours.

I came from Maranhão in an English steamer, the "Brandenburg", leaving on Wednesday evg. and arriving here yesterday, Friday, noon. Landing at Ceará is a fearful undertaking.

There is no harbour, and the sea comes in in heavy rollers and breaks on the sandy beach into a churning surf. The boats, which are large and strong, have two or more men to row and one with an oar of the stern to steer by. A rudder would be useless. With the oar the steersman can turn the boat half round with one stroke, and that is necessary to prevent her from getting broadside on and being capsized. As you come to where the surf begins to break, it is "steady all!" and wait for a big wave on the top of which you go sweeping in, then "row hard" against the back-wash and advance some yards before the next breaker comes tumbling in on the top of you. Meanwhile a crowd of twenty or thirty jabbering scantily-clad natives – more or less black – rush in to the water to meet you. Some pull the boat up on the next wave, and the others fight for possession of passengers and baggage. One big nigger lifted me high in his arms and then a wave nearly bowled him over. However he steadied himself and staggered up to the dry sand without dropping me.

I saw one boat turned right over, bottom-up, and passengers and trunks bowled over and over in the surf till they were rescued by the niggers. Our steamer was anchored in deep water quite close in, but we had to wait for an hour while several futile attempts were made to launch the health boat. Finally just as they got over the last breaker I saw one of the sailors sent spinning head over heels out of the boat. The wave had evidently caught his oar and the oar him. He dived and swam ashore.

I was fortunate in being landed with only a very slight wetting.

You are not fond of boats at any time, but I wonder what your feelings would be if you had to face a landing through the Ceará surf.

An English Company has spent a very large amount of money in the attempt to make a harbour for Ceará by building a breakwater, with the result that they have only made bad worse, for the sand silted in behind the breakwater and made it almost dry land.[2] There the dredges are, banked up inside, and it is very doubtful if they will ever come out again.

The town of Ceará is rather picturesque viewed from the sea. Behind the broad beach the land rises in a steep slope

---

1. Theodor (Theo) Just, agent. See Index to People.
2. This was probably the start of the Port of Fortaleza. The first attempt to create a port at Fortaleza was around the beginning of the 19th century.

to a height of one or two hundred feet. On this slope, in the centre, there is a beautiful garden, with palms of many sorts, and trees which are one mass of splendid crimson bloom. Along the top there is a line of rather imposing public buildings which are, I believe, Naval and Military School Barracks, and so on. Above there is also one of the finest public gardens in Brazil, forming the fashionable promenade on Thursday and Sunday evenings, when the band plays.[3]

The streets are well-paved, broad, and clean; the houses rather small but painted with bright colours. Altogether the town produces rather a favorable impression, though how they came to choose such a place to build a town, with no approach from the sea but through the surf, I really cannot guess, unless it was because this is one of the few hilly spots along the northern coast and therefore healthier and more easily defended. The climate is said to be very good. In fact many invalids from north and south come to Ceará as a sort of health resort.

Though I praise the town, and the climate, I am sorry to say I cannot praise the "best hotel in the place". In my room I can scarcely turn round without knocking against the walls; my deck chair stands half in the room and half on the lobby outside; overhead are the bare tiles; the bed would form a cot for an average-sized infant but it was never built for legs like mine. One must clean one's own boots or go with them dirty. Mosquitoes flourish and bats abound. About the food and attendance I shall say nothing, but fortunately after dinner last night I discovered a place where one can get a ham-sandwich and a glass of beer.

The proprietor of this leading Hotel, Senhor Sylvester, walks round the dining-room with his hat on his head and slaps his guests on the back.

Well, I may as well make the best of it all for I shall have to stay here for a fortnight I suppose.

I have not made any acquaintances so far, but I have a couple of introductions to present.

The rainy season has begun here within the last few days, much to the content of the inhabitants. It is about two months behind time and they had begun to fear another "secca".[4] They have had terrible experiences of a drought in this province, notably in the sadly memorable years of 1882/1883 when it is calculated over five hundred thousand people died of starvation and of the small-pox epidemic that ensued. There is a graphic description of these horrors in that book on Brazil I mentioned in a former letter.

What address shall I give you now? I think you had better send one more letter to Pernambuco c/o Theo Just. After that I shall probably ask you to write to Rio.

Love to all,

Jack

---

3. The Public Garden in Fortaleza is set in the oldest square of the town and dates from 1890.
4. The Grande Seca, the Great Drought, of 1877–1878 was the largest and most devastating drought in Brazilian history so far. It caused the deaths of between 400,000 and 500,000 people. By June 1879, all relief governmental relief was discontinued, although the drought did not end until 1880. After the Great Drought, the northeast was constantly plagued by recurrent drought, (1888-89, 1900, 1903-4) and in 1909, the government created an Inspetoria de Obras Contra as Secas (IOCS) headquartered at Fortaleza, the state capital of Ceará. This governmental department has focused mainly on increasing water storage infrastructure. In 1945 it was renamed the Departamento Nacional de Obras Contra as Secas (DNOCS): https://en.wikipedia.org/wiki/Grande_Seca

122. Letter from Ceará, 28th February 1895

18950228 See an image of this letter, https://doi.org/10.17613/ns95-gr73

Ceará,   28th Feby. 1895

My dear Mother,

There has been no mail since I wrote you on the 16th. It was then too early to send you a birthday letter, and now I am afraid it is a couple of days too late. It is not easy to hit it off right. The steamers from here are so irregular. However there is one leaving today – the make shift for <u>my</u> birthday – and by it I send you my very best wishes for many happy returns of <u>yours</u>, and may the coincidence be of happy augury.[1]

I am not writing any business letters for this mail. The boat is a slow one but I shall wait for the next via Pernambuco. Besides I have unfortunately very little to write about. Business here is very up-hill work. The place is new to me and I know nobody, and a couple of introductions I brought were not of much value. Then carnival came in and everyone went masquerading. I have not seen it celebrated to the same extent anywhere else. Two afternoons a procession paraded the town. There were some fifty young men on horseback in fancy costume, – plumed hats, capes, knickerbockers, buckled shoes, colours white and red; – it was rather picturesque. Then followed a number of carnival cars – mostly humorous critiques of notable incidents and people in the Ceará life of the past year. One of the best was a reproduction of a steam dredger that is making-believe to dredge the harbour. In it were three fellows masked in burlesque imitation of the English engineers in charge, – a capital take-off; fair fierce moustaches, florid faces, sun-helmets, whiskey-flasks, and pipes. Outside the car was an inscription to the effect that so long as the Government paid the guaranteed interest this cow would give milk.

A comic butcher with chopper and joints of beef, in another cart, had reference to some attempt of the municipality to fix the price of meat.

The politicians were not spared, nor the official newspaper. There were several triumphal cars with prettily-dressed children, and two structures ridiculing the efforts of a rival carnival club. Then some thirty boys in fancy dress riding on donkeys. Two or three bands accompanied the procession, and altogether it was well worth seeing, although I have a very small opinion of the people who indulge in the tom-foolery that prevails at this time. Pretty fancy dresses I like to see and witty burlesques are amusing, but mere buffoonery is imbecile.

I had cards for four mask-balls at the two leading clubs, and I went to two of them. At each there was a crowd of over four hundred people, mostly in fancy dress, – really a very pretty sight. Some of the girls had invented most tasteful and striking costumes. I cannot give anything like an adequate description but I noticed a "Carrier Pigeon" – wings from the shoulders and on the head and a letter fastened to a necklace, – "Railway" – head-dress imitating a locomotive funnel, semaphores on the shoulders and rails round the skirt, a lady "Jockey"; a "Duchess of Devonshire" costume with a very pretty hat and a very pretty face under it; a military costume – gold epaulettes etc. very "fetching"; – a "Magicienne" with a towering conical head-dress; shepherdesses and dominos galore. Flowers were very popular too. One of the prettiest was a little girl with a cap of an inverted pale blue convolvulus, and dress to match. The men mostly went in for comic masks, and of course there was the usual badinage and mystification. Dancing was kept up vigorously from nine o'clock till after three.

---

1. Birthdays: JMcC 29th February 1864 (31st birthday). Jane 17th March 1836 (61st birthday).

I have made the acquaintance of an English family, – very nice people, – Mrs Saunders, three daughters and a small boy. The husband was drowned some few year ago on the coast. He was employed under the Brazilian Government, fortunately – for the widow draws a pension and otherwise their means are not large.

When I write again I shall probably be about to start for Pernambuco. The English cable clerk tells me there were conversational enquiries along the wire about me from friends there. I often send and receive messages in this way along the coast, as I know almost all the staff of the Cable Coy.

Well, I shall drink to your good health on St. Patrick's day and may be I shall get a sprig of shamrock to drown, for little Mrs Wilson (from Cork) says she has discovered it or something very like it growing in Pernambuco.

Best love

Jack

123. Letter from Ceará, 12th March 1895

18950312 See an image of this letter, https://doi.org/10.17613/2bb3-r044

Ceará,   12th March 1895

My dear Mother,

I wrote you on the 7th, 16th, & 28th Feby. For a very long time I had been without any news from you and I was very glad indeed to get, just half an hour ago, a batch of fourteen letters from Mr Just in Pernambuco, including your three of 28th Jan., 4th & 11th Feby. (21st Jan. must be on the way to Maranhão by a very slow steamer). These long delays are very difficult to avoid unless you are thoroughly posted in the sailing dates of the various steamers. From Pernambuco the coasting boats come slowly north every ten days. A mail from Europe may just fail to connect with one of these, and then there is a great loss of time.

But don't worry about Xmas or birthday letters not coming in time. I know that it is not your fault and that the good wishes are there all the same. Many thanks to Addie, Annie, Emma, Olga, Julie and Jim for exceedingly welcome letters and to everybody for kind birthday greeting.[1] I spent the day same as other days and had no celebration but the fellows with whom I lunch and dine wished me many happy returns and I told them you would be drinking to my health at home. From Bahia I had a business telegram on that day and at the end of it congratulations from Eggers, Hoyer and Tonita, the little daughter (aged 10) of the proprietor of the restaurant where we all lunched in Bahia, with whom I carried on a desperate flirtation.[2] Very kind of them to remember.

The rainy season continues in full swing here. Three days ago there was one of the heaviest falls on record – nearly three inches in a few hours. You can have no idea what that means till you see it come down.

Leppin, I was told, had gone to the West Indies, but some one else told me since he had gone south again to Pernambuco – perhaps on his way home.[3]

I should like to have been at some of those dances described in the various letters, – and particularly to have met Miss Boxwell again.[4] I shall see her people very soon again in Pernambuco if they have not left for England meanwhile. But to drive 40 miles for a hop requires an amount of enthusiasm worthy of a better cause. 20 dances is a very good record for a couple of months.

The "Bonnie Briar-bush" has not come yet. It is not a tract is it? Perhaps I shall have it this afternoon.[5]

The only papers I have had of late were "New York Heralds" – till Feb 12th – ; what excitement over the delay of the

1. All JMcC's siblings.
2. John C Eggers Commission agent of German trading houses in Bahia (in 1899 Bahia Registry) and his colleague George Hoyer. See Index to People.
3. Ernest Leppin, ex-employee of Moore & Weinberg in Belfast. See Index to People.
4. Ada Boxwell (b 18th September 1870 Liverpool), niece of John Harvey Boxwell (b 1845), "Merchant" based in Pernambuco. Her brothers John Harvey (b 1868) and William E.G. (b 1870) were also merchants based in Brazil. Her sister was Edith Ann Williams née Boxwell. JMcC had already met them in Pernambuco in 1893. See Index to People.
5. As the scribbled last line of the letter records, the book indeed arrived. *Beside the Bonnie Brier Bush* is a book of short stories by Ian Maclaren's published in 1894. It became a hugely popular bestseller: https://www.gutenberg.org/cache/epub/7179/pg7179.html and https://en.wikipedia.org/wiki/Beside_the_Bonnie_Brier_Bush.

"Gascogne" – coming after the fearful catastrophe of the "Elbe".[6] And what phenomal records of cold.[7] On a steamer that arrived at Pernambuco the other day the coal was still frozen solid, and the barefooted natives could not be induced to work at it. Here, if I come to my room for fifteen minutes, I immediately take off coat and vest, collar and tie, and turn up in my shirt-sleeves, and "mop" frequently.

French Liner La Gascogne is safe. Line drawing from The New York Times, February 12, 1895

For about a month I have been looking forward with expectant interest to a total eclipse of the moon. I had talked about it with several fellows and we were to sit up last night till one o'clock to observe it. Alas it had taken place the night before!

Since I wrote you last nothing of interest has occurred to be entered in my last log and reported. The usual work during the day and, in the evening, a walk on the promenade. Then, sometimes to bed at nine, sometimes a penny tram-ride, sometimes a game of cards – whist (one of the four has played about a dozen times and rather fancies himself, another just knows the values of the cards) or mild poker. At our table in the hotel we have Mardock, U.S. Consular Agent and Cable Superintendent, Page, an American, and Wengorovius (Carlos for short) a Polo-Anglo-Portuguese.[8] Page is

6. The New York Times of 12th February 1895 reported: "La Gascogne, the big French Line steamship, whose long absence has caused so much anxiety, is safe. The vessel made port last night under her own steam, and none of her passengers is any the worse for the protracted journey. A broken piston rod and bad weather caused the delay. Heavy southerly gales drove her out of her course and drifted her to the northward of the steamship lane." https://nyti.ms/3FFcs0E. The SS Elbe was a transatlantic ocean liner built in the Govan Shipyard of John Elder & Company, Ltd, Glasgow, in 1881 for the Norddeutscher Lloyd of Bremen. She foundered on the night of 30th January 1895 following a collision in the North Sea with the loss of 334 lives. https://en.m.wikipedia.org/wiki/SS_Elbe_(1881)

7. "phenomal" JMcC's misspelling. The winter of 1894–1895 was severe for the British Isles with a Central England temperature (CET) of 1.27 °C or 34.3 °F. Many climatologists have come to view this winter as the end of the Little Ice Age and the culmination of a decade of harsh winters in Britain: https://en.wikipedia.org/wiki/Winter_of_1894%E2%80%9395_in_the_United_Kingdom

8. William H. Mardock (b 1860) US Consular Agent in Ceará. Charles Francis Wengorovius (b 13th August 1869 Oporto).

here to buy a sort of wax collected from the Carnahuba palm-tree.[9] Carlos represents a Manchester firm. We have small jokes at one another's expense and we join in abusing the waiters and the hotel, and so the time passes.

I expected to leave for P'buco abt. 7th inst. but no steamer has come since. There will be one in a few days. Meanwhile I have been turning the time to account though unfortunately rather for Dundee than Belfast. Still for myself I have earned £5 or £10 in the last few days – according to the commission Dundee sees fit to pay me.

I mean to write a lot of "family" letters very soon tell them all. I am now considerably in arrears.

Bye-bye. I must trot out now and look after business. It is one o'clock and the folks will be back from breakfast.

Best love

Jack

The book has come – many thanks.

9. Carnaúba palm a species of palm tree native to northeastern Brazil (mainly the states of Ceará, Piauí, Maranhão, Rio Grande do Norte and Bahia). The most important product of the Carnauba tree is the wax extracted from its leaves. It can be used in floor, leather, furniture, car and shoe polish, and in the manufacture of carbon paper, candles, chalk, matches, soap and woodwork stains: https://en.wikipedia.org/wiki/Copernicia_prunifera

124. Letter from Pernambuco, 23rd March 1895

18950323 See an image of this letter, https://doi.org/10.17613/1d2h-0z41

Pernambuco, 23rd March 1895

My dear Mother,

My last letter was from Ceará 12th inst.; since then I have returned to P'buco and here I received the missing letter of 21st Jan. and three later ones, 18th & 26th Feby., and 4th March, for all of which many thanks, as well as for the shamrock; it was withered but Mrs Latham is trying to see if she can revive the roots.[1] I was at sea on the 17th but I happened to find a little plant very like shamrock growing in a flower-box in the stern of the steamer and I decorated myself with a sprig of it.[2] An Englishman on board, whom I did not know, came up to speak to me and said how he had forgotten it was St. Patrick's day till he saw my shamrock. I drank your good health and I hope my wishes were effectual and that you have shaken off that bad cold.

I am at Mrs Latham's again. The house is full and meanwhile I am sharing a room with Youle.[3] To-night I go to the Gatises for dinner and whist and I have an invitation for Tuesday from Williams.[4] Mrs Williams is a sister of that Miss Boxwell.[5] Her uncle, Mr Boxwell, leaves for home to-day. I have just been on board the Roy. Mail steamer, "Magdalena"; several people I know are homeward-bound, and I had a friendly greeting from several officers with whom I have sailed on various occasions.

I shall likely go down to Bahia on the steamer with Bertie Weinberg.[6]

Keiller is all right but business is not going very well with him I think.[7]

Love to all.

Jack

Address

c/o Messrs Adolf Spann & Co[8]

Caixa 1

Rio de Janeiro

1. Mrs Latham runs an English boarding house in Pernambuco. See Index to People.
2. 17th March being St Patrick's Day.
3. Frank Schwind Youle. See Index to People.
4. Mr G C Gatis, Mrs Mary Fredina Gatis, and their seven children.
5. Mrs Edith Ann Williams née Boxwell, sister of "that" Miss Boxwell (Ada Boxwell). See Index to People.
6. Bertie Weinberg: Herbert James Weinberg), died Perth, Scotland 1896 (the year after letter, aged 28). See Index to People.
7. John Gibson Keiller (b 9th July 1865 Dundee, d 1897 Pernambuco). Fred Weinberg's brother in law. See Index to People.
8. Adolf Spann = Moore & Weinberg agent in Rio de Janeiro.

125. Letter from Pernambuco, 31st March 1895

18950331 See an image of this letter, https://doi.org/10.17613/7xwe-ya26

Pernambuco, 31st March 1895

My dear Mother,

I wrote to you about a week ago. To-day, Sunday I was in town all morning as there was a mail from home & another leaves for England early to-morrow morning. The "Galicia" brought your welcome letter of March 11th, and I had still later news from the office. I am very sorry to hear you were still poorly when you wrote and I hope in your next letter you will be able to give a better report of yourself.

Here we have had ten days almost continuous rain and colds are very prevalent too. Three of four people had to remain in their rooms in the house for several days and Miss Davis, Mrs Latham's sister, an old lady of 76, is seriously ill with bronchitis. I am all right. I scarcely remember having had a cold in South America though I usually have one at intervals at home.

The rainfall has been very heavy. In one spell of some thirty hours it was twelve inches. Up country the downpour must have been of exceptional severity too; for to-day the river has flooded all the low lying districts in the suburbs and the houses there must have several feet of water in the ground-floors. Communication is interrupted on the three or four suburban railway lines that connect the scattered districts which, all together, go to form the straggling town of Pernambuco. I hear that the water was so high on one line that it put out the engine-fires and one train stuck. What the passengers did I have not been told.

Perhaps the floods are partly owing to the tears shed over "The bonny Briar-bush".[1] A tough old Scotchman, judged incapable of any display of emotion, took the book to his room and admitted having wept over it. I myself found it very wearing on the back of the throat. Briny tears came to the Parson's eyes and I am sure that Mrs Latham wept "buckets full". It is very well written. Several people have heard of it and were anxious to read it but hitherto no one had received a copy. It seems the Author is a presbyterian clergyman in Liverpool, – Mr or Dr Watson.[2] Mrs Latham has heard him preach there. Mrs Macfadyen, the sermon-taster, is inimitable.[3] "We will now consider Satan in all his offices and characteristics", and "Am I a goat?", and that other about heaven being a place where "we shall sook the juicy pear and looscious meelow", are stories deliciously told.

I dined out twice this week – on Tuesday with the (Boxwell) Williamses, a "diplomatic dinner" – there were four consuls present, no ladies except Mrs Williams who I had the honour of taking in, much to my surprise.[4] Mr Williams has been

---

1. *Beside the Bonnie Brier Bush* was a book of short stories by Ian Maclaren's published in 1894. It became a hugely popular bestseller: https://en.wikipedia.org/wiki/Beside_the_Bonnie_Brier_Bush and https://www.gutenberg.org/ebooks/7179
2. The man behind the pseudonym Ian Maclaren was John Watson (b 3rd November 1850, d 6th May 1907). He was a minister of the Free Church of Scotland. In 1880 he became minister of Sefton Park Presbyterian Church in Liverpool, from which he retired in 1905. https://en.wikipedia.org/wiki/Ian_Maclaren
3. Mrs Macfadyen is a character in *Beside the Bonnie Brier Bush*, described as "our recognized sermon taster, who criticized everything in the technique of the pulpit, from the number of heads in a sermon to the air with which a probationer used his pocket-handkerchief."
4. Edith Ann Williams (née Boxwell) was Ada Boxwell's sister, married and living in Pernambuco. Her husband was Arthur Llewellyn Griffith-Williams (b ~1857), a Sugar Planter in Pernambuco. See Index to People.

very generous with his Havana cigars of late – gives me one when we happen to meet – and as they are about the best cigars I have smoked (cost 90/- a hundred in bond, someone told me) I do not care to hurt his feelings by refusing. The consuls were rather slow company – one did not speak Portuguese, and one did not speak English – but the dinner was good and the wines excellent.

The other dinner was at the Ellises and was also a bachelor entertainment, as some charming young ladies were not able to accept Mrs Ellis' invitation.

The frogs are in their element in this rainy weather, and they make a terrific noise all round the place. You cannot form an idea of it without hearing it. In addition to those that croak there are ever so many other kinds that have peculiar calls. One of the noisiest calls Hey! Hey! in a loud and most human tone, – so much so that Youle and the Parson said the other night they had turned round to see who was calling them. Another has a shrill whistle, another barks; then there is the cooper-frog and the anvil-frog, that make noises exactly like a cooper and a blacksmith at work.

I intend going down to Bahia on Thursday next on the same boat with Bertie W.[5]

Best love.

Jack.

Letters
c/o Messrs. Adolf Spann Co
Caixa 1
Rio de Janeiro

5. Herbert Weinberg. See Index to People.

126. Letter from Bahia, 10th April 1895

18950410 See an image of this letter, https://doi.org/10.17613/wz1x-6696

Bahia, 10th April 1895

My dear Mother,

Last mail brought me your letter of Mar.18th. Influenza seems to be terribly prevalent. I suppose old Mrs Moore is dead meanwhile. I think I remember hearing once that in such an event "Dalchoolin" would be sold.[1]

You were going to tell me "two great secrets", but you only told me one – about Robert Watt.[2] My Congratulations to him. The absence of haste in his case gives hope that there will be no ground for repentance. What is the other secret?

I came down on the "Thames" with Bertie W. from Pernambuco to Bahia.[3] He was very well and jolly. Among the other passengers was Mrs Jackson of Rio, Miss McKisack's friend, whom I was very pleased to see again. She is one of the "nice little women" whom I like, and Mrs Ellis of Pernambuco is another. By the way I have an invite for this day week to a dinnerparty chez Mawsons – Mrs Ellis's people – I know of some six or eight guests so it will be full war-paint.

The night before leaving Pernambuco we had a whist meeting at Mr Comber's.[4] I have been to his house several times for whist and he always has liberal supplies of cigars and liquid refreshments but he has never invited me to dinner – he never entertains anyone. He is very wealthy – worth £120,000 I was told, but he is not given to extravagance, and they say his wife, whom no one ever sees, is a tarter. He is scarcely popular, but I have always found him very agreeable, and when we meet he is always keen on arranging whist-parties.

1. Mrs Moore was the widow of James Moore, a founding partner of Moore & Weinberg. "Dalchoolin" must have been the Moore's family home. Dalchoolin Park in Holywood, Co Down, is today the grounds of "a 19th-century house, now demolished." Fine trees and a walled garden remain, with the site serving as part of the Ulster Folk and Transport Museum: https://www.parksandgardens.org/places/dalchoolin
2. Likely Dr Robert Watt (GP). Born Scotland ~1862, died Malone Road, Belfast 1950.
3. Herbert Weinberg. See Index to People.
4. There was a Comber family in Pernambuco – Edward and Eleanor (Edward died in 1865) – and they had 4 sons who survived beyond childhood – but it is not clear if any of them lived in Pernambuco when JMcC was there . . .

The "Barra" beaches at Salvador, Bahia, in 1885. A photograph by Rudolph Lindemann.

On arrival here Hoyer and Eggers came off to meet me.[5] I had written Eggers that I did not wish to impost on Hoyer's hospitality and I said not to tell Hoyer I was coming, but to take a room at the hotel. But it was of no use. Hoyer knew was coming and would not hear of any such arrangement but simply marched me off to his house. There were sundry small jokes about the room they had reserved at the hotel, – Nº 184, – my luggage was to be sent there and so on, but as soon as I saw Hoyer in the boat I knew how it would be. Since I was here he has removed to a new house. It is further up town, in a fine situation, and much larger. He says he chose it with the extra accommodation with a view to my coming here next year with Mrs John L. Unfortunately it is not near the "Barra" and I miss the morning swim very much.[6]

This is "Holy Week". To-morrow, Thursday, is a half-holiday, and Friday is the strictest holiday in the year, – everyone goes dressed in black.

I shall go on to Rio by first steamer – end of next week. Business is very dull all round and reports from there are bad. I am writing to Buenos Aires and Montevideo to know if it would pay to go there before returning home. If not I shall likely start for England in six or eight weeks, unless the powers rule otherwise.

Best love,

Jack

5. Georg Hoyer and John C Eggers. See Index to People.
6. Barra is a neighbourhood located in the south zone of the city of Salvador, Bahia, Brazil. It is one of the most traditional neighbourhoods of the city, and famous for its beaches.

127. Letter from Rio de Janeiro, 22nd April 1895

18950422 See an image of this letter, https://doi.org/10.17613/yzmk-5831

Rio, 22nd April 1895

My dear Mother,

Here I am in Rio at last. The Easter Holidays which are very strictly observed in Brazil robbed me of some working days in Bahia, but I made a push, finished the most important part of my business and caught the "Nile", arriving here yesterday. By the same steamer your welcome letters of 25th and 31st March came. So you were about to revel in the delights of "Spring Cleaning"! – hunting in out of the way places for the innocent dirt that is not doing any harm to anyone. No doubt all my belongings will have been turned out except my Davenport, the repertory of some of my many love-letters and other private chattels, comfortably embedded in the dust of years.[1] Wouldn't you like to get at it with your dusters and ill-smelling varnish paste?

I have come up to the same hotel at which I stayed before – beautifully situated in the hills overlooking the Bay. The place is quite full, – there are several English families living here whom I know so the evenings will be pleasant. This evening, for instance, we started dancing in the drawing-room after dinner and kept it up till 11 o'clock. Up here it is deliciously cool – at nights so chilly that a blanket is welcome. This summer has been an immensely healthy one in Rio; there has been no yellow fever to speak of. I only heard of one mild case among all the English residents.

The steamers are going home crowded just now, – not a berth to be had, they say, on the next two Royal Mail boats. At this time of year there always is a homeward rush, but never before so much as this year. The "Nile" is the steamer I came out on last time. She brought very few passengers this outward trip – no one I knew, which I thought rather remarkable for I scarcely ever go on a Royal Mail steamer without meeting several acquaintances.

I have not been in Rio – to stay – since Dec. '92; I have passed through a couple of times, – once in Sep. '93 when the Revolution had just broken out.[2] Still I did quite a lot of hand shaking in town to-day. Several people remembered me whom I had forgotten – "travelled home with you in such a year", or "on this steamer or that". It is sometimes awkward enough for me, not being able to remember all the faces, but I see new people every day and I am so constantly on the move that it is utterly impossible for me to remember everybody and to say when and where we met. It is much easier for folk who live in one place to remember strangers who have passed through.

I saw Fred Youle in town.[3] He asked me to dinner to-morrow night. They still keep up their Tuesday night whist-meetings.

The foreign residents have lately started a very good lunch-club in the city. Formerly one had to go to noisy restaurants which were not so clean and orderly as Europeans like. I have been put up for four weeks.

---

1. A Davenport desk, (sometimes originally known as a Devonport desk) is a small desk with an inclined lifting desktop attached with hinges to the back of the body. Lifting the desktop accesses a large compartment with storage space for paper and other writing implements and smaller spaces in the form of small drawers and pigeonholes. The Davenport has drawers on one of its sides, which are sometimes concealed by a panel. This stack of side drawers holds up the back of the desk and most of its weight.

2. The Federalist Riograndense Revolution was a civil war which occurred in southern Brazil, between 1893 and 1895, against the recently-formed Republic: https://en.wikipedia.org/wiki/Federalist_Riograndense_Revolution

3. Frederick Louis Youle (b 1857, d 8th December 1900 Rio De Janeiro – buried in Cemiterio dos Ingleses Gaboa). The Brother of Frank Youle. See Index to People.

I have written down to B. Aires & Montevideo to know if the agents think a visit from me at the present time would "pay". I shall know in about a fortnight.

Anyway you can still write to Rio c/o

Adolf Spann & Co

Caixa 1

Rio de Janeiro

Love to all

Jack

128. Letter from Rio de Janeiro, 21st May and 1st June 1895

18950521 See an image of this letter, https://doi.org/10.17613/e2k8-3364

Rio Janeiro, 21st May 1895

My dear Mother,

By the last mail I only sent you a couple of lines, along with two photos of myself taken here. I hope the latter arrived all right.

By yesterday's mail I was glad to have two letters from you, 22nd & 29th Apl. By the paper I see that Mrs Moore was 82 when she died.[1] She was a wonderful old lady, with a clear head, able to manage everything herself up to the end.

Of course it would be well for Julie to know French, & Bradshaw is a fairly good teacher, but for travelling in South America both Portuguese and German are more useful. I seldom have occasion to speak French, except sometimes to waiters who always understand some other language too – , but in Brazil of course Portuguese is the language and one cannot manage well without it, and I speak a great deal of German, – there are so many German agents, clerks, travellers, and merchants all over South America.

Our agent in Buenos Aires reports that business there is rather better than it was and since I am not very far away he wishes me to go there. So I shall leave for the Plate in about a fortnight, and counting six weeks for Buenos Aires and Montevideo I expect to leave for home end of July. Please write ^c/_o O. Letzgus, Casilla 1296.[2]

You were having alternate summer and winter weather at home. Here the mornings and evenings are cool and the nights quite cold – so much so that I use a blanket. In the early mornings up here in the hills we are sometimes enveloped in clouds and to go under the cold shower-bath requires an effort between 6 and 7 a.m.

Business is very bad and very uphill work here, but I shall leave that for my business letters. Friends have been very kind as usual in inviting me. Four families have dined me and put me up for the night or kept me over Sunday and I have refused several similar invitations that would have encroached on business hours.

I paid a most pleasant visit to the Jacksons – Miss McKisack's friend as I told you. They have a fine old house beautifully situated near the water on a small bay on the far side. They have a couple of small pleasure-boats, one called the "Bicycle" because "built for two", and from the landing stage one can have a header into five feet of water. They made one awfully comfortable and invited me to return. In the next "chacara", or country house, there are seven Englishmen living, among them some of the nicest fellows in Rio.[3] The house is a picture – something in the "Queen Anne" style, with steep roof and broad eves, and massive brown beams in the white walls. There is a broad verandah at one end with palms and vines. A trim lawn slopes down to the sea and one or two huge tropical trees give a pleasant shade over the garden seats. Behind, the rising ground is bright with flowers and the top of a small hill has been cut away to make a fine cemented tennis-court, from which there is a view all over the bay. I don't suppose there is another court with such a view and such surrounding in the whole world.

---

1. Eliza Moore née Gunning (b ~1813, d 19th April 1895) was the widow of James Moore, founding partner of Moore & Weinberg, who had died 11 years earlier. See Index to People.
2. Ottmar Letzgus. See Index to People.
3. Chácara = Portuguese for FARM.

I was at a pleasant ball at the English Club, and some small dances have been given here in the hotel by the English families. At the Youles' I have a room always ready for me and I keep a suit of pyjamas and a tooth-brush there.[4] If business were better I should be happy enough. I hope the Pater has done well in Berlin. Emma is in luck getting to London,[5] and the other girls seem to have had a good time at the Sintons'.[6]

Bye-bye. Love to all,

Jack

Rio, 1st June 1895

My dear Mother,

Just a few lines before I turn in, for it is close on midnight & I have to be up at 3.30 to catch a steamer going to a little place on the coast where there is a jute factory. Recv^d y'day your letter of 6th May. I sh^d like very much to have you meet me in London. I will stand treat for a week. I expect to be there in August, & I will let you know in time, so as to arrange details. It is not the best time but we can go nice drives to Windsor, Richmond, Kew, on coaches, & so on.

I hope your head was quickly well again & you had no return of the pain.

You should not tell one things by halves. Either all or say nothing about them, but don't leave me to guess.

I shall be away from Rio for 4-6 days. On my return I shall take first steamer for the Riv. Plate.   I have packed my things & written to M.&W.[7] since dinner & now I think I shall go to the land of Nod for 3 hours   so bye-bye

Best love

Jack

4. The Youles were brothers – Frederick (b 1857) and Frank (b 1866) – from Lancashire, both merchants in Rio De Janeiro (both died there in 1900). See Index to People.

5. I think she was visiting Eduard and Anna Derenberg. Eduard was Julius' first cousin (and Elsa Iklé's uncle).

6. Important Quaker linen family from Tamnaghmore with whom the Loewenthals were friends. Thomas Sinton had established the village of Laurelvale to house workers at his linen factory "Thomas Sinton & Co". See Index to People.

7. M&W = Moore & Weinberg so a business letter.

129. Letter from Rio de Janeiro, 16th June 1895

18950616 See an image of this letter, https://doi.org/10.17613/4tsv-0122

Rio,   16th June   1895

My dear Mother,

I have just returned from my expedition up country and am on the eve of leaving for Buenos Aires. The excursion to the factory took longer than I had counted on. I went with the Director of the Company starting at 4 o'clock on the Sunday morning by a little paddle steamer about the size of an ordinary tug-boat. All Monday one lay at a little place called Angra,[1] and on Tuesday we landed at the village of Paraty,[2] where horses were waiting to take us to the factory five miles inland. We were there a week, there being no return steamer sooner, and it took us three days to come back a distance of certainly not over 100 miles, – in all 12 days. I must leave till my next letter a description of the place and people. I have been packing and doing my correspondence all night, but I shall have time to write private letters on the steamer "Thames" during the next three days. All I can say now is that my visit was of very great use to the Compy. and to M.&W. Dundee. They had lost a very important customer who was very wild with them, and I was able to put matters straight and reopen the account with a good order, besides putting the people here in a grateful frame of mind by making a lot of calculations and showing them how to do a number of things which they, in their inexperience of manufacturing, had not before understood. I hope D^{ee}[3] will prove as grateful.

I was glad to get today your letters of 14th and 20th May. Of course you will come to London to meet me. It won't be the season but there will still be one or two people left in London. I will buy you a cap in New Bond St. and – if you like- "something nautical, for the river" at Redfern's.[4]

In my next letter from B. Aires, I hope to be able to say what steamer I shall take to come home by, and when you must start. I suppose you can manage up to London by yourself all right.

I really must have an hour or two's sleep now so bye-bye.

Best love.

Jack

Address $^{c}/_{o}$ O.Letzgus, Casilla 1296, Buenos Aires.[5]

then after that you can send a letter to Rio to meet me.

---

1. Angra dos Reis (Portuguese for "cove" or "bay of the Kings") is a Brazilian municipality located in the southern part of Rio de Janeiro state. Angra is located at an altitude of 6 meters and includes in its territory many offshore islands, the largest being the Ilha Grande.
2. Paraty (or Parati) is a preserved Portuguese colonial (1500–1822) and Brazilian Imperial (1822–1889) municipality. It is located on the Costa Verde (Green Coast), a lush green corridor that runs along the coastline of the state of Rio de Janeiro.
3. Abbreviation for Dundee, and the office of Moore & Weinberg there.
4. Redfern & Sons (later Redfern Ltd), was a British tailoring firm founded by John Redfern (b 1820, d 1895) in Cowes on the Isle of Wight that developed into a leading European couture house (active: 1855–1932; 1936–1940). By the early 1890s the business had branches in London, Edinburgh, Paris and New York. The Redferns are credited with making tailored clothing chic for women.
5. Ottmar Letzgus, "Merchant", (b 1861 Germany), resident in Buenos Aires. See Index to People.

130. Letter from Buenos Aires, 5th July 1895

Printed letter head:
O. LETZGUS
CASILLA DE CORREO 1296
Telegramas LETZGUS

Buenos Aires..........5th July.......... de 189 5....
ALSINA 555

My dear Mother,

I had a letter from you the other day – it is in my "digs" so I can't say what date, but it was about a month ago.   So they say over there that the mails never go out from Brazilian ports before the advertised time. Well perhaps they know best & I must be mistaken in thinking I was once on a Royal Mail steamer that left Rio a day and a half before the time announced, and that such an occurrence is not infrequent. Anyway I have not missed this mail, but have sent them some nice orders. I must try to get some more so that I may be well received on my return.

I visited Hirschbergs on Sunday. Mrs H. & the children are flourishing. There are two boys and a girl – all healthy, fat and pretty.[1]

I have been dining out a couple of times and there are several invitations pending I know. Bertie's partner was married two days ago.[2] We went to the wedding, – church 8.30 p.m. all in swallow tail, reception afterwards – awful frost! Bad port-wine, – no champagne, thick sandwiches. The bride is rather nice and her sister is pretty, but the old father is as sour as unripe gooseberries and as glum a mute at a funeral. We had carriages to drive us out to the house in the suburbs and back to town. When Bertie and I were ready to come home – towards midnight – our coachman was sound asleep in the carriage & could not be wakened. I think someone had given him whiskey. So Bertie and I got on the box seat and he drove me home – 3 or 4 miles. We were stopped several times by policemen because we had no lights – the candles were burnt out, but after some conversation and a caution they let us pass. Meanwhile the jarvy slept blissfully though the coupé jolted fearfully over the rough roads.[3] When we arrived I had to shake him for several minutes before I could bring him to his senses enough to let him take charge of the horses. I hope he got safely to the stables.

I have given them a note – to the office – of the dates at which I expect to be in the various ports on the way home and I shall expect letters from you to meet me on the way. It takes letters a fortnight to Pernambuco & 3 weeks to Rio, more or less.

Best love
Jack

1. Edward and Selma Hischberg, among their children at the time were Erika aged 8, and Frederick aged 5. See Index to People.
2. Herbert Weinberg's business partner.
3. "jarvey" = a hackney coach driver (17th and 18th century idiom). A coupé was a four-wheeled carriage with outside front seat for the driver and enclosed passenger seats for two persons.

131. Letter from Buenos Aires, 18th July 1895

18950718 See an image of this letter, https://doi.org/10.17613/20fm-zt58

Printed letterhead:
O. LETZGUS
CASILLA DE CORREO 1296
Telegramas LETZGUS

*Buenos Aires..*18th July....*de 189* 5......
ALSINA 555

My dear Mother,

No more long letters from me now, for when this reaches you I hope to be on my way home. I have been rather busy & have sent home some orders. Bertie is still in bed with an abscess that had to be cut – not very pleasant.[1] Julian turned up some days ago – did I tell you – on his way from one part of the Camp to another.[2] He looked strong & well, much improved in every way.

I have been out little – writing later once or twice – but last night I went to an English subscription Cinderella – about 500 people, – the best dance I have been to for a long time. I met a number of nice girls, – some old acquaintances, some new. There were many pretty faces & lots of handsome & striking "frocks", an excellent string-band, a fine hall most beautifully decorated. I enjoyed it all very much.

The "Clyde" sails 25th July. The steamer of 8th Aug. will be "Magdalena" I think, both good boats. I shall go by one or other. I really require the 2 weeks to finish, but the Pater seems to want me back middle August, so I suppose that means that I cannot give you a trip to London now. Never mind, we shall have it at the earliest possible moment I promise you. I expect a wire now to say which boat I am to take.

Best love to all

Jack

---

1. Bertie = Herbert Weinberg. See Index to People.
2. Julian Weinberg. A gaucho manqué. Enjoying The Camp, "El Campo" – equivalent of "the bush" in Australia – out in the countryside.
   See Index to People.

From Miss Sissy Weinberg, 2nd September 1895

See an image of the letter from Sissy Weinberg, https://doi.org/10.17613/h4xx-dx26

Printed letterhead
LOYAL[1]
ALYTH, NB.[2]
2nd September

My dear Jack.

So you are back in the old country. I thought I would write you a line to welcome you back. I hope we will soon have the pleasure of seeing you over here. I was just saying yesterday that the last time I had seen you was on the evening of the wedding day a year ago.[3] By the way did you get the letter I wrote you about a month ago or had you left B.A. already? I wasn't quite sure whether you would get it or not. I suppose you had a very pleasant time on the voyage over, you generally do have a good time I think. Are you going to stay in Auld Irland for a bit now, I should think you have had enough wandering to last you for the rest of your life. My love to all your people.

Ever affect. yours
Sissy Weinberg[4]

1. This is a property Sissy's father Isaac Julius Weinberg rented for the family to spend the summer at. From his memoir (privately published in 1909): "After my sons had more or less grown up, for several years I took places in the country with some shooting and fishing. . . . The next year I took Loyal, near Alyth, which belonged then to Prof. Ramsay. It is a very nice place, with excellent gardens. . . . It was not exactly a holiday for my wife as we had the house full of visitors all the time, but she enjoyed it and so did we all. [a couple of years] after I again took Loyal; Prof. Ramsay had sold the place in the interval to Mr.Grieve of the Balmoral Hotel, Edinburgh, a very different man from our former landlord, which made the stay not as pleasant as it had been before, owing greatly to the interference of Mrs. Grieve, who wanted us to feed her pigs and asked my keeper to supply her with hares and rabbits, but as he mentioned the matter to me, Mrs. Grieve had to supply herself elsewhere." "The house had originally been built for Commander William Ogilvy in the 1850s who after a triumphant time on the battlefields of Waterloo returned to the area of his birth. As son of the Earl of Airlie from Cortachy Castle near Kirriemuir, Ogilvy was fortunate to be a man of means and enlisted the local architects A & A Heiton to design Loyal House complete with adjacent stables and coach house, and there he lived out his days, unfortunately alone. Loyal House remained in the Ogilvy family until the 1870s when it was sold to George Gilbert Ramsay of Bamff, a Professor of Humanities at Glasgow University. During the Ramsays' time the footprint of the house more than doubled in size, when with the help of Andrew Heiton Jr a large extension was built in 1877 - 1878. *Leslie's directory for Perth and Perthshire* lists George Gilbert Ramsay, Professor of Humanity at the University of Glasgow, as proprietor in 1895-1896: https://en.wikipedia.org/wiki/George_Gilbert_Ramsay
2. Alyth, a town in East Perthshire, was famous for the manufacture of brown and other linens with two mills, one of which, Smith & Sons (1873), spun jute and flax. There was also a woollen factory: https://www.scottish-places.info/towns/townhistory141.html
3. This must have been the marriage of Frederick Simon Weinberg (her brother b 5th August 1865) and Grace Keiller. They married on the 14th August 1894 in London. See Index to People.
4. Sissy Weinberg (see Index to People). Zerline Adele Weinberg (b 1872) nicknamed "Sissy", the daughter of Isaac Julius and Agnes Weinberg, the fourth of their seven children, and the elder of their 2 daughters – closest in age to JMcC. This could have been a perfect match! Two of her brothers were part of JMcC's South American travels: Julian Weinberg (b 12th August 1871 Dundee, d 1936 London) and Bertie (Herbert James) Weinberg (b 1868 Belfast, d Perth, Scotland 1896). JMcC and Sissy did not marry each other however. JMcC married Elsa Iklé in Hamburg on the 21st April 1903. It is from this marriage that all the editors and textual contributors to this book descend.

Family Tree

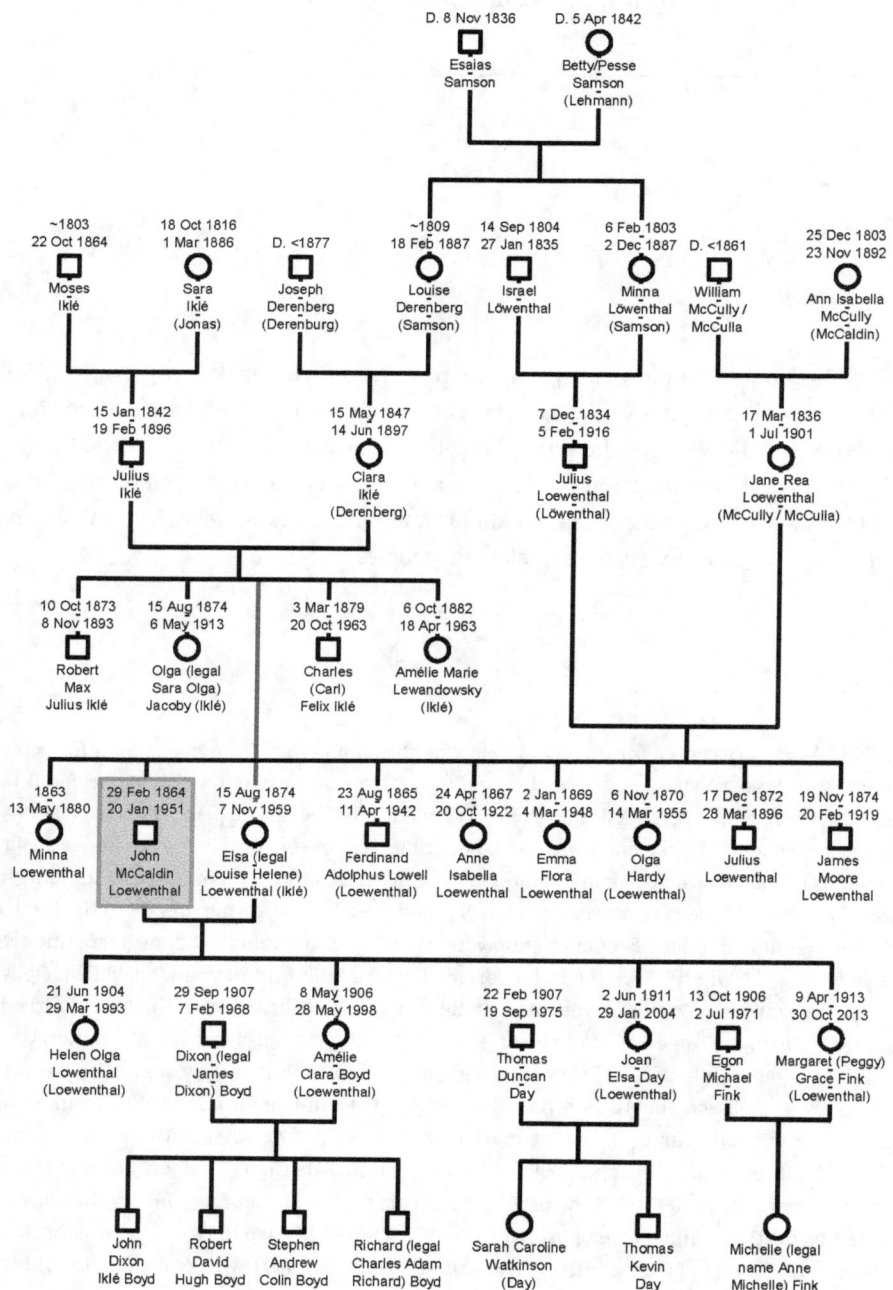

This is the family tree of
John McCaldin
Loewenthal (name
shaded). Original
diagram by Alex Belous.
A printable version can
be found online at
https://doi.org/10.17613/
81pp-kn36

Index to People

The Index of People provides a list of individuals referred to in the letters (in bold, in alphabetical order by last name) and some details about them.

Aepli, Eberbach & Co in Barranquilla, Colombia

Importers and Exporters and General Merchants.

From Colombia a Handbook *published by International Bureau of American Republics 1892), an article on* "Hanseatic Barranquilla":

"The tobacco boom that Colombia had, more specifically Carmen de Bolívar, starting in the 1850s, prompted the arrival of German commercial houses and shipping agencies to Barranquilla. In addition, at the same time, there was a reduction in shipping rates for some European companies, which meant a boost to trade and migration from Germany. In the last decades of the last century, the German firms with the highest economic activity in Barranquilla were, among others, those of J. Helm, O. Berne, Hoenisberg & Wessels, Müller & Siefken, Hollman & Merkel, Aepli & Eberbach, and Gieseken & Held."

See also *The German Barranquilla Colony*, by Enrique Yidi Daccarett: http://ref.scielo.org/gmfcd6

Mr & Mrs Allen, in Rio de Janeiro

John Roscoe Allen (b 14th January 1859 Lancashire, d 10th August 1946 in Rio De Janeiro). He is buried in the Cimiterio do Ingleses Gamboa. Married Grace Elizabeth Williams (b 1867, d 1923) in 1888. Daughter Grace Muriel Allen (b 1890).

Ashby boys (in *Recollections, Robert Boyd*)

Sons of Eric Ashby (b 1904, d 1992); botanist, university administrator, public scientist. His specific legacy in Ulster was based on his incomparable tenure as Vice-Chancellor of Queen's University, Belfast, for the entire decade of the 1950s.

Mr Bilton

Mr W. H. Bilton, Manager of the London and Brazilian Bank in Pernambuco, lived at Mrs Latham's when JMcC was there in February 1893 ("Mr Bilton, manager of the London & Brazilian Bank, is living here now, & there are in all eight boarders, – all gentlemen. The tone of the house is excellent." he wrote on 18th Feb 1893). The "hubby" of Mrs B – they were both on the passenger list travelling from Southampton to Pernambuco in May 1897. Retired from his position and returned to England in 1898.

From The Brazilian Review *of the 23rd August 1898:*

"We regret to hear that Mr. Bilton so long and favourably known in Pernambuco is leaving the London & Brazilian Bank to retire to England. He will be much missed in that community. The brokers presented him with a handsome farewell gift in token of their friendly appreciation and good will. Mr. N. J. Harding the accountant has been named to take Mr. Bilton's place pro tem, and Mr. R. King to substitute Mr. Harding as accountant. It is thought that Mr Harding who has shown great ability will probably be definitely confirmed in the post."

Mr Birtner

Friedrich Wilhelm Birtner (b 3rd February 1854 Bremen, m 15th December 1883 to Flor de Maia Baldo Jara). "Mrs Birtner is a native lady . . ." wrote JMcC.

The Blacks

The "heiresses" from "across the way." It sounds like their mother was a widow. Possibly related to James Black who got married in New York in Jan 1891.

Dora Boas

Dora Rosetta Boas (b 30th March 1865 Antrim). Her parents were Hermann Boas & Caroline, née Spiers, (b ~1840 Holland, d 13th November 1916 Belfast). She married Bernard Israel Catz (b ~ 1857 Groningen), son of Israel Catz and Jannetje (née van Aalten) on 12th February 1891 in Groningen. Her parents were Hermann Boas (b ~ 1828 Germany) and Caroline Boas. They were recorded as living in Windsor Park, Belfast, in the 1901 Census. See also "Mrs Catz."

Fred Boas

Dora's brother (Hermann and Caroline's son) was Frederick Samuel Boas, OBE, FRSL (b 1862, d 1957), an English scholar of early modern drama. He was born on 24th July 1862, the eldest son of Hermann Boas of Belfast. His family was Jewish. He attended Clifton College as a scholar and went up to Balliol College, Oxford, in 1881 (matriculated 18th October 1881). He was baptized in London 6th June 1890 (age 28). In late 1892 in Oxford he married Henrietta O'Brien, daughter of S. J. Owen, Reader in Indian History at the University of Oxford; they had one son. Frederick Boas died on 1 September 1957. https://en.wikipedia.org/wiki/Frederick_S._Boas

The Boxwells, in Pernambuco

"**Miss Boxwell**" (Ada Boxwell) was born in 1870 in Liverpool (baptized 18th September 1870). She was the daughter of William James Boxwell, "Cotton Broker", (b ~1833 Co Wexford, Ireland) and his wife Mary Boxwell.

Ada was the sister of **Edith Ann Williams** (b ~ 1862, née Boxwell) who is referred to as "Mrs Williams" of Pernambuco (see "The Williams' of Pernambuco"). **John Harvey Boxwell** "Brazilian Merchant", (b ~1845 Co Wexford, Ireland) was based in Pernambuco during the time JMcC was visiting. He was the uncle of "Miss Boxwell" (Ada Boxwell) and Mrs Williams (Edith Ann, née Boxwell); the brother of their father William James Boxwell.

When JMcC refers to "Mr Harvey Boxwell (old) & 2 nephews," this would be most likely John Harvey Boxwell (Ada's uncle) and his nephews John Harvey Boxwell (b ~1868) and William E. G. Boxwell (b~ 1870), both of whom are listed as "Cotton & Sugar Agent Broker" and "Cotton & Sugar Merchant in Brazil" in the 1901 Birkenhead Census. They would be his brother William's sons, and thus Ada's brothers.

From the passenger list of the "Clyde" coming from South America, we see the Boxwell clan arriving in Southampton on 28th April 1893 (2 months after the letter from Pernambuco in February 1893): "Embarked in Rio de Janeiro: Mr W J Boxwell age 60 (b ~ 1833); Miss Ada Boxwell age 22 (b~ 1871). Embarked in Pernambuco: Mrs Williams age 32 (b ~1862); Her 4 children: Henry age 6 (b ~1887); Alice age 4 (b ~1889); John age 3 (b ~1890); Annie age 1 ½ (b ~1891); Mr John Harvey Boxwell age 48 (b ~1845)."

Miss Braga

Constance Mary Braga was the Governess who came out to Pernambuco with Mrs Elizabeth Ding (whose husband the Rev William Ding died of yellow fever on 24th Feb 1893, see "Rev William Ding"). Constance (born ~1871 Pernambuco) married Benjamin Howard Tuckniss in 1893. Her father was José Fernandes Marquis Braga, "Brazilian Merchant", (b 1839 Pernambuco, naturalized), and her moth was Barbara Braga (b 1840 Lancashire). As listed in the 1881 England Census entry for Formby, Lancashire.

Brocklehurst

See: Singlehurst, Brocklehurst and Co

Miss Browning

The Governess to the Gatis family (see "The Gatis") was Clara Annette Browning (b 1st August 1864 New Brompton, Kent). She arrived in the USA in 1904 and married William Wright Wesley in New York City in April 1927. She became a naturalized US citizen in 1940.

Mrs Catz

Presumably Dora Boas (to be Catz) as there is no reference to suggest that her mother-in-law (Mrs Catz) lived outside of Holland.

The Chappells, of Rockway Avenue, Brooklyn

Good friends of Addie's in NY (see the letters of January 1891) were Mr & Mrs J. H. Chappell and their daughter Millie, age 13-14. Mrs Chappell is described as being much younger than Mr Chappell. The *Brooklyn Daily Eagle* reported a party at their house on Rockaway Avenue on 18th February 1891.

young Clark(e)

Mentioned as a traveller for "York Street" in JMcC's letter from Barranquilla on 21st February 1891. Also as a response to his mother writing of Clark's death in late 1893/early 1894 (letter from Pernambuco, 29th January 1894, "York St. will not easily find another man as good a traveller"). "York Street" probably refers to the "York Street Flax Spinning Company."

Copperthwaite

The "young engineer" met aboard ship (the "Australian") between Trinidad and Curaçao in 1890. He was on board going to Columbia and had worked in Mexico in charge of railway works. This is William Charles Copperthwaite, "civil engineer", (b 7th March 1861). He is recorded in the Membership of Institution of Civil Engineers (2nd April 1896) and as marrying Alice (née Hobroyd) in Mexico City on 22nd April 1889.

Mr and Mrs Da Costa who live at "Dalkeith"

This is the Da Costa Family of Barbados. Darnley Da Costa (b 1844, d 1911 London) had taken over the business and had married Ellen Mary Jeanie Clements on 15th December 1875. Darnley and Ellen Mary are likely to have been the Da Costas JMcC visited first in December 1889 (they both would have been 46 then).

> More about the Da Costas is recorded online: http://freepages.rootsweb.com/~wheelwright/genealogy/dacosta.htm
>
> ". . . The Da Costa family is believed to be of Portuguese origin and the earliest Da Costas in the Caribbean are thought to have been Sephardic Jews from Europe.
>
> . . . 7 Sept 1868 David (Da Costa b 1819) . . . bought out the remaining partners and renamed the firm Da Costa & Company, with offices at Broad St, Bridgetown. His new partners were his son-in-law, William Phillips Clarke, and his eldest son Darnley. The firm sold a wide range of commodities and David became known as "The Napoleon of Commerce". He helped the planters by taking over from two US firms in selling their sugar and molasses. The company enjoyed extensive business across the southern Caribbean and Suriname. A particular coup was in persuading the Liverpool Steamship Co. (which later became the Harrison Line) to send their ships to the West Indies.
>
> . . . the family home was Dalkeith House, a large mansion in the centre of Bridgetown."

Rev William Ding

William Ding (b 20th November 1854 Papworth St Everard [Cambridgeshire], d 24th November 1893 Pernambuco) was British Consular Chaplain in Pernambuco. He died aged 38 of Yellow Fever which he contracted while taking Holy Communion with a sick parishioner. His wife Elizabeth was on board ship with their young children William Rowland (8 years old, b 1885) and Doris Mary (3 years old, b 1890) en route to Brazil when he became ill. He died only days after her arrival. She was 36 (Elizabeth Isabella née Lowe b 1856, m 2nd November 1884, d 1944).

Duff

See: "Power & Duff"

Violet Dunlop

Violet Madoline Dunlop (b 22nd June 1872 Castlereagh [Belfast], m Elliott Hill 1898, d 20th August 1947 Belfast). She was the daughter of Dr Archibald Dunlop and Elizabeth who were listed as residing in Holywood, Co Down in the 1901 Census. Violent went to school with Ada Boxwell.

Harry George Estill

". . . a fellow called Estil, who lives with Youles in Rio, . . ." was probably Harry George Estill (b 14th November 1866 Madras [India]). He grew up in Lancashire but lived most of his adult life in Brazil working as a coffee exporter. In 1897 Harry married a woman 5 years older than him (Edith Jeavons) in Hounslow (he was then 30 and already listed as resident in Rio de Janeiro). They both died in Rio de Janeiro; she on 20th August 1932 and he on 10th May 1955.

Eggers

John C Eggers was a commission agent for German trading houses in Bahia (as listed in the 1899 Bahia Registry). He was born on 28th May 1860 in Buxtehude, Hanover, but became a naturalized US citizen in 1882, the same year he married Antonia Meister of Chicago.

Mr Fensohn

Carl Fensohn (b 20th September 1850 Hamburg, d 1st June 1942 Curaçao). He was the German Consul in Curaçao, "acting as agent for the Red D Line and who as such was one of the leading businessmen on the island." Carl married Marianna Léonore née Esteva (b 24th February 1862 Paris) in Curaçao on 23rd February 1881. He was a secret German agent in World War II: https://udspace.udel.edu/bitstream/handle/19716/7896/mss0109_1930-00.pdf See also "Rivas Fensohn & Co"

Fuhr

"Harry" and "Bob" Fuhr were the sons of Ernest Augustus Fuhr and Dorothea Hannay (b 1836, d 1894). Dorothea was the daughter of Robert Strickland Hannay MD of Lurgan (d 21st June 1894). She and Earnest married on 9th December 1863 in Shankill, Armagh. They had a very large family ranging in age from older to younger than those of Julius and Jane. In 1880 they lived at 1 Mount Pleasant, Strandmillis Road (9 minutes walk from Lennoxvale), and in 1901 one unmarried daughter lived in 52 Malone Avenue (4 minutes walk away). **"Harry" Fuhr** was Henry Augustus Robert Fuhr, "civil engineer", (b 17th May 1868 Belfast, d 1942 King William's Town, Cape Colony, South Africa). He was four years younger than JMcC. Harry married Marie Elise Knox-Niven in South Africa on 30 July 1895. Her grandfather Richard Niven came from Lisburn (*The Belfast Newsletter* 5th August 1895). He was mentioned on the *List of Associate Members of The Institution of Civil Engineers* in 1900, with the date of his election showing as 5th December 1893. **"Bob" Fuhr** was Dr Robert Strickland Hannay Fuhr, LRCP, LRCS Edin (b 27th August 1871). He was baptized on 9th December 1895 (!) and married on 1st January 1896. He served as a Lieutenant Colonel in Royal Army Medical Corps in WW I. Harry and Bob had a brother, Ernest Augustus Fuhr (b 1864) who was a surgeon and had changed his name to "Farr."

The Gatis'

Mr G C Gatis & Mrs Mary Fredina Gatis b 1854. They had 7 children. Lived in Pernambuco. "Miss Browning" (see separate entry) was their governess.

Miss Gilling-Lax

Referred to by JMcC as "Miss Sealingwax," she was the sister of Ellen Gwendoline Wallace (see "The Wallaces in Buenos Aires"). She was either Katherine Emma (b 1859 Bedfordshire, d 1943 Dorset, unmarried) or Agnes Maud Gilling-Lax (b 1862 Somerset, d 1924 Aylesbury, Bucks, unmarried) or Olive Mary Gilling-Lax (b 1866 Somerset, d 1942 Tunbridge Wells, unmarried) or Ethel Gilling-Lax (b 1872 Somerset, m April 1893, d 1957 in Surrey) or Edith Margaret Gilling-Lax (b 1873 Somerset, d 1945 Sussex).

Gotto

Edward Gotto, civil engineer (b 1822, d 1897) was the father of **Arthur Charles Gotto** and **Percy Murly Gotto**. Between 1860 and 1890, Edward Gotto was in partnership with Frederick Beesley and carried out important drainage works in Rio de Janeiro, Seaford, Trowbridge, Evesham, Huyton and Roby, Redditch, Brentford and Cheshunt. Gotto and Beasley also worked on the water supply of Campos (Brazil), Oswestry, Leominster and Cinderford. In 1862, Edward Gotto founded the Rio de Janeiro City Improvements Company.

Two "**Mrs Gottos**" are mentioned by JMcC: (1) Margaret Gotto (b 1853) wife of Arthur Charles Gotto (b 1853). They lived on the Malone Road, Belfast. (2) Jane Tulloch Fiddes Murly Gotto (née Laing) (b 1862 Glasgow, d 1934 Romsey, Hants) was the wife of Percy. She was the "young and pretty" Mrs Gotto who was hostess to JMcC in Rio de Janeiro. **Percy Murly Gotto** (b 18 April 1859, d 20th July 1935 Stockbridge) was also a civil engineer and directed the Rio de Janeiro City Improvements Company founded in 1862 by his father Edward Gotto. He was married in London to Jane on 15th December 1888.

The wedding announcement in The Belfast Newsletter *on the 20th December 1888:* GOTTO – LAING – December 15, at St. Peter's, Cranley Gardens, South Kensington, London, by the Rev. E. R. Gotto, Rector of Bradford, Devon, brother of the bridegroom, and the Rev. the Honourable F. E. C. Dyng, and the Rev. J. Faringdon Downes, Percy Murly, fourth son of Edward Grotto, M. Inst. C. E., J. P. for Middlesex, of Hamstead and Rio de Janeiro, to Jane Tulloch Fiddes, eldest daughter of James Robert Laing, of Earl's Court Square, London.

Alfred Guimarães

Alfred Lopes Guimarães, Merchant, (b~ 1855) had a business in Manchester listed in *Slater's Manchester, Salford, & Suburban Directory* of 1903 as "Antunes, Guimarães & Co" in Milverton, Alderley Edge.

GYK

See: George Young Kinnaird

Hirschbergs

Edward Hirschberg (Merchant) was naturalized in Dundee in 1887. He arrived in Dundee having been recommended to Isaac J Weinberg by his father in law Philip Simon from Hamburg. Eduard Hirschberg (b 30th December 1851 Lauenberg, Pomerania, d 1914 Lancashire). "Itzig Eduard Hirschberg" married Selma Hedwig Hirschberg (née Zander) (b

1861 Belgard, Pomerania, d 1946). Belgard was about 15 km north of Lauenburg. Edward and Selma had three children: Alfred Ewald (b 1885, d 1885 aged 3 months), Erika Josephine (b 1887, d 1940), and Frederick Rudolf (b 4th June 1890 Badenweiler [Germany], d 15th December 1963, ?Argentina).

Hoyer

Georg(e) Frederick Hoyer (b ~1860 ?Germany, d 26th April 1910 Rio de Janeiro). He died at the age of 49/50 and was buried in the Cemitéria São João Batista, Botafogo, Município de Rio de Janeiro. He lived at Rua Milo Pecanha; No 17 Sao Domingos. https://www.findagrave.com/memorial/136507117/george-hoyer George was a Merchant who married Margaret (b ~1869). They had three children: Vera (b ~1888), Alice (b ~1890), and Olga (b ~1892). All are on the passenger list from Hamburg to Bahia, Brazil (departed 28th Sept 1893) and listed as resident in Bahia, Brazil: George Hoyer (33); Margarethe Hoyer (24); Vera (5); Alice (3); Olga (1). Vera married Walter Malcolm Bevan Williams in Shepherds Bush in 1916. By this time George was deceased and her sisters Margaret and Alice were witnesses.

Adam Jenkins

Probably Adam Primrose Jenkins (b ~1865 Belfast). He was an usher at James Black's wedding in New York City. He is listed as a "Merchant" arriving in New York on 17th January 1891 on the "Celtic", 10 days before James Black's wedding.

Mr von Jess

Eduard von Jess (b 7th May 1863 Hamburg, d 13th July 1935 Maracaibo) married Ana Julia Lossada Diaz in Maracaibo on 7th May 1897. Eduard was a Merchant and Consul who partnered in the early 1900s with Breuer, Möller & Co of Maracaibo (who had split off in 1895 from Minlos, Breuer & Co, a company founded in 1860).

Albert Josephy

Albert was born in Schwerin, Mecklenburg 18th January 1859. He died in Monifieth on 19th November 1918. He was the son of Simon and Franziska (née Jaffé) Josephy. Registered in Mecklenburg-Schwerin census 1867 and naturalized in January 1899, he was shown as residing in Broughty Ferry and working as a linen and yarn merchant. He was a "Subscriber" to Moore and Weinberg and connected to the management of the firm.

From the Edinburgh Gazette of January 2nd 1903:

NOTICE: The firm of MOORE AND WEINBERG, Merchants of Dundee, of which the Subscribers Isaac Julius Weinberg and Frederick Simon Weinberg were the sole Partners, has of this date been dissolved by the retirement therefrom of the said Isaac Julius Weinberg. The Subscriber Frederick Simon Weinberg, the remaining Partner, and the Subscribers George Ivan Weinberg and Albert Josephy, both Merchants, Dundee, who have been connected with the Management of the later firm for many years, will carry on the business for their own behoof under the same name of Moore and Weinberg, and in every respect as heretofore. The new firm will collect all outstanding accounts due to the late firm, and discharge all its liabilities.

Dundee 31st December 1902.

I. J. WEINBERG, FRED. S. WEINBERG, GEO. I. WEINBERG, A. JOSEPHY

Albert was married in Hamburg on 27th April 1899 to Edith Lieben (born 11th January 1872 Manchester) who was the daughter of merchant Joseph Lieben and Selly (née Hahn). The parents, originally from Hamburg, had naturalized in 1864 and "assimilated" in Manchester, probably including conversion to Protestantism (like Julius Löwenthal). Edith was the fifth of their eight daughters. Albert Josephy was connected to the prominent Belfast family of Jaffe by birth. His mother was Franziska Jaffe, born in Schwerin, daughter of Selig Joseph Jaffe (b 1802, d 1884). His father was Simon Josephy (b 1826, d 1898), the son of Chaim (Heymann) Josephy (b 1795, d 1867). Sir Otto Moses Jaffe was born in Hamburg in 1846. In 1852 his parent Daniel Joseph and Frederike Rahel (née Josephy in 1819, daughter of Joseph Isaac Josephy) brought the family to Belfast. Daniel Joseph Jaffe set up a business exporting linen. So there seems to be a multifactorial Jaffe/Josephy connection from the "old country".

Theo Just

Theodor Just (b 23rd May 1839 Zittau, Saxony, Germany) was the Moore & Weinberg agent in Pernambuco. He was German with a Brazilian wife.

Victor Kamcke

(William) Victor Rung Kamcke (b ~1863) served as a missionary in Bengal after marrying Mabel Eliza Lloyd in Lichfield on 10th April 1902 (Marriage notice in *The Belfast Newsletter* 12 April 1902). They had a son born in Bengal on 3rd April 1907. Victor's parents were William Roderick Kamcke (b 9th May 1825 Danzig, d 27th November 1896) and Helene Emilie Rung (b Danzig, d 26th January 1894 Belfast). They were married in Danzig on 28th July 1861 (a marriage notice was printed in *The Belfast Newsletter* on 3rd August 1861). William Roderick Kamcke had arrived in Belfast on 28th June 1848 as an "apprentice to a merchant." He later established "Kamcke, W.R., & Co., flax, linen yarn, and linen merchants" and lived with Helene lived at 73 University Road, Belfast.

Ernest Kanthak

Ernest was a merchant (b 26th May 1866 in Ceará, Brazil) who was naturalized with his father and siblings in Liverpool in 1885. He married Josephine Maria (née Dowsley) (b 19th March 1869) in Pernambuco around 1893/4. Both died in Bournemouth; he in 1953, she in 1946.

Keiller

John Gibson Keiller (b 9th July 1865 Dundee, d 24th February 1897 Pernambuco) was the brother of Grace Keiller. Frederick Simon "Fred" Weinberg (son of Isaac Julius Weinberg) married Grace. Benjamin Howard Tuckniss, Accountant in Pernambuco, and Frederick Simon Weinberg, Merchant in Dundee were the Executors of John Gibson Keiller's will.

George Young Kinnaird (GYK)

Owned George Kinnaird & Co, linen merchants, Belfast; Kinnaird, George Y & Co., collar & cuff manufacturers. He was born ~1854 and died on 6th January 1921. On 2nd June 1892, he married Letitia Mathews (she was 16 years younger than him), daughter of Johan Mathews, Coleraine. Their eldest daughter Margaret Kinnaird was born ~early 1893 (he was the ripe old age of 39) and her sister Elizabeth H. Kinnaird (a close friend of JMcC's 4 daughters) was born 2nd June 1894. They had eight children in total; including their son John Loewenthal Kinnaird, born on 19th April 1896, (the latter was High Sherriff for Co. Londonderry in 1960, when he was listed as Major John Loewenthal Kinnaird, residing at The Old Rectory, Culmore); another son George Young Kinnaird Jr born in 1902 (d 1951) owned Carrowdore Castle, Co Down.

Mr van Kleunen

Probably Jacob van Kleunen ("Merchant"), (b 27th November 1859, m 31st August 1881 Margaretha Louisa née Moors, d 25th October 1912 Curaçao). He was a Dutch citizen. JMcC notes "in mourning for Mrs van K's mother," Margarita Luisa Moors née Rees.

Kölkenbeck

Likely to be one of 2 brothers – both merchants and naturalized British subjects, and resident in Belfast: Eduard or Alfred (see more below). Their parents were Hermann Ignatz Ludwig Kölkenbeck (b ~1827 Prussia, arrived London 1852, d Yorkshire 1899) and Emma Sophie née Munster (b Belfast 1830, m 1861 Co Down).

Eduard (Edward) William Emil Kölkenbeck (b June 1865 St Petersburg in Russia) lived in Frankfurt before moving to Belfast and naturalizing in 1887. Listed as residing in Belfast at 26 Ponsonby Avenue and working as a "Commercial Traveller". He married Marion Frances Atkin in Frankfurt am Main in 1891. Her parents resided in Dublin, but Marion lived in Hamburg. He also appears on the ship's manifest returning to Southampton from Las Palmas in 1896.

Alfred Edward Julius George Kölkenbeck (b 1864 Germany [or Belgium!]). He was naturalized in Belfast aged 24 on 20th February 1888 (b~ 1864). He was ALSO resident at 26 Ponsonby Avenue and worked as a "Commercial Clerk". He was married to Eva also born ~1864.

Eduard and Alfred were brothers to Harriet Mary (b ~1868), Paul Magnus (b ~1870), Frederick William Bismarck (b ~1872), Emma Sophie (b ~1873), and Mary Emily Magna (b ~1875). All of the other siblings naturalized in Belfast on 15th May 1888 and also resided at 26 Ponsonby Avenue, Belfast.

Mr & Mrs Landsberg, Petropolis, Rio de Janeiro

Mr Albert Landsberg (b 1851, d 21st November 1923, Petrópolis, Rio de Janeiro). Lived at Praca Liberdade; No 28, Petropolis and buried in Rio de Janeiro. Mrs Lucy Ethel Landsberg (née Williams) (b 1869, d 1951 Rio de Janeiro). Albert and Lucy married in 1886. She was 17 (hence "young, handsome and lively") and he was twice her age. She was the daughter of Captain John Smith Williams and Laura Ursula Williams.

Mrs Latham (née Davis)

We don't know much about Mrs Latham as a person, but she was mentioned in JMcC's letter of 18th February 1893 and then often thereafter:

"Through Mr Guimarães I have been lucky enough to secure a room in an exceedingly nice English boarding-house owned by a Mrs Latham . . . Mrs Latham is a kind motherly woman, & a lady. Her husband had formerly considerable means but he came to grief. He is in Ceará on business just now. They have one daughter & three sons." In another of 31st March 1895, "Miss Davis, Mrs Latham's sister, an old lady of 76."

Leppin

Ernest Leppin (b ~1861 Germany?) a commercial agent and disgruntled ex-employee of Moore & Weinberg in Belfast who regrets he hadn't appreciated how good Julius had been to him . . . (reported in JMcC's letter from Rio de Janeiro of 27th December 1892. He appears often in the later correspondence from Brazil.)

Mr O Letzgus

This is Ottmar Letzgus, "Merchant", (b 1861 Germany), resident in Buenos Aires and married to Magdalena (from Switzerland).

Mr Levy

Probably Enrico Salvator (Harry S) Levy, "Merchant", (b ~ 1861 USA) and now a citizen of Malta. Mentioned as being in Pernambuco in JMcC's letter of 29th January 1894.

Emma Löwenthal

"Aunt Emma" was Julius Loewenthal's older sister. She was three years older than Julius. She was born on 28th October 1831 in Ludwigslust and died there on 30th November 1913, aged 82. She was never married.

MacCallums

Likely James MacCallum, "merchant" (b ~1849 Scotland) and baby Doris (b 1892 Buenos Aires). In the Buenos Aires 1895 Census are listed Doris MacCallum (3 ½), thus born around 1892 so no doubt the baby in the letter, and her parents "Diego" (probably James) MacCallum from Scotland and Emily from England (b~ 1865) plus a baby brother, Hector.

On the passenger manifest sailing to Southampton from Buenos Aires in July 1895 are listed James MacCallum with daughter Doris and son Hector. On the passenger list to Liverpool from Montevideo in 1901 are listed James with wife EMILY and children Doris and Hector.

Rev Andrew McCaldin

Jane's mother Ann Isabella McCully was née McCaldin. Jane had both an uncle and a cousin called Andrew McCaldin. However, neither were the retired Presbyterian minister who died on 29th November 1894 aged 75 (thus b ~1819) at his residence, The Manse, Richhill. He was likely a more distant relative. https://apps.proni.gov.uk/WillsCalendar_IE/willsSearchResultsDetails.aspx

"Letters of Administration of the personal estate of the Reverend Andrew M'Caldin late of Corcreevy County Armagh Retired Presbyterian Minister who died 29 November 1894 at same place were granted at Armagh to Marshal M'Caldin of Corcreevy Gentleman the Brother."

Martha McCaldin

Martha (b 1808, d 23rd December 1897) was JMcC's great-aunt, his mother Jane Loewenthal's Aunt. Martha was the sister of Jane's mother Ann Isabella McCully (née McCaldin), the granny who lived with them at Lennoxvale.

Ann Isabella McCully/McCulla (née McCaldin)

Ann (b 25th December 1803, d 23rd November 1892 Lennoxvale, Belfast) was the mother of Jane Rea Loewenthal (née McCulla), JMcC's mother and the recipient of the letters. Reported in *The Belfast Newsletter* (25th November 1892), this Death Notice: "McCulla – November 23, at the residence of her son-in-law, Lennoxvale, Mrs Ann McCulla, aged 90 years."

Mr & Mrs McKinnel

Met in Rio de Janeiro 1890 and 1892. He English (? an engineer), she American.

Meili & Roesli

Listed as "commission merchants" in Buenos Aires. The individual partners are shown below.

From the International Bureau of the American Republics Argentina Handbook *of 1894*:

"*Manufacture of bags and sacks*. This industry, owing largely to the spread of agriculture, has increased to such an extent that from 30,000,000 to 50,000,000 of sacks are now sold annually (according to the year and the crops) in the country. The five principal factories are capable of producing more than 100,000,000 sacks. The importation of manufactured sacks is thus rendered impossible."

(The five factories include: "Meili & Roesli, Buenos Ayres" – manufactured 6,000,000 sacks in 1897.)

Augusto Meili (b Zürich 1853, m Mathilde Haack Meili, d Buenos Aires 1935) was listed as an "Industrialist" in the Buenos Aires census of 1895). He is mentioned by JMcC in his letter from Buenos Aires, 4th September 1892. Isaac Weinberg mentions in his memoir that Augusto Meili was his first representative in Buenos Aires ~1885. **Eugen Roesli-Bidermann** (b 15th February 1857 Zürich, m Anna b ~1869, d 7th November 1923 Zürich) is also listed as an "Industrialist" in the Buenos Aires census of 1895). JMcC travelled to Rosario with him in 1890. He had been a traveller for Moore & Weinberg in Dundee and was recruited by Meili in Buenos Aires to join him in business, although Roesli "was bound to M&W by written agreement" according to I. J. Weinberg's memoir.

Moore & Weinberg

A partnership between James Moore and Isaac Julius Weinberg, established in Belfast on 1 January 1855.

James Moore

James Moore (b 1811 County Down, d 14th October 1884 Holywood, Co Down) is buried in Holywood churchyard. He was a Justice of the Peace as well as a partner in Messrs. Moore & Weinberg, Linenhall Street, Belfast. His obituary appeared in the *Belfast Newsletter*, 16th October 1884, page 4, and an account of his funeral in the same paper, 20 October 1884, page 7. In around 1837 James Moore married Eliza Gunning (b 1813, d 1895), **Mrs Moore**. They had a son, John Byers Gunning-Moore, and lived in Dalchoolin, near Craigavad, Holywood, County Down. The grounds are now Dalchoolin Park, "grounds of a 19th-century house, now demolished." Fine trees and a walled garden remain, with the site serving as part of the Ulster Folk and Transport Museum. https://www.parksandgardens.org/places/dalchoolin

Miss Petulla or Petullo

Mentioned in JMcC's letter from Buenos Aires on 15th June 1890, the name was likely to be "Patullo," as there were no Petullas in Dundee – but plenty of Patullos. Most likely Catherine Patullo, listed as a single Scottish lady aged 32 sailing back to Southampton from Buenos Aires arriving on 5th August 1890. JMcC was 26 years old at the time, so she was six years his senior. She was friendly with the Weinbergs and was at Frederick Simon Weinberg's coming of age party at Fernbrae.

Power & Duff

JMcC talks about them very effusively when he wrote home from Pará on 30th March 1893). Power was the former manager of the London & Brazilian Bank and Duff from Aberdeen, "where his people have a nice house, judging from photos he showed me." In the letter of 19-26 April 1893, JMcC expands on his description of Mr Power (who describes himself as "once a bank-manager & a gentleman, now a broker, but makes as broker twice as much as he made when manager of the London & Brazilian Bank") and mentions Mr Duff, his partner. And in the letter of 4th March 1894, he writes of them again, this time mentioning that Duff comes from Inverness, where his people have a nice place, to judge by photographs. And on 4th January 1895 from Pará, JMcC adds that Power is now manager of the London & River Plate Bank in Pará, and Duff is an exchange-broker.

Renny

Likely to have been William John Renny (b 11th February 1841 Russia, later naturalized British) a Flax Merchant and Artist in Dundee. Willian John was the son of William Warden Renny of Broughty Ferry (b 26th March 1809 Arbroath, Scotland, d 1882 Broughty Ferry) who was "one of the oldest and most honourable of Dundee's merchants. He lived a life steeped in the knowledge, workings and trading of flax, both here in Scotland and also in Russia . . . . William Warden Renny enjoyed a long and successful career as a flax merchant. Known as a peace-maker, he was frequently sought as an arbiter in disputes where his opinions and decisions carried weight. His name was as familiar in the flax trade throughout Russia as it was at home on the streets of Dundee . . . "https://mcmanus168.org.uk/mcmanus168entry/w-w-renny-esq/#source2 This suggests that Julius' trips to Russia may have been linked to the flax trade for Moore & Weinberg.

Rivas Fensohn & Co

Partnership composed of Carl Fensohn, the German consul in Curaçao, and Jorge Rivas, of Puerto Cabello, Venezuela. Said to be a strong firm. Local business in Curaçao is principally that of agent for the American Red D Line. Trading company in Curaçao that issued private paper money in 1893.

The Rodriguez family, Puerto Cabello

Mentioned in JMcC's letter of 17th May 1891. They are mentioned again in a much later letter dated 29th April 1894: "At Puerto Cabello, where our steamer also called, I went to see a Mrs Rodriguez with her son & daughter, who were very kind to me before."

Roesli

See: "Meili & Roesli".

Mrs Simmelkiaer

The widow who offered to give Addie music lessons in New York in January 1901.

Singlehurst, Brocklehurst and Co

When JMcC was in Pará the company was "Singlehurst, Brocklehurst & Co." As of 1st January 1892, it was run by Henry and Septimus Brocklehurst (I have been unable to find which one is the chess player). Septimus was born in Liverpool in 1840 – in the census listed as a "retired shipbuilder." He died in 1914 -VERY WEALTHY!

From the London Gazette *5th July 1892*:

NOTICE is hereby given, that the Partnership sometime subsisting between the undersigned, Robert Singlehurst, Robert Brocklehurst, George William Brocklehurst, Henry Brocklehurst, and Septimus Brocklehurst, as Merchants and Shipowners, at Liverpool, under the firm of R. Singlehurst and Co., as Merchants, at Para, in Brazil, under the firm of Singlehurst, Brocklehurst, and Co., and as Merchants, at Manaos, in Brazil, under the firm of Brocklehurst and Co., has been dissolved, by mutual consent, as regards Robert Singlehurst, Robert Brocklehurst, and George William Brocklehurst, as from 31st day of December, 1891. The business has been since the last mentioned date and will in future be carried on by Henry Brocklehurst and Septimus Brocklehurst, at the same places and under the like firms' names, and they will pay the debts and collect the assets of the late firms. – Dated the 30th day of June, 1892.

ROBT. SINGLEHURST.

BROCKLEHURST.

WM. BROCKLEHURST.

BROCKLEHURST

BROCKLEHURST

The Sintons

The Sintons, like so many of Northern Ireland's linen families, were Quakers, in this case of Scottish descent; although the Sintons had been settled at Tamnaghmore for several hundred years. Thomas Sinton, JP (b February 1826, d 20 August 1887) was an Irish industrialist and magistrate. Sinton made a significant impact upon the Irish linen trade; not least establishing the village of Laurelvale, County Armagh. This was a model village named due to the abundance of laurel bushes in the area. Also known as Laurel Vale, the village housed workers at the large linen factory of "Thomas Sinton & Co." The factory was started in the early 1850s and by the 1880s it employed around 700 workers, responsible for manufacturing very high-grade heavy linen. The Laurelvale factory closed in 1944 when it was acquired by the Ministry of Defence: https://en.wikipedia.org/wiki/Thomas_Sinton

Dora Sinton

Dora is mentioned frequently in the letters – and must be related to the Quaker linen and flax Sinton family – but I have been unable to identify her with certainty. She may have been Dorothy Hesilridge Sinton (b 29th June 1863 in Laurelvale, never married, d 5th October 1949 Laurelvale), the daughter of Thomas Sinton and Elizabeth Hesilridge Buckby (m 1859): https://www.genealogy.com/forum/surnames/topics/sinton/14/

Adolf Spann & Co

Registered in Rio de Janeiro as commercial agent of foreign businesses and manufacturers.

Taylor of Dundee

John Brown Taylor (b 5th December 1853, m Julie Anne née Duff [b~1859], d 19th May 1932). Living at Affleck Castle, Monikie, Dundee, John was a Linen & Jute Manufacturer and Merchant.

> *From Probate Calendar*:
>
> TAYLOR, John Brown, sometime Merchant, Dundee, latterly of Gowanlea, Alyth, died 19 May 1932 at Alyth, testate. Confirmation Perth, 11 January, to Mrs. Julie Anne Duff Taylor, Gowanlea aforesaid, Executrix. Will dated 12 August 1918 recorded Perth 5 January 1933. Value of Estate, £325: 9: 3.

Mr Tripp of Trinidad

(Albert) Edgar Tripp (b 1847 Kent, d 1921 Trinidad). He emigrated to Trinidad in 1870 and established Trinidad's "Electric Light and Power Company" in 1894. He was the co-author of *Fauna of Trinidad* with P. L. Guppy, published by the Agricultural Society of Trinidad and Tobago: https://www.ancestrylibrary.com.au/family-tree/person/tree/174670247/person/172269495626/

Miss Troutbeck

Possibly Victoria Troutbeck (b 27th March 1874 Buenos Aires), daughter of John Brown Troutbeck from Lancashire and Mary Ann Linay. Her parents married in Buenos Aires in 1856. JMcC met her at a dinner party at the "Goodwins" in Buenos Aires in October 1893. Victoria would have been 19. She later married Robert Lawrence Scott-Moncrieff in Buenos Aires on 1st June 1897 and died in Sussex on 11th December 1937. Victoria had several sisters, so could have been one of them but they were probably all too old, except for Charlotte Anne Manuela (b 1872, d 1955 Chelsea) who would have been 21. The other sisters were Annette (b 1857, d 1848), Agnes (b 1858, d 1897), Mary Jane (b 1860, d 1863 aged 3), Margaret Watson (b 1862, d 1830).

The Tucknisses

Mr Benjamin Tuckniss (b 1826, d 1896) was the son of Benjamin Fuller Tuckniss and Mary Jane Tuckniss. Mary Jane was the daughter of Richard Tyndall, clergyman and slave owner, of Barbados and Leonora Eliza Taylor (b 1842, d 1931). Keiller lodged with them in Pernambuco.

Benjamin **Howard Tuckniss**, "Accountant", (b 1863, d 24th December 1924) lived and died in Pernambuco. He married Constance Mary née Braga (see "Miss Braga") in Liverpool on 15th November 1893. He is described as a "friend of Keiller's" in JMcC's letter of 18th February 1893. His daughters were Irene Mary Barbara Tuckniss (b 1894, d 1968) and Mary Tuckniss (b 1903, d 1983).

Twose

Robert Warren Twose (b 1858 Exeter, d between 1926-1930 Panama). Found on the passenger list from Southampton to Savanilla in 1893. Involved with late 19th Century Transportation modernization (rail and riverboats on the Magdalena) in Colombia. Possibly in a clerical capacity (several times occupation described as "secretary", including on the passenger list where he was in transit through New York City in 1906 on his way to Cartagena, Colombia. See article by Hernán Horna in *Journal of Latina American Studies*, 1982: 14(1), 33-54, which describes Twose's involvement with the Barranquilla Line rail line which by the end of the century handled nearly all of Colombia's foreign trade was needed to facilitate coffee export. Later, in the *London Gazette* of 23rd October 1900, Robert Warren Twose is named as one of the liquidators of Penang Steam Tramways Ltd.

Mr Tyndale

Probably Andrew Tyndall, "Engineer", (b ~1853) listed among passengers sailing on the "Nile" from Buenos Aires to Southampton, arriving 17th December 1893.

Tom Wallace

In New York (mentioned in JMcC's letters of 29th January and 4th February 1891) and sounds like a Belfast man, possibly a friend of Julius Sr. Probably Thomas Parker Wallace (b 8th June 1846 Irvine, Ayrshire, m Jane Anderson [29th June 1868] Belfast, d 1931 Brooklyn). He arrived in the USA in 1868, worked as a Commission Merchant, was naturalized as a US citizen in 1874, and was recorded as living in Brooklyn in 1930.

The Wallaces, Buenos Aires

Frederick L'Estrange Wallace (b 1853 Brooklyn, d 1925 Buenos Aires), wife Ellen Gwendoline Gilling-Lax (b 1860 Bedfordshire, d 1850 Buenos Aires).

Weinberg family

Isaac Julius Weinberg, Jute merchant in Dundee, (b 1832 Hamburg, d 1st January 1912 in Sussex and buried in Dundee). According to his privately published memoir (http://dx.doi.org/10.17613/ch97-0r17), Isaac was apprenticed to brothers Isaac and Daniel Jaffé and sent to Belfast to represent the Jaffé Brothers company in 1850. He became Partner in Moore & Weinberg of Belfast and Dundee from 1855. He married Agnes Weinberg, née Simon, who was his cousin (b 1846 Hamburg, d 26th November 1936 Lancashire). Agnes was around twenty when she married and Isaac was already a wealthy jute merchant fourteen years her senior. Isaac originated from Germany but became a naturalized British subject in August 1857. Isaac and Agnes had two residences, the family home at Fernbrae in Dundee and a residence at 9 St Andrew's Place, Regent's Park in London. They had eight children. The first three, Frederick Simon, Philip Charles and Herbert James were born between 1865 and 1868 in Belfast, Ireland, where Isaac had business interests; he moved to Dundee, Scotland in 1870, where Julian, Zerline Adele, George Ivan, Henry Leo and Gertrude Auguste were born between 1871 and 1882. The Weinberg children therefore were:

Frederick Simon ("Fred") (b 5th August 1865 Belfast, m Grace Keiller (1894), d 1921 Broughty Ferry).
Philip Charles (b 19th October 1866 Belfast, d 21st November 1881 Fernbrae, Dundee). He died of lung disease.
Herbert James ("Bertie") (b 11th May 1868 Belfast, d 25th June 1896 Perth, Scotland). He committed suicide.
Julian (b 12th August 1871 Dundee, m Audrey, d 1936 Portsmouth). He was a banker and travelled to Buenos Aires.
Zerline Adele ("Sissy") (b 2nd November 1872 Dundee, m Hayward, d 25th March 1934 Cheltenham).
George Ivan (b 11th April 1875 Dundee, m Paula, d 8th July 1950 Reading).
Harry Leo (b 8th April 1878 Dundee, m Leonore, d 1944 Eastbourne). Publisher, also known as "Henry Leo Wynne".
Gertrude Augusta ("Trudy") (b 20th February 1882 Dundee, d 13th November 1966 Reading).

"Fred" Weinberg

Frederick Simon Weinberg was born on the 6th August 1865 in Cromac, Antrim and died in 1921 at Broughty Ferry. He married Grace Keiller in Hamstead Parish Church on 14th August 1894. Grace (b 31st May 1870 in Dundee) was the daughter of George Clark and Grace Ann Keiller of Dundee, and sister of John Gibson Keiller (the "Keiller" who worked in Pernambuco). She died 5th of November 1935 in London and is buried at The Howff in Dundee. Fred and Grace were the parents of Philip David Weinberg (b 28th May 1895 Dundee, d 9th May 1915 in France, a casualty of WW I), Agnes Moffat (b 14th June 1896 Dundee, d 10th January 1982 Leeds), and Grace Ida Weinberg (b 27th May 1898 Dundee, d 24th February 1971 London) known to JMcC's daughters and families as "Grace Weinberg".

"Bertie" Weinberg

Herbert James Weinberg was born in Dundee 11th May 1868 and died 26th June 1896 aged 28, by suicide. He worked as a ship's engineer and is frequently mentioned in JMcC's letters. The *Dundee Courier & Argus* reported his death on 26th June 1896 reported his death the previous day. The *Belfast News-Letter* the following Monday carried a similar announcement.

> The Aberdeen Weekly Journal *of 26th June 1896 gave the following graphic account:* "Shocking Suicide near Perth – Early yesterday morning two fishermen, while engaged fishing near Perth, observed the body of a man lying at the edge of the River Tay. On removing the body they discovered a revolver lying beside the deceased's right hand. The deceased looked over 30 years of age. A number of articles, including a gold watch and about £4 in money, were found on the body, and a passport signed by the Earl of Kimberley and bearing the name "Herbert James Weinberg". A bullet had pierced the head behind the right ear. The body was conveyed to Perth, and in course of the day was identified as that of Herbert James Weinberg (mentioned above), commission agent, Buenos Ayres. It appears he is the son of I J Weinberg, jute merchant, Dundee."

Bertie was on his way home from a business trip to Buenos Ayres in South America and a fuller account is given in Isaac Julius Weinberg's memoir (http://dx.doi.org/10.17613/ch97-0r17).

Julian Weinberg

Julian was born on 12th August 1871 in Dundee and died on 5th October 1936 in Portsmouth. He started working in his father's business but Isaac J Weinberg's memoir records that this was for a short period: "In the year 1891 he [John Loewenthal] induced me to send out my son Julian with him, who at that time was twenty years of age and too young for what he was expected to perform. After a while Julian lost his health; office work did not seem to agree with him at that time and he went out to a ranch."

Julian married Audrey Burton Barber in Marylebone in 1907. The couple had a daughter, Joan Gertrude, who was born at 43 Belsize Park Gardens on 10th March 1909 and a son, John, who was born at 76 Adelaide Road in Hampstead on 15th July 1912 (both births announced in *The Times*). In the 1911 census, the family was residing at 76 Adelaide Road in Hampstead and Julian was a bank manager.

> *The* Dundee Courier *of 5th December 1916 carried the following article: "Military Cross for Dundee Officer.* The list of Mesopotamia honours published on Saturday included the name of Major Julian Weinberg, 6th Royal Lancaster Regiment (King's Own) who has been awarded the Military Cross. Major Weinberg is a son of the late Mr. I. J. Weinberg, J.P., Fernbrae, Perth Road, and is a former pupil of the High School. He went through the South African War, and rejoined at the outbreak of the war. His regiment first went to Gallipoli, where he was wounded, and from there to Mesopotamia where he was wounded for the second time. He is at present on light duty in this country."

Major Julian Weinberg of Stream Cottage, Farnham in Surrey, died in Southsea on 5th October 1936, a month before his mother Agnes Weinberg. He was aged 65 years old.

"Sissy" Weinberg

Zerline Adele Weinberg was born on 2nd November 1872 in Dundee and died on 25th March 1934 in Cheltenham. She was named after her father's mother, Zerline Simon. Sissy married Dr William Curling Hayward (b 1866, d 1946), surgeon, on 14th September 1904 and became known as Adele Hayward. The couple had no children. Sissy died on 25th March 1934 at the Imperial Nursing Home in Cheltenham (she had previously lived at Eversley, Eldorado Road, Cheltenham).

Sissy met her husband after she spent two winters in Egypt to recuperate after a severe chill that damaged her health. The first winter she met Dr Hayward (the youngest son of Samuel Haywood, of London and Burrow Lodge, Ilfracombe, Devon). The following winter the couple became engaged, and on 14th September 1904 were married at Fernbrae.

> *The* Dundee Evening Post *that evening, and the* Dundee Courier *the following day, gave the same long account of the fashionable wedding:* "Today at Fernbrae, the Rev H. Philip Wickstead, M. A., London, solemnized the marriage of Miss Weinberg, elder daughter of Mr. I. J. Weinberg, Fernbrae, Dundee, and Dr. Curling Hayward, Cairo. The bridal gown was of white satin, handsomely trimmed with Carrickmacross lace,

and a deep veil of tulle was worn . . .. " There follows a list of some of the over 200 presents the couple received, including a list of some familiar names:

- Bridegroom to Bride: Diamond and Turquoise brooch.
- Bride to Bridegroom: Gold watch with monogram.
- Mr I. J. Weinberg: Diamond tiara.
- Mrs I. J. Weinberg: Two suites of inlaid mahogany bedroom furniture.
- Parents of the bride: Suite of walnut dining-room furniture.
- Mrs Augustin Simon (the bride's grandmother): Bechstein piano and cheque.
- Mr and Mrs I. Lewenz: Silver entrée dishes and sauceboat (Iwan Lewenz).
- Mr and Mrs Carl Simon: Solid silver new art tea service (Carl was Agnes and Ida's brother).
- Mr and Mrs Fred Weinberg: Dessert Service.
- Mr and Mrs George Weinberg: Cut crystal table service.
- Miss Weinberg, Mr Julian Weinberg, and Mr Harry Weinberg: Dinner Service.
- Herr and Frau Max Stauenhagen: Solid bronze figure, "Le Pecheur" (the wife was the daughter of Carl Simon).
- Dr and Mrs Martin Goldschmidt: Bohemian glass ice service (the wife was Agnes and Ida's sister Martha).
- Mr and Mrs Carl Calmohn: Crystal and gilt salt cellars (Auguste Simon's sister née Behrens, Fredericke).
- Mr P Lewenz: Worcester vase (Pius Lewenz).
- Mrs Berman, London: Large silver photo frame (Pius Lewenz's daughter).
- Mr I L Lewenz, Calais: A marble and bronze inkstand (John Leo Lewenz).
- Miss G A Weinberg: A leather writing case.
- Mrs Friedlander: A Japanese Gong (Moritz Lewenz's daughter).

George Ivan Weinberg

George was born at Fernbrae on 11th April 1875, the sixth of the eight children born to Isaac Julius Weinberg and Agnes Simon. He married Paula Lewenz at a Jewish marriage ceremony conducted in the bride's home, 33 Belsize Avenue, Hampstead in London, on 18th April 1901. As the bride's mother and the groom's mother were sisters, Paula and George were first cousins as well as husband and wife. Both families were very comfortably situated. George was a merchant in his father's company Moore & Weinberg. In 1903, when George's father Isaac Julius Weinberg retired, George became a partner alongside his elder brother Frederick. The young couple set up home at Belsize, Broughty Ferry, in Dundee, where they had two children; James Lewenz Weinberg on 2nd September 1902 and Joyce Paula Weinberg in 1905.

George was an active member of the Scottish Bulldog Club, arranging an event in 1907 where he carried off numerous prizes for six of his dogs, continuing his involvement with the Club up to 1911. In August 1914, Paula was one of several Dundee citizens who intimated her willingness to the Red Cross to accommodate a number of patients. However, in June 1916 she placed an advert in the *Dundee Courier* for an experienced table maid to work in London as one of three servants, and advertised again in May 1922 for an experienced housekeeper to do the entire work for two ladies in a London flat.

In late 1923, George and Paula disposed of their Belsize mansion in Broughty Ferry and auctioned off their valuable antiques. They moved to Invermark in Broughty Ferry, from where their daughter Joyce Paula Weinberg married the son of James Robertson, the new owner of Belsize on 11th May 1931. Shortly after, they moved to England, perhaps to be closer to their elderly mothers, Agnes Weinberg and Ida Lewenz, and their sisters Gertrude Augusta Weinberg and Marie Adele Lewenz. Paula and George lived at 65 Whitley Court, Woburn Place, London, up until Paula's death in The London Clinic after a short illness on 26 October 1943. George died on 8th July 1950 at 2 Star Road, Caversham in Reading after a long illness. He left £31,219.

> The Dundee Courier *of 11th July 1950 carried the following announcement*: "Member of Noted Dundee Family: Mr George Weinberg, member of a family which was well known in the Dundee jute industry, has died at Caversham, near Reading. He was the youngest son of the late Mr Julius Weinberg, a partner in the firm of Moore & Weinberg, which was taken over by A & S Henry & Co Ltd. He resided in Broughty Ferry, but left there for England nearly 20 years ago. He was 75. Mrs Weinberg died some years ago. He is survived by a son and a daughter."

Harry Leo Weinberg

Harry was Isaac and Agnes' youngest son. The *Dundee Courier* of 14th April 1896 reported that he passed in English and Latin at the University of St Andrews. He became a partner alongside William Heinemann and Sydney Southgate Pawling in the publishing firm of William Heinemann but left the partnership in September 1909. He was the last of the Weinberg children to wed. He married Leonore Ford, the youngest daughter of John Ford of Holyoke and Springfield, MA, on 16th November 1910 in Manhattan, NY, and put an announcement in *The Times* of London. The following year in the 1911 census, Henry and Leonore were at 31 Albany Street in Regent's Park in London, where Henry was listed as a book publisher. They had at least one child, Mary, in 1912. When Leonore sailed to New York in January 1914, she gave as her nearest relative her husband, Mr H. L. Weinberg of 6 Finchley Road, London.

Henry was appointed a temporary lieutenant on 17 September 1915. In the *London Gazette* of 26th July 1918, it was announced that on 10th June 1918, Henry Leo Weinberg of 1a Regent's Court, London, a Captain in the 19th London Regiment, had changed his name by deed poll to Henry Leo Wynne. Henry Leo Wynne, of Went Hill Cottage East Dean Eastbourne, died on 19th March 1944 at the Redoubt Nursing Home, Royal Parade, Eastbourne, with probate to Gwendolen Wynne, widow, and his sister Gertrude Augusta Weinberg ("Trudy"), leaving £11,577.

"Trudy" Weinberg

Robert Boyd writes: "I met Gertrude, known as Trudy. She left Grace (Fred W's daughter Grace Ida) quite a lot of money. When Grace was dying in 1971 her solicitor made her buy a farm or farms so as to avoid death duties in her legacy to Moffatt girls! She was already semi-comatose, in Central Middlesex Hospital, and said to me in a confused state 'But Rob, I don't want a farm'. I ignored the remark though I was an executor . . ."

Lieut. Welles U.S.N.

Roger Welles (b 1862, d 1932) was a US Naval Officer https://en.wikipedia.org/wiki/Roger_Welles. In 1891 he was sent to Venezuela and the Guianas to explore the Orinoco River as U.S. special representative for the World's Columbian

Exposition in Chicago. Between 1925 and 1926 he was Commander, U.S. Naval Forces in Europe. He retired from the Navy in 1926: https://snaccooperative.org/ark:/99166/w6gt77hq

Dr Whitla

Sir William Whitla (b 13th September 1851, d 11th December 1933) was an Irish physician and politician. He was born at the family home in the Diamond, Monaghan. On leaving school in 1866, at the age of 15, he was apprenticed to his eldest brother, James, who was a pharmaceutical chemist with a shop on the Dublin Road, Monaghan. Two years later he moved to Belfast, where he continued his apprenticeship with the leading firm of dispensing chemists in the city, Messrs. Wheeler & Whittaker. In 1870, while still employed by Wheeler & Whittaker, he matriculated and embarked on his medical curriculum at Queen's College, Belfast; a common transition in those days. In 1873 he graduated, obtaining the Licentiate of the Royal College of Physicians and Surgeons of Edinburgh.

William was appointed physician to the Belfast Royal Hospital and the Ulster Hospital for Children and Women in 1882. He held the post at the Belfast Royal Hospital and in the Royal Victoria Hospital, of which it was the forerunner, until his retirement in 1918. He succeeded Seaton Reid as professor of Materia Medica at the Queen's College in 1890, retiring in 1919. He was twice president of the Ulster Medical Society (1886–1887, 1901–1902) and also served the British Medical Association as president, presenting each member who attended the annual meeting held in Belfast in 1909 with a copy of his most recent book *The Theory and Practice of Medicine*. He was appointed a Knight Bachelor in the 1902 Coronation Honours list published on 26th June 1902, he was knighted by the Lord Lieutenant of Ireland, Earl Cadogan, at Dublin Castle on 11th August 1902: https://en.wikipedia.org/wiki/William_Whitla and https://www.ums.ac.uk/whitla_w.html

Captain and Mrs Williams, Rio de Janeiro

John Smith Williams (b ~1835, New Orleans) and Laura Ursula Williams née Gilbert (b ~1844) were the parents of Mrs Grace Elizabeth Allen and Mrs Lucy Ethel Landsberg. They married in Duxbury, MA, in 1864.

The Williams, Pernambuco

Mrs Williams was Edith Ann Williams née Boxwell (see Boxwell). Born in ~ 1862, Edith was Ada Boxwell's sister. She married Arthur Llewellyn Griffith-Williams and had four children: Henry (b ~1887), Alice (b ~1889), John (b ~1890), Annie (b ~1891).

Youle

Frederick "Fred" (b 1856) and **Frank Youle** (b 1866) appear several times in JMcC's letters. They were brothers, two sons of Alfred Phillips Youle, "South American Merchant", (b 24th July 1824 Hackney, d July 1905 Hackney) and Annie Stewart Schwind (b 1835, d 1871). Alfred and Annie were married in Bahia, Brazil, in 1852.
   They had 12 children, including 10 boys (the ones who JMcC mentions are underlined below):

Alfred Francis Youle (b 10th July 1853 Pernambuco, d 6th June 1929 Surrey)
Henry Stewart Youle (b 1855 Lancashire, d 1856 Hackney)
Frederick Louis Youle (b 6th April 1856 Lancashire, d 8th December 1900 Rio de Janeiro).
Charles Youle (b Manchester 1857, d 1880)
Arthur Goolden Youle (b Manchester 1860, d 1905)
Anne Schwind Youle (b 1861 Broughton, Lancashire, d 1934)

Edward Schwind Youle (b ~1864 Lancashire, d 1926)

Mary Louisa Schwind Youle (b 1st June 1864 Prestwich, Lancashire, d 29th January 1952 Croydon, Surrey)

Frank Schwind Youle (b around September 1866 Ormskirk, Lancashire, d 9th March 1900).

Albert Schwind Youle (b 21st April 1868 Manchester, d 1909)

Ernest Schwind Youle (b 21st April 1868 Lancashire, d 8th April 1914 Santos)

Percy Schwind Youle (b July 1869 Manchester, d December 1895 New York)

Smith & Youle:

"A firm registered as Brazilian but founded by British expatriate entrepreneurs, which was very important in transferring marketing knowledge, technological knowledge and entrepreneurial knowledge. This firm was established in Brazil in 1880 by two British expatriates who also acted as managers. These entrepreneurs had strong international networks derived from their work as agents for British trading companies. The firm imported textiles into Brazil (wool, cotton and linen cloth), and also other goods and services including iron, steel and copper, and insurance. One of its shareholders, Frederick Youle, became a manager of Companhia Manufactora Fluminense in 1891."

From: da Silva Lopes, T. *et al* 2018 "The 'disguised' foreign investor: Brands, trademarks and the British expatriate entrepreneur in Brazil," *Business History*, 60.8, pp. 1171-1195. http://dx.doi.org/10.1080/00076791.2017.1287174

Coda

The letters contained in this book are available digitally in the Humanities Commons digital repository as part of the Loewenthal Letters Project, https://hcommons.org/groups/loewenthal-letters-project/. Humanities Commons is a non-profit network that enables scholars and practitioners to share and discuss their work in a stable, academy-owned and -governed online space. The creation of Humanities Commons was made possible by support from the Andrew W. Mellon Foundation and the National Endowment for the Humanities. Thanks to the financial contribution of participating organizations, fully-featured accounts are always free for individual users.

A collection of the letters in a box file, laid out to photograph.